O9-BUB-796

WELLINGTON

The Maras, the Giants, and the City of New York

⁓

Carlo DeVito

TRIUMPH
B O O K S

Library of Congress Cataloging-in-Publication Data

DeVito, Carlo.
     Wellington : the Maras, the Giants, and the City of New York/Carlo DeVito.
          p. cm.
     Includes bibliographical references and index.
     ISBN-13: 978-1-57243-872-9
     ISBN-10: 1-57243-872-X
          1. Mara, Wellington Timothy, 1916–2005—Family. 2. Football team owners—
     United States—Biography. 3. New York Giants (Football team)—History 4.
     Football—New York (State)—New York—History. I. Title.

     GV939.M2898D48 2006
     0796.332'092'2—dc22
     [B]
                                                                    2006010482

This book is available in quantity at special discounts for your group or organization.
For further information, contact:

     Triumph Books
     542 South Dearborn Street
     Suite 750
     Chicago, Illinois 60605
     (312) 939-3330
     Fax (312) 663-3557

Printed in U.S.A.
ISBN-13: 978-1-57243-872-9
ISBN-10: 1-57243-872-X
Design by Chris Mulligan

This book is dedicated to my father, Philip DeVito, who bequeathed to me my inheritance, a love of the New York Football Giants.

This book is also dedicated to Fredrick Exley, with apologies, and to my drunken, reprobate dog, whom I named after Exley.

And finally to my sons, whom I love very much, and who enjoy the grace and competition that athletics provide us.

CONTENTS

FOREWORD

Wellington Mara, in my opinion, was the most important man ever to be involved with the NFL. He was in favor of expansion and revenue sharing. When I was a rookie, in 1956, there were 12 teams in the NFL. Now there are 32, and the NFL is one of the richest sports leagues in the world. His foresight and willingness to share television revenue and other monies with all the existing teams helped to ensure financial stability and growth.

Mara was like a father to every player. He was always on the side-line watching his team practice. He was there every time it took the field. Wellington Mara was always there, and that is why he will never be forgotten. If you played for the Giants, you were part of his family.

Back then, when it came time, we negotiated with the owner, and often he stepped into a fatherly role with us. We didn't play the game for money—you can't play the game of football just for money. You put your body on the line. We played it back then because we loved it.

One year I walked into Mr. Mara's office at training camp and he said, "Here's your contract, and here's your extra $500." I was supposed to sign, and that was it. I wasn't supposed to ask questions. That year I told him I was going to hold out for more money. He stood up, and he threw papers around the office. "You'll sign the contract, and that's all you're getting!"

"Yes sir, Mr. Mara," I said. I signed, and I got out of there. As I said, that's when he was most like a dad to me.

At one point I heard that Kyle Rote and Frank Gifford were having an easier time of negotiations with Jack Mara, Wellington's brother.

I said to Wellington, "I don't want to talk with you anymore. I want to talk with Jack."

"I handle the tough guys. And you're one of the tough guys," he said.

He used to drive this old, beat-up Chevette to practice every day. And he showed up for every practice. That was who he was. And I remember his wife, Ann, would show up in a limousine. He offered me a ride one time, and I said, "I don't want to ride in that Chevette. I want to ride with Ann."

My years with the Giants coincided with a great time in the world of sports—and the world of New York sports, especially. I remember when Wellington decided he was going to trade for Y.A. Tittle. We were at Fairfield University, in the defensive locker room. The defense and offense had separate locker rooms. (We didn't let the offensive guys in because they didn't score enough.) Mr. Mara walked in.

"I have to talk to you players," he said to us. "I have a chance to get Y.A. Tittle. I want your opinion."

"Who do you have to give up?" someone asked.

"Lou Cordileone."

"Lou?" we asked. Lou was a good offensive lineman, but this was Y.A.

On a West Coast swing after the trade, training at Salem University, Y.A. said to me, "I thought you were pretty dirty when I played with the 49ers, but now I think you're pretty good."

I told him: "Y.A., we win here, and we win with defense. You've played with the 49ers. You played on an all-offense type team, but we play defense here. Don't be afraid to throw the ball because no one's going to score anyway."

Y.A. had some of his best years when he was with us. It was the greatest deal anyone ever made in the NFL. He was a smart football man.

In 2003 Frank Gifford and Ann Mara threw a party for Wellington at Tavern on the Green. The guys who played for him over the years were there. They were all there for him, which is typical of the Giants organization. Some of the former players still lived in and around New York and New Jersey. Some not. And all the big names were there: Lawrence Taylor, Phil Simms, Andy Robustelli. All the greats were there to pay tribute to him. Because that's the kind of guy he was.

The game just after his death, when the Redskins played the Giants, was a somber day for me. It was like the death of a father. It was an emotional day. And it was orchestrated in a way only the Giants could pull off. Wellington's granddaughter Kate sang the national anthem. She was fantastic. Emotion means so much in football, and there was no way the Giants were going to lose. That was his game.

As an announcer for the Washington Redskins, I covered both of the games between the Redskins and Giants each year. I always made a point of seeing Mr. Mara. I saw him at every game. I made a point to visit him out of respect. He was very much like a father to me and to the other players. I remember every meeting with him every day of my life.

—Sam Huff

PREFACE

F rank Gifford told the Newark *Star-Ledger*'s Paul Needell, "He built the team into what they are now, but the money never meant anything to him. He always drove the same Ford from the same Ford dealer. That was Wellington. A very simple man who had it all in perspective."

In 2003 Gifford attempted something that had never been done before. He planned a surprise party for his old mentor. Wellington Mara was someone special to him.

"He was my owner and boss, then he became a father figure, and then really a brother figure," Gifford said. "We were very, very close. He was my presenter when I went into the Hall of Fame, and I was his."

Gifford knew Well didn't much care for parties. He was a homebody. So Gifford told Well, no, Ann was in on it and that it was a surprise party for Gifford's wife, Kathie Lee.

"Mara acquiesced, just for Gifford," Needell wrote. "He remembered how Gifford had flown back from Hawaii in 1965 to attend the funeral of Wellington's brother and partner, Jack Mara. Friends don't forget."

With the help of Wellington's son, John, and other family and Giants employees, they put together a group of Giants that had never been assembled before. Many had not been back in many years.

"We made a little bit of a mistake because it was September 6, the night before the season opener. Ann was my coconspirator and had convinced him that he was coming to the Tavern on the Green for something totally different. And he was one grumpy camper."

Ann told Gifford, "He hasn't spoken to me since we left."

"But we walked into the patio at the Tavern on the Green and Well looked around and the first person he saw was Lawrence Taylor," Gifford said. "And then Wellington saw Sam Huff, Andy Robustelli, Y.A. Tittle, and a number of other famous former Giants, and some not so famous, the guys who played for a few years, guys like John Amberg and Cutter Thompson. It took a while for it all to sink in for Well.

"It was a beautiful night," Gifford said. "And a beautiful night for Wellington Mara because what I remember about that night is each of the players got up to say a few words and said that he had touched each and every one of their lives. For many of them it was in an economic way, but for many more of them, it was just being there at the right time"

ACKNOWLEDGMENTS

T he author must acknowledge and commend Ken Samelson, who offered my name up to Triumph to write this book. I thank him for his advice, his researching assistance, and his fact-checking. Without Ken, this book would not have happened, and I am grateful for his friendship and his advice.

Any author of such an effort also owes a huge debt of gratitude to those who went before him. Several writers' works have proved invaluable to me. Among the many valuable volumes I used were Frank Gifford's *The Whole Ten Yards*, Dave Klein's *The New York Giants*, Jerry Izenberg's *No Medals for Trying*, Michael Eisen's *Stadium Stories: New York Giants*, David Maraniss's *When Pride Still Mattered*, Michael MacCambridge's *America's Game*, Jeff Miller's *Going Long*, Gerald Eskanazi's *There Were Giants in Those Days*, Elliot Asinof's *Seven Days to Sunday*, David Harris's *The League*, Roger Kahn's *A Flame of Pure Fire*, Andrew O'Toole's *Smiling Irish Eyes*, and Richard Whittingham's numerous tomes on the New York Giants organization.

Of course, as I pored over almost 1,000 newspaper and magazine articles, it is impossible to imagine writing this work without the dedicated and hard-working beat writers who have covered the Giants on a daily basis over the decades, from Arthur Daley to Larry Merchant, from George Vecsey to Dave Anderson, Mike Lupica, Bill Handleman, Larry Fox, Mike Freeman, Ian O'Connor, Vinny DiTriani, Bill Pennington, Wayne Coffey, Ralph Vacchino, Michael Eisen, Frank Litsky, and the many other writers who have covered the Giants over the years. Without their dedicated coverage and investigative reporting, this book could not have been written. My apologies to anyone whose name was inadvertently left off this list— you can probably be found in the notes at the end of this book.

As ever, I owe a debt of special thanks in all my professional endeavors to Gilbert King for his ear, opinions, advice, general good cheer, and encouragement.

I would of course like to thank my editor, Tom Bast at Triumph Books, who helped make this book a reality. Were it not for his excitement and enthusiasm, I might have given up under the massive weight of such an undertaking. He was cheerleader, coach, and friend. I thank him for his tireless editing and opinions. He was truly the best editor a writer could ever hope to have. I thank him, as well as everyone at Triumph Books, for this opportunity. I would also like to thank Kelley White for all her help and efforts, as well as her patience.

I would like to thank my agent and friend Edward Claflin of James Peter Associates. I thank him for his encouragement and assistance, and for his belief in me.

I would like to thank my two sons, whose patience has been stretched between my day job and the call of our barn, wherein the writing of this work took place. I owe them a great debt of time that might be well spent in more important pursuits in their eyes— swordplay, T-ball, the making of paper airplanes, riding bicycles, and many other pastimes. I thank them for letting me do this, and I pledge to become more competent at Game Boy, GameCube, and PlayStation.

And finally I would like to thank my wife, Dominique. She is a fanatical and dedicated Philadelphia Eagles fan. She makes watching football fun, exciting, and controversial. But she is always a good sport and a great wife, mother, and den leader to our family menagerie of pets. She was my friend, counselor, confessor, secretary, expert, confidant, and pillar during the writing of this book. I am sure if she could, she would trade any of my books for some more time spent with me and our kids. My successes in my job and work are a result of her effort, love, and understanding. She makes my failures and disappointments seem inconsequential. I thank her most of all.

INTRODUCTION

When Wellington Mara died, many NFL fans were shocked by the turnout for this beloved owner. League executives, Hall of Famers, fellow owners, and players both past and present attended his funeral, as well as many well-wishers who were part of the "Giants family" (as Well liked to call them).

Some newer owners were not always fans of Wellington Mara. He was too old-fashioned, too married to the previous generation's vision of what the NFL was.

Some fans did not like him because they thought he did not demand enough of his players, coaches, and executives, like other more hotheaded owners did.

Some players saw him as paternalistic, rather than the benevolent, fatherly presence he wanted to be.

The sum of Wellington Mara's life was greater than its parts. He knew that. He also knew that were it not for the sum of those parts, he would not have been the man he was.

Wellington Mara was a man of faith. He was a man of conviction (whether you agreed with that conviction or not). He would not demur, he would not flaunt his convictions, but he would not give ground either.

Wellington Mara believed in his God, his wife and family, his league, his team, and his fans—pretty much in that order. In the 1960s and 1970s, while his team was floundering, Giants fans asked what had gone wrong. The problem was simple. The times had changed, and Wellington, a lifelong innovator, was trapped under the weight of trying to run his team like a small-time operation in an era when the NFL was growing by leaps and bounds. In that era, he was spending more time at the NFL offices than he was at the Giants executive offices.

Wellington's vision of the NFL had changed drastically in the early 1960s through the influence of his brother Jack, who taught him that league came before team. That the sharing of the wealth meant that if they shared in kind they would profit in kind—that they would survive in kind. Well was instrumental in league affairs for many years, preferring a behind-the-scenes kind of power that few realized. When many owners die, obervers say that the owners had an impact on the NFL. But Wellington Mara lived the NFL. He was involved in the introduction of filming football games for the purposes of coaching, he was the first to take photographs during games to show how defenses were lining up, he knew how to recruit and draft the best players, and he assembled the teams that went to the championship game six out of eight straight years between 1956 and 1963 (a feat not equaled before or since).

But he also spent time helping Pete Rozelle get elected commissioner of the NFL, and then he worked with the brilliant young NFL executive. When previous commissioner Burt Bell (who operated out of his Philadelphia home) died, Rozelle moved to New York to head up the NFL offices, create the licensing department, share the immense television revenues, and lead league labor negotiations for years to come. Mara was his confidant, his advisor, his sounding board, and his most effective warrior. When newer owners puzzled over Mara's stodgy ways, they assumed he was still stuck in the past. Wellington Mara was not lost in the past—he was defending one of the best and most successful sports leagues in the world, which he had helped to build with his own two hands. There would not have been the same kind of growth and opportunity in the NFL had it not been for Wellington Mara.

వ్యৎ

As a lifelong Giants fan and as a fellow Fordham graduate, I was both honored and awed when asked to write about the life of Wellington Mara and indeed the Mara family. And what I came to understand about Wellington Mara was that you could not write about him without writing about his family and the city he loved and helped to shape.

Wellington Mara's story is not his own, and he would have been the first to tell you that. There were too many people that made up the many parts of him. His father and mother, his brother Jack, Steve Owen, Jim Lee Howell, Vince Lombardi, Tom Landry, Frank Gifford, and even his nephew Tim, with whom he quarreled for the better part of a quarter of a century, could all be counted as positive influences on the building of Wellington Mara. Without them, he would not have accomplished what he did.

And his influence was felt by numerous city institutions, such as St. Ignatius Church, St. Patrick's Cathedral, Loyola Preparatory School, Fordham University, St. Vincent's Hospital, the New York Catholic Youth Organization, and numerous other charities he was involved in through donations of time, effort, and money. He was an integral part of New York City's power structure, like his father and brother before him, on a first-name basis with politicians, fellow sports owners, and other influential Gotham-ites.

On the other hand, Wellington was not a saint. He was well known for his wit (a trait he shared with his father, brother, and nephew), but it could also be used with rapier-like effect, eviscerating to some. He could holler and scream with the best of them, breaking chairs or other items. But his humility and his religion helped him keep a check on those qualities.

Wellington Mara wasn't as outrageous as Papa Bear Halas, as controversial as Al Davis, as colorful as Carroll Rosenbloom, or as much of a maverick as Jerry Jones or Daniel Snyder.

He was a scion who wished to remain as anonymous as possible, a member of that greatest generation whose accomplishments stand taller with every successive year. He was a man who never drove fancy cars, just the same car from the same dealership, every year. He lived like any other working stiff, although his lifestyle could have afforded him more fancy luxury automobiles. He was a man who preferred to wear the same gray sweat suit and rumpled old hat every day, instead of quality suits and finer garments, and he didn't give a damn what others thought. He preferred to be home rather than at fancy banquets, whether they were held at the New York Athletic Club, the Waldorf-Astoria, the Plaza Hotel, Tavern on the Green, or at Winged Foot Country Club.

For his God, his family, and his Giants family, Wellington Mara was a private man. He aspired to be one of the people he courted—he aspired to be a Giants fan. Whether you liked him or not, he wanted you to respect him, and you could not do less than that.

PART I

1925–1965

CHAPTER 1

A Son of Ireland

At the height of the Potato Famine, in 1850, Orestes Brownson, a celebrated convert to Catholicism, stated, "Out of these narrow lanes, dirty streets, damp cellars, and suffocating garrets will come forth some of the noblest sons of our country, whom she will delight to own and honor."

The Irish immigrants of the time hoped he was right. For those who could not stand the deprivations that Ireland afforded them in the 1850s, 1860s, and 1870s, the prospect of America was a mixed blessing. Certainly the hunger and want and oppression that were their constant companions in Ireland could not follow them to these new shores. But if these kinds of pestilence were not hounding them in the new world, they still would not be more than an arm's length away in America. Those leaving for these new shores were fêted with what became known as the American Wake, for they knew they would probably not see Ireland again. And they came over in what were called coffin ships, so named because the conditions were awful: overpacked and undersupplied. Many people would die on the voyage over.

In the 1860s and 1870s, New York saw hundreds of coffin ships choke the ports in a year. As the ships approached their docks, large greedy men known as runners, "wearing bright green neckties and speaking in thick accents," descended on the unknowing new immigrants, grabbing their bags and herding them toward this tenement or that, where outrageous fees would be foisted upon them for their living space.

"When city authorities proved unwilling or unable to provide even minimal protection to the new immigrants, associations of older ones stepped forward," wrote historians Edwin G. Burrows and Mike Wallace in their Pulitzer Prize–winning history of New York, *Gotham*. "The friendly Sons of St. Patrick busied itself with its compatriots' problems. Most notably, the Irish Emigrant Society (1841) offered information about jobs and lodgings, filed complaints against charlatans, protested shipboard conditions, remitted money and prepaid tickets back to Ireland, and in 1850 established an Emigrant Industrial Savings Bank.

"Beside the din and disorder and sheer misery of it all, large numbers of those coming ashore had been exposed to typhus, cholera, smallpox, and other infectious diseases that ran rampant on immigrant ships." Many new immigrants were eventually reduced to begging because many shops and other places of employment featured the infamous No Irish Need Apply signs in their windows. In many cases those hoping to find employment in service were also shunned because African Americans were seen as preferable to Irish immigrants.

This condition was replicated in many great cities across the country. An editor at the *Chicago Post* once opined, "The Irish fill our prisons, our poor houses. ... Scratch a convict or a pauper, and the chances are that you tickle the skin of an Irish Catholic. Putting them on a boat and sending them home would end crime in this country."

At one point in Philadelphia, a number of Catholic churches, strongholds of the Irish communities, were burned. Deadly riots resulted. The mayor of New York asked Archbishop Hughes, "Do you fear that some of your churches will be burned?"

"No sir, but I am afraid some of yours will be. We can protect our own."

Later, public officials asked the archbishop to restrain New York's Irish. "I have not the power," he replied. "You must take care that they are not provoked." No Catholic church burned in New York.

By the 1870s, New York City featured its own St. Patrick's Day Parade. Numerous Irish Americans had found their ways into brutal manual labor, but had also worked their way into the Catholic clergy, the New York police force, and positions of low-ranking political office.

Irish Americans were finding some success and making inroads into the ranks of the city's middle class. The city was filled with immigrants from all over the world. New York was the premiere melting pot of the United States, where people of many different cultures were forced by dint of geography to live side by side. In a walk downtown one could hear languages and accents from all over the world, creating a street-wide symphony filled with Yiddish, Chinese, Italian, German, Irish brogues, and many other languages and accents.

And in New York, each ethnic group had its own neighborhood. While Hell's Kitchen eventually became the last bastion of the Irish neighborhoods in New York City, the area in and around the Five Points in lower Manhattan was, at that time, the landing site and main Irish neighborhood.

The district of the Lower East Side, between City Hall and Houston Street, was known as Little Ireland. In the late 1800s this New York City neighborhood had more Irish residents than Dublin. In this neighborhood today there are such existing spots as the founding site of the Ancient Order of Hibernians, Al Smith's childhood home, the former Five Points, and sites associated with Tammany Hall, Thomas Addis Emmet, and many others.

Not all the streets were paved. In fact, there were more paved streets uptown and over by Wall Street, but around this area there was little development. This was the voting block, ignored for years by politicians, which eventually became the backbone of Tammany Hall. Eventually, one of the new neighborhoods populated by the Irish became Greenwich Village.

❧

Into this hectic, rough-and-tumble neighborhood was born Timothy James Mara on July 29, 1887. "A poor boy from Greenwich Village, he began running bets as a messenger when he was only a 12-year-old newsboy," wrote Pro Football Hall of Fame and *New York Times* reporter Arthur Daley, a longtime friend of the Mara clan. In fact, Tim was a very successful newspaper boy. According to Daley, Tim quit school when his father, a policeman, died, in order to help his brother, John J. Mara, and his mother survive (several searches of the city's records and of the newspaper's incomplete obituary and death notices did not yield any confirmation of this fact). Aside from being a newspaper boy, he was also an usher at the Ziegfeld Theater, sold programs at Madison Square Garden, sold law books, and was a runner for professional bookmakers. As a newspaper boy, his route ran along Broadway from the old Wannamaker's store up to Union Square. That route just happened to be studded with a large number of bookmaking establishments. According to later reports, Tim was impressed by the bookmakers.

At one point, Mara attended Public School 14 during the day and worked in the mornings and evenings to earn money. A former newspaper boy and friend of Mara's jockied a horse. Tim bet on him for good luck. "The horse lost, but the experience started Mr. Mara on the pathway of his life," *The New York Times* reported sometime later. He began as a runner of bets between the hotel guests to whom he delivered papers and the bookmakers.

Tim, even at a young age, was extremely clever. He worked both sides of the streets, so to speak. He was paid 5¢ for every losing bet placed by one of his newspaper route players. Of course he also received tips, sometimes very generous ones, from those same people when he delivered their winnings.

Another benefit of his paper route was that many of his customers were the colorful old Democratic figures of the time. Some of these men rose to great heights and led to many political associations for Tim that would have incredible sway over the rest of his life.

"Being as smart as he was ingenuous, he began booking the bets himself and eventually became one of the town's most respected 'wagering commissioners' when this was a legal profession, reported *The New York Times*."

As a reliable young boy, Mara gained the trust of Thomas O'Brien. O'Brien was an acolyte of the famed gambler Arnold Rothstein. The trustworthy Mara soon gained a reputation as a successful numbers runner. "In the morning Mara worked his newspaper route, and in the evening he picked up payments from O'Brien's customers and delivered winnings to the lucky few whose number had hit," wrote sports biographer Andrew O'Toole. "Mara soon learned that, by his own description, bookmakers 'lived best and worked the least.' He began covering small wagers on his own and by the time he was 16, Mara had his own clientele.

"On leaving school, Mr. Mara took a job with a law-book firm on Nassau Street. The contacts he made with lawyers to whom he delivered the books helped him to extend his betting business," the *Times* continued. "When he opened his own place, the New York Law Bindery, someone remarked that 'more than bookbinding goes on there.'"

"[Mara] became a bookie in 1910," wrote Pulitzer Prize–winning author James Agee in *Fortune* magazine. By 1921 he had closed his Manhattan business and had firmly planted himself in the enclosure at Belmont Racetrack. "Some of his avocations: customers' man in Wall Street for Al Smith's pal Mike Meehan (1927–30); coal business (Mara Fuel Co., still listed); liquor business (Kenny-Mara Importers Co., 1933, still listed); [and] a Scotch labeled Timara."

Mara, throughout his life, was always involved in more than one business, or one profession, at any given time. Out of his constantly moving offices he would run as many as two or three businesses while at the same time promoting events around town, or a number of other things.

The one constant in his life remained his love of horse racing and gambling. However he was not a gambler; he did not make his money, like Art Rooney, owner of the Pittsburgh Steelers, gambling on events (though Mara often boasted of large wagers). Rather, Tim Mara was a bookmaker. Eventually Mara became one of the biggest bookmakers on the East Coast. Today, the word bookmaker has a negative connotation as a profession that is largely legally banned. But until the 1930s being a bookmaker was a legal profession, much in the same way it is legal today in the United Kingdom and elsewhere.

At racetracks throughout the New York metro region, Mara ran one of the most well-thought-of and successful companies. Bookmakers had their own offices, or stands, at each racecourse, including Belmont and Saratoga Springs. This single business afforded Mara a lifestyle few could match. As has been said before, horse racing is the sport of kings. It is also the sport of very rich people. Through his associations with horse racing, Mara was able to rub shoulders with the Vanderbilts, the Astors, the Belmonts, and many of New York's best families. His name often appeared in the society columns in *The*

New York Times. It also gave him entry into the sporting world, as well as a Damon Runyon–esque world of New York characters.

His high-rolling customers, whether downstate or in Saratoga, included such big players as Arnold Rothstein, Harry Payne Whitney, Colonel E.R. Bradley, Harry Sinclair, Nick the Greek, Remy Dorr, Sam Rosoff, Isidore Bieber, and others. The only bigger name was Art Rooney, who rarely bet with Tim in the years he cleaned up. In fact, Tim often helped Art out in his betting schemes.

"[Mara] has a place at Lake Luzerne, near Saratoga," James Agee once wrote about Mara. "He is variously known about the tracks as (a) just a big, good-natured guy and (b) the ultimate truculent mug. But everyone agrees that as a mental mathematician he's second only to [Long Tom] Shaw and, as a bookie, among the most imminently successful."

"Tim Mara was a big man in every way," wrote Phil Bieber, brother of Isidore Bieber, a popular gambler and a sometimes handicapper, to Red Smith once. "Big in stature and big in gambling undertakings. Back in the 1930s, when New York racing ended in October and reopened in April, a few bookmakers opened shop in private rooms, taking action on New Orleans races. They catered mainly to their regular racetrack clients, which provided a winter income and kept them in touch with their customers."

Many hotels in Times Square, including the Knickerbocker and the Times Square Metropole, drew a crowd of men looking for action, as several other suites there also offered recreational gambling, including card games and other casino-type games in the 1920s and 1930s. Rothstein had once taken over a gambling concern at the Knickerbocker, and was a regular in its restaurant and bar. Regardless of whether Mara and Rothstein ever did business, it would seem they certainly must have known each other socially, especially since Rothstein also enjoyed the comforts of Saratoga in the summer, and was known to wager there liberally. And they certainly had a large number of friends in common, including Tammany Hall associates like Jimmy Walker and Al Smith, and shared such friends as Thomas O'Brien, Billy Gibson, baseball legend John McGraw, and others. However, no record exists of any transactions between them, and Rothstein was known for his dislike of football (one of the few things he rarely, if ever, bet on).

In the 1920s Rothstein's establishment at the Metropole drew the likes of William Vanderbilt, Julius Fleischmann, Joseph Seagram, and many other wealthy high rollers. Tim's operation was similar.

"Tim operated a large, well-furnished suite in the Knickerbocker Hotel at Broadway and forty-second Street, continued Bieber." This was an old-fashioned betting parlor, not unlike something right out of a movie. The right knock at the door got you in. Palm trees, spittoons, a small bar. "There was a wire service for prices, track conditions, off times, etc., but communications often broke down and it was never certain whether the delay would be one of minutes or hours." This created problems for bookmakers and players alike. A player could bet, but might have to wait some time to collect his money. The player also had difficulty trying to figure how to wager his bets—by size, etc. The bookmaker didn't know if he had won or lost, and it was difficult trying to lay those bets off on other bookies around town.

One day Isidore and Phil Bieber came to Mara's to lay down a few bets. Isidore and Tim were good friends. It was smoky, and neither brother wanted to stay. The wire was down in New Orleans. Isidore placed "a series of wagers with provisos to increase the bets in the event he had winners, and he added a few parlays as well." The two then left together to take in a film. They returned at 5:30 PM, and Mara was at his desk, the only man left in the suite of rooms, feet up with his hands behind his desk.

"How was the movie?" asked Mara. "Hope you enjoyed it."

"Come on, give us the results and let's go out to eat," Isidore said to Tim. Tim then got up and invited Isidore to sit in his chair so he could show him the figures. Isidore went around and sat down. Then Mara told him to put his feet up on the desk. Isidore was flustered.

"Shut up!" said big Tim, laughing. "Relax," he continued, a little quieter now. "You own the joint. All five of your horses came in. I still haven't figured out how much I owe you, but Beeb, it's more than I have. Got any questions?"

"Come on, I'm starved," said Isidore. And so the three went to dinner at a place called Paddells, on Forty-second Street and Broadway. They picked a table near the back to have some privacy. They ordered dinner and began to eat. They traded a little small talk. Then Tim spoke up.

"Beeb, how are we going to settle this? I can give you part of it tomorrow, but..."

"Don't give me any buts," said Iz, as Isidore was called. "You know how much you need to keep your joint going. Play it safe, and give me what you can spare. We'll settle the balance after you get in action at the track in the spring."

"Mara sat staring at my big brother," Phil wrote to Red. He was "shaking his head slowly from side to side." Mara then rose, put his arm around his friend's shoulders, and laughed until their cheeks almost touched. He then strode laughing out of the restaurant. Phil was all choked up until his brother spoke.

"Look, Phil," said Iz, "the guy stuck us with the bill."

They waited for spring. Racing returned to New York. The spring had been good to Tim. "Of course he settled the debt," wrote Phil. "Almost $65,000 in real, old-time dollars. A smile and a hug had sealed it."

Mara lived most of his life in New York. He associated with the most fascinating circles of people. By dint of necessity, he and Mrs. Mara spent every summer in Saratoga Springs, where he ran his extensive betting business and interacted with the finest people of New York society. Not bad for a poor Irish boy from Greenwich Village.

Throughout his life, Tim Mara remained a successful businessman who was never afraid to dabble in businesses about which he knew nothing. At one time he was even a successful investment banker, which was something that truly suited his entrepreneurial nature. He had been a successful stockbroker. He was also briefly in the coal business, making his offices at Twenty-third Street and Lexington Avenue.

Another constant in Mara's life was his love of boxing. For a period, Mara was one of the city's premiere boxing promoters. He promoted many matches. It was no surprise to those who knew him that promoting boxing was his favorite chore among his many occupations. Firstly, boxing was purely speculative. Sometimes he made scads of money from these events, and a few times he lost huge sums. But by and large, Tim Mara was known as a very successful promoter who made lots of money setting up matches. Secondly, boxing made him a star. It was not a bad thing to be a businessman who could offer the best seats in town to his customers, business and political associates, etc. It put him at the absolute center of the New York back-scratching world. He became a man to know. And lastly, boxing often added a spike to his betting operations, so when things broke just right, he made money on the event and the book.

"Tim Mara was a white-haired, curly haired Irishman with a brogue. I don't think he'd gone very far in school though," said Hall of Fame Giants player Tuffy Leemans. "But he enjoyed everything he ever did, and win or lose, there was no long face on him. My best friend was the old man."

"Tim Mara is a large, curly headed, thick-fleshed Irishman with the wide, relaxed, dimpled, big-mouthed, and keen type of Irish face," observed Agee. "Timothy James Mara's life is too colorfully involved to bear writing on a thumbnail." Agee also observed that Tim hadn't driven a car since 1915, when he was injured in a disastrous car accident, and was an avid player of golf.

Toots Shor, the famous saloonkeeper who catered to New York's sporting scene for at least two generations, was a great friend of Tim Mara. "The big thing about Tim was his imagination. You could tell him he had to make germs the most popular thing in town, and he'd find a way. He'd get everybody in New York absolutely nuts to have the most germs on their block. He was a promotional genius...and a very close, dear friend."

"I never passed up the chance to promote anything," Mara once said. "Not just because of the profit but for the challenge of promoting something."

Perhaps the real center of Mara's world was his closest friends. William "Bill" Kenny was one of Mara's best customers and a good friend. Kenny was a childhood friend of politician Al Smith. Kenny had made millions as a contractor in the city. By 1926 he was estimated to be worth $30 million. At one point Kenny built an opulent room called the "Tiger Room" atop his office building at Twenty-third Street and Park Avenue South. "A private clubhouse retreat. Named for the 'Tammany Tigers,' the lavish penthouse featured a huge fireplace, tiger skins, brass tigers, and tiger paintings. Entertainment was provided by Al Jolson, Will Rogers, and, on one occasion, the entire cast of the Ziegfeld Follies," reported *New York* magazine years later. "But politics dominated. 'You could no more get up to that Tiger Room than you could get into heaven, unless you were a damn good contributor,' producer Eddie Dowling once said."

"There was 24-hour food and drink service, and guests could comfortably be put up overnight," wrote political biographer George Walsh. "Here Kenny and his three brothers (who likewise became wealthy in his business) would gather for poker parties with Smith and New York's mostly Irish political leaders, as well as Irish entrepreneurs like banker James J. Riordan and bookmaker Timothy Mara." Other visitors included well-known banker Herbert H. Lehman and shipbuilder William H. Todd. Several prominent Irish politicians, such as Mara's good friend Jimmy Walker, future mayor of New York City, were also patrons of the Tiger Room.

Eventually Mara married Lizette Barclay, and they had two sons. First born was John V. Mara on March 21, 1908, who came to be known as Jack. Second came Wellington Timothy Mara, born on August 14, 1916. According to Wellington, his name was an accident. He claimed later in life he had been named Timothy Wellington Mara by his parents, but his birth certificate reversed the order. His parents never bothered to rectify the mistake, and the change stuck. Wellington soon developed the nickname "Duke," which came from people associating Well's name with the "Duke of Wellington." And that stuck, too.

Timothy and Lizette were, among many things, devout Catholics and they passed on to their children a deep sense of religion. They were very involved in the Catholic community in New York City and its environs, whether they were in Westchester, Saratoga, or in Spring Lake, New Jersey, where Mrs. Mara liked to summer in later life. This would play an important role in their sons' lives. Both were sent to private Catholic schools, including the Jesuit Fordham University in New York, an important building block in each man's life. Both Jack and Well continued their involvement in Catholic churches throughout their lives in the metro region. Even into his old age, Wellington would impress upon his grandchildren, more than 50 years later, the need to go to confession and attend mass, tying it to rewards from their devoted grandfather. While visiting each of his 40 grandchildren, he would leave notes on refrigerator doors during the Advent season of the Catholic church, writing, "No confession. No Christmas."

Through both their religious charities, as well as secular ones, Tim and Lizette also impressed upon both their boys the need for involvement in helping the less fortunate. Any kind of charity involvement was a good one. Many of the charities, foundations, and other good works in which the Maras were involved included the Catholic church, but not always. However, they almost always centered on kids, athletics, and sportsmanship. Later, medical concerns and charities also attracted the family's attention.

On a windy, cold, late evening in 1923, Tim Mara was lost in Rockland County, out by West Nyack, when his car died in Blauvelt, New York. Stranded, cold, and hungry, Tim wandered the dark, deserted back roads until he came upon a convent. The Sisters of Saint Dominic of Blauvelt opened their door to the stranger and fed him a hot meal in their kitchen. The Dominican convent was devoted to helping less-fortunate children. Tim became a great benefactor of the convent from that night on. And when Tim died, Jack made sure the convent was well taken care of. When Jack passed on, Wellington carried on the tradition until the day he died.

Though Tim shed many of his business interests late in life, he passed on to Jack and Well a devotion to the family's football franchise—the New York Giants. Or maybe they passed it on to him. But there is no denying that the Giants were the single unifying magnet that held a huge, and at times warring, Irish clan together for almost a century, or at least for four generations of Maras.

THE ROARING TWENTIES

"The 1920s in the United States [were] called 'roaring' because of the exuberant, freewheeling popular culture of the decade," states *The New Dictionary of Cultural Literacy,* Third Edition. "The Roaring Twenties was a time when many people defied Prohibition, indulged in new styles of dancing and dressing, and rejected many traditional moral standards."

Prohibition jump-started the Jazz Age. As songwriter Hoagy Carmichael put it, the 1920s came in "with a bang of bad booze, flappers with bare legs, jangled morals, and wild weekends." According to novelist F. Scott Fitzgerald, during Prohibition, "The parties were bigger...the pace was faster...and the morals were looser."

With the ending of the Great War, many veterans came home disillusioned, and sought new truths. The 1920s also ushered in the Jazz Age, a period in which new music helped to dismantle the last conventions of the Victorian age. It was epitomized by writers like Fitzgerald, who waded fully clothed into the fountain in front of the Plaza Hotel, and Edna St. Vincent Millay, who wrote the Jazz Age credo:

> My candle burns at both ends
> It will not last the night;
> But ah, my foes, and oh, my friends—
> It gives a lovely light.

Speakeasies were the norm. New York soon became known as the "City on the Still," as it was noted there were probably 100,000 of them in the metro region, including Brooklyn. Speakeasies were popular because people of all stripes came to drink the bad bathtub gin, enjoy the jazz, and rub elbows with all manner of people. Famous clubs included the Cotton Club, Small's Paradise, and the Trocadero, among many. And from these joints, large and small, rang loudly the music of Louis Armstrong, Bix Beiderbecke, and bandleaders like Duke Ellington and Jim Cullum (of the Jim Cullum Jazz Band). Popular dances were soon replaced with more lascivious gyrations, including the tango, the blackbottom, and, of course, the Charleston.

Broadway was known then as "the Great White Way," counting at its peak more than 100 theaters. Plays were still very much in vogue, and movies were still silent. *If You Knew Suzie, Sweet Georgia Brown,* and *I'm Sitting on Top of the World* were the three big hits of 1925. Fitzgerald published his masterpiece, *The Great Gatsby,* while Ernest Hemingway's greatest accomplishments still lay ahead of him. The Pierce Arrow was America's most luxurious car. And there was a small trial down in Tennessee being fought by William Jennings Bryant and Clarence Darrow that would become known as the Scopes Monkey Trial. It pitted America's fundamentalist Christian beliefs against the cold science of Charles Darwin's *Theory of Evolution*.

This was also the golden age of sports, popularized by sportswriters like Ring Lardner, Damon Runyon, and the granddaddy of all popularizers, Grantland Rice. The king of American sports was baseball. And the town was dominated by two bigger-than-life legends, old John McGraw of the New York Giants (a friend of Mara's) and George Herman "Babe" Ruth, the "Sultan of Swat" of the New York Yankees. With three teams in the city at the time—the New York Giants, the New York Yankees, and the Brooklyn Dodgers—baseball was king.

"I remember as a kid I was taken down to the Yankees dugout and introduced to Babe Ruth and Lou Gehrig," Wellington said. "This was before you had a public-address system. The public-address system consisted of one or two men with megaphones who walked around the periphery who would say, 'Now pitching for New York is so and so.' One of them was named Jack Lenz, who was a friend of my father's. He got me down to the dugout so I could meet Ruth and Gehrig."

But when the pennants of October snapped for the last time in the autumn wind, the new sportswriters raised new legends. And those were the men of college football.

The 1920s were the heyday of college football. Men like Knute Rockne and the Four Horsemen, Red Grange, and many more ruled the landscape. Teams like Notre Dame, Army, Navy, Michigan, Ohio State, and many more dominated the nation's attention in the fall. College games drew huge crowds, from 50,000 to 100,000 spectators, depending on the size of the stadium. Newspapers devoted great amounts of coverage to these sporting events.

And of course, by this time, boxing had names like Jack Dempsey (the "Manassa Mauler") and Gene Tunney. It was the heyday of the American sportsman. And it was during a visit to one of Tim's closest friends and fellow boxing promoter Billy Gibson to discuss a possible match between the popular Dempsey and Tunney that the football Giants were born.

"I remember it was a hot, steamy day," Mara later recalled of his visit in August 1925, "and it was so damned uncomfortable I wasn't sure I could sit there for very long to deal. I had to keep moving, but I went because I had already started out for his office and I wanted some of Tunney. I really did."

As Wellington pointed out later, "My father had actually been instrumental in Tunney's early career. He also had been very friendly from boyhood with Al Smith, and through him with the political organization in New York City and the state, and boxing at that time was very politically oriented. My father helped Tunney to get some fights that he otherwise might not have been able to get."

Already inside Gibson's office were Joe Carr, the commissioner of the infant National Football League, and Dr. Harry March, one of the more outspoken proponents of "postgraduate football." They had come in an effort to get Gibson to purchase and establish a franchise in New York, which the new league desperately needed as one of its linchpins. Gibson was busy waving the men off when he saw Mara enter his offices.

"Last year we fielded 18 clubs. We want to make it 20 this year," Carr was saying. "Including New York...we need a club in New York, where the action is. Madison Square Garden, the Polo Grounds...Yankee Stadium, Babe Ruth, Jamaica Race Track, Belmont..."

"No, no, I don't think it will promote," Gibson reportedly said. Gibson had owned an earlier rendition of the football team, which had failed spectacularly years earlier. "Maybe my friend Tim here would like to buy it."

"Buy what?" asked the hot, exasperated Mara.

"A franchise for New York City in a professional football league," Carr replied.

"How much?" asked Mara.

"Five hundred dollars," Carr said.

"Sure. Any sports franchise for New York ought to be worth $500. Even football. I'll take it." And he wrote them a check, and the New York Football Giants were brought into existence. But there was one problem—Tim Mara had never even seen a football game.

"The Giants were founded on a combination of brute strength and ignorance. The players supplied the brute strength, and I supplied the ignorance," Mara said years later. "But you have to remember that New York City in the 1920s was virgin area for a smart promoter. There was money around, and people would buy anything, or at least they would come to see or hear it." As Arthur Daley once opined about Mara, "He couldn't distinguish the difference between an end run and a goal post. But he had intelligence, personal integrity, and a blazing competitive fire."

Truth be known, over the expanse of time, and in the hands of an expert promoter like Tim Mara, the story of the $500 was a little bit of blarney. The sum was probably more than that—the number $2,500 has also been bandied about, both by Mara and others. Either figure today is a paltry sum, especially when one considers the current value of the New York Football Giants or their brethren, the New York Jets, or the fees associated with gaining entry into the National Football League in the 21st century.

"In New York, even if only for an empty room with two chairs is worth that kind of money," Mara himself once said of the sum.

"I was betting on the city of New York," Mara later said. "Sports have always been important in New York, and the franchise was worth that money even if it had been in the shoe-shine league."

"The professional game was looked down upon: college football was not minor league then, but the true sport, and Westbrook Pegler could reflect the general disdain by writing of 'the alleged Giants.' The pro owners were 'sportsmen,' which meant they sometimes owned horses and bet baseball, and they often held league meetings in hotel rooms, breaking for card games across the twin beds, and for serious drinking," wrote Robert Lipsyte in *The New York Times*. Professional football was played in places like Canton, Ohio; Latrobe, Pennsylvania; Hammond, Indiana; and other places far out in rural America. It reminded folks of farm laborers and mud. It wasn't something New Yorkers were looking for. In truth, Mara was taking an awful gamble. It was the kind of big gamble he was dying to take. It was the giant challenge he was interested in matching his skills against. He relished the moment.

It later turned out that Gibson relented and decided to throw in with his good friend Tim. Mara would remain the official owner, and Gibson an investor. But Mara owned the team, and little did anyone know or care that it would be 66 years before anyone other than a Mara family member would ever own a piece of the Giants again.

Mara started by hiring Dr. Harry March. He was hired as club secretary, and was given the job of organizing the club. He was to find the players, assemble the necessary equipment, and other necessities. Mara and March looked for a coach and found Bob Folwell, a longtime college football coach whose most recent stop had been the football team at Annapolis for the Naval Institute.

The team realized they needed a name to attract the necessary crowds to make it worth their while in New York City. They set their sights on Jim Thorpe. Thorpe was one of the most recognizable celebrity athletes in America. He had won the pentathlon and the decathlon in the 1912 Olympics, and the King of Sweden said to him, "Sir, you are the greatest athlete in the world." His accomplishments on the gridiron placed him on the 1911 and 1912 All-American football teams. Thorpe eventually became the first president of the American Professional Football Association in 1920.

But by 1925 Thorpe was 37 years old and nicked up. Mara thought they would be able to get Thorpe relatively cheaply, and that his presence would mean a lot to fans and give the franchise credibility, even if his greatest feats on the football field were far behind him. And so they signed him to one of the most unique contracts in the history of professional sports. Owing to the fact that he could probably not play an entire game anyway, he was signed to a contract that paid him $250 per half.

While Thorpe's name gave the team glitz, a series of other signings gave the Giants their backbone. Mara and March signed up Yale All-American tackle Century Milstead, Penn State star running back Henry "Hinkey" Haines, and from Syracuse, star running back Jack McBride and star tackle Joe "Doc" Alexander. Alexander had retired from football to pursue a medical career.

Being a football player in those days was a different kind of experience. Most of these fellows held regular jobs during the day. A few did not. Some worked full time after the season was over. Even by the mid to late 1930s, pro football players were still not making a lot of money.

"The only trouble with being a pro football player in New York was that you were bored to death. You had too much leisure time on your hands. We didn't have all those meetings these guys have today," said Hall of Fame running back Tuffy Leemans years later. "Oh, sure, New York was the big city, but your ball players weren't making enough money to be whooping it up all the time."

At best, really good players in those days made $400 per game. There were many things that had to be done, and by the time the season ended, Mara and Gibson found themselves on the hook for more than $25,000, including salaries, equipment, and other extras—a goodly sum in those days.

The first two games on the Giants schedule were road games, and then the team would host nine straight home games. The first game was up in Rhode Island against the Providence Steam Roller, another new franchise in 1925. The Giants went down 14–0. In their second game, also on the road, they lost to the Frankford Yellow Jackets in Philadelphia, Pennsylvania, with a score of 5–3. The next game was a home game.

"Tickets were a problem," Mara once said. "They must have been, because nobody wanted them."

"I can remember how he used to walk around the streets handing out free tickets and half-price tickets," Wellington told Newark *Star Ledger* writer David Klein. "And if he couldn't get half price, those became free too. All he wanted was to get some people into the stands. He had to do that before he could hope to get their money, I suppose." Wellington admitted New Yorkers only seemed to care about Army, Navy, and Notre Dame. "Besides, the professionals had an unsavory air about them, much like professional baseball players had when they first started touring the country." Both Mara and March were known to walk into restaurants, theaters, subways, and any other venue where they knew they could attract attention and hand out free tickets to get people to show up at the games.

According to football historian Dick Whittingham, "It was Sunday morning in New York, a clear, sunny October day in 1925. Mass was just letting out at Our Lady of Esperanza Roman Catholic Church up on 156th Street, between Broadway and Riverside Drive." Among the congregation were Mara, Lizette, and the Maras' two young sons. Folks were chatting, and Wellington stood by his father. His father turned to a friend and said, "I'm gonna try to put pro football over in New York today." Dressed in a dark overcoat with a velvet collar and wearing a derby hat, as he often wore up until his death, Mr. Mara went off to stake his fortune.

The first home game was at the Polo Grounds in New York, home of baseball's New York Giants. Mara had gotten people there. Paid or not, there were almost 25,000 people in the stands. Mara could only hold his breath. He had gotten them here on the strength of his name and reputation. You could lead a horse to water, but you couldn't make him drink. Mara had gotten the people there, but would they drink? Only time would tell. But from an attendance standpoint only, he had succeeded.

Tim paced the sideline. He had brought 17-year-old Jack with him, who sat on the sideline. Lizette and nine-year-old Wellington sat in the stands. "We were sitting on the Giants side, and it was a little chilly," said Wellington years later. And Lizette complained to Tim that the team's side was in the shade. Why couldn't the home team sit on the other side of the stadium, Lizette reasoned, in the sun, where it was nice and warm? "So the next game, and from then on, the Giants sideline in the Polo Grounds was in the sun."

And the Giants sideline has remained on the sunny side of the field ever since.

Wellington was sure his father had never seen a professional football game before. "I had seen one or two. My brother Jack had taken me to a couple of Fordham games."

Journalist John Steinbreder tells a story that after Frankford scored its first touchdown of the game and fans roared, Mara, the old race-tracker, turned to his son Jack, and asked, "What's a touchdown?"

Unfortunately the Giants flopped again, and started the season with a 0–3 record. To add insult to injury, Thorpe was so out of shape that he could not even play a full half. He was paid his full pay and was released after the game.

Would the crowds come back? Jack Mara estimated that his father handed over "at least 5,000 tickets to every game, and sometimes our crowds didn't add up to that many." Jack noted that many people didn't want to come—even for free—and most folks didn't even know what they were talking about when the Maras mentioned the football Giants. "Most of our friends wouldn't even come around.

They thought we meant the baseball Giants, and then they'd look at us like we were crazy, because they knew the baseball Giants didn't play football, and even if they did, they knew we sure as hell didn't own them."

"I used to pass out free tickets at school when I was a kid," Wellington said in later years, talking about one of those games from the late 1920s. "I was up in the stadium offices when I looked out to the field and saw some kid walking in the snow. It turned out to be my buddy Bill Colihan writing his name in the snow to prove to me he had been there."

The team eventually turned it around, and began a winning streak. But the franchise was not making money. By midseason Mara realized he was spending more each week than the Giants were bringing in. He needed to do something that would draw paying customers.

HAROLD "RED" GRANGE

Mara looked around for an idea, and it did not take him long. There was no bigger celebrity, no bigger draw in college football, than Harold "Red" Grange. With a shock of red hair, Grange had single-handedly captivated enormous crowds with his incredible abilities, and the writers of the golden age of sports were more than happy to praise his victories.

Grantland Rice once wrote of Grange that he was "three or four men and a horse rolled into one for football purposes." Rice also opined, "He is Jack Dempsey, Babe Ruth, Paavo Nurmi, and Man O'War."

The Illinois running back had dominated the field of play. In 1924 Grange was pitted against the great Michigan team coached by Fielding Yost. Michigan had not lost since 1921. Grange sliced and pounded his way through the Michigan team at will. He began his barrage with a 95-yard kickoff return. In the fourth quarter he scored on three con-secutive drives. He put up scoring runs of 67, 56, and 44 yards—all in the first quarter. In all Grange scored five touchdowns and threw for another in an incredible 39–14 win. It is important to understand that in their 21 previous games, Michigan had allowed a total of only 32 points, and it gave up only 24 points in its following 17 games. Red

Grange was the real thing. And crowds showed up in fantastic numbers to watch him perform these prodigious feats.

One of the key lines from the articles in the *Chicago Tribune* relating the events of the game stated, "They knew he was coming; they saw him start; he made no secret of his direction; he was in their midst, and he was gone!" When Grange garnered 63,000 fans when the Illini played the Penn Quakers at Philadelphia, and then another 72,000 showed up at Ohio State to watch him, his status as a superstar was sealed.

Mara decided it was time for Red Grange to leave college. He told Dr. March and the boys about his plan, then left for Chicago.

"Mara's plan was to sign him and get him into a Giants uniform to play against the Chicago Bears at the Polo grounds. 'It would save the franchise,' Mara told March," wrote Whittingham. "Mara then promptly reserved a drawing room aboard the 20th Century Limited."

The problem was, Red Grange had a representative, and his name was C.C. Pyle. He was soon to become known as "Cash and Carry" Pyle, because he got tremendous amounts of cash for Grange's services, even out of the toughest promoters.

Dr. March and the boys received a telegram. It read:

> Partially successful STOP
> Returning on train tomorrow STOP
> Will explain STOP
> Tim Mara

"We couldn't figure out what 'partially successful' meant," Wellington later told Whittingham. Well's father explained when he got back.

"He'll be playing in the Giants-Bears game here," he exclaimed. "Only he'll be playing for the Bears," he said less enthusiastically. Mara had been too late. Cash and Carry Pyle had extracted one of the most infamous deals in all of professional team sports. He had made a deal with Bears co-owners George Halas and Dutch Sternaman in which he split the gate receipts with the Bears for two years—17 games—50/50. In 1925 Pyle and Grange took home more than $250,000. There was no way Mara could compete.

But he was thrilled that one of Grange's stops was going to be the Polo Grounds. He had made sure of that. The barnstorming would begin at the end of the college football season in 1925.

In the meantime the New York Football Giants had run up a record of 7–3 and were considered a solid team within the new league. They just weren't making any money. Mara estimated he was down about $40,000 toward the end of the season. He was lamenting his losses to his visiting friend, Governor Al Smith, when Smith rejoined, "Pro football will never amount to anything. Why don't you give it up?"

Mara nodded his head toward his two sons, who happened to be near, and said, "The boys would run me right out of the house if I did."

Grange and the Bears were playing their way through the Midwest en route to New York. With engagements in Detroit, Pittsburgh, Washington, D.C., Providence, and other cities between Thanksgiving and his date with the Giants, Grange and the Bears played seven games in 11 days.

No matter, though. The publicity of his games across the country and in the local newspapers leading up to the game made sure every New Yorker knew Grange was coming to the big city.

The date was December 6, 1925. The day before had been the Army vs. Navy game, and the Polo Grounds had numerous seats still set up because that game annually drew enormous crowds. Mara was worried that the Giants wouldn't fill the extra stands. He and a few fellow employees manned the ticket office and waited. And New York showed up, 70,000 strong. The Polo Grounds were packed.

"It looked like an invasion. People had brought ladders and were scaling the walls, and for everyone who was caught and ejected, 10 more made it in and saw the game for free standing in the aisles," Mara later said.

"When I saw that crowd and knew that half the cash in the house was mine, I said to myself, 'Timothy, how long has this gravy train been running?'"

Not surprisingly, the New York Giants lost to Grange's Bears, 19–7. On the final play of the game, Grange, who also played defense, intercepted a pass and ran it back for a touchdown. The Giants finished the year 8–4, but ending the season with a loss didn't mean much compared to Tim's victorious accomplishment. Grange had made a whopping $30,000 that day alone. The Bears walked away with $56,000. And Tim Mara had not only wiped out his $40,000 of debt, he ended the season with a tidy profit of $18,000.

Tim had made it work. He had "put professional football over in New York." He had found his biggest professional challenge, and he had come out victorious. To top even that, he had finally seen that if he were successful, if football were successful in New York, it might not be as huge as professional baseball, but it could indeed come close. He was like Moses and knew what the promised land might hold—but would he ever get to see it?

He had one successful season in 1925. Could he pull it off again?

CHAPTER 2

A Season of Woes

THE GRANGE WAR OF 1926 (AND THEN SOME)

If putting together a successful season the first year was another accomplishment in Timothy Mara's already sensational career, then repeating that success would be a long time in coming. Or so it seemed.

C.C. Pyle and Red Grange had made a fortune in 1925. They made a lot more than the owners did. And Grange's success had garnered Pyle new—and just as famous—players as clients from the college ranks. He controlled the talent, and now he wanted control of the league. Cash and Carry saw dollar signs. He tried to extort Halas and Sternaman, asking for unacceptable terms that were even pricier than those of the year before. He wanted a piece of the team for Grange and himself. The co-owners drew the line. It was exactly what Pyle was hoping to hear—it had been a calculated move.

The real prize, as Pyle saw it, was New York, the most successful stop on the Grange tour. Of course, were it not for Mara's promoting panache, Grange and Pyle would not have profited so handsomely. But Halas's loss was not to be Mara's gain. Pyle wanted his own franchise in New York.

Grange and Pyle arrived on February 26, 1926, for the NFL owners meeting at the Hotel Statler in Detroit, Michigan. As most owners saw it then, Grange was just a good, All-American kid with incredible talent who was being dangerously misled by this incredible charlatan, Pyle. And Pyle might as well have been named Rasputin, for the NFL owners did everything to antagonize him and vilify him in their conversations.

Nothing could have been further from the truth. Grange knew the owners would make money off of him, and this encouraged Pyle to extraordinary heights of brashness. And to his credit, Pyle was trying to help the owners make as much money as they could off the gridiron star, but first he wanted to make sure his star got the lion's share of the profits. He controlled what every man in the room wanted, and he would have exploited them if given half the chance. The fact that Pyle's demeanor was seen as arrogant only made his declarations more despised.

After some pleasant introductions, the afternoon got off to an awful start for Tim, and it was only going to get worse. According to NFL historian Bob Carroll, "He announced that he and Red had secured a five-year lease on Yankee Stadium for all the Sunday and holiday dates from October 15 to December 31. They proposed running their own franchise. C.C. painted a convincing picture...the league members all stood to profit greatly."

"I have the biggest star in football. I have a lease on the biggest stadium in the country. And I am coming into your league whether you like it or not," Pyle told the assemblage.

Several owners didn't even wince, instead offering to sign up right away. Mara balked. He had paid for an exclusive franchise. Few owners sided with Mara. Pyle claimed 19 of the 20 owners acquiesced to him—only Mara declined. Out of respect for Mara, a number of fellow owners hesitated.

That Saturday night several owners tried to get Pyle and Mara to sit down and talk out their differences. Grange's inclusion in the league would be a boon to the fledgling organization. And of course two strong franchises in New York would only help the league overall. The city supported *three* baseball teams, but Mara knew it meant that there would be one loser, and that the Giants would be the "second" team in New York City.

A compromise was offered. What if Pyle moved his team to Brooklyn? It would be another 10 miles from the Polo Grounds, and that was where the Dodgers played.

"It was doomed. Mara had developed a healthy dislike for Pyle's arrogance the year before when negotiating the Grange Tour into the Polo Grounds. Now C.C. was treating him as a tiresome obstacle to a New Dawn and Tim had his Irish up," Carroll wrote.

According to Dr. March, "Mister Pyle's chin narrowly missed a massaging several times."

In any case, Pyle's fate was sealed. The NFL barred his joining the league. Pyle went to work trying to place his stable of stars across a new league he founded—the American Football League. And his new team with Red Grange became the New York Football Yankees.

George Halas was quoted years later as saying that after the owners meeting disintegrated, Pyle told Grange, "No blasted Irishman is going to keep me out of New York!"

Pyle controlled Grange, of course, and worked at placing players like Wildcat Wilson and the Four Horsemen of Notre Dame. One of college football's biggest stars in 1925 had been Ernie Nevers. Since their first meetings, both Pyle and the league members assumed Nevers would play for Pyle.

❦

What the pompous Pyle didn't know was that the West Coast's most prolific back of 1925, Stanford's Nevers, had pledged his allegiance to the unlikeliest of all NFL owners—Ole Haugsrud. Ole was of Swedish extraction and was the quiet owner of the Duluth Eskimoes. He'd bought the franchise for the price of $1, which the previous owners accepted, and then invested in 25¢ beers all in the same sitting.

Haugsrud had been skeptical of Pyle's claim that Nevers was locked up, so Haugsrud went to St. Louis, where Nevers was pitching for the St. Louis Browns. The famed Stanford head coach, Pop Warner, proclaimed Nevers the best back he had ever coached.

"Ernie was very glad to see me, and I was glad to see him," Haugsrud told writer Myron Cope. "I met with him and his wife at their apartment, and Ernie showed me a letter he had from C.C. Pyle."

"Ole, if you can meet the terms Pyle is offering in this letter, it's Okay with me. I'll play for Duluth," Nevers had told him. The terms were steep. Pyle had promised Nevers a salary of $15,000 a year, plus a percentage of some of the larger gates. Haugsrud was game, but he didn't know if his fellow owners were up for it.

Ole scheduled a meeting with his friend, and fellow owner/confidant, Tim Mara to develop a strategy. Ole was 23 years old and counted on the older, more successful Mara for advice. Both were headed for another owners meeting, this time held in August at the Morrison Hotel in Chicago.

"I'll tell you, kid," said Mara. "We got to do something here to make this a *league*." He now leaned in with a conspiratorial nod. "Now, we'll go through with the regular meeting, and when it gets halfway through and you got two, three ballgames, I will give you the high sign." With 22 teams in the league, there would be plenty of comers once they knew Ole had Nevers. And Mara hoped the news would energize the other owners. Many were skeptical and scared of the threat of Pyle's new league.

"Wait 'til I highball you, and then go up to the league president with your option on Nevers," Mara told Haugsrud at the meeting. And Ole did exactly as instructed. At the right moment during a lull in the meetings, Mara gave Ole the high sign, and Ole walked the option up to Joe Carr.

Carr read the documents and then interrupted the meeting. "Gentlemen! I got a surprise for you!" he bellowed, and then he told the owners the news. According to Haugsrud, the owners yelled like little children. Carr turned toward the young Swede and said, "You saved the league!"

After much commotion, Mara hollered to the owners, "Now let's start over and have a new draft." By this he meant that they would draft another schedule. "What we've got to do is to fill the ballparks in the big cities. So we've got to make road teams out of the Duluth Eskimoes and the Kansas City Cowboys."

But Pyle was still a force to be reckoned with. He stole Mara's coach, Bob Folwell, for his own New York Football Yankees. Another painful loss for the Giants was that of Century Milstead, who also defected to the new league. And so battle plans were drawn up. It would be the NFL, standing by Mara's Giants, while Pyle and Grange would roam the field at Yankee Stadium as the New York Football Yankees. No matter how you looked at it, it was going to be a tough season.

28

A LOT OF BALLS IN THE AIR

As if owning a fledgling football team wasn't enough of a challenge, Tim Mara involved himself in another endeavor. On March 8, 1926, *The New York Times* announced that Carr had been voted the president of the newly formed American Basketball League. It was the first professional basketball league in America.

There would be two franchises in the metro region, Tim Mara's New York Basketball Giants and a squad that would play in Brooklyn. Other cities included Philadelphia; Washington, D.C.; Boston; Detroit; Chicago; Cleveland; Fort Wayne, Indiana; Rochester, New York; and Buffalo, New York.

Generally sponsored by promoters or companies, the ABL was much more ethnic and "big city". By contrast, the later National Basketball League was made up of smaller-town teams.

Teams that succeeded in the league's first few years included the Cleveland Rosenblums, the New York Celtics, the Boston Whirlwinds, and the Philadelphia Sphas. "Players were generally the children of first-generation immigrants, many being Jewish, Italian, and Irish. Nat Holman, Harry Boykoff, Bobby McDermott, and Harry Litwak were but a few early stars," wrote Mike Selinker.

The major accomplishments of the league were banning the double dribble and eliminating the use of rope or chicken wire surrounding the court where the athletes played. The New York Basketball Giants never amounted to much and eventually were disbanded. And in 1931, the American Basketball League itself disbanded.

Nonetheless, the attempt to own a basketball franchise severely cut into Mara's war chests as he attempted to restock his football Giants. But having lots of balls in the air was what he was always about. The basketball Giants would be only a minor distraction over the coming years, as other endeavors were soon to plague him.

GENE TUNNEY AND JACK DEMPSEY

In August 1926, Gene Tunney was training in Speculator, New York, near Lake Pleasant, getting ready for his momentous bout with famed heavyweight champion Jack Dempsey. Dempsey was a sledgehammer of a boxer. The Manassa Mauler, as he was called, had dominated the

1920s as boxing's most feared and disliked champion. His brutal strength, lightning-fast hands, and ruddy looks were well known around the world, and he was easily as famous as Babe Ruth.

James Joseph "Gene" Tunney had been fighting since he was 17 years old. Where Dempsey was a former laborer turned athlete, Tunney was a smart individual. He had more schooling than Dempsey had and was extremely well-spoken.

During 1925, Tunney had been writing to Mara privately. He was trying to convince Mara to sign him up for a Dempsey fight. He would not fight the African American boxer Harry Wills, who was New York boxing commissioner James A. Farley's preferred choice for a tune-up before Dempsey. Tunney was hoping to skip Farley's preference and get right to the main event.

Mara responded to one of Tunney's letters, hoping not to antagonize Farley, for Farley was ensconced in the political machinery that Mara knew all too well. Farley was a dangerous man with lots of influence. Mara wrote an erudite letter in 1925 wherein he built a case point by point to try to mollify Tunney. Mara ended the letter, "By the way, Gene, who have you fought that justifies you getting a Dempsey rematch?"

But that was nonsense. Tunney was the only clear challenger Dempsey had not yet disposed of. As Roger Kahn pointed out in his biography of Dempsey, *A Flame of Pure Fire*, "Mara's disparagement was a business tactic. He had convinced Tunney that he alone could deliver Dempsey for a fight at the Polo Grounds, and that he wanted to be paid as much as possible for his services. Knocking Tunney was one of Mara's devices to stress his own importance."

"No record shows how Mara proposed to produce Dempsey, but moving money under the table was a reasonable supposition," continued Kahn. "Mara probably intended to offer...cash to the boxing commissioners and to Governor Alfred E. Smith...to license the Tunney fight." According to Kahn, Mara "warmly" mentioned the possibility of a $3 million gate. Mara was a persuasive individual. "The gilded picture impressed Tunney. He signed a contract promising Mara 10 percent of his purse for fighting Dempsey and...25 percent of his future earnings as heavyweight champion." Of course, Tunney probably had a similar deal with Billy Gibson, Mara's friend and investor in the New York Football Giants.

As Kahn pointed out in his exceptional 1920s biography, it was not unusual—especially given the world of shady boxing promoters—that a boxer should sell more than 100 percent of himself. Jack Dempsey was one boxer who had done this.

Once the match materialized, Mara began promoting the new young boxer to the press. On August 30, 1926, *The New York Times* reported, "Tim Mara, well-known sporting man, motored over to Lake Pleasant with the closing of the Saratoga racing season yesterday. Mara is associated with Billy Gibson...and a great friend of Gene Tunney's. Last week he bet $10,000 on Tunney against $15,000 put up by Tom Shaw." The article also went on to say, "He watched Gene carefully today and at the conclusion of the sparring declared he was ready to bet another $25,000 on the challenger at any odds."

Gibson himself was a great friend of Mara's and was also a well-known associate of Arnold Rothstein, the man who had organized the 1919 "Black Sox" World Series conspiracy. When Gibson managed Benny Leonard (World Lightweight Champion from 1917 to 1925), Gibson had trouble getting a boxing license in New York. Rothstein contacted Tammany's "Big Tom" Foley and secured a license for Gibson. After that, Rothstein collected 10 percent of everything Leonard earned while he was with Gibson. Gibson and Rothstein remained connected until Rothstein's untimely demise in 1928.

A little more than two weeks later, Mara's name was back in print at *The New York Times,* which reported that Dempsey remained a firm favorite. Babe Ruth, Ty Cobb, Tony Lazzeri, Bill Tilden, and even Ethel Barrymore proclaimed loudly that the Manassa Mauler was just too overwhelming a champion. However, Mara stood by his man: "Tunney will beat Dempsey. He is the cleverest and shiftiest boxer Dempsey ever faced. I have a big bet on Tunney," he was quoted in *The New York Times.*

On September 28, 1926, Gene Tunney met Jack Dempsey for the heavyweight championship of the world.

"On the morning of the fight, Dempsey's bodyguard Mike Trent gave the champ a small glass of olive oil, a habit meant to aid digestion," wrote David Pietrusza in his highly acclaimed biography of Rothstein. "Dempsey suffered something akin to food poisoning."

The fight took place in Philadelphia under the auspices of Tex Rickard, with more than 144,000 in attendance. The crowd at Philadelphia's Sesquicentennial Stadium (subsequently renamed Municipal, then JFK Stadium) included three cabinet members and six governors. Tunney won in 10 rounds. It was one of the biggest upsets in sports. It was also the single biggest payday in boxing—the gate was a record $1,895,733. Dempsey got the lion's share, taking home approximately $700,000. Tunney took $200,000. And Rickard got the rest.

"I was laughed to scorn by almost everybody when I insisted Gene would win," said a proud Gibson after the fight. "Gene will defend his title against whatever opponents are recognized as logical challengers for the title. And he will be ready to return to the ring next year."

When Tunney came to New York the next day from Philadelphia by train, the head of the welcoming committee, as noted by *The New York Times,* was one "Big Tim Mara." According to the *Times,* Mara whisked Tunney off to a luncheon with that other famous Irish son of Greenwich Village, Mayor Jimmy Walker.

"Writer Ring Lardner (who lost $500 on Dempsey) was among the many with suspicions. Damon Runyon didn't know what to think, but the whole set up bothered him," wrote Pietrusza. As Pietrusza reported, Rothstein and Abe Atell (also of the Black Sox scandal) were all over the fight.

No one thought either Tunney or Dempsey were in on it. But it was apparent something might not be right. Atell and Rothstein were bad news, and "Billy Gibson was, of course, very used to transacting business with Arnold Rothstein." And Atell and Tunney were good friends.

A former boxer of note, Grantland Rice was attributed with saving Tunney's life after Tunney's loss to Harry Greb, his only professional loss. Rice raced to a local pharmacy to "get enough adrenaline chloride to staunch Tunney's bleeding." Atell was also friends with

Gibson, and was seen in Tunney's corner, with Gibson, moments before the fight started. Atell was also tight with another man, Boo Boo Hoff, a Philadelphia crime lord whose name would soon surface in connection with Tunney. Gibson also met with Hoff after a call from Rothstein. When Hoffa ssured Rothstein he was betting $125,000 on Tunney ("I sent the word out," he told Rothstein), Rothstein did the same.

When Rothstein was shot to death in the Park Central Hotel in New York, his "private papers revealed a secret." Among the people hiding the dead man's assets were his wife, his mistress, his office functionaries, and his Broadway henchmen. Only one name came as a real surprise: "William Gibson of No. 505 Fifth Avenue."

THE END OF 1926

Three weeks later Mayor Jimmy Walker was the guest of honor at the Polo Grounds, where he was supposed to kick off the New York Football Giants' home opener by punting the ball from the stands to the field. Mara had also hired baseball clowns to entertain the crowd which was around 25,000 strong. However, His Honor arrived almost two hours late. After an hour Mara got tired of waiting for his erstwhile friend and began the game. Walker showed up just in time to watch the Frankford Yellow Jackets score the winning touchdown in the second quarter. The Giants eventually lost 6–0.

With Doc Alexander now doing double duty as player and coach, the Giants went on to compile a record of 8–4–1. This was good enough to place them seventh in a 22-team league. The Giants were a respectable football team.

On November 1, 1926, summonses were handed to the captains of the team and to Dr. Harry March with a complaint filed against the franchise. The complaint stated that both the Cleveland and New York clubs, the teams opposing each other that day, were playing on the Sabbath, and were therefore violating the "blue laws" of the period. The judge who eventually heard the case, Judge James Barnett of Washington Heights, was a regular at the Polo Grounds. "I attend the games myself, and fail to see any basis for such charges," said the judge. As he saw no disturbing of the peace in the playing of the games, he summarily dismissed the charges against the two clubs.

The season, as expected, was ugly. Attendance was so low Mara thought of folding up the team again. And even with the free tickets, it was hard to fill up the stands. The team was losing money. The only good news was that Pyle's team was doing even worse. The crowds for Pyle's and Grange's Yankees team never materialized. It also didn't help that most of Grange's games that year were played on rainy days, which kept even the slightly interested casual fans away.

At the low points in the season the Giants were drawing 3,000–4,000 people per game. Halas remembered, "Mara would look through binoculars at Yankee Stadium and say, 'There's no one over there, either.'"

The Yankees ended up 14–5–1 overall, and 10–5 in AFL play, which was good enough for second place. The champions of the AFL that year were the Philadelphia Quakers. In an effort to scare up some extra money and publicity, Mara challenged Pyle to a little intracity game, pitting his Giants against Pyle's Yankees. Pyle rose to the bait at first, but then begged off. So Mara challenged the Philadelphia club to a little interleague scrimmage, and the folks in Philadelphia were more receptive. As champions of the AFL, many had no doubt in their minds that they could take some seventh-place club. Some Quakers even boasted in the newspapers how they would beat the Giants.

The game started off at a stalemate, with not much happening until the Giants went up 6–0 just before halftime. But in the second half New York exploded, both offensively and defensively. The final score was 31–0, with the Giants making fast work of the AFL champs.

"Everyone on the Giants wanted to win that one. The Quakers thought the Giants were pushovers, but we kicked the shit out of them," said Babe Parnell, a tackle who played the entire 60 minutes.

The final outcome of the football season was disastrous. The Giants had lost $40,000 in total. Grange had not come to save them again. And without the big draw, it was a hard year. The only good news came from across town. Pyle's Yankees had lost $100,000 for the year. And there was even better news—the American Football League was disbanding. It was great news for everyone but Mara.

Mara negotiated as best he could, but the NFL agreed to admit Pyle's Yankees into their league. Out of 16 games in 1927, the Yankees would only be allowed to play four games in New York

City. And those games were only scheduled when the Giants were away. It was a deal Mara could live with.

Later, after analyzing the year, Dr. March realized that attendance for the two teams combined in 1926 was the same number the Giants had attracted all by themselves the year before. Attendance had been 25,000 people per game on average in 1925 for the Giants, and averaged just 15,000 people per game in 1926. The Yankees brought in the other 10,000.

In late December an article appeared in *The New York Times* with the headline: "Pro Football Here to Stay, Says Mara." Tim was still pitching, and still committed. But Wellington admitted years later that his father consistently wavered over the status of the franchise. "Many times my father had second thoughts about football, advancing money and writing off losses...but he stayed firm."

Two other pieces appeared in the papers before December ended.

The first was very brief. Tucked on page 31 of the December 16, 1926, edition of *The New York Times* was a thumb-sized bit of column that read, in part:

> Gibson Gets Subpoena
> Billy Gibson, manager of Gene Tunney, yesterday was made codefendant with the world's heavyweight champion in the suit to recover $18,000 from Tunney instituted by Tim Mara [...] for alleged breach of contract.

The other piece was a small society page column titled: "Christmas Spirit Pervades City." The article noted that, "Christmas celebrations by a city aglow with the holiday spirit began yesterday, hearty and widespread, and will be continued today, with agencies searching out the dark corners to make certain no one is overlooked." As a member of the Social and Community Welfare Committee, Timothy J. Mara and others hosted a large party for disadvantaged children.

CHAPTER 3

The Lean Years

A CHAMPIONSHIP SEASON

The steeling of the NFL came in 1927. In two years the league had dwindled from 20 teams to 12. Many of these would go on to become the teams the NFL was founded on, and from whence many of its great names emanate. That season, the best teams were thought to be the Chicago Bears, the Green Bay Packers, and the Cleveland Bulldogs.

Chicago was led by owner/player/coach George Halas, owner/player Joey Sternaman, and Paddy Driscoll. The Packers were led by the indomitable Earl "Curly" Lambeau and Joseph "Red" Dunn. And Cleveland had new rookie sensation Benny Friedman. Many of the surviving NFL teams benefited by bringing in quality players left stranded by the liquidated clubs.

The Giants were no slouches that year. First and foremost, Tim and Dr. March replaced head coach Doc Anderson (whose medical practice was interfering with coaching the team) with Earl Potteiger. Potteiger had played for coach Nig Berry's Conshohocken 11 in 1919 and 1920. In 1919 he was a highly touted, multisport athlete and a very successful running back. In a major upset of the Holmesburg Athletic Club—the Philadelphia city champions of 1919 and 1920—Potteiger rushed for two touchdowns during a 19–7 victory over the Holmesburg 11. He knew hard-nosed football.

Already anchoring the team was Steve Owen. Owen was 5'10" and 255 pounds and he was rock solid. He appeared on the Giants roster in 1926, and little did anyone suspect then that he would be with the club for the next 28 years. He was known as a brutal player who liked to inflict punishment on his opponents. He had been the anchor of the team's defense in 1926, and for the 1927 season he would be paired with Centenary College's All-American lineman Cal Hubbard as well as Century Milstead, who had happily rejoined his comrades after his Yankee defection a year earlier. Also joined by Al Nesser, Hec Garvey, Mickey Murtaugh, and Chuck Corgan, the New York Football Giants easily had one of the best defenses in the league. It would be the backbone of their season.

The offense was also solid and featured backs Bill "Mule" Wilson, the indomitable Hinkey Haines and Jack McBride, and the crafty, although aging, Native American signal caller Joe Guyon.

The beginning of the season was an up-and-down affair. By the time the gun sounded on the fourth game of the season, the Giants were 2–1–1, and their prospects seemed questionable. But things were just about to turn around. They swept a home-and-away series with the Frankford Yellow Jackets, then beat Pottsville, Duluth, Providence, and the Chicago Cardinals in the next four games. At 8–1–1, they headed into a home-game showdown against the vaunted Chicago Bears.

The teams were separated by two wins when Halas's Bears showed up at the Polo Grounds with a record of 6–2–2 and the hope of beating the Giants—finding a way to take the title before the season ended. The Bears had a new star, Red Grange, whom they had reacquired without the assistance of Mr. Pyle.

The beginning of the game looked bad for the Giants from the outset, when the Bears got the ball and marched it methodically down the field. But in a heroic defensive stand, the Giants turned back the Bears at the goal line. The Bears forced their way deep into Giants territory several times, but the defense held strong each time. By the half, the game was still scoreless. Then, in the third quarter, the Giants drew first blood when, from the 2-yard line, McBride finally penetrated the Bears defense. However, they botched the point after. McBride repeated his feat later in the third, from the 1-yard line, to give the Giants a commanding lead in a defensive struggle. The Bears, not to be outdone, answered in the fourth quarter, with a pass play that brought the score to 13–7.

The game became a brutal, defensive affair filled with blood and mud.

Chicago lineman Ed Healey who retired after the 1927 season, recounted that Giants game as the toughest game in which he'd ever played. Both teams wanted it bad. "On defense, I came into contact with the great Cal Hubbard," he complained, and "on offense I came into contact with Whitey Nesser.... All the time there was Joe Guyon, all elbows, knees, feet, cleats, everything. If he didn't scratch you up, he'd break a bone. It was a tough day for me."

At one point in the game, Bears defensive end and owner Halas came at Guyon on a backside blitz. He had Guyon in his sights. Halas was hoping to make a play, cause a fumble, a sack—anything to shift the momentum. Guyon stood poised in the pocket, and at the last minute he threw a pass and, in the same motion, turned toward Halas, throwing a knee into his chest. The hit took Halas's breath away as he lay supine on the ground.

"Come on, Halas," said the wily Guyon, "you should know better than to try to sneak up on an Indian." Halas wasn't sure what hurt more, the 15-yard penalty for attempting to clip Guyon or the several broken ribs he had to nurse the rest of the game.

"It was the roughest game I ever played," Owen would later recall. Owen played opposite Jim McMillen, who later went on to become a famous wrestling champion. "When the gun went off, both of us just sat on the ground in the middle of the field. He smiled in a tired way, reached over to me, and we shook hands. We didn't say a word. We couldn't. It was fully five minutes before we got up to go to the dressing room."

The team went on to sweep a home-and-away series with their hated crosstown rival, C.C. Pyle's New York Yankees. The Giants finished 11–1–1, compared to the Bears' 9–3–2 and Green Bay's 7–2–1. To the Giants' delight, the Yankees finished the season 7–8–1. With no championship game at that time in the league, the New York Football Giants had finished first and were crowned champions of the NFL in 1927.

The championship was great publicity and the Bears game had been decently attended. But for Mara, while the championship had been sweet vindication, especially when coupled with Pyle's further unraveling, the fact of the matter was that Mara was still losing money on the Giants, even in years when they won.

After winning the championship, Mara proclaimed the Giants "the greatest football team in the world."

It was his love of the team, his sons' love of the team, and his belief that professional football would eventually make it that kept him on his course despite the obstacles. Revenues from his other businesses were being used to float the franchise.

"Only the winner comes to dinner," Tim Mara used to say, which was an old racetrack saying that Tim loved to use about the Giants.

TIM MARA VERSUS GENE TUNNEY: ROUND 1

While Dempsey may have had cause to be afraid of Tunney in the ring, and while Tunney may have been the heavyweight champion of the world, Tim Mara was not especially afraid of him in a court of law. After his victory in Philadelphia over Dempsey, Tunney was beset on all sides with men to whom he had made many promises, and men who had made many promises to him. Each held an intractable position. This was not unusual.

However, Tunney had three men who claimed they now had a piece of him: Tim Mara of New York, Chicago fight promoter Jim Mullen, who had helped to legalize boxing in Chicago, and alleged Philadelphia mobster Max "Boo Boo" Hoff.

It was largely acknowledged that Hoff was involved in the mafia in Philadelphia, but many also knew him as a premiere boxing promoter. Boxing was his passion. And it was no coincidence that Hoff was involved in the first Tunney-Dempsey match, fought in the City of Brotherly Love.

In Philadelphia in the late 1920s Hoff "had the largest stable of prizefighters in the nation, and he staged boxing matches for many years at several sites in Philadelphia." While his group boasted no champions, its ranks were filled with well-known contenders. By 1928 Hoff was calling his star-studded stable Max Hoff Inc., making it the first incorporation of a group of fighters in the nation.

On the day before the first Tunney-Dempsey affair, Hoff filed a lawsuit for $350,000 against Tunney and Gibson. Hoff claimed he had a document signed by Gibson and Tunney entitling him to a cut of the proceeds.

Hoff said that he had loaned Gibson and Tunney $20,000 to cover training expenses that they owed to Tex Rickard. In exchange for the loan, Gibson and Tunney were said to have traded 20 percent of Tunney's earnings from the bout in Philadelphia, and that Hoff would then gain some control of Tunney as a joint manager.

Syndicated New York columnist Mel Heimer told the story of Gibson arriving at Tunney's Philadelphia apartment days before the fight, after Tunney had arrived for the weigh-in. Gibson had arrived at Tunney's apartment with Hoff in tow, along with Hoff's lawyer.

"First Gibson asked Tunney to witness an agreement between Hoff and himself, which Gene did, and then he produced another document—the small print of which turned out to be a long-term agreement between Gibson and Tunney. Tunney even then was dissatisfied with some aspects of Gibson's behavior; he threw the papers at his manager and ordered him to leave."

"According to newspaper accounts, Hoff and Gibson signed the contract, but Tunney wrote 'Eugene Joseph Tunney' on the document. His real name was James Joseph Tunney," explained Philadelphia mafia historian Parry Desmond. "Despite his insistence that he had a strong case, Boo Boo mysteriously dropped the suit in 1931, reportedly without discussing a possible settlement with Tunney's lawyers."

Few thought Tunney was capable of such chicanery, but it was not above Gibson. Gibson had always been a shifty and cunning old promoter. In those days, managers and promoters often took advantage of young, uneducated boxers, paying them with percentages and fees. And Gibson was no slouch. He had promoted numerous fights at Madison Square Garden and in Havana, Cuba, and in his career he had managed such fighters as Tunney, Leonard, Paulino Uzcudun, Louis "Kid" Kaplan (Featherweight Champion from 1925 to 1927), Joe Barlow, and Johnny Grosso (who was most famous for his murder in 1932).

But few of Gibson's boxers were as smart and wily as Tunney was.

Mara was not impressed by his old friend's shenanigans and pressed ahead with his suit against Tunney. On July 26, 1927, Mara's complaint was filed with the New York State Supreme Court. Mara claimed Tunney had signed a contract with him in April 1926 in which Mara was to receive 10 percent of the boxer's championship winnings and a subsequent 25 percent of all his exhibitions afterward. Mara and his lawyers had attached a signed contract to their suit. The total value of the suit was now up to $26,250.

In September 1927 in Chicago, Tunney faced Dempsey again. This time Dempsey was devastating. While Tunney had always been a game fighter, he was mostly considered a smart boxer. But Dempsey tried to make the ring smaller and was determined to pound on his crafty opponent. What resulted was the infamous "long count," in which Tunney was stunned by a barrage of Dempsey's punishing blows. But the referee took time to fight with Dempsey, insisting Jack go to a neutral corner before he started counting. Tunney was thereby afforded approximately 10 seconds before the referee began the count. As a result, Tunney recovered and later took the fight to Dempsey. Any review of the film today clearly shows Dempsey won the fight, but was cheated by one of the most infamous calls in boxing history.

The Chicago bout was even more successful than the Philadelphia bout had been, and as a result, Gibson and Tunney made even more money. In a subsequent court filing, as reported on March 1, 1929, Mara raised the amount of damages against them to $405,000. Mara and his lawyers claimed that the $1.54 million that Tunney and Gibson had earned from exhibitions between the two championship bouts, Tunney's victory over Tom Heeney in another match, and the rematch with Dempsey were all subject to the contract in question.

On October 4, 1929, Tunney and his lawyers revealed that Tunney had earned approximately $1,715,863 to date since his victory in the first fight with Dempsey. According to *The New York Times,* "The figures were disclosed yesterday when Mara objected to the inclusion in the statement of earnings of large 'professional expenses.' He told the court he asked only for the exact amount of income." The statement also disclosed that Gibson had earned $5,275 in 1926 and approximately $135,508 in 1927.

The trial's biggest bombshells still lay ahead, as the sleazy, back-room underbelly of boxing was exposed. Another small distraction outside the courtroom was the crash of the New York Stock Exchange, which began on October 28, 1929, "Black Monday," and continued on October 29, 1929, known as "Black Tuesday," two of the worst days in financial market history. In two days the stock market lost 25 percent of its overall value, and the news would only get worse.

The first witness on the stand was attorney Allen Cruthers, followed by Mrs. Rose L. Salzberg, former secretary to Cruthers. Cruthers and Salzberg corroborated the story that Mara's services had been "engaged for the specific purpose of inducing the New York State Boxing Commission to reverse its stand and permit the Dempsey-Tunney match to be held" in New York City, "a purpose not accomplished."

According to Salzberg, to whom the contract was dictated by Gibson and Mara together in Mr. Cruthers's office, Mara was to receive 10 percent of Tunney's purse from the Dempsey fight if it was held in New York during that year.

"At that point," she said, "Mr. Mara interrupted the dictation to say he thought it was best to leave out the reference to New York, because if the boxing commission or the newspapers got a hold of it, there might be trouble."

"Mr. Mara said to Mr. Gibson, 'We understand each other; we're friends,'" she testified.

"Mr. Gibson said, 'Yes, we understand each other.'"

The contract was recorded and completed but reputedly never signed by Tunney, according to Salzberg, who was appearing for the defense and whose expenses were being paid by Tunney and Gibson. Gibson, however, did sign a contract, on behalf of Tunney, to give 25 percent of all Tunney's winnings to Mara. Mara had a written and an oral agreement.

Then Tunney took the stand. Gene told the story of his days of working for peanuts and becoming the champion of the American Expeditionary Force, and of Rickard's promise to get him a bout with Dempsey. Essentially Rickard had positioned himself as the only man who could make the match happen.

"'Dempsey fought for another promoter once and he hasn't been paid for it yet,'" Tunney said, quoting Rickard. "We shook hands across the table and Rickard said to me, 'Do you think you can live on $70,000 a year after you become champion?' When I left I had a gentleman's agreement with Rickard to fight Dempsey," he told the court. Mara's lawyer objected strenuously. Rickard had died, and none of Tunney's conversations could be corroborated by any other witnesses.

"Tunney can say anything he likes, and we can't do anything about it," cried Mara's mouthpiece, Martin W. Littleton.

Tunney explained that he had fought in New York long before he met Mara. But Mara had helped Tunney with the restoration of his boxing license in the state of New York, and for that Tunney admitted he was thankful.

In the next day's deliberations, the late Rickard's machinations were grotesquely exposed when a series of telegrams revealed how he was playing Tunney and Dempsey against one another to his own benefit. As testimony had already shown, Rickard promised to make Tunney a champion. Further testimony and telegrams showed that Rickard had told Tunney that Dempsey was in failing health and was ripe to fall.

At the same time, the shrewd Rickard was telling Dempsey to ignore the New York State Boxing Commission's number-one ranked contender, African American Harry Wills, and take the easy money with Tunney.

If anyone came out of the courtroom looking good, it was Dempsey. While Rickard, Tunney, Gibson, and Mara were all working the backrooms together, Dempsey came across as a plainspoken and honest man who was sure of his value as a box-office draw and was willing to wait for his price.

The telegrams also showed that Rickard had approached Dempsey a full three months before the alleged contract between Mara and Tunney was drawn up. In his telegram to Dempsey, Rickard was trying to place the fight in New York. After offering Dempsey $400,000, Rickard wrote to Dempsey, "Please keep this absolutely confidential until I sign Tunney, as he will want too much if he learns you have agreed to box him." The negotiations went back and forth between Rickard and Dempsey, with Dempsey pressing Rickard with threats of offers to fight Wills for "big dollars."

Dempsey once countered one of Rickard's telegrams with the fact that a separate promoter had offered him a Jersey City match for $500,000. "Can you compete with this offer?" Dempsey demanded in a return telegram.

With Tunney back in the chair under cross-examination, Littleton laid into the now ex-champion Tunney pretty well. Tunney kept trying to sidestep questions. "The question was put again and again," reported *The New York Times,* "with Tunney refusing to give a direct answer and Mr. Littleton angrily asking him to quit arguing and quit making speeches." Later Tunney complained vehemently, "You can't get me to admit to things I don't want to and that are not in accordance with the facts."

Later, Tunney's usual clearheadedness was called into question when Littleton tried to get Tunney to relate details from his meeting with Mara and General John Phelan, the New York boxing commissioner, regarding his license to box in the state.

"My memory's not infallible!" Tunney snorted.

"I thought it was," retorted Littleton.

"Did you really?" Tunney drawled.

"Yes, really," said Littleton.

"Go on," said Tunney in reply.

Littleton got Tunney to admit that he had experienced a falling out with Gibson. For fear of exposing this rift, Tunney refused to answer questions, and the judge finally asked Tunney why he couldn't give a straight answer. The prosecution had clearly won the round, with the ex-champion looking like he had something to hide.

Later, Tunney's former counsel, Dudley Field Malone, related a story of how Mara, Tunney, and he had met to discuss Mara's claim. He recounted how Tunney warmly resisted Mara's claim, stating the fight had not taken place in New York and so Mara was not due anything.

Then it was the prosecution's chance to tell their side of the story. Mara absolutely denied he had been in the office with Cruthers and Gibson for the dictation of the contract.

Mara also denied the charge that he had pressed the fight out of New York after Tunney refused Mara's demand for 25 percent of Tunney's earnings after the bout. Emory R. Bruckner, Tunney's lawyer, sided with Mara on this testimony, but then used it against him. Bruckner inferred that Gibson and Mara were in league to compel Tunney into signing over a "huge slice" of his future earnings.

"Tunney was being besieged from both sides!" Bruckner exclaimed.

However, Tunney had one strike against him. On June 6, 1926, before it became known that New York would not allow the fight, Tunney had written a letter to Mara saying he knew Billy and Tim were "trying to overcome certain angles." This letter assured Mara that the reward would be worth the effort.

"Of this you can be sure, you will receive 25 percent of all moneys [sic] earned by the exploitation of Gene Tunney after he wins the championship from Jack Dempsey on September 16, 1926," Tunney wrote to Mara. Mara thought he now had a piece of Tunney. Mara thought he had gotten in, and that he was truly on the way to managing Tunney.

In the summations, Littleton described Tunney as a man who would do anything—make any deal—to take the championship. Mara contended that he and Tunney had met in his office on April 3, 1926, and that, in a gentleman's agreement, Mara was "to assist, advise, and cooperate with Tunney in a general way." Littleton also pointed out that Tunney's contract with Gibson had all but run out, and both men knew it. Littleton said that Tunney had essentially botched the changing of managers.

"Tunney was willing to promise anything to get the championship," Littleton cried out, "but when he got it, it was a different story. When the battle was won, when he had walked to glory on the bodies of his friends, he told Mara, 'See my lawyer,' and he told Gibson, 'I'll give you 15 percent.'"

Bruckner described his own client as a "sucker" who had been duped by his own manager and coerced by a wily promoter. The defense's stance was Tunney's stance. Tunney wanted to fight in New York, where he could win by out-pointing Dempsey. Tunney knew that in New Jersey he would have to knock out the champion to take the crown, and he did not want to risk it. When Mara failed to produce a

New York match because the commission insisted Wills was rightfully next in line, Tunney claimed that Mara did not deliver and was not due the monies.

Justice Peter A. Hatting presided over the case and instructed the jury to deliberate on the facts. Hatting instructed the jury that an oral agreement can be just as binding as a written one. He insisted there were only two possible verdicts: that Mara receive his full amount or nothing. The jury was out for a little more than an hour and a half, but took only 30 minutes to decide the case.

"Gentlemen, have you agreed on a verdict?" the court attendant asked.

"Verdict for the defendant," said jury foreman Joseph Goldberg. The courtroom burst into applause. Throngs outside heard the news and erupted. Newspapermen and motion picture cameras greeted Tunney on his way out of court. Neither Mara nor Littleton were there, but a spokesperson for them announced the verdict would be appealed.

To be sure, here was also the great underhanded power and genius of Billy Gibson.

According to Ed Fitzgerald, who wrote for *Sport* magazine, "Slowly, it came out in court that Gene's manager, Billy Gibson, had signed away approximately 83 percent of Tunney's earnings before Gene stepped into the ring against Dempsey." And Fitzgerald pointed to *New York Herald Tribune* writer Alva Johnston, who wrote of the trial, "There was no particular surprise in the front row of spectators, which was composed chiefly of fighters and managers, at the news that Tunney had given away pieces of himself to the extent of over 75 percent.... It is said that many fighters have given away as much as 150 percent of themselves in similar contracts, while one fighter is known to have signed away 250 percent of himself."

Whatever the outcome of the trial, it is a difficult conundrum to consider here. Mara was clearly being shifty, if not underhanded, but in subsequent dealings a handshake deal was always honored by Mara for the rest of his life. He was uniformly remembered by many as someone who could be trusted once he gave his word. Indeed, Owen never had a contract for the 28 years he worked for the Giants. It was always just a handshake between Tim and Owen and that was the agreement. All proper expenses and salaries were paid. They never went to court. And Tim operated in that same way with many employees, especially in the first dozen years of the organization, and was generally reported to be an honest businessman. He could be intimidating and tough, but he was known to be honest. And just because you're honest doesn't mean you can't be shrewd.

Round two was yet to come.

BENNY AND THE GIANTS

What a difference a year makes. In 1928 there was no suspicion that the Giants would fall so far from their incredible perch of just a year before. But despite having exactly the same coach and players, the Giants fooled no one: they were an awful football club.

The defense was inconsistent. They had eight games where they gave up a touchdown or less. But they had five games where they gave up solid double-digit points. The team that had given up 20 points the year before allowed 136 points in 1928. And the offense, which had scored 197 points in 1927, earned only an anemic 79 points in 1928.

Potteiger faced an attitude and morale problem. The players were overconfident in 1928, and that had not been the case the previous year. During the 1928 season, the Giants often refused to practice or did not exhibit enthusiasm when they did practice.

Some said they were in fact spoiled and lazy.

Part of the bad attitude that was pervasive throughout the team was no doubt a reaction to a tightening of the financial reins (which were already tight according to many) because the franchise was hemorrhaging cash. Mara and Dr. March were trying to stanch the bleeding. Whereas the players had ridden in a private Pullman car the year before, they were now being transported like cattle in an old, used bus that broke down on the way to one game, making the Giants late. On a trip to play the Bears that year, the team stayed at the local YMCA instead of a hotel. March resorted to berating the players to try to motivate them. It worked for a time, but eventually the Giants sank under their own weight. The Giants finished 4–7–2 and lost $40,000 that year. The only bright spots in the season were Owen and Hubbard.

Something had to be done. Mara had become embittered by the thing he loved most—his football team. He promised swift and decisive action, and he delivered.

Mara took matters into his own hands and fired Potteiger and 18 team veterans. The one difficult pill to swallow was Hubbard's request to be traded to Green Bay, a terrible loss for the club. It was the most sweeping change in professional football for years to come. And now Mara wanted to start over. And he would start over with Benny Friedman.

According to football historian Bob Curran, "Benny Friedman did as much to popularize the forward pass as any man who has played the game." Friedman was a graduate of Michigan, where he was an All American, and played alongside Benny Oosterbaan for famed coach Fielding Yost. The two had become a devastating tandem in the college ranks. Friedman graduated in 1927 and went to play for the Cleveland Bulldogs. Eventually the Bulldogs moved north to Detroit and were renamed the Wolverines. Twenty investors put in $500 each, and at the end of the year, they got $350 back. It hadn't been too bad a year.

"After that year, Tim Mara, who was a wonderful, wonderful individual, wanted me to come to New York, and Leroy Andrews, who was still coaching and managing the ballclub, made the deal with him. So we joined up with the Giants," Friedman later said.

Friedman's version is plainspoken if a little simplistic. The Wolverines were insolvent and were ready to close up shop. Mara's arrival to woo Benny could not have come at a more auspicious time.

"We need Friedman," Mara told Dr. March. "Spend what you have to spend, but get him."

Four times the Giants were rebuffed by the Detroit team, until a unique arrangement was worked out—Mara would buy the entire roster and the Wolverines would go out of buisness. Mara and March combined the best of their existing players with those of the Wolverines, which was a 7–2–1 club in 1928 with a stingy defense. Lyle Munn, who was a wonderful offensive end and Friedman's favorite target in Detroit, came along, as well as other Wolverines including Les Caywood, Joe Westoupal, and Bob Howard.

"I was paid $10,000 a year with the Giants," Friedman said later. The salary was astronomical in a time when the highest paid players were getting $125 per game. But Friedman would be worth it. He was going to revolutionize the professional game, and interesting things were about to start happening.

Friedman went on the offensive with the publicity machine. He spoke at every high school in New York City, promoting professional football in general. Then he and former *Cleveland News* editor Ed Bang hit the numerous newspapers.

"Ed would buy two bottles of whiskey and we'd walk into a newspaper office. He'd hand one bottle to the sports editor and the other to the sports columnist, and then we'd kibitz. That was the way we got publicity," Friedman said. "It was real barnstorming." Friedman was everything Mara had hoped for. He was handsome, well-spoken, and intelligent.

And on the football field he could do wonderful things. With Owen, George Murtaugh, Jack Hagerty, Wilson, Tony Plansky, and Dale Moran, among others, the Giants were set to hit new heights.

"He made us believers. He was a natural leader who came to us with a great reputation, someone we were able to respect right away because he had already proven himself," said Owen years later.

Passing in the 1920s was a true art. The ball was more round in shape compared to the streamlined version used today, making throwing more difficult. And rules governing the area from which the quarterback could throw were also difficult. But Friedman didn't let any of this stop him. He thrilled audiences with his deep, long passes down the field. Opponents, especially in 1929, were shocked. And the Giants were reborn.

The first two games showed glimpses of the team's potential, but resulted in an unimpressive 1–0–1 record. There was a tie with the Orange Tornadoes and a 7–0 win over Providence. Then things started to get interesting. People were talking about Friedman and the Giants. Twenty thousand people came to see the Giants beat the Staten Island Stapletons 19–9, and then another 30,000 fans showed up the following week to see the Giants put on an offensive explosion, walloping the Frankford Yellow Jackets 32–0. The Giants were hot.

But the market was not. In the midst of a resurgent 1929 Giants football season, the stock market crashed and Tim Mara was devastated. Mara, with his incredible appetite for speculation, had invested wholeheartedly in a wide array of speculative stocks. He was crippled financially, and the Giants as a business were now on the hook. Mara no longer had the oozing streams of money that had helped to float the Giants boat. The Giants would need to sink or swim on their own.

But a funny thing happened on the way to the stock market crash—the Giants became one of the biggest draws in football. With Friedman unleashed as never before, he and the Giants became news. In the next five games, two against the Chicago Bears, one each against Providence, Buffalo, and Orange, the Giants outscored their competition 146 points to 20 and won all five games. Friedman had one of the greatest passing seasons in the history of the NFL. That year he threw for a league-record 20 touchdown passes for the season. The record would not be broken until 1942.

And then came one of the biggest games in the entire league that year. On November 24 the Packers and the Giants met as two undefeated teams. The Packers were 9–0 and the Giants 8–0–1. The winner would probably take the championship.

That year the Packers were awesome. A traditionally built football team, they were a ground-rushing juggernaut and had a stiff defense to boot. The Green Bay roster was an NFL who's who. Coached by Curly Lambeau, the lineup included former Giants standout Hubbard, running sensation Johnny "Blood" McNally, and lineman Mike Michalske (a former Yankee who made the club that summer), all three of whom were future Hall of Fame players. Other standouts included Verne Lewellen, Lavie Dilweg, and Bo Molenda. Lewellen, Molenda, and Blood each rushed for more than 400 yards that season, which was quite a feat in those days.

On game day, in late November, more than 25,000 paying customers showed up to see what would happen when these two mighty teams met. Michalske and Hubbard harassed Friedman all game long; the Giants line was not able to hold off the two forces of nature. And Lewellen's booming punts kept the Giants pinned down on their side of the field all day. Lambeau was so determined to win, he made only one substitution all game, in the final minute, meaning the 11 Packers played almost the entire game. The Packers won 20–6, but it was a hard-fought game.

"We had no problems with anyone else," Friedman later said, "but the Packers were special. They were so big, and yet they were so fast, that they almost won their games before they took the field."

The Giants won their remaining five games, scoring another 102 points and crushing their opponents. But it was to no avail: the Green Bay Packers didn't lose any of their games either, and they took the 1929 title. Mara had mixed emotions. With victories so numerous, it was a shame the team had not won the championship. But there was lots of good news to go around.

The Yankees were gone. So was Pyle. And the Staten Island Stapletons and the Brooklyn Lions both now operated under Mara's franchise license. Both paid homage to him, since he owned all rights to the NFL franchise in New York City.

But what of the Giants' financial woes? Thanks to Friedman, those days were gone. The team would still struggle. It wasn't an automatic money machine, but the team started surviving on its own.

"In 1928, the year before I came with the Giants, Tim Mara lost $54,000. In 1929, the first year I was with him, he made $8,500. In 1930 he made $23,000 and in 1931 he made $35,000," Friedman said. His quote is somewhat misleading, because while his explosive offense was the reason people kept coming back, the numbers were also due to cost-cutting measures, some of them quite silly, that enabled the franchise to bank some of the money the Giants were generating. For years after the Giants were known for their penurious ways in that era. And while good times were not exactly here, the team had started to become part of the landscape of New York. They were beginning to catch on. Fans were coming back. It seemed the NFL—professional, "postgraduate" football— was starting to catch on around the country and in New York, and the franchise was starting to turn around.

Mara himself had lots more to worry about that was not connected to his team at all, and many other issues and fronts were about to confront him. But for a brief, shining moment, the Giants were one of the bright spots.

In 1930 the Giants once again played with abandon, but fell short. Recording a 13–4 record, they ultimately lost the league title to the

Green Bay Packers again. Green Bay finished with a 10–3–1 record. In the third week of the season, the Giants had gone to Green Bay and lost 14–7. But they avenged that loss on November 23, when they returned the favor, 13–6. The Giants led the league in scoring with 308 points and had three scorers in the top 10 NFL leaders. Friedman passed for 1,246 yards that year. And Friedman and Moran led the team in rushing.

Morris "Red" Badgro's first season with the Giants came in 1930. "Tim Mara signed me to my first contract with the Giants. He was a good owner. I never had any trouble with him," said Badgro years later. Badgro remembered that during one practice, he split his chin. It was bleeding pretty badly, and needed stitches. He went up to see Dr. March, whom he called "a grand old fellow." March had no medical equipment with him, related Badgro years later, "so he got a plain needle and sewing thread out of his drawer and sewed up my chin. He liked football more than the practice of medicine, I believe."

"Red Badgro was a rugged, fierce competitor," Wellington said years later, "and a 190-pound defensive end was pretty big in those days. He was a very mild-mannered guy, but murder on the field. He was a clean player. You had to be because there were only three or four officials and the other guy could get back at you without the officials catching on."

"In those days, players had to supply their own shoes, just as in baseball then. He didn't have money to buy extra football shoes, so he worked out in baseball spikes. Everyone gave him a lot of room so he wouldn't step on their toes. When we had a scrimmage, he had to change his shoes."

SANTA ROCKNE IS COMIN' TO TOWN

The 1930 season ended with a charity game that was slated to raise money for Mara's Tammany Hall political friend, Mayor Jimmy Walker. As the Great Depression started to gain momentum, more and more New Yorkers were out of work. Walker had started a New York City unemployment fund to help those who found themselves in the long bread lines that became famous in urban centers across America.

One day Walker called Mara to ask, "Tim, would you be willing to schedule a charity game and turn over the receipts to the unemployment relief fund?"

"You name the team, and we'll play them," Well reportedly responded. The idea had been dreamed up for the Giants to play Notre Dame. The Fighting Irish of Notre Dame and their celebrity coach, Knute Rockne, were one of the biggest draws in all of football, college or professional. The idea was that Rockne would lead a Notre Dame all-star team, made up of seniors and former Notre Dame men, which included the famous Four Horsemen, to face Mara's hometown 11. It was thought that Rockne's team would have an easy victory.

However, the Giants players and organization thought the charity game would be a great opportunity to showcase how professional football was indeed the better version of the game. Then came rumblings from Norte Dame. Headlines hit New York on December 2 that Rockne might withdraw his team from the exhibition. Privately, Rockne was unsure of what he'd gotten himself into. He told reporters he was reconsidering because the expenses for the trip would come to more than $3,400, and he thought it was too much. Well expressed shock to the New York press, claiming 50,000 tickets already had been sold to the charity game and that expenses and receipts had been negotiated and were being handled. Rockne had backed himself into a corner.

The stage was set.

The game was played on December 14, 1930. True to its reputation, Notre Dame proved to be the best draw of the year, with a crowd of 55,000 paying customers showing up to cheer on the Notre Dame alumni.

Before the game, Rockne confidently told reporters, "The Giants are big, but slow. Score two or three quick ones on passes, then play defense. Don't get hurt." Rockne's braggadocio was a well-known personality trait.

Then Rockne went into the Giants locker room to talk with Benny Friedman. Friedman admitted that Rockne was his idol.

After pleasantries were exchanged and some small talk, Friedman asked, "What can I do for you?"

Rockne started in on a long list of small injuries from which his impromptu all-star team was suffering. Rockne eventually concluded, "I think we ought to have free substitution," which was not the rules in those days. Friedman agreed.

"I think we ought to cut the quarters down to 10 minutes from 15."

"Oh, Lord, we can't do that. There are 55,000 people out there who paid $5 apiece...we'll cut it down to 12 minutes and a half. ..." Rockne shook his head in agreement.

"Anything else?" asked the amused Friedman.

"Yes, for Pete's sake, take it easy!"

One famous story came from the kickoff, when star Notre Dame lineman Johnny Law walked over to an official after watching the huge Giants lumber onto the field. Awed, Law reportedly went over to an official and asked him, "How much time is there left to play?"

The Giants led 14–0 at the half. The Giants were so overpowering that Notre Dame didn't have a first down the entire half. Reportedly, Rockne asked Dr. March to call off the dogs. The second and third string played in the second half, scoring another touchdown, and the Giants won 22–0.

"That was the greatest football machine I ever saw," said Rockne afterward. "I'm just glad we got out alive."

The proceeds came to $116,000 raised for the unemployed after all expenses were deducted and the players paid, including $5,000 in expenses for the Notre Dame players, which a bitter Rockne announced to Mara and March in the Polo Grounds offices after the game. Mara was miffed. A few days later Friedman met Mara at his offices in New York. Mara had asked Friedman to go downtown with him to present the proceeds to Mayor Walker.

It was not the first time Walker or, for that matter, other Tammany Hall hangers-on took advantage of Mara's kindnesses. When the team was winning, Tammany politicos, including Walker and Governor Al Smith, showed up for team photos and other photo ops. Mara's team and its games created great opportunities for politicians to show up and get their pictures taken at Giants games, the way they did for baseball games in the summer.

"We have no arrangement with them as to how we'd pay them. So why don't we keep the $16,000. We can use the money," Friedman pleaded with Mara. "We'll give them the even $100,000. You know what's going to happen to that money."

Friedman said years later in his own defense, "Remember, this was the heyday of Tammany—Tin Box Farley—and all those characters." Friedman was sure not all of this money would end up in the fund for use by the unemployed. But Mara was a good Tammany man.

"We can't do that!" admonished Mara. And so the two went down to city hall and presented the check for $116,000. The press was impressed, and Mara and the Giants became heroes. They had also proven that professional football was taking its place in the sports world.

Sometime later Friedman walked into Mara's office and saw the cancelled check framed on Mara's wall. The two looked at the frame and sighed. Friedman said, "I know what you're thinking."

"I'm thinking of how much I could use $16,000 right now," Mara answered. "You, my friend, are looking at a dumb Irishman!" This was only an omen of Mara's future troubles with the Tammany machine.

OTHER DISTRACTIONS

While the 1931 and 1932 Giants clubs turned in some forgettable seasons despite having some intriguing stars, Mara was involved in numerous other affairs. Mara was back at one of his favorite involvements—promoting boxing events.

Mara promoted one of the biggest fights in New York that year —Jimmy McLarnin (the future welterweight champion) versus Lou Brouillard (who held the New England light heavyweight title) on August 4, 1932, at Yankee Stadium. It was a much-anticipated fight, with two exciting boxers. Brouillard won by decision in the 10th round. One judge voted for McLarnin while the other judge and the referee gave the nod to Brouillard. *The New York Times* noted that Brouillard "pounded and battered McLarnin through 10 rounds of primitive fighting to gain a decision that met with the undivided support of the onlookers."

The *Times'* John Kieran pointed out in the late summer of 1932 that, "Tim Mara lost $4,800 promoting the McLarnin-Brouillard fight and went back to Saratoga Springs laughing about it. His good humor apparently incurable."

In September 1932 Mayor Walker's brother, George F. Walker, died, and Mara was one of the notable attendees.

In December 1932 Tim, now president of Aram, A.C., which held leases on Yankee Stadium and the Polo Grounds, signed up one of the biggest fights he would ever promote, getting stadium rights for the marquee match up of Max Baer versus Max Schmeling. Baer fought with a Star of David embroidered on his trunks. Schmeling, the hard-hitting German, had lost his world heavyweight title to Jack Sharkey the year before in a very controversial bout that, spawned his manager's famous outcry, "We was robbed!"

The match had been organized by none other than Dempsey, the former heavyweight champion. Dempsey had been determined to hold the bout in Chicago, Philadelphia, or Pittsburgh, but was stymied in his efforts to promote the fight in any of those cities. Since Mara controlled the rights to the two largest forums in the New York City metro region, he and Dempsey came to terms and the match was eventually approved by the New York State Athletic Commission on March 15, 1933.

That year Dempsey promoted numerous fights, and Mara staged many of them. He also staged many others that year with other promoters. Mara and Dempsey were seen at events and boxing matches all that spring and summer. In April, Dempsey was invited to address the faculty of Columbia University, and Mara was there. That same month the two were approved by the New York State Athletic Commission, led by General Phelan, to host a series of boxing matches throughout the summer. In addition to Baer versus Schmeling, they also promoted the Jack Sharkey–Primo Carnera fight. Schmeling, Baer, and Dempsey were feted in late April by the New York Athletic Club, where Tim was among the notables. Mara, and later his sons and grandsons, would attend New York Athletic Club black-tie events well into the next century.

April 1933 also saw Mara's name spread around the press as he fought a proposed law known as the "O'Brien Bill." The bill was sponsored in the New York state house by Duncan T. O'Brien, a New York Democrat, who wanted to increase the license fees for anyone connected to the sport of boxing and to raise gross revenues that the state could cull from such events. The bill was introduced as a reaction to Carnera's lethal defeat of Boston heavyweight Ernie Schaaf, who died as a result of their bout. The bill was aimed against professional wrestling as well.

Mara was vehemently against the bill, which he saw as an attempt to kill the sport in the state. Not only would it mean the death of boxing in New York, but it would mean huge sums of revenue would leave the city and go to places like Philadelphia, Pittsburgh, Chicago, or worse yet, their own backyard—New Jersey. Mara personally implored Governor Herbert Lehman, and Lehman vetoed the bill in late April.

Baer was on his way up. His arrival in New York was covered by the press, and the first men to greet Baer as he got off the train were Dempsey and Mara. And that night, on June 8, 1933, he fought the best fight of his life. In front of 60,000 rabid boxing fans at Yankee Stadium, Baer battered Schmeling. Schmeling took such a beating from Baer that referee Arthur Donovan called the fight in the 10th round on Baer's behalf. The night had been a terrific success for everyone but Schmeling.

Mara promoted a fight between the Hammering Hollander—Bep van Klavern—and Billy Petrolle, which took place at the Polo Grounds on July 12, 1933. "He hasn't much hope of reaping a fortune in this Petrolle bout," Kieran opined again, "because promoter Tim Mara is putting it on at 'popular prices,' meaning 'popular' as far as the spectators are concerned. With the fighters, such prices are highly unpopular."

A TAMMANY TIGER BY THE TAIL

Alfred E. Smith was one of the dominant Democratic politicians in New York state politics between 1903 and 1928. Smith, who grew up on the Lower East Side, came from a middle-class family. However he was forced to quit school upon the death of his father when he was 14 years old. Smith used his Lower East Side roots and early working career to identify with lower-class and immigrant voters who flocked to his side over the years.

Although he owed a certain amount of his political success to Tammany Hall and its political machine, Smith remained clean of the political scandals surrounding many of the other Tammany puppets.

In 1903 he was elected to the New York State Assembly. He also served as vice chairman of the investigating committee that uncovered the conditions that led to the horrific Triangle Shirtwaist Company fire in 1911. This pivotal moment in his career only hardened his views on labor and the need for pro-labor causes. Smith served briefly as the New York county sheriff, and was then elected governor of New York in 1918. He was not reelected in 1920, but regained the office in 1922 and held onto it for two more terms. In 1924 he failed to gain the Democratic party nomination for president of the United States.

In 1928, however, Smith had reached the pinnacle of his career, and finally secured the Democratic presidential nomination. The plan was simple. Smith would help up-and-comer Franklin Delano Roosevelt take the office of governor. In return, FDR, with the help of his wife Eleanor, would help Smith keep a stranglehold on New York for the election.

Timothy J. Mara was often mentioned in articles about Smith. Mara showed up at major gatherings and even traveled with the governor during the campaign. Mara was a Tiger Room man, which meant he was in the inner circle of Tammany life. And he was a true friend of Smith's. There was no mistaking that Smith's friends were very glad for him. Smith was using them and they were using him. Smith and Mara were seen going to the same church from time to time and playing golf together. Mara was noted as being an "investment banker" at the time.

Smith's bid was a difficult one. As an Irish Catholic, he suffered because of a backlash of anti-Catholic and anti-Irish sentiment. His connections to Tammany were exaggerated. Also, the 1920s had been the heyday of the conservative philosophy, which Calvin Coolidge had so succinctly summed up as, "the business of America is business."

Smith and Mara's friendship was about to be tested. John J. Raskob was the chairman of the Democratic National Committee, and in mid- to late-1928 Raskob realized there would be a $1 million shortfall in Smith's campaign finances. Raskob and James J. Riordan, president of the County Trust Company Bank, concocted a scheme.

The bank itself, within the confines of the law, could not donate that much money to the campaign. So they asked many of their friends, including Tim Mara, to cover notes amounting to that total sum. Mara was asked to sign a note for $50,000, being told that he would never have to pay it. Other notables were told the same, including Herbert Lehman, Michael Meehan, Pierre DuPont, August Hecksher, George Van Namee, and many other major and minor stars of the Tiger Club, including a Yonkers plumbing contractor named William Kenny (no relation to the well-known William Kenny). With the signed notes, the campaign was fully funded. Riordan, in the heady days of New York finance and the height of the roaring '20s, figured he could keep the shell game going for quite a long time. They would continue to roll notes over until enough money had come into the party, when they could finally cover the difference. With the $1 million in hand, Raskob ran a reckless campaign, and Smith lost to Herbert Hoover in the fall of 1928, although his friend and future enemy, FDR, did indeed take the governor's mansion.

But with the crash of the New York Stock Exchange in October 1929, the scheme imploded entirely. The first to fall was Riordan. At the height of its power, on May 1, 1929, the County Trust Company, which Riordan had founded, was worth $36 million, and a single share was valued at more than $1,000. Two days after the crash, Riordan realized he was ruined. He paid a single margin call of $200,000 and had little other money left, with plenty of other debtors in line.

On Friday, November 8, 1929, the 47-year-old Riordan went home and put a .38-caliber gun to his head while sitting in a wing-backed chair in his Twelfth Street house. Smith and Kenny were the first to arrive at the house. Smith was visibly shaken. The headline in *The New York Times* the following day read: "James J. Riordan, President of the County Trust Company and Intimate Friend of Former Governor Alfred E. Smith, Committed Suicide." This was only the beginning of an avalanche of stories *The New York Times* would print in its coverage of what was about to become a major regional and national scandal.

In April 1929 Riordan himself had begun calling in the notes the trust had issued to the signers. Kenny, Lehman, Meehan, and DuPont all had the means and paid fairly quickly. "For others it was not so easy," wrote historian Robert A. Slayton in his book *Empire Statesman: The Rise and Redemption of Al Smith*. "Men like T.J.

Mara, who owed $50,000, or Patrick Keeney, who signed for $25,000, simply could not afford it."

After Riordan's death, Raskob hoped he could continue the ruse, as he had become acting director of Riordan's bank. However Mara and others refused to sign subsequent notes, realizing that the game was over. "By November [1930], Raskob was sending out notarized letters calling on them to honor their debts." Eventually Raskob brought suit against the two hold-out leaders, Patrick Kenny and Mara. The two fought back.

Raskob fired the first shot by releasing his treasurer's notes to the Democratic National Committee, which noted the forgiveness of $100,000 on notes signed by Kenny and Mara. In covering the story, *The New York Times* reported, "Messers. Mara and Kenny replied that they had understood that they were not to pay this money, but had signed the notes to 'cover' allegedly illegal contribution to the 1928 Smith campaign fund."

While the suit was brought on Kenny and Mara in June 1931, the media circus did not start to peak until March 1932. Each day brought new allegations and new accusations. Headline after headline scarred the Democrats' reputation. The "1928 Fraud Charged in Democrats' Fund" appeared in big, bold letters on the front page, above the fold. "Mara Backs Charge of Campaign Fraud" screamed a similar headline.

Kenny had struck first in the fight against Raskob by going public with the entire story, explaining how Riordan and Raskob had brought it to him and how the scheme had finally unraveled. Mara claimed he signed the notes as an "accommodation," and that the notes were part of a "fraudulent" scheme to illegally fund the campaign. Both Kenny and Mara said neither would have donated anywhere close to the amount of the notes to the campaign from their personal funds. Eleven of the original 23 underwriters had gathered behind Kenny and Mara. The *Times* referred to Mara as "a long-standing friend of the former governor."

Indeed, Mara and Smith had been seen together in Miami as late as February and March 1929, and at the Hialeah Park racetrack along with Tiger Room owner William Kenny.

By March 25, 1932, the scandal had reached Washington and *The New York Times* blared the headline: "Urge Senate Inquiry into Smith

Financing." Senators and congressmen alike demanded a Capitol Hill investigation into the Smith campaign financing schemes, which were now being referred to as the "Tiger Room" financing scandal." The Republicans smelled blood, and Mara decided to throw more chum in the water by issuing a public statement on March 26. Mara pointed out that after the Democratic Party had raised $4 million, the 23 underwriters were told they were relieved of their debts. The fact that Raskob had overspent by $1.4 million was not their responsibility.

"When we met with Mr. Raskob concerning the letter, I personally explained to Mr. Raskob the feeling of the group, which was that they had fulfilled their obligations. Thus Mr. Raskob knew before the later signing of the notes that we did not intend to pay, and for the reasons already stated," Mara's statement read. Mara pointed out that in some cases, Raskob had endorsed notes for people he had never even met. To add to that, Raskob had questioned Mara's friendship of Smith.

Mara shot back, "The name should never have been mentioned in this matter, because I do not think Mr. Raskob has any more love and devotion for [Al] than any of the men in this group, and I think the group will continue their love and admiration for him much longer than Mr. Raskob."

The circus continued to grow, culminating in the appearance of Smith himself on October 20, 1933. "Smith testified in open court that as chairman of the board, he had to advise the two men that they must pay for his own aspirations," wrote Slayton.

On October 25, 1933, *The New York Times* headline read: "Mara Is Cleared of Campaign Debt." Mara had won. Raskob immediately set about to fight the verdict, but as Slayton pointed out, "Eventually, John Raskob accepted that he could not get money from businessmen all but bankrupt, and quietly wrote off the bills, taking a tax loss. But Al had been terribly, terribly hurt."

TIM MARA VERSUS GENE TUNNEY: ROUND 2

In the summer of 1932 the appellate division of the New York State Supreme Court agreed to hear arguments in the Mara and Tunney case. And on July 2, 1932, that division voted to retry the case. Not all justices concurred, but the majority found in Mara's favor. The appellate division argued that the major point in the case was whether or not Mara's responsibilities were to be solely directed at getting the match sanctioned in the state of New York.

"The majority opinion held that the omission of such a condition in Tunney's June 6 letter showed it was not a condition of the agreement. Mara denied there had been such a condition," *The New York Times* explained.

Tunney had admitted that the reference to New York was purposely omitted so as not to draw suspicion to Mara's efforts to keep the bout in the state, which, according to Tunney, were to be kept secret.

The appellate division also found fault with Hatting's instructions to the jury regarding Mara's mission, which was specified by Tunney as exerting undue influence on public officials. If the jury decided that was an illegal act, then the jury must find for Tunney.

Eventually Tunney contacted Mara's lawyers. Negotiations were begun and a settlement was reached. The conversations went on for weeks, as Tunney and Mara and the lawyers talked.

From his home in Greenwich, Connecticut, Tunney announced a settlement with Mara in January 1933. "I have no resentment against Tim," Tunney said. He said he felt comfortable with the fact that the jury had found in his favor, and he saw that as vindication. Tunney also said, "For one thing, I have a sick wife, and I must take her to Arizona. Secondly the payment of $30,000 is small compared to the amount for which he sued, and is less than it would have cost me to defend the case again." Tunney was happy the case was over. "Finally, I do not want the publicity that a new trial would mean."

"The lawyers have been dickering for weeks, and I have signed a release of all claims," Mara said.

In accepting the sum of $30,000 in lieu of the original $405,000, Mara's new lawyer, I. Gainsburg, said, "It was urged upon me during the settlement negotiations that Mr. Tunney had not been working for the past few years."

"In these times, that's a lot of money for Tunney or for anyone else to pay. All I wanted was vindication. Now I've got it, Mara told the press."

Now Mara could concentrate on his various businesses, including racing and his beloved New York Giants.

CHAPTER 4

The Sons of the Father

In 1930, because of his financial woes and his many litigious involvements, Tim officially transferred ownership of the team to his sons Jack and Wellington. Jack was 22 years old and Wellington was 14. The boys loved the team, and the players were heroes to them. Jack graduated from Fordham University in 1930, and within a few years, he was traveling with the club on away games regularly. He tended to fraternize with the players more as he got closer and closer in age to them. Wellington looked up to his older brother and the football players as well. As Wellington later recalled, "I was permitted to take the trip...when I was still in school, if it wouldn't interfere with my Friday afternoon classes." Jack, too, had school—he was studying to be a lawyer at Fordham Law School.

Until the day he died, Tim kept a letter he got from Wellington in 1930. It was a scouting report on the Staten Island Stapletons that Well had written at age 14. The report was a solid one, with descriptions of the way the Stapletons played and a discussion of how the Giants players should not be overconfident. In a side note he also brought up for discussion the idea of raising ticket prices and calculated the effect on customer draw.

"You can see," Tim once said in the 1950s, "that Well was a pretty good scout then, and now there isn't anyone any better."

During the early and mid-1930s, football was catching on, and players were demanding more money. Other teams had greater attendance and therefore could pay better. Historically, Green Bay and Chicago were the class of the league, and they generally commanded the biggest crowds at home as well as on the road. They could afford larger salary structures and attempted to recruit the biggest stars. New York usually finished somewhere in the middle of the league regarding attendance.

Even more so than today, New York was a baseball town. Baseball was king, and the Yankees were easily the royalty of the baseball world in those days. The men in pinstripes were the hated Yankees by 1933, and their legend would only grow from that point on. But New York had always been a National League town, and Horace Stoneham's baseball Giants and Brooklyn's Dodgers occupied two thirds of the town's heart. It had been the tough, shrewd John McGraw who had led the early baseball Giants to pennants and prominence. It was said that the city's loyalties were divided approximately thusly: Wall Street and Park Avenue types rooted for the Yankees; small, independent store owners and the like often rooted for the Giants; and all the workers rooted for the Dodgers. Each group lampooned and jabbed at the other two.

College football still dominated the national landscape, though the professional game was gaining fans. Still, pro football was largely viewed the same way as professional wrestling was in the late 1950s and 1960s: as a sideshow filled with freaks and a smattering of real athletes, former college stars, etc. Many football teams barnstormed when the season was over. In many cases the clubs made better profits on the road than they did during the season.

For the football Giants, home crowds were still stingy in their attendance. But according to Wellington, the senior Mara believed that sports, especially boxing, baseball, and football, "prospered during the Depression because they really offered the best entertainment for the money."

Another woe hit the Giants around this time. Friedman was a smart player and budding businessman, and he approached Tim one day in 1932 with a case for being made part owner of the Giants. How much was up for discussion? Friedman's inquiry was not out of the realm of possibility. Several stars of his stature had similar deals, especially with the smaller teams. Sharing pieces of the gate or admission, like Grange's deal, were still in vogue. Tim was disconsolate and adamant. He did not want to lose his biggest star, but the answer was a flat-out no: "You're a good friend and a great quarterback. If you cannot play any longer, we'll always have a place for you here. But this is a family business. The Giants are for my sons."

However, Mara came to a deal with NFL star running back Johnny Blood. For a small rights fee, Mara allowed Blood and another player to found the Brooklyn football Dodgers, who would play at Ebbetts Field in Brooklyn. Like the Pyle deal, the Dodgers and Giants would rarely play in a town the same weekend. Benny Friedman signed a lucrative deal with Blood and joined his friend in Brooklyn. Financially, Mara made out well from the deal, but talent-wise, it was a huge blow to the Giants team.

But the team had been busy signing as many up-and-coming stars as possible. With the new additions of Ken Strong and Harry Newman, the Giants were stacked with fresh, raw, young talent and drive.

"I don't know if I want to hire you. I hear you're a trouble-maker," Tim said to Strong, who was available because the Staten Island Stapletons had disbanded after the 1931 season.

"What does that mean?" Strong asked.

"I understand you bawl the other players out."

Strong explained he hollered when people didn't block. "I play to win. If you don't want a winner, you better not hire me," Strong retorted back.

"You are three years too late. I never understood why you went over there for less money than we offered you," Tim told Strong during the negotiations.

"What do you mean?"

"We offered you $10,000 a year."

"No you didn't. You offered me $5,000."

"Apparently," Wellington told Whittingham years later, "our employee was going to pocket the $5,000 difference or else he thought he was going to save the club some money and make some points for himself." Tim was livid for years after he found out about Strong and the bungled offer.

Also remarkable among the new recruits was one of the great Giants legends of all time, Mel Hein. In 1930 Hein was named to Grantland Rice's All-American team. At Washington State, Hein was one of the stars who led the team to the 1930 Rose Bowl. Hein's

Washington State team had come to Philadelphia to play Villanova, and as a result Hein became friendly with several Giants players. The Giants were hot to get Hein, but he almost slipped away.

Other teams were hot after Hein, too. And in the days before the draft, offers poured in. Providence offered $135 per game. Hein waited, but the Giants' contract, despite the team's promises, never appeared. So Hein signed a contract with Providence and put it in the mail.

That same day he went to Spokane, Washington, as he was on the men's varsity basketball team and they were playing Gonzaga that night. After the game, Gonzaga coach Ray Flaherty, who was also a well-known Giants defensive end, asked Hein, "Did you get the contract from our club yet?" Hein told him he had never heard from the Giants, and had that very day signed the Providence contract and sent it back. Flaherty immediately demanded to know how much Hein had signed for. When Hein reported he had signed for $135 per game, Flaherty shot back, "The Giants will give you at least $150 per game. I'll get in touch with the club tomorrow and see if they will send you a contract right away. In the meantime you better find some way to get that Steamroller contract back."

Hein did as he was told and asked a postmaster in Pullman what to do. The postmaster advised Hein to send a telegram to the Providence postmaster regarding the letter, asking him to return the contract. Luckily for Hein and the Giants, the Rhode Island postmaster intercepted the contract and returned it to Hein, who signed with New York shortly thereafter.

From 1933 to 1940 Hein was named first-team All-NFL center eight years in a row. He also played linebacker for most of his career. When he suffered a broken nose during a 1941 game, he requested the only timeout of his career, after which he continued to play.

Later in his career Hein earned the nickname "Cappy," as he was the Giants team captain for 10 straight years. He would play for the New York Giants his entire career, lasting 15 years. Hein was considered aggressive, ruthless, and always a gentleman. He rarely started fights, and was well liked or well regarded by teammates and opposing players alike. Hein would be the linchpin to some of the Giants' high points for the next decade and a half.

This was a crucial year in the NFL. Restructuring had made it an exciting league. First the league was split into two divisions—the Eastern Division and the Western Division. The Eastern included New York, Brooklyn, Boston, Philadelphia, and Pittsburgh. The Western included Chicago, Green Bay, Portsmouth, Cincinnati, and the Chicago Cardinals. The second innovation was to add a championship game to decide the league's winner.

By now Jack was really making his presence felt at the club. He left player personnel moves and team management to his father and Wellington. Jack was an executive, and was happy in that role. He busied himself with the finances and administrative duties of the club. Even at an early age, Wellington was showing a flare for spotting talent, and some of his biggest finds were not far off.

"Well was much more interested in the team than Jack. Jack wanted to see the ledgers, the balance sheets," said Tim one time. "He hated to spend money, just as I did."

"I'm just a businessman," Jack said later. "I let Well run the team and talk to the sportswriters. I'm only doing what I feel I can do best. If I tried to mix in elsewhere, I might hurt the team. And the team is the family. I'm just doing my job."

Jack was like any number of businessmen of the day. He loved his family and he loved the country club. He was a golfing fanatic, playing as often as he could, regardless of his abilities (as his published golfing handicaps attested).

"Golf relaxes me," Jack said. "When I go to the office, I get all wound up in the business. Even if we're making money, I find myself worrying. So I get out to the golf course. But sometimes I get myself to the racetrack," said Tim Mara's boy. "Either way, I can relax from the office."

The exclusive Winged Foot Country Club in Mamaroneck, New York, is one of the great, classic bastions of golf on the East Coast. Situated with several challenging courses, the club was personified by its immense, sprawling English Tudor clubhouse. It was home to scores of very wealthy merchants, bankers, and entrepreneurs. The courses were designed by one of history's premiere golf architects, A.W. Tillinghast, who also designed such prestigious courses as Baltusrol Golf Club, Bethpage State Park, Brooklawn Country Club, and Quaker Ridge Golf Club. Winged Foot is supposed to be among his crowning achievements, and today is still considered among North America's greatest courses. Winged Foot has been the site of the 2006, 1984, 1974, and 1959 U.S. Open golf championships. And no member was fonder of testing the courses' or clubhouses' limits than Jack Mara was. Jack played as often as he could, competing in well-publicized pro-am and amateur tournaments, as well as club round robins. He was also fond of entertaining in the club's celebrated dining room.

During the warmer months the family preferred to summer at Spring Lake, New Jersey, a coastal town populated by huge, sprawling Victorian mansions and blessed with cooling seaside breezes. It was sometimes jokingly referred to as the Irish Riviera, since the town was so densely populated by wealthy Irish merchants and bankers. Almost 40 percent of the town was of Irish ancestry.

For more than 100 years the seaside community played host to the rich and famous. Dominating the resort scene were giant, classic Victorian seaside resort hotels with hundreds of rooms. The opulent New Monmouth Hotel and the Essex and Sussex Hotels dominated the two-mile stretch of shore, which was capped by the longest non-commercial boardwalk in New Jersey. The well-known sprawling Tudor hotel called the Warren was the sight of many Jazz Age parties, and, up until its demise in the 1990s, it exuded an old-time country club atmosphere with its manicured lawns, sprawling tennis courts, and elegant poolside cabanas.

"Jack, who befriended sportswriters and players alike, was a fun-loving man," wrote Dave Klein, a former sportswriter for the Newark *Star-Ledger*. "Unlike Wellington, he found no difficulty at all in separating his football life from his social life, perhaps for the simple reason that Well was so obsessed with the Giants that Jack knew the team was in capable hands."

"His religion was his strength," wrote Arthur Daley. "He was a good man, kind, generous, and thoughtful. He had all the virtues. On top of that he had a glowing personality, a quick smile, and a ready quip that drew people to him, high and low. Everyone liked Jack Mara."

Lizette was very involved with the Spring Lake community and local churches. When at all possible, Jack availed himself of the neighboring golf clubs here, too. "I'm not a football player," he once joked. "I wish I were as good at it [golf] as the Giants are at football."

In 1933 the Giants were a machine again. Though Chicago led the league in yardage gained, the Giants were a close second. The team stumbled out of the gate and went 2–2, and then lost to the Bears three weeks later. After that, they finished 11–3–0, and had gained a split with Chicago later in that year.

Since the Bears had won the Western Division, the Giants would play them again. Since the Bears had finished with a better regular-season record, the game was played at Wrigley Field.

On a foggy day in Chicago the Bears opened with two field goals, and the Giants answered with a touchdown pass from Newman to Badgro. The teams went into the half 7–6 in a hard-fought game. The Bears opened the second half with a field goal, and the Giants immediately answered with another touchdown. The Bears did the same right back, making the score 16–14, Bears. The Giants then scored again in the opening of the fourth quarter, making the score 21–16 in favor of the Giants.

Late in the fourth quarter the Bears' Bronko Nagurski threw a pass to Bill Hewitt, who gained 14 yards before subsequently lateraling the ball to Bill Karr, who scored the winning, and heartbreaking, touchdown. Chicago won, 23–21.

In October 1933 Smith and Mara were linked once again, this time in headlines that read: "Smith Is Named in Company Row...Oust T.J. Mara as Official." Mara, among his many positions in and around New York, was vice president and director of the Meenan Coal Company. The company had been formed in 1928 with Kenny, Meenan, and other Tammany friends, with 4,500 shares of common stock and 4,500 shares of preferred stock. Some 563 shares of each stock were in Lizette's name. Tim's brother, John J., was also a stockholder on his brother's behalf. On October 4, Alfred E. Smith, the former governor and Mara's friend, and William F. Kenny, of Tiger Room fame and majority stockholder, held a secret shareholders meeting, without the Maras, and ousted Tim from the company. At the meeting, Kenny, his son-in-law Arthur Smith (Al Smith's son), and T.A. Kenny were substituted as the new slate of company officers. To add insult to injury, Jack was supplanted as secretary. I. Gainsburg, who filed suit on behalf of Mrs. Mara, said the election was illegal because it was called by a nonstockholder and that she, as a substantial shareholder, should have been invited to the special election. The lawyers also pointed out that the results had not been disclosed. The courts agreed, and eventually terms were reached by the warring parties. One must wonder if this was an unsettling attempt at retribution against Mara for tainting Smith and other Tammany faithful in the Raskob scandal.

Young Wellington was maturing. Roman Catholic Bishop William McCormack grew up just across Park Avenue and Eighty-third Street from Mara. Young Billy McCormack was Wellington's oldest friend. "I was a 10-year-old brat when he was 17 or 18, and I remember thinking, 'This guy is something special.' And that's the impression I had of him my whole life," McCormack said 71 years later.

In the fall of 1933, a very interesting young man, Vincent Lombardi, accepted a scholarship to Fordham University. Lombardi was a well-respected athlete who played vasity football and later won national fame as one of the vaunted "seven blocks of granite," as the Rams offensive was known. Also in attendance that fall was Wellington Mara. "The Fordham campus and its surroundings seemed isolated from the grit of the metropolis," wrote David Maraniss in his acclaimed bestselling biography of Lombardi, *When Pride Still Mattered*. "A calming preserve of natural beauty extended from the world famous zoo to the New York Botanical Gardens and onto the school property itself, 70 acres of cobblestone paths, gray stone Gothic buildings, and rolling greenswards shaded by graceful elms."

But their circumstances could not have been more different. Among the 432 boys in that freshman class, Lombardi was from an immigrant, lower-middle-class working family and was one of the few boys commuting to and from the school from New Jersey. Lombardi's cousin had entered Fordham the year before and had convinced his cousin to follow suit. Every day, to get to Fordham, Lombardi took a series of connecting trains and ferries. Well's commute was slightly different. According to Maraniss, Wellington "was occasionally seen riding up from his family's luxurious residence at 975 Park Avenue in the back of a chauffeur-driven limousine."

According to Maraniss, "Contrary to later reports that they were close college chums, Wellington Mara had known Vince only casually during their Fordham years, when he spent most of his spare time scouting pro talent for his father's team. Vince and Well were in Ignatius Cox's ethics class together. ... In their senior year Mara was sports editor of the Maroon yearbook and wrote stories about the exploits of the Seven Blocks of Granite, but considered Lombardi the least talented of the seven and never interviewed him."

Also according to Maraniss, it was Owen who first spotted Lombardi's talent as a coach. Once, when Owen went to a football dinner in the mid-1940s, he reportly came back and said to Well, "You know that guy Lombardi who was in your class at school? They win the championship every year!" referring to St. Celia High School in Englewood, New Jersey.

A year ahead of both Lombardi and Well was a devastating halfback named Ed Danowski. Danowski was an All-American halfback in 1932 and 1933. In 1934 he signed to play for the New York Football Giants. His presence would make 1934 one of the most memorable seasons in the history of NFL football.

December 1933 showed how small the glitzy world of sports really was in New York City. At the Hotel Astor, John Hay Whitney, the famous American sportsman more commonly known as Jock, sponsored a black-tie fund-raiser for the coal fund for the needy of New York City. Five hundred notables and wealthy people attended the star-studded dinner. Mingling at the tables and bars were such notables as Dempsey, Tunney, former Governor Smith, Friedman, A.A.U. and future American Olympic Committee president Avery Brundage, McGraw, W.A. Harriman, Hamilton Fish, and a list of Guggenheims, Vanderbilts, Whitneys, and other glitterati of the New York social scene. And of course, Mr. and Mrs. Timothy J. Mara. Indeed it seemed charity, like politics, made for strange bedfellows.

THE DUKE OF WELLINGTON

In the early years Wellington Mara was a ballboy for his father's team. Always curious and always interested, he attended all the training camps and ferried balls and equipment while watching the players. During one such incident Wellington was running around the field and shagging balls for future Hall of Fame lineman Mel Hein. Hein was a center and was practicing long snapping.

"I got too close when he was snapping the ball," Wellington ruefully remembered. "I would get the loose balls on the field and bring them to him, and each time he snapped he'd run through a fake blocking drill. Well, he didn't see me, and he charged off the line with his elbows and his fists churning. Boy, did he catch me. It might have been the first time Mel blindsided anybody," Mara chuckled. It resulted in a black eye and some bruised ribs.

Especially in the early years, Wellington was seen as something of a mascot by the players—a good luck charm. By players and fellow owners alike he was dubbed "the Duke," "the Duke of Mara," and even "the Duke of Wellington." Tim, ever the Irishman, told writers and players that Well had been named after the Duke of Wellington, a man Mara referred to as "the fightingest of all Irishmen," since Arthur Wellesley, the original Duke of Wellington, was born in Dublin in 1769. Eventually, Well's nickname was shortened to "the Duke," and it stuck.

"It was interesting because most of the guys I went to school with called me Tim," Wellington said years later. "I picked up the nickname when I was around the team, and the players called me 'the Duke.' It didn't bother me. I preferred it to Wellington."

And Duke soon shared his nickname with the newly developed oblong football, a revision of the old, round style. The official NFL football was supplied by the Thorp Corporation. Ed Thorp, the company's founder and president, was a longtime friend of Tim Mara's. Thorp developed the final shape and length that satisfied him as well as coaches and players, and called it "the Duke" in honor of his friend's football-obsessed son. Thorp created the new official NFL ball in 1941, and that ball would be used in professional football games for decades to come.

"I'm pretty sure my father had something to do with it," Wellington said with a smile years later.

Well's parents impressed upon him the importance of his Catholic faith and the need to earn a good education. He was an excellent student and showed promise early when he skipped the fifth grade because of his academic performance. He later went to Loyola High School in New York City.

THE SNEAKERS GAME

In 1932, Owen was made the head coach. He would become one of the most influential coaches in the league. He was the first among a string of innovators the Maras would hire over the next 70 years.

"I wasn't sure then," Tim Mara later said on why Owen was made head coach. "But he seemed to get along with all the other players, and he seemed to take his word seriously. He was the kind you could have a lot of confidence in. Besides, he had worked as a foreman for my coal company [the Harlem River Coal Company]. He knew how to handle rough customers with tact."

When told he had been made head coach, Owen, a brawny, tough customer, asked Mara to stop kidding and tell him who the coach really was. It went back and forth. Finally, Mara demurred, "It's you! I'm tired of buying you new uniforms. You're the coach." Owen was only 34 years old, and he would remain with the team for another 23 years. In the entire time he coached, he never had a written contract. Tim's handshake was Owen's bond.

Owen was devoted to defense, and his 23-year reign forever left a stamp on the club that thrived on its defense. If anyone gave the team its backbone, its character, its mystique on the playing field, it was Owen. Owen's smothering defenses were the scourge of the NFL and a signature of some of the great Giants teams. As late as 1950, he was still an innovator and was the architect of the "umbrella defense," which would revolutionize professional football, and the first to improvise a two-platoon system, rotating fresh and/or rested men into the game. His stamp on a young lineman named Jim Lee Howell would ensure that Owen's influence on the team would be felt for generations to come.

"The teams are usually nervous before a game starts," Owen once reasoned. "They are prone to make errors. I want us to be able to capitalize on their mistakes." While innovators around the league, such as Washington's Slingin' Sammy Baugh, thought Owen pushed back the football hands of time, Owen didn't care. He was out to win. And it seemed he preferred an ugly win to a pretty loss. "I'd rather win 3–0 than lose 43–42. If the other team has a great offense or a superstar athlete, we have to stop him."

In 1934 the season got off to a bad start with losses to Detroit and Green Bay, but then the Giants went on a five-game winning streak. They had a strong defense, led by All-Pros Hein, Badgro, Butch Gibson, Potsy Jones, and Bill Morgan. And the offense shone brightly with Strong and Newman.

A pivotal game came when New York visited Chicago on November 18, 1934. It was, as usual, a hard-hitting affair—an ugly, tight game. During the game Newman's season ended catastrophically when he suffered two broken vertebrae. The Giants were visibly shaken by the crushing blow Newman had received, and the team went on to lose 10–9 to the Bears.

The team rallied to win two more games before blowing their final game to Philadelphia. Still, with the 8–5–0 finish, they were good enough to take the Eastern Division for a second year in a row, and they would have to play the Bears—who had won the Western Division with a record of 13–0–0—for the championship.

The Giants had only the fifth-best offense in the 10-team league. Chicago's brutal machine had consumed 3,783 yards in the season, and Chicago's star, Beattie Feathers, had amassed more than 1,000 yards. By contrast, the Giants had only advanced the ball 2,775 yards, and their best rusher had gained only 483 yards, not even best in the conference. On paper, it seemed like a gruesome mismatch.

The game was to be played at the Polo Grounds on December 9, 1934. The night before, a driving rainstorm mixed with ice had drenched the city. A freeze followed it directly, so that the field was frozen solid. It was a blustery, cold day, marked by violent gusts of wind and bitterly cold weather.

"When I went to mass, the thermometer showed 9 degrees. Street puddles turned to ice," Halas remembered years later.

Jack arrived at the field first. He walked the field and immediately phoned Coach Owen. "It's bad," Jack told Owen. "You can't even walk without slipping. I don't know what we're going to be able to do."

Owen talked to the players. This was going to be a makeshift game. Badgro and Newman were out with injuries, and Strong had a badly sprained ankle. Could they run on this field? Could they pass? Could they defend?

It was then that Flaherty spoke up, mentioning that at Gonzaga they had played on a field like this in 1925 and had won because they wore sneakers. The sneakers were able to get better traction. But where to get sneakers on a Sunday? Back then the blue laws forbade stores to be open on Sundays.

"We had a little fellow on the payroll named Abe Cohen, a sort of jack-of-all-trades," Wellington later recalled. "Abe was a tailor by profession and he also worked for Chick Meehan, who was a famous coach at Manhattan College."

Owen asked Abe Cohen to go over to the Manhattan campus. Cohen had keys to the school's equipment room and gymnasium. He was given instructions to bring back as many pairs of sneakers as possible.

"Abe got in a taxi and went to Manhattan. I think he had to break into the lockers."

In the meantime, the game had begun without the sneakers. The Bears were surely the superior team. The Giants struck first with a field goal, which put them up 3–0. But then the Bears scored 10 points before the end of the half. The Bears had driven the length of the field twice during the second quarter. Their size and strength were the difference in the game.

"We were pretty discouraged at halftime," Hein said years later. "Bronko Nagurski and Pug Manders three-yarded us to death." And still no one had heard from Cohen.

As the second half was about to begin, Cohen showed up.

"Some of the players didn't want to put them on, but those who did had so much success that eventually most of our players put them on," said Wellington.

The Bears scored again, and now the Giants had an awesome task ahead of them. They were down 13–3 to the Bears in a game they had been pushed around in for three quarters. By the late third quarter most of the Giants players were wearing sneakers and finding comfortable footing. At one point the Bears players began to take notice of the Giants' surer footing and noticed the sneakers. One Bears player pointed out the change in footwear.

Halas barked back, "Good, step on their toes!"

"Dammit," said another lineman, "we couldn't get close enough to even see their toes." Some Bears players had resorted to taking off their cleats so they could get better footing. But nothing helped.

"We were helpless," Hall of Fame fullback Nagurski later said of the second half. "We had to mince about. We were down more than we were up."

Dame Fortune had struck. First, former Fordham star Danowski threw a 28-yard pass to Ike Frankian, and suddenly the Giants were back in the game.

When a timeout was called, Gus Mauch, the famous New York sports trainer who also was the trainer for the New York Yankees, ran out onto the field with paper cups filled with whiskey. The water buckets had frozen, so Mauch had asked Jack Mara for the whiskey he kept in his office. On the next play, Strong scored.

Strong had broken off a 42-yard touchdown run that put the Giants ahead. Mauch brought another tray out and the men drank it down. Then Strong tore off another 11-yard touchdown run, and Danowski added insult to injury and ran one in himself from nine yards out a little later in the quarter.

"By that time the bottle was empty," Mauch recalled for the *Pro Football Inquirer* in 1976. He sent Jack into the field boxes looking for more. Jack went to see Well, his father, General Phelan (the New York state boxing commissioner), Mayor Jimmy Walker, and James Farley, who were fortifying themselves against the cold but happily forfeited their stash for the team. On the next timeout the players told Mauch they were trying to win the game, not get drunk. "They chased me off the field."

The Giants had scored 27 points in the fourth quarter and were now world champions. The contest was immediately dubbed "the Sneakers Game," and has gone down in NFL history as one of the most incredible comebacks in championship play.

"I still say we had no business winning it," Strong said 35 years later.

Wellington told Whittingham years later that a week after the Sneakers Game the Bears were doing a little barnstorming, playing in Philadelphia after the championship game. "Steve Owen and I went down to see the game. We went into the Bears' dressing room, I guess to crow up a little bit, and the first thing we saw was about 24 pairs of sneakers on top of the lockers.

"I'll never get caught like that again," Halas said to Well and Owen. Later he wrote in his autobiography, "I wish I could forget the fourth quarter."

"My father and Halas were so often on opposite sides that I grew up looking upon Halas as an enemy," said Wellington of Halas years later. "They had deep feelings. Neither was afraid to take positive positions and let his position be known." Wellington's love of his team and family could at times make him myopic. Where the older Jack got along well with many of the other owners, whom he saw as fellow businessmen, Wellington saw only bitter rivals. However, as youth gave way to wisdom, Wellington changed some. "Now I see Halas in a different light," Mara said in 1979. "I realize he and my father were on the same side, working for the good of the league."

Hein told a great story of a time when the team had traveled to California for an exhibition game, as was the custom in those days, to do a little barnstorming after the 1934 championship. Tim had accompanied the team to Los Angeles, where the first of two games was scheduled to be played. Two days after arriving, Mara announced he had to return home. When pressed as to why, Mara admitted to Hein that the quiet was driving him crazy. The birds were waking Mara at 6:00 AM. "Tim said he needed to get back to New York, where he was raised on the East Side, and where he could hear the subway and the fire engines and all the racket. He couldn't sleep unless he heard all the noises of New York."

At the annual meeting, when the championship trophy was awarded, it was not Tim who accepted the trophy, it was Jack. And in the background was his father. It was more than symbolic. Tim Mara wasn't dead yet. His brogue would be heard and his hand would be felt for another 24 years, but his sons were making a solid contribution to the organization. And that contribution would only grow. For the next 24 years the Mara's would run the Giants as a family concern. Jack and Wellington were about to help their father in incalculable ways.

And what of Cohen? The 140-pound, 5'2", diminutive tailor went back to his quiet life and to rooting for the Giants. But his name was not forgotten. Lewis Burton of the *New York American* immortalized Cohen forever, writing on December 10, 1934, "To the heroes of antiquity, to the Greek who raced across the Marathon plain, and to Paul Revere, add now the name of Abe Cohen."

JACK GROWS INTO THE ROLE

While Tim garnered some attention in 1934 as the first bookmaker to take a bet under the new horse racing betting laws enacted in 1934, the year clearly belonged to Jack.

The mid to late 1930s were a good period for Jack Mara, and the years would only get better after that. He graduated from Fordham Law School in 1933 and passed the New York state bar examination two years later in May 1935. Although he would never practice law professionally his skills were put to good use by his father on behalf of the Giants and many other companies in which Tim was involved.

There is a great story that illustrates how Jack and Tim operated in those days. Strong told about how, after the 1934 season and "the Sneakers Game," he figured he was due for a good raise. The Maras stonewalled him by telling him he wasn't even the best back in the league by a large margin, and that his contract shouldn't be adjusted too grossly.

"The next time I went to his office I brought a lawyer with me. When Mr. Mara saw him, he said, 'I don't want to talk to you when you have a lawyer.'"

"Why not? You have one with you," Strong's lawyer retorted, motioning toward Jack. Reluctantly, the Maras gave him a deal that included a small salary increase and a percentage of the gate, over a certain amount, but with a ceiling of $6,000. The Maras kept the deal quiet, as they had with Harry Newmans similar deal the year before. With Newman, they thought they had gotten themselves off cheap, but their threshold number hadn't been low enough, and Tim got burned for some serious cash. They were tougher on Strong, and he knew it because he and Newman were friends. In the end Strong did well, but the Giants had figured it out. Strong had capped out with two games left to go in the season. As he figured it, he played the last two games for free, including one against the strong-drawing Chicago Bears.

Newman also remembers when he tried to hold out for more money that year . He recalled that the Maras were still smarting from paying so much money from the year before. "They had to pay me a lot of dough," he said. Despite playing for nothing in a charity game to help raise funds for World War I hero Major Frank Cavanaugh, Newman could not slay their ire. He held out until two games into the season, and finally relented and ended up playing for less money than he wanted.

Hein remembered dealing with Jack, too. Hein remembered that Jack was originally put on the payroll as the team's lawyer the year he graduated from law school. "Tim was easier to deal with as far as a contract was concerned. Jack, being a lawyer, was a bit tougher to get anything out of. I think Tim was a little more generous and, needless to say, I preferred to deal with him if I wanted to get a raise or anything like that. He would listen to me longer."

Among the closest of the Mara's family friends was Major General John J. Phelan, who was, not by coincidence, the chairman of the New York State Athletic Commission from 1926 to 1927 and again in 1930 after a brief interlude when he was supplanted by Tammany Tiger James J. Farley.

Phelan was a constant in the New York sports and society world. His name comes up more than Mara's in cross-referencing his appearances in the press. He was known as a serious man of influence and power. He could make or break matches. He could (and did) withhold purses, and he oversaw all aspects of sports licensing in the state of New York.

He had served as a general in World War I, during which he commanded the Sixty-ninth Regiment, known as New York's "Fighting Irish." He later commanded the same regiment of the National Guard after he returned home.

He married in 1907 and had five children. His wife, Miss Mary Irene Bradley, died in Paris in 1920. He remained a widower for many years and raised his children by himself. He had a son, Lieutenant John J. Phelan Jr., and four daughters, Lillian, Helen, Jeanne, and Marie.

Jack Mara and Helen Phelan were married on May 5, 1934, at St. Patrick's Cathedral by Reverend John J. Nestor. Marie Phelan was her sister's only bridesmaid, and 20-year-old Wellington served as Jack's best man. Jack was now coming into his own.

Jack was tall and thin. Though many of the linemen were taller and more solidly built, Jack nonetheless always cut a tall, dashing figure. He dressed like a businessman, always wearing suits and ties. He looked like he belonged more on Wall Street than at the Polo Grounds. He was conservative in many of his views, and he had an excellent sense of humor. On several occasions, when seeing a very highly touted new player, he might laughingly say, "Gee, I thought he should have been bigger—at least bigger than I am."

As *The New York Times* wrote of Jack many years later, "In the 1930s Mr. Mara was of a trio that included George Halas of the Chicago Bears and George Preston Marshall of the Washington Redskins that kept the National Football League alive through the lean years. When other owners wanted to quit at the start of World War II, he insisted that the league continue, using what players it could find."

Always rabid fans of their own team, Well and Jack often watched the game from high up in the stadium. One story about Jack from years later told of him watching a game at Texas Stadium from the glass-enclosed press box. Chided for his loud applauding of his own team, he shot back loudly, "If you're going to sit near me, you're going to hear me."

The 1935 season was just as exciting as the 1934 season had been. Actually, it was better. The season was seen as a rebuilding year, with Owen eventually easing Newman, Strong, Badgro, and Flaherty to the sideline in favor of younger, faster, hungrier kids.

One of the highlights that year was a game with Chicago. Strong kicked two game-winning field goals, only to have each nullified by penalties. A third attempt was good, but a scuffle occurred when several players went after the ball and struggled in the mud. To everyone's amazement, who should come up with the muddy pigskin but the bedecked owner of the Giants himself, Tim Mara. His shoes, topcoat, and suit were caked with mud as he hugged the slimy ball next to his chest, smiled, and clucked, "Now I know I'm some kind of crazy Irishman. I give away a hundred new footballs every year, and here I am fighting for a muddy one."

The Giants went 9–3–0 and won the Eastern Division for the third year in a row. They led the division in overall offense and had a solid defense to boot. Again, the stalwarts in the West had been the Bears and the Packers. But in the 1935 championship game the New York Giants played neither of them; instead they faced the upstart Detroit Lions in only their second year of play.

The Giants went to Detroit, Michigan, and played the Lions at the University of Detroit Stadium, on December 15, 1935. The talent-rich Lions drubbed the "Maramen," as they sometimes were called in the press, 26–7. Still, the Giants had appeared in the first three NFL championship games.

The owners meetings followed. These affairs could yield almost anything. In the early 1930s these meetings were the source of new rule changes that would profoundly change the way football was played, including the use of hash marks, the placement of field-goal posts, and other innovations to the game.

In 1933 Tim had gone public with his fight to institute an overtime period in an effort to eliminate the number of ties occurring during the regular season.

"In every sport but football the authorities have sought to avoid a tie score," declared Mara. "No matter whom you are rooting for, you don't want to see a game end in a tie." Mara opined, "This plan might not be feasible for collegians, but I think it would work out for the professionals. I believe that our men are in better physical condition and that it would not affect them as much." However, Mara was stumped as to what should be done in case the overtime period yielded nothing. "I guess they would have to allow the tie to remain," he said.

"At the league meeting in 1934, some members wanted to make a dropped lateral a live ball. George [Halas] was bitterly opposed. He gave one of his most passionate speeches," Wellington said. Since the Bears ran a T-formation, which included lots of player movement, their weapon of choice for their ground game was the lateral pass. And there were lots of drops.

"You gentlemen will destroy me," Halas said.

"He really cried. Real tears. He had his way," said Wellington.

In 1936, at one of the league meetings, Bert Bell had proposed that the league establish a draft. Each team would create a list of graduating players of whom it thought highly. The lists would be posted. And then the selection process would begin. The teams finishing last would pick first, and so on, until the champion picked last. The proposal was meant to allow the teams to negotiate one-on-one with the players. And if terms still could not be reached, the league president would arbitrate. If terms still could not be reached then, the team could trade the player to a more suitable team, or the player would have to wait a year before entering the league as a free agent. All those not selected could go to any team of their choosing.

This draft concept was a double-edged sword. The NFL wanted to show outsiders that they would only take graduated students, an issue that had become a bit of a publicity sore point because many college athletes were leaving school early for the fame and fortune of professional sports. It was also designed to help the less-fortunate clubs compete.

On the other hand, it was easy to see that the owners wanted to hold down salaries. By stopping clubs from competing against each other for a player's services, the league could sidestep ugly bidding wars and keep salaries down. The players coming out of college were not happy, as salaries dropped by almost half.

"I thought the proposal sound. I thought it made sense," wrote Halas. "Mara also approved. He and I had more to lose than any other team."

"People come to see a competition. We could give them a competition only if the teams had some sort of equality, if the teams went up and down with the fortunes of life," Tim Mara said. "Of course that meant no team would win the championship every third year and people would start saying, 'What's happened to the Giants? They aren't the team they used to be.' That was a hazard we had to accept for the benefit of the league, of professional football and for everyone in it."

"With our support, the proposal was adopted unanimously," Halas said of Mara and himself.

That year was the first time Wellington would have an impact on the franchise. Wellington was obsessed with football, often taking in a Fordham game on a Saturday morning when possible and then going to a Giants home game on a Sunday. By this time Wellington was keeping files on dozens of players around the country every year, analyzing who was the best, who fit the team's needs, etc. He would cull newspapers and magazines, searching for anyone he thought might be able to contribute to the team.

"We had no scouting budget. I would buy all the college football magazines and subscribe to a whole bunch of out-of-town papers," Mara said years later.

Mara would often write to college administrators, coaches, and professors for information on those in whom he was keenly interested. He had been an avid supporter of Fordham's Danowski, and now Mara was pouring himself into the work of signing him. And in addition to Danowski's love of football, he was also among those singled óut by his school for having superior grades.

One Saturday Well and a friend went to Washington, D.C., to see a bruising fullback named Alphonse "Tuffy" Leemans. Even though Leemans played for a small school—George Washington—Well thought that Tuffy had what it took to make it in the NFL. Tim encouraged his son to approach Leemans.

"I sent him a telegram setting up a meeting and signed my father's name," Wellington recalled. The two were set to meet in front of the small school's gymnasium. "When I got there, he thought I was a kid who wanted his autograph. He looked at me strangely suspicious." Leemans insisted he was meeting Tim Mara, the owner of the New York Giants. "But I was able to eventually convince him that I was in fact a legitimate emissary, and he did listen to me."

Leemans was always relatively happy with the Maras. "With Tim Mara...you never really needed a contract. His word always held good. One year I got hurt pretty badly and New York paid my salary in the hospital, which I understand was the kind of situation in which some of the fellows around the league had a tough time collecting."

Leemans would not only go on to eventually lead the Giants to a championship, but would be the first among many Hall of Famers Wellington would scout for the team.

In 1936 the Giants saw the defection of some of their veterans who'd been making fewer and fewer contributions. It was a mass migration: Badgro, Strong, and Newman all left. And Flaherty became the new coach of the Boston Redskins, working for George Preston Marshall.

The 1936 Giants were a disappointment. The younger players did not grow into their roles, and many of the veterans were gone. The Giants finished 5–6–1, and the Boston Redskins, with Flaherty as coach, won the Eastern Division with a record of 7–5–0. The only good news for the New York fans was that they got to see a championship game anyway, as the mercurial Marshall simply folded up his tent in Boston and changed the venue to New York, where he thought he could make more money. The NFL championship game was played at the Polo Grounds, with Tim helping to make the deal with the Stonehams, owners of the baseball Giants and the Polo Grounds. Mara brokered the deal despite his lifelong tenuous relationship with Marshall.

Despite a tight race at one point, the Redskins, now based in Washington, took the division in 1937 with a record of 8–3–0. The Giants finished second with a 6-3-2 record, two of those losses having been inflicted by Marshall's hated Redskins. Washington went on to beat the Bears in the championship game to take the league title.

After the championship game Flaherty stopped by to say hello to Jack. Flaherty was headed out West for some traditional Washington barnstorming and some scouting. Flaherty mentioned his scouting thoughts to Jack.

"He'd look pretty sweet in my backfield next year," Flaherty said, of an unnamed player.

"No, Ray, I personally think he would look much better in a Giants uniform," said Jack enthusiastically.

"There's nothing you can do about that," said a grinning Flaherty. "I'll see him first."

Jack warned Flaherty, laughing, "The split second you step out of this office, I'm going to wire that fellow and tell him to be on his guard. I'll advise him that a red-headed lunatic who says his name is Flaherty has escaped from his keeper and is roaming around the country with a football complex, trying to sign up players. They'll put you in an asylum if you go near him."

"We'll see," declared the grinning Flaherty. "Happy New Year, Jack!" said Red, and with a chuckle he was gone.

This is the kind of exchange Wellington could not understand. Maybe in his later years he could have relished the moment—his former player talking to his late brother about the old days. In the spirit of the moment, Jack could be humorous and convivial. To Wellington, this moment might have seemed maddening—a former player, who now worked for the hated Redskins, nodding with a grin about the new talent they were going to sign up. For Jack, by all accounts, these moments were not to be suffered. There was money to be made and golf to be played.

On February 13, 1937, Marshall officially moved the Redskins to Washington. By 1937 there had been many changes within the Mara family that would have great impact in years to come.

Happily for Jack and Helen, 1936 saw the birth of Timothy J. Mara, their first child, named for Jack's father. Their daughter, Maura Mara, was born at the Harkness Pavillion Medical Center a year later. John and Helen now had a burgeoning family. Also in 1937, Wellington graduated from Fordham University. Unlike his brother, Wellington had decided he was going to be a lifelong employee of the Giants organization. He wanted no law degree— Jack's law degree was enough for the organization. He had grown up in football for more than 11 years. His course was set, and Mara Sr. was not about to derail his youngest son's aspirations.

"When my father owned it, he objected when I wanted to be a part of the team," Wellington said. "He wanted me to go to law school. My brother Jack had gone. I said, 'Look, I skipped a class in grammar school. I'm going to take that year off, work with the football team, then I'll go to law school.'

"About 12 years later he said, 'I guess you're not going to law school.'"

In 1936 Tim had officially named Jack the president of the New York Giants organization. Nothing really changed except that now he started dealing with more of the administrative duties that had previously been split between Dr. Harry March and Tim himself. Their two jobs had been married into one in Jack.

Jack was garnering more and more press, as the business/frontman of the operation. Tim was surely the fatherly hand guiding his sons, but Jack was more and more a fixture on the sports and social circuit as well.

When Art Rooney hit it big in August 1937 at Saratoga, cleaning up somewhere around $250,000–$380,000, he was being followed by the press. "Art used information given to him by Tim Mara, the kind of tips a fellow could usually count on. He didn't completely follow Mara's word though," wrote Rooney biographer Andrew O'Toole.

"I'd see something the charts didn't see, like a change of jockeys, a post position, and I'd use my own judgement," Rooney said.

Always feeling just as comfortable at a racetrack as he did on the golf course, Jack was no stranger to racing and his name appeared in racing sections of the papers from time to time. When Rooney was on his winning streak, winning as much as $100,000 in one day, he took a little time off to meet with Jack. The press followed them.

"We always wanted to know what a fellow who won a hundred grand on the races would do with his evening," wrote Bill Corum for the *New York Journal American*. "Rooney met Jack Mara...at a picture show in Lake Lucerne, and when the show was over said, 'Let's go someplace and have a dish of ice cream.' That's what ruins those fast-gaited guys. Nibbling on ice cream at 9:30 at night when sober, hard-working folk are in the shucks."

"Even without inside information, Art's success at the track was unmistakable. Tim Mara liked to joke that Rooney picked his horses by the flip of a coin, basking in the merriment of telling people that Art was nothing but a lucky rube. The charge drew a harrumph from the irritated Rooney," wrote O'Toole.

"That was a lot of bunk. I may have been more reckless in betting in those days, but I was no amateur," Rooney said. Regardless of this ribbing, Art and his son Dan remained close with Tim, Jack, and Wellington for decades to come, and the Rooneys and the Maras would be inextricably linked for many years.

Rooney never publicly released how much he actually won in that famous run. "I was up at Saratoga with my father that year," Wellington recalled. "The next day I was at the track with him when Art Rooney came over to bet the first race. I've forgotten whether he bet $10,000 or stood to win $10,000, but his horse was disqualified. He turned to me and said, 'I think it's time to go home.' And he did."

When Jack was named president and treasurer of the New York Football Giants, Wellington was named secretary. Wellington, his father, and Steve Owen worried about the actual team. Wellington by now was gaining a reputation as a spotter of talent. He listened in team meetings intently. He rarely spoke up. But he attended all strategy meetings, planning meetings, etc. And he was instrumental in the draft, setting up standards that would make the Giants, regardless of wins, one of the best scouting organizations in the NFL for years to come. It was not unusual at all to see Well and Owen sitting together in the stands watching a college football game or scouting another pro team.

"Jack was an attorney, and he was the conservative member of the family," noted Wellington. During a typical discussion we would have about a player's contract, I'd be in favor of giving the player an amount of money. And Jack would say, 'Suppose we have a bad year?' And my father would say, 'How can we have a bad year?' Jack was pretty conservative, and my father and I both wanted to take a chance."

Well often traveled with the team in those years. "When you went to Pittsburgh, instead of getting on a plane and flying for an hour, we'd get on a train, and I think it was a nine-hour trip. We played cards. I was part of a regular group that included [Ward] Cuff; Orville Tuttle, who was a guard; Ed Danowski—there were maybe four or five of us. We played hearts, or pitch...we played from one year to the next. At the end of the year you might have won five dollars or lost six. We were a pretty close unit, brought on by going on those long trips together."

These were the happy years. The father and the sons had found a happy medium, and this quartet of men (for Owen was family) would lead the Giants for the next 20–25 years as one of the strongest organizations in the NFL. With the Mara clan it was family, Giants, God. Blood was thicker than water, and what bound you outside of that was the team itself, followed by God. This cocoon, this moat around them, made them impervious to almost anything. Like that other famous Irish family of the 1930s to 1960s, the Kennedys of Boston, the Mara clan wielded unprecedented influence in the city of New York, although their field of choice was sports rather than politics. But be that as it may, the Maras had friends on Wall Street and at city hall, in the athletic commission, the racing commission, and with the Roman Catholic churches of the metro region. Connected with some of the most influential country clubs of the area, they were also popular guests on the society and dinner circuits, as well as the horse circuit. This vast array of social contacts gave them unprecedented power and influence.

While Lizette was no football maven, she was no small cog. She kept the family involved with charity, society, and other circles that added depth and glamour to their ranks. She made donations to seminaries in the region, was involved in numerous churches the family attended, and also donated her time to other charities around the city. She was well liked in society circles, where she kept the Mara name in league with many well-known power brokers of the period.

The Giants as a team had not made the family any real money yet. But they had an expanding organization, that turned over more and more cash every year. Each year, it seemed, promised to be the breakout season when finally they would make money. But it would be a little while still before that crop would finally begin to flourish.

CHAPTER 5

The Third Brother

The Maras and Owen now formed a brain trust that would help revolutionize football and transform the struggling Giants franchise into one of the pillars of the sports industry alongside teams like the Yankees, the Cardinals, and other famous American sports franchises. But there was still work to do. And right in front of them lay the 1938 season.

By 1938, according to David Neft and Richard Cohen, authors of *The Football Encyclopedia*, "Coach Owen had stockpiled so much talent, he formed two separate squads that alternated in the game by quarters, and after two early losses to the Eagles and the Pirates, the deep Giants marched undefeated through the bulk of their schedule."

This was the first of Owen's innovations. With All-Pros Hein, Danowski, and Ed Widseth, and with Leemans, who had just missed the All-Pro tag, the Giants were indeed deep, as well as powerful and fast.

These were the years when Wellington began to come into his own, defining himself during his early twenties. No longer the little boy, Wellington was now the age of many of the stars on the team. "All the fellows were my age," said Mara of the Giants of the late 1930s. "I was close to them, part of them." And during the 1937 and 1938 seasons, Mara even roomed with one of the team's star running backs, Ward Cuff, who also doubled as the place-kicker for point-after attempts and field goals.

In 1938 Well was officially named the club's secretary. As such he was responsible for everything from travel arrangements to purchasing game equipment to evaluating talent to negotiating

91

contracts. He even filmed the team's games with a 16mm camera his parents gave him as a Christmas present and ran the projector during team meetings.

"Back in 1935 I shot the first game films we ever had. My parents gave me one of those old bulky Bell and Howell cameras for my birthday and I would climb on the rickety press box roof at the Polo Grounds, shoot on Sunday, then rush them in for special developing that night, and then we would show them at the hotel the next morning," Wellington remembered.

"I knew all our plays, so I knew where the ball was going. The other cameraman knew little abut football and nothing about our team. I knew what the coach wanted."

But Steve Owen "was a rough, tough character," Wellington remembered. "Most of the time he'd look at them [the films] for a few minutes and walk out, although he did show them in the locker room to the players. But it was so different then: no offensive and defensive meeting, a single scout named Jack Lavelle who would watch next week's opponent and come back with a written report, and a bundle of newspapers from the next opponent's town so Owen could study the game accounts."

Marshall's Washington Redskins were keen to retain their crown and were no slouches themselves. However, Slingin' Sammy Baugh, the best passer since Benny Friedman, was injured at the beginning of the year. While Bill Hartman and Andy Farkas came to the Redskins' rescue in the backfield, Washington's two powerful linemen, Turk Edwards and Jim Barber, anchored Washington's offensive and defensive lines.

The Giants were 7–2–1 and the Redskins 6–2–2. It would come down to the final game of the season, Mara versus Marshall, in one of the first of many memorable showdowns.

George Preston Marshall was known as the "Laundry King," as he had made his fortune in the laundry business. His company's slogan was "Long Live Linen." He sold his laundry business in 1945, and held on to the Redskins until 1963. It was reported that he rooted for his beloved Redskins until his death in 1969.

Marshall, born in West Virginia in 1896, was a consummate showman. In 1938 he formed the Redskins Marching Band and was quoted as saying, "Football without a band is like a musical without an orchestra."

And on the Saturday before the game Marshall assembled his band in New York City and marched that huge orchestra down the city's streets. At the front of that Redskins parade was none other than Marshall himself with his full-length raccoon coat and always-at-the-ready chauffer-driven automobile trailing at his heels, cheering on the Redskins.

The New York Journal American relayed the sight for its readers when Marshall arrived in town for the big showdown. Bill Corum wrote of the spectacle, "At the head of a 150-piece brass band and 12,000 fans, George Preston Marshall slipped unobtrusively into New York today. ..."

"George Preston Marshall was a dashing fellow whose love of show business manifested itself in many ways," wrote famed writer Shirley Povich. "It was evident in his own failed fling at acting, in his first marriage to a former Ziegfeld Follies girl, and in his second to silent screen goddess Corinne Griffith. It was apparent in his invention of halftime extravaganzas worthy of Hollywood and in his groundbreaking radio and television broadcasts of football games." In fact, it was Griffith who penned the official fight song, "Hail to the Redskins," which made its debut on August 17, 1938.

Tim and Marshall did not like one another and often needled each other at league meetings and during showdowns throughout the season.

"Charlie [Bidwill], Bert [Bell], and I just used to sit back and watch the two of them get redder and redder as they yelled at each other," Art Rooney recalled with a laugh. "Maybe it was the schedule or a change in the rules. It didn't make no difference. They just liked to fight." Rooney also recalled of his friend Tim, "Tim always carried this prayer in his pocket. It was a prayer on hate and he used to pull it out and read it every time he flew off the handle."

This was one season Tim would have the bragging rights. While there are a multitude of highlights from the game, there was little drama to it, as New York stomped the Redskins, 36–0. It was a classic drubbing.

What loomed beyond Marshall's histrionics were the Green Bay Packers. While in previous seasons Green Bay had been an old-fashioned running club, the 1938 edition featured the pass-catching duo of Arnie Herber and Cecil Isbell. Isbell was a rookie running back sensation who could race though the line or haul in passes downfield and rumble for extra yards.

The stage was set as the Giants hosted the Packers at the Polo Grounds on December 11, 1938. More than 48,000 people came to watch, making this the most highly attended title game in NFL history up to that time. The crowd was electric. The Giants scored the first nine points, a field goal and a touchdown (the point after was missed). Herber heaved a 40-yard touchdown pass to make it 9–7 and get the Packers right back in it. Danowski answered that with a 20-yard scoring pass of his own. But Green Bay ended the half with a one-yard plunge by running back Clarke Hinkle to make the score 16–14 in the Giants' favor.

After the half Green Bay went right back to work and put up a field goal, putting the Packers ahead. But the championship was decided in the last quarter, with the Giants driving the ball. Danowski let lose a 23-yard pass to Hank Soar. Soar took in the pass and rumbled toward the goal line. Hinkle made a diving tackle and came up with one of Soar's legs. But Soar summoned all his might and pulled Hinkle over the goal line with him. With the successful point after, the Giants swallowed up the rest of the game and won the 1938 championship 23–17.

Owen, a bear of a man, had helped the Giants achieve great things, including capturing two championship pennants for their club. He was like a third brother, and among one of the closest and most trusted of family friends. This win would solidify him as the largest moon in the Mara family orbit. Francis J. Sweeny, Owen's brother-in-law, was the team physician for almost three decades. And the other lesser orb in the family's transit was the Reverend Benedict Dudley. For several decades he would also be seen about the locker rooms, practice fields, and other family events.

"The relationship between the large Mr. Owen and Tim, Jack, and Well Mara is absolutely unique in sports. Steve's contract will not be renewed at the end of the current season for the simple reason that he has never had a contract," Arthur Daley once wrote. "They are friends indeed."

"This has been a 25-year vacation for me," said Owen many years later. "I'm being well paid for doing something that I love for real people I love to do it for. Never a worry. Never a contract," he said proudly.

Though the family would place great trust in him for years to come, Owen's success as a coach had already peaked.

❦❧

The year 1939 started off quickly as the Giants played in the first All-Pro game that January. Instead of stars from the two leagues playing against each other, the NFL decided to have the previous year's champion versus an all-pro team made up of players from around the league. That way fans would see the championship team and the greatest stars of the league. The New York Giants defeated the Pro All-Stars 13–10 in the first Pro Bowl at Wrigley Field in Los Angeles, on January 15, 1939.

On May 20, 1939, Carr, NFL president since 1921 and the man who had sold Tim the team in 1925, died in Columbus, Ohio. Carl Storck was named acting president on May 25. All three Maras and Owen attended Carr's funeral. Eventually, Elmer Layden was named the first commissioner of the NFL.

In 1939, fresh out of college, Wellington was given a great honor. He was asked to run the 1939 NFL draft for the Giants. "The success of the Giants is their organization. Tim Mara is a smart businessman, Jack Mara is a great executive, Steve Owen coaches the hell out of them, and then there is that damn little Wellington," said Bert Bell, former Philadelphia Eagles coach and later NFL commissioner. "Nobody ever beats him on some unknown player who can be a star, and he won't take a well-known player if he feels the man won't produce. The little son-of-a-gun is never wrong."

Wellington did as asked and assembled the list from the players each team submitted. And with their first pick the Giants chose someone who wasn't on the list: Walt Nielson. When asked about it, Wellington replied with a grin and a shrug, "I didn't think I had to put every name on that list." For the 1939 squad the Giants would have three sensational new rookies as well as the returning Ken Strong, who was coming back from a two-year stay in the AFL. The Giants seemed poised for success.

Years later, no matter his accomplishments, Wellington always deferred to his father and older brother. "He laid down the standards and principles according to which he wanted the business operated," said Wellington of his father. "Jack took those practices and embellished those standards far beyond any abilities of mine."

❧

On September 1, 1939, Hitler's Blitzkrieg brought Europe from the brink of war to utter chaos. Many Americans now saw U.S. involvement in the war as only a matter of time. Each week the Giants vanquised foes, and the same could be said for the Germans. The 1939 and 1940 football seasons were odd times for men who played football. The players were champions on the gridiron, while overseas, men were being killed. Football's clichés and war analogies seemed silly banter next to the front-page headlines that reported a world at war. In war, many heroes die. And the military draft, if it came, would call on teammates and schoolboy friends.

In 1939 the Giants came back stronger than ever and seemed poised to repeat as champions. Again, the Giants and Redskins were pitted against each other on the last day of the season. Again, the final game would be at the Polo Grounds.

The regular-season match, played in Washington, had resulted in an ugly tie, one of only two blemishes on an otherwise spotless record posted by the New York 11. "Mud, oodles of it, and an underrated Redskins team held New York's champion Giants to a 0–0 tie yesterday in the young bog that driving rains had made of Griffith Stadium. Oilskins and umbrellas dotted the stands as 26,341 of Washington's professional football fans braved the elements," wrote Shirley Povich in the next day's *Washington Post*. "Down on the field the two teams slogged in a bitter battle for yardage, mud-caked from the opening whistle, and it was the Redskins who struck hardest. ... They smothered every Giant assault, hammered viciously at the vaunted New

York line, and forced it to give ground. But inside their own 20-yard line, the Giants braced rigidly, took advantage of the mud, and kept their goal line inviolate."

Now, as the winds of December swirled, a championship banner had yet to be claimed. Both teams had an identical 8–1–1 record, and people wanted to see what would happen. Marshall and his army of mad, traveling fans showed up in New York City again. Parades. Bands. Anticipation was growing.

"Ten years ago promoters of professional football were unable to fill a good-sized stadium, even with Annie Oakleys. Last Sunday 62,000 football fans jam-packed Manhattan's Polo Grounds for a championship game between the New York Giants and the Washington Redskins," reported *Time* magazine a week later. *Time* noted that the attendance was not near the more than 100,000-strong crowd that had filed into a stadium in Philadelphia the day prior to see the Army-Navy game, "But more than 50,000 applications for tickets had been turned down, and speculators had little difficulty in getting $25 a seat from fans eager to see what they considered the best football game of the year."

Anyone looking for an offensive show was sorely disappointed, but it was easily one of the hardest-fought games of the year. Each team pushed, fought, and clawed its way across the field. Near the end of the fourth quarter, with the Giants up 9–7, Washington drove the ball to within field-goal range. With only seven seconds left in the game, Bo Russell, a lineman for the Redskins and the team's best kicker, strode onto the field. On point-after attempts, Russell had been almost automatic, with a kicking average of 94 percent, but his field-goal percentage was a wanting 17 percent. The players lined up and Russell aligned himself. The ball was snapped, the kick went up, and what happened next is still under discussion.

Of the 60,000-plus fans who braved the winter chill that day, roughly half saw the ball sail wide. The other half would insist to their graves that the ball went through the goal posts. The game ended in controversy, and referee Bill Halloran ruled the kick no good. The Giants had won, 9–7.

But Marshall was apoplectic. He screamed, shouted, and insisted that Russell's kick was good and that Halloran was wrong. He complained to the league office, to the newspapers, and to anyone who would listen. Marshall declared that Halloran should be banned from officiating any NFL games. "Halloran never did referee again," wrote Povich, "though it was not clear whether that was because of Marshall's fury."

Povich later ran a quote from a rabid (and probably inebriated) Redskins fan who insisted, "I was sitting on the 50-yard line. I saw two balls and two sets of goal posts, and I know damn well one of those balls went through one set of those posts."

The Giants were the Redskins' Eastern Division archrivals, and they were headed to the championship game. This time the Packers would host the championship event. The Giants, fresh off their brutal game against Washington, had to pull up stakes and head for Green Bay. More than 32,000 fans showed up at the State Fair Grounds in Milwaukee in frosty, 35-mph wind conditions to watch the game. The game itself was anticlimactic for Giants fans, as the Packers completely shut down their Gotham counterparts en route to a 27–0 championship victory. It was the Packers' fifth NFL title, and it was the first NFL championship game to end in a shutout.

The problem with playing in Milwaukee Stadium was that it lacked facilities in which the players could wash up after the game. Still bloodied, players got on the bus bound for the local airport. At one point an overzealous Packers fan threw a brick through the window. While no one was badly injured, it sent glass flying everywhere.

"The only thing I regret," Tim told the press, "is that we didn't lose last week to Washington. Then Marshall and his team would have had to take this beating and this indignity, not us."

⤜⤛

In March 1940 the public saw Tim Mara back in court. It was another scandal, but this time he was just a witness. It seemed Assemblyman Lawrence J. Murray of Rockland County had bet heavily on horse races in 1937 and 1938. It was later exposed that he had lost thousands of dollars beyond his salary and income. He had embezzled more than $49,102 from a Miss May A.V. Dunnigan of Haverstraw, New York.

Tim Mara was called in with several other bookmakers to reveal the accounts of Mr. Murray's betting habits and ledger losses. Of the $13,600 Murray still owed, Mara was owed the most: a sum of $6,000.

While Murray served as Miss Dunnigan's attorney, he was also rifling her bank accounts to play the horses. Murray insisted that he was betting on behalf of Miss Dunnigan. Murray was betting anywhere from $100 to $500 per race and easily tallying up $1,500 a day.

Tim testified that he had spoken with Murray at a Turf Writer's dinner in August 1938. He said he had warned Murray that he was "foolish" to bet races as recklessly as he did. Mara said that Murray claimed he was betting in someone's stead "who could afford to lose."

"He was betting wildly and losing a lot of money," Tim told the court. When asked by the prosecutor, Irving G. Kennedy, if Mara could produce a record of those wagers, Tim replied, "The only thing those records will prove is that a player loses more than he wins."

Mara's name was used in the headlines a few times more before the story finally died. Whether he recouped his money was never disclosed.

☙❧

The 1940 season was a forgettable one. Although laden with talent, the Giants often played without passion and were sluggish in the big games, finishing 6–4–1, third in the Eastern Division. In 1941 the team was resolved to get better and started strong, reeling off five straight wins.

On October 19, 1941, a strange thing happened. Umpire C.W. Rupp fired once into the air to indicate the expiration of the first quarter. A few seconds later another shot rang out, and it seemed Rupp had accidently shot himself in the hand. He was rushed to a local hospital. It had always been assumed that officials were using blanks—not so, it seemed.

"The fact that there was no score at the time was just a coincidence," reported *The Times*.

"I've seen a lot of football officials that I thought oughta be shot," said Giants coach Owen. "But it was the first time I've seen an official take that duty on himself."

"Mr. John V. Mara, the president of the Football Giants, said he couldn't understand a football official shooting himself, but he was sure that G. Preston Marshall would approve such a plan on a wide scale," wrote sportswriter John Kiernan.

The season was already won when they played the Brooklyn Dodgers football club at the Polo Grounds, celebrating Tuffy Leemans Day. While Leemans was considered a great back in his day, few know his name now. However, the Giants organization was grateful for his services and wanted to honor Leemans in his last game, before retirement. Today, existing programs of the game are considered extremely desirable, if not for Leemans visage on the cover then for the date on that program: December 7, 1941.

In the first quarter, the public-address system uttered the words, "Attention please. Here is an urgent message. Will Colonel William J. Donovan call Operator 19 in Washington immediately?" In the press box there was chatter, as the Cardinals were beating the Bears.

"At halftime, Father Benedict Dudley, who was our team chaplain, told me the Japs had bombed Pearl Harbor," Wellington recalled 60 years later. Father Dudley was among those in the inner circle of the family. "Within two weeks I was notified that my V-12 [training] program would begin in February."

Near the fourth quarter, the public-address system sounded again, and this time it was more ominous. "All officers and men of the army and navy are to report to their stations immediately. We repeat. All armed forces personnel will report to their stations immediately."

With more important issues at hand, some players questioned why they should even finish the game, but the game was finished, with the Giants losing 21–7. For the Dodgers it was a Pyrrhic victory, as the Giants were already Eastern Division champions.

The Bears and the Packers finished in a tie for the Western Division championship, setting up the first divisional playoff game in league history. The Bears won 33–14. On December 21, 1941, the Giants and the Bears faced each other for the NFL championship in Chicago. The Giants were soundly beaten, 37–9.

What waited next was the war.

THE WAR YEARS

Wellington reported for duty in January 1942. That July and August were the first times in his life he had ever missed a Giants' training camp. He would spend 1942–1945 in the navy. He was originally sent to the Atlantic on aircraft carrier duty, and was then transferred to the Pacific fleet. During this period Well was not involved with the team in any capacity, but it seems he must have tried to follow the team's exploits no matter where he was on the globe. It would have been odd for a man who followed little-known prospects from halfway across a continent not to have inquired about absolutely everything about his beloved team.

Wellington was enlisted as a lieutenant on January 28, 1942. His first assignment was the U.S.S. *Santee*, an aircraft escort vessel that performed escort duties along the North African Coast and later saw action on many sorties. The first was against the North Coast of Africa. Then the *Santee* took part in the Palau, Yap, Ulithi, and Woleai Raid actions, which were followed by the Western New Guinea Operation.

In July 1944 *The New York Times* did a story on Lieutenant Mara. He was an early graduate of Columbia's Midshipmen's School. By that time he was a radar officer on an aircraft carrier and he had earned two medals—one for North Africa landings and one for landings in New Guinea.

In the navy, Wellington came across Jim Poole: "The wild man who used to play end for us. Jim is now as big as a house, at least 250 pounds. Except for his heft, though, he hasn't changed much," said Well.

Mara described the meeting. "Our carrier anchored off this island, and we had been observing strict naval etiquette all the time. We had to wear ties and be dressed properly at all times. Then one day this huge man came aboard.

"For a moment I thought it was some beachcomber trying to trade coral reef for a can of sardines. He was dressed only in shorts, a raincoat, and a sun helmet," Wellington said. "He took one look at our well-dressed officers before blurting out, 'By golly, these are the first ties I've seen in nine months!'" Wellington then knew who it was.

"Jim, it strikes me you'll never play end for us again. You're now big enough to be a tackle or a standing guard."

Poole was horrified. "Me not an end! Don't worry, I'll be back to playing weight in time."

While such kinds of interludes were probably rare, run-ins with familiar faces like Poole's surely broke up the long periods of inactivity. But the men of the *Santee* were about to be thrust into the center of the war in the Battle for Leyte Gulf, which has been considered the largest naval battle ever fought.

Wellington and his shipmates received presidential citations for their involvement in the battle.

At one point Mara was transferred to the U.S.S. *Randolph,* which also saw action in the Pacific theater. Of Mara, FOX sports anchor Bob Fiscella once wrote, "My father served under his command on the aircraft carrier U.S.S. *Randolph* in World War II. Mara was his lieutenant, in command of 30 men. They were stationed in the South Pacific during the latter two years of the war, seeing some combat action. My father has nothing but glowing things to say about Mara. And the time their ship docked in New York, Mara treated all the men to a Giants game."

At the end of the war Wellington had earned the American Theater Medal, the European–African–Middle Eastern Medal (two Service Stars), the Asiatic-Pacific Medal (five Service stars), the Philippine Liberation medal, the World War II Victory medal, and the Presidential Unit medal.

ON THE HOME FRONT

In the meantime Jack, Tim, and Owen kept the Giants, and the NFL, in business. The 1942 Giants were not very good. The league had been drained of many of its stars, and the Giants yielded few highlights that year. They went on to a dul 5–5–1 record, while Washington finished 10–1–0, winning the NFL championship by defeating the Chicago Bears 14–6. In 1943 the Giants improved only slightly, tying for first with a 6–3–1 record before losing a playoff to the Redskins 28–0 for the division title. Again the Redskins faced the Bears, but this time the Bears routed Washington 41–21.

At one point—and this story must be taken with a grain of salt considering Wellington's dislike of the irascible Papa Bear—several owners, led by Halas, suggested they shut down professional football until the war ended, and then they would resume operations. Attendance, which had surpassed one million spectators in the years prior to the war, had shrunk to an all-time low. Some other owners were away fighting the war, most noticeably Halas, Dan Reeves, and Fred Levy. With players, coaches, and owners fighting the war, there were few men qualified to play the game—and few men in the stands to watch them.

The holdouts against this idea were Tim and Jack Mara, Marshall, and Bert Bell. The alliance must have been a strange sight to the other executives and owners. Tim and Jack pointed to Major League Baseball—especially in their town, where there were three teams—as a league that had not slacked off at all in its attempts to earn money, regardless of the on-field product. It was also their duty, the trio reasoned, to continue life as it had always been here at home. The owners had worked so hard to establish their league and to make a going concern of it, and there was no guarantee they would get back what little edge they had if they suspended operations.

They felt it was better to keep the league going. "Even if we had to play 4Fs and high school players," said Wellington years later. And they did both.

Recruiting in this period was difficult. The better athletes were joining the war. One letter exists from this period, during which Jack was doubling as a scout and personnel man. These letters were addressed to James Carol Hecker, a student-athlete at Brigham Young University. According to Brigham Young ROTC files: "On more than one account, Hecker received letters from John V. Mara, who, at the time, was the president of the New York Football Giants. [Hecker's] courage and leadership on the football field is illustrated in a portion of a letter from Mara dated 5 March 1943: 'We like to have boys who have confidence in themselves, as you seem to have.'"

"Despite several entreaties to a good job in one of the nation's major cities, Hecker served on a different field, and paid the ultimate price for freedom," the ROTC office wrote.

It was Jack's ability to communicate across the aisle that made him so valuable to both the team and the league. As he approached it, they were all just businessmen. Where Wellington, and sometimes Tim, could let their anger get the better of them, Jack would find the common ground—the business perspective—and friends or not, he could in fact make sense to other owners by appealing to their bottom line and common interests.

According to *The New York Times*, it was Jack, among others, who "kept the National Football League alive through the lean years. When other owners wanted to quit at the start of World War II, he insisted that the league continue, using what players it could find."

The weakened owners relented to the unholy New York–Washington alliance, with certain provisos in place. They would lessen the schedule to 10 games for teams that were really hurting, rosters could be as small as 28 players, and most teams, who usually trained far away, would instead stay close to home. The Cleveland Rams did not play the 1943 season. The Philadelphia Eagles and the Pittsburgh Steelers merged into the "Steagles" in 1943. The Eagles decided to go it alone in 1944, and Pittsburgh and the Chicago Cardinals banded together to become "Card-Pitt" in 1944.

The 1944 season did not get off to a great start. Owen and Mara had convinced Arnie Herber, the retired Green Bay star, to make a comeback. It was not an unusual move in those war-torn years. The league was bereft of talent because most men of playing age were being swallowed up by the war effort. Herber showed up after three years of retirement, 30 pounds overweight. One of the leading papers called him a "tub of lard." But he worked his way back into shape and led the team on an improbable run. Along with old-timer Strong, who also came out of retirement, Owen cobbled together a team that could compete. The season was such a surprise that the newspapers dubbed the New York 11 "the Miracle Men of Mara Tech."

With the exception of one stumble, against Philadelphia, the Giants went 8–1–1 overall, which was good enough for the Eastern

Division crown. The Giants met Curly Lambeau's Packers at the Polo Grounds on December 17, 1944. Although the Giants successfully prevented famed pass catcher Don Hutson from beating them for any big plays, the Packers' crushing ground attack led by Ted Fritsch pummeled them. Fritsch made a one-yard dive for a touchdown and hauled in a 28-yard pass for another touchdown, while the Giants remained on their side of the 50-yard line until late in the third period. Cuff pushed the ball into the end zone within the first minute of the fourth quarter, but that was as close as the Giants were going to get and the Packers won it convincingly, 14–7.

There was one funny story from this period reported by Bill Corum of the *New York Journal-American*. Corum had a little fun at Tim's expense. Apparently, Mara had taken over a ticket-selling window when his ticket seller was out of the office. Shortly, a young man came up to the window, brandished a $100 bill, and asked for 25 boxed seats.

"The only boxed seats left are in the lower stands back of the goal posts," Mara responded. The young man nodded, and handed over the bill. Mara counted out the tickets and then handed the man back his change of $10.

"Stick this in your kick," the man said, pressing the $10 bill back into Mara's hand. Mara refused the tip.

"You mean you don't want $10?" said the man, surprised.

"Not as a tip," replied Mara. "You see, I happen to be owner of the Giants."

"Are you Tim Mara?" asked the young man.

"That's right," Mara replied.

"Well, keep the $10 anyhow. It's worth that to meet you," said the young man, and then he walked off.

The nadir of football in New York during the war years came in 1945, as the Giants finished an appalling 3–6–1. But with the war in the Atlantic and Pacific theaters all but over, many millions of returning GIs were looking forward to some fun football in 1946. The nation was looking to lick its wounds and get back to commerce. While the returning GIs were facing unemployment woes with so many men returning from the armed forces, the NFL and the Giants would see the opening of a new front, and a new war at home.

THE ALL-AMERICAN FOOTBALL CONFERENCE

With the start of the new season in 1946 the Giants faced not only a league of foes on their usual slate but a new league altogether called the All-American Football Conference (AAFC). The new league was led by Jim Crowley and included such teams as the Brooklyn Dodgers, the Buffalo Bisons (later the Bills), the Chicago Rockets (later the Hornets), the Cleveland Browns, the Los Angeles Dons, the Miami Seahawks (later the Baltimore Colts), the New York Yankees, and the San Francisco 49ers.

The new league had great stars and offered a very competitive product. The Yankees and the Dodgers put a great strain yet again on the Maras' family franchise. The player salaries escalated because of competition with another league. Ticket prices went a little higher and audiences were cut in half by competing playing dates. As with all other leagues, before and after, the Giants bore the brunt of the new challenger's blow because New York was the nation's largest market. The smaller market teams usually did not suffer these hard hits. Chicago was generally the only other city to face this kind of competition. These new teams hurt the Giants, whose profits were wrung tight, and whose expenses had to be wrung even tighter.

What made matters worse was the defection of the Brooklyn Football Dodgers. Topping, the owner of the Dodgers, was also the owner of the New York Yankees baseball team. He and the Maras, especially Tim, had a cantankerous relationship. Scheduling home and away games became a grotesque game of one-upmanship between the two camps. Now in another league, Topping could schedule his home contests whenever he wanted. Eventually many NFL owners blamed their situation on Elmer Layden, the NFL commissioner. Led by Marshall, Layden was ousted, and Bell was made commissioner.

"It was hoped the well-liked Bell could bring some equanimity to the proceedings, but both the 1946 and 1947 meetings deteriorated into the usual protracted discussions in which nothing was settled," pointed out sports columnist and historian Michael MacCambridge.

"The schedules would always take several days and Bert always found time to be politic," said Wellington. "All the clubs were very jealous of the schedules and no one trusted anyone. After a while people

started walking out of the league meetings and saying 'Let Bert do it.'"
Bell would be the league's scheduler for the next dozen seasons.

Bell's jocular persona belied a shrewd operator. "He'd have his delegates staked out in advance; he always knew how many votes he needed to pass something," Wellington said of Bell.

While the NFL eventually defeated and merged with the AAFC in 1949, the victory came at a high price. The NFL accepted three teams into the league: the Cleveland Browns (a renowned team that instantly and easily competed in the NFL), the San Francisco 49ers, and the Baltimore Colts. All the other teams disbanded, and many of the talented players were absorbed by the remaining teams.

"I think that it may very well be that playing under those circumstances," Wellington said later, regarding the league's wartime decision to keep playing, "helped to save the NFL, because when the war was over, Arch Ward started the All-American Football Conference. It started at a terrible disadvantage, even though they had some fine teams and excellent players, because we were already established. I think if we had suspended operations for three or four years and then tried to start it up again, the AAFC would have started on more equal terms with us, and the league might be a very different one from what it is today."

The teams banded together as much as they could in those years. Squabbling was still very much a part of league affairs, but their view on outsiders usually pulled them together. The Maras believed in the longevity of the league, and they put there money where their mouth was on more than one occasion.

Earl "Greasy" Neale, coach of the Philadelphia Eagles, once said, "I have to say that in those early days, I had a lot of help from Steve Owen and Wellington Mara of the Giants. They wanted to see the Philadelphia club make a go of it and they gave me some good tips on how to draft."

SCANDAL!

The 1946 season was an up-and-down affair for the Giants organization. The team was bereft of the talents of aging stars such as Hein, Cuff, and Herber. But the team featured a strong defense and an aggressive offense. Filchock, a former Redskins player who'd spent his pro career behind Baugh, finally got a chance to show his considerable wares in front of the Gotham faithful. And the defense was stalwart.

The Giants split with Philadelphia and Washington, and their third loss to the Los Angeles Rams. The well-balanced Giants led their division in neither passing nor rushing, but led in scoring and gave up the second-least amount of points. They finished the season 7–3–1, ahead of Philadelphia and Washington respectively. They were set to face the Chicago Bears on December 15, 1946. However, there was a problem.

The Saturday before the game, Bell was notified that two Giants stars had been contacted by professional gamblers. They had been offered money in exchange for throwing the game, à la the infamous Chicago Black Sox scandal.

"I cannot discuss this on the phone, but something is wrong," Bell told Tim Mara. "Get over here right away. You have to be told immediately."

Tim learned the gruesome details from Bell. Merle Hapes and Filchock had been offered $2,500 per game, as well as a $1,000 bet on their game against the underdog Bears. Hapes had admitted the whole thing to Bell; Filchock denied any knowledge of the events, but did admit to knowing Alvin Paris, having dined with the known gambler on several occasions.

Both players had been released by the police since both had refused the bribe offers. Mara offered to bench the players for the game. As commissioner, the long shadow of the Black Sox scandal could not be ignored by Bell. To insure the league remain legitimate in the public's eyes, the league could show no pity. Bell took the players at their word. He suspended Hapes, who had received an offer but had not reported it. And Filchock, who denied receiving a bribe, was allowed to play, with his players' share reduced. The loss of Hapes was a death knell for the Giants. The dazzling back had been a superb balance to Filchock.

Dave Klein tells the story of how Father Benedict was asked to address the team on Sunday morning concerning the matter. "I didn't know what to say. Nothing like this had ever happened. I was bitterly disappointed myself," the priest said. Dudley and the team knew what the loss of Hapes meant.

According to Klein, the priest walked into a silent locker room. Filchock was in the room. Hapes was not. "This game of yours has always been played in sunlight. Because of this incident, today's game will be played in the shadows of doubt. It is up to you to restore the faith of the fans in professional football and in the New York Giants."

Both fans and newspapermen were angry. When Filchock took the field at the Polo Grounds—he who had led the team to this pinnacle—the crowd booed loudly and lustily. And Grantland Rice wrote in his column, "Unfortunately, too much money has come into sport. Call it big business—football, baseball, or tennis—but don't call it sport."

Time magazine noted, "The newspapers played it as the worst scandal since the 'Black' Sox threw the 1919 World Series. Alvin Paris, the tinhorn gambler who tried to fix last fortnight's pro football championship game, was still in jail. Who was behind him? The papers hinted darkly of a big-time Jersey gambling ring, which was not above fixing prizefights and college basketball games." The article went on to mention, "The Giants' boss, Tim Mara, once one of the biggest of the bookies, wondered why his two players, Merle Hapes and Frank Filchock, had failed to tell anyone they had been offered bribes."

In fact, *The New York Times* eventually opined that the Giants' debacle was "the biggest sport scandal since the 1919 World Series."

In the first quarter the Bears scored two quick touchdowns, one coming off a Giants fumble and the other an interception returned for a touchdown. Before the half ended the Giants scored a touchdown and went into halftime with the score 14–7, Bears.

The Giants tied the game when they recovered a Bears fumble and eventually scored a touchdown. The game went into the fourth quarter tied 14–14. After a poor punt by Howie Livingston, the Bears drove to the Giants' 19-yard line. Then came one of the most famous plays of the era. Chicago quarterback Sid Luckman faked a handoff to George McAfee and then, with the ball hidden behind his hip, ran a bootleg and raced all the way to the end zone. Luckman had never run the ball like that. It was his first rushing touchdown of the year. Frank Maznicki added a field goal later in the quarter and Chicago won 24–14.

Few spectators questioned Filchock's attempt to vindicate himself. According to most accounts, even with a broken nose and six interceptions, Filchock played with great heart and was more valiant in defeat than he had ever been in victory. It was the last game he would ever play for the Giants.

The man behind Paris's scheme to fix the 1946 NFL championship game by proffering bribes to two key Giants players was an Elizabeth, New Jersey, bookmaker named Eddie Ginsburg. Ginsburg was Paris's father-in-law. During the off-season Hapes worked for Paris as a salesman for the latter's metal novelties company. Hapes was worried he would lose his position, and so never reported the bribe to proper authorities. Hapes refused the offer, but referred Filchock to Paris.

Wiretaps had recorded conversations between Paris and his father-in-law. Frank S. Hogan was the district attorney of New York City at the time. He was also soon to be one of the heroes of Malcolm Johnson's Pulitzer Prize–winning series on dockside corruption, which would eventually come to be known as *On the Waterfront*. What eventually came out of Hogan's investigation entertained newspaper readers for months to come.

As it turned out, Paris had wined and dined Hapes and Filchock on numerous occasions. Paris often took Hapes and Filchock to posh nightspots such as Studio Club in Westchester, the Carnival, the Martinique, and the Copacabana. Paris also threw lavish cocktail parties at his novelties showroom and apartment at 56 West Fifty-sixth Street. The most shocking of details was that sometimes the trio took their wives, while at other times Paris instead procured attractive female companions to escort them on their 'gay rounds.' Sometime female film actress Ida McGuire was the most notable of three or four women identified during the proceedings.

The papers covered McGuire's appearance as if Gloria Swanson herself was appearing. The press followed her trek from the West Coast to New York, covering each whistle-stop. Even the old Gray Lady herself, *The New York Times*, got into the act with headlines like, "Film Actress Here for Trial of Paris." The article had quotes by Ms. McGuire, again maintaining that she had heard no discussion of bribes or football. "Making the last stage of her journey by train from Chicago after a flight from the West Coast, Ida McGuire, dancer and film bit player, arrived here yesterday to testify in the bribery trial of Alvin J. Paris." McGuire's two most notable (although forgettable) roles were her screen credits after the trial, when she appeared as the majorette at the beginning of *Miracle on 34th Street*, and her role as Miss Roberts in *Boomerang!*

The February 10, 1947, issue of *Life* magazine also carried a very alluring photo of Ms. McGuire, whom they referred to as a professional contortionist who was offered as an "inducement" to the intrigued players.

The trial became a series of damaging circuses. Hundreds of onlookers swamped the courthouse each day, as they had during the Dempsey trial. Hundreds were turned away from the media circus. The wiretap tapes were played.

"Over the defense's repeated objections, the State yesterday placed into evidence 17 tapped telephone talks that purportedly linked David (Pete) Krakauer, Harvey Stemmer, and Jerome Zarowitz to the football 'fix' deal," reported *The Times* of the trial.

Hapes and Filchock proved to be embarrassments to the league.

On January 8, 1947, *The New York Times* ran a front-page story with the headline: "Filchock Admits He Lied to Mayor on Football 'Fix.'" Filchock had lied. He had indeed been propositioned. He had turned Paris down, telling him "No soap," according to the tapes. But he had ruined himself, because on the night before the game, he and Hapes had been brought before New York City Mayor William O'Dwyer, where Filchock had lied right to the mayor's face.

At one point the papers released the fact that District Attorney Hogan had received a death threat. And there was no hope that the story would die when on January 10, 1947, *The Times* ran the headline: "Paris Trial Data Sought by Jersey." According to the *Times*, "Attorney General Walter D. Van Riper of New Jersey moved into the Alvin Paris football-fixing case yesterday. Twenty-four hours after Paris's conviction by a jury of having attempted to fix the championship game between the New York Giants and the Chicago Bears, the New Jersey official asked District Attorney Frank S. Hogan of New York County to send him a transcript of all portions of" the trial.

In New Jersey the case went even deeper and provided just as much amusement for the public and press. There were four alleged gamblers, and three were convicted.

Harvey Stemmer, and David Krakauer received sentences of five to 10 years. Paris turned informer, turning state's evidence and received a reduced sentence of one year. As if things weren't bad enough for the Maras and the NFL, the convicted felons appealed their loss all the way up to the Supreme Court, keeping the story alive in the press for some time.

Hogan argued against the appeals. He wrote, "Despite the tie vote and also that the court refrained from writing opinions of the law, the case was considered a landmark in wiretapping cases, which would tend to increase the use of wiretapping. ...."

While serving time at Riker's Island, Paris's life was threatened, and he eventually served out the rest of his sentence at the Tombs. While Hapes and Filchock were banned from professional football in the United States, Filchock eventually continued a stellar career in the Canadian Football League. Both were eventually reinstated to the NFL years later.

Jack spoke to the press in April 1947, saying he approved of Bell's decision and thought his actions right. "Bert Bell made a fair examination of all the facts, cooperated with the district attorney 1,000 percent, and made the only decision open to him. We are now busy trying to strengthen our backfield and have a couple of deals in the fire" to replace the two players.

At the time, the scandal was a brutal black eye on the Maras, the team, and the league. For the Maras, it was an ugly smear against them, the team, and their reputation. For the league it was a near brush with death. One can only assume that the founding fathers must have held their collective breath. The Maras and the Rooneys were involved in legal gambling, but there could be no mistaking their businesses with gangsters trying to spoil their league. These kinds of actions could not be allowed to stain their game.

Luckily for the league and the team, the more the trial went on, the more it was apparent that a small ring of gamblers were the real root and cause of it. Nothing had come up during the trial that would touch or taint the reputations of the Maras.

Still, with another league challenging them, this was a bullet dodged.

CONERLY AND TUNNELL

Some of the worst teams in New York Football Giants history came in 1947, 1948, and 1949. These were rebuilding years. Two bright spots were two young players who would be the building blocks of the great New York dynasty that was just over the next hill.

The first was University of Mississippi sensation Charlie Conerly. A consensus All-American in 1947, Conerly led the NCAA in passing attempts, completion percentage, and touchdowns. Conerly was the prize pick of the 1947 season. The Giants drafted him, but so did the AAFC. While the Giants were in the more established NFL, the owner/manager of the Brooklyn Dodgers in those years was Branch Rickey, the famed baseball man who also was the general manager of the perennial World Series runner-up Brooklyn Dodgers. Regardless of which team was more established, Rickey's interest conferred instant celebrity on Conerly.

The attention he drew was not good. The Giants had offered $62,500. Rickey offered $110,000. Conerly turned down Rickey and joined the Giants. Rickey was upset and went public. As *New York Herald Tribune* columnist Red Smith described the tirade, "[Rickey] predicted the Giants would always have a 'morale problem' with Conerly because he would remember that he had not been allowed to make a better deal. 'It seems un-American to me,' declaimed the Reverend [Rickey]."

In the meantime, Rickey's paltry offer for the services of 21-game winning pitcher Ralph Branca had also been released to the press. Rickey had offered the well-known and beloved pitcher $14,000. "Maybe the kid figures he'll have greater security with the Giants than with an organization that puts such a price on a 21-game winner," Mara replied in the press. Then Tim took a parting shot at the AAFC, saying, "Maybe he's looked over the All-America Conference and realized we've been here 24 years, whereas Brooklyn's had three, four owners.... I don't know where this guy gets off talking about morale problems and stuff, considering the business he's in."

By this time the Giants had come to be known as a soft touch organization. It seemed that Jack and Well had inherited their father's generous nature. Particularly in Jack's tenure, the organization was especially kind to cut players, injured players, and former players. Conerly said to his wife, Perian, who wrote about Charlie more than 12 years later, "I don't know about other clubs, but I do know that the Giants have been known to slip a hard-put family man a little extra while he is finding other employment."

Conerly would go on to play for the Giants from 1948 to 1961. His Hall of Fame career was marked by a series of yearly negotiations with Jack and Well. Perian said years later that her husband agonized over each negotiation. After one particularly remarkable season, he insisted to her that in his upcoming meeting with Well, he would press the penurious Mara family for more money. "And if they don't want to give it to me, I'll tell Well that I'll..." mumbled Conerly to his wife, and then trailed off talking to himself. Conerly talked with his wife throughout the night, insisting this would be the drawing line. He had his number and he was going to stick to it.

Conerly went to meet Well in Mobile, who was scouting the Senior Bowl that year. "The following night Charlie called me from Mobile," said Perian. "'Did you talk to Well?' I asked finally..."

"Yes, and you know what happened?" said Conerly sheepishly. Conerly explained he went up to Mara's room, resolved to fight for the money he felt he had earned. Mara welcomed him warmly, and before Charlie could light up a cigarette and go into his spiel, Well spoke up, saying, "Charlie, you had such a good year, we think you ought to have a raise."

"He handed me a contract already filled out for the exact amount I was going to ask for—down to the last penny! Makes me wonder if I should have asked for more!"

Perian related in later years that she had "lost count of the times the Giants offer turned out to be the figure which Charlie had in mind. The whole thing got to be downright spooky...such a meeting of the minds is but one of the many reasons we think the Maras are the pleasantest of people—and by far the best bosses in the NFL."

While this viewpoint was somewhat skewed because Conerly seemed to improve almost every year and played at an extremely high level, the Giants were known around the league as a paternalistic organization that took care of its own despite their eccentricities over costs and other picayune items. Over and over again during the first 30 or 40 years of the NFL, this reputation stood them in good stead with players throughout the league.

In 1948 Emlen Tunnell showed up at the Giants' training camp and asked for a tryout. Tunnell had played one year of college football, but had broken his neck. He recuperated but, as with others his age, including Conerly, the war had interrupted his college days. He went to school for one year at Iowa and decided he might try out for the Giants. He liked to say that he had $1.50 to his name the day he walked in the Giants offices. He would walk out that same day with a contract.

"If you have enough guts to come in here and ask for a job, I'm going to give you a chance," Wellington said to the outspoken Tunnell.

Tunnell, who went on to a Hall of Fame career, is considered one of the greatest defensive backfield players ever to play the game. He would play in eight Pro-Bowl games by the end of his career, and held four league records at the time of his retirement from playing in 1961 (his last three years were with Green Bay). He went on to coach on the Giants staff from 1963–1973. He was the first African American player ever signed by Mara Tech, and would become the first African American full-time coach. He was one of a handful of trusted Giants who would spend almost three decades with the club.

Conerly and Tunnell were two of the most crucial linchpins of what would become the golden age of Giants football. While the late 1940s didn't seem so gilt-edged at the time, things were about to change.

CHAPTER 6

The Golden Age of New York Sports

THE CITY OF CHAMPIONS

Tim Mara had now been a fixture on the New York sports scene as long as people could remember. And the Giants had been a part of that scene for 25 years in 1950. But as anyone can tell you, the 1950s were the heyday of sport in New York City.

From 1949 to 1956, the New York Yankees, the Brooklyn Dodgers, and the New York Giants would rule baseball and make the World Series their own local playground, taking every major league baseball championship in that period. And New York, as a city—its subways, more than a dozen newspapers, checker cabs, clubs and dinner parties, and bars—became their personal playground. The city was theirs for the asking, and they took it.

The mayor of New York sports in those days was a tall fellow with a big head and rounder belly, whose name was Toots Shor. Shor was a giant of a man who stood about 6'3" and weighed a whopping 270 pounds. Shor was the product of a tough neighborhood in Philadelphia, which was made all the tougher by his mother's death when young Shor was only 15 and his father's suicide when he was 20 years old. He had made his way to New York, where he ran a series of speakeasies until he founded his famed spot, called simply Toots Shor's.

"The slab face and meatcutters' hands," wrote Pulitzer Prize–winning author Don DeLillo. "You look at Toots and see a speakeasy vet, dense of body, with slicked-back hair and a set of chinky eyes that summon up a warning in a hurry. This is an ex-bouncer that throws innocent people out of his club when he is drinking."

Despite his rakish repartee with his famous guests, Shor knew how to run a restaurant and bar. He catered to stars and introduced famous people to each other all the time. No matter his fame, Shor always referred to himself as a saloon keeper.

"Show me a man that don't drink, and I'll show you somebody I don't want to be with," said Shor. His bar, located near Madison Square Garden, was the hub of the sports world—owners, coaches, players, sportswriters, and hangers-on were found there. Entertainers such as Frank Sinatra and the "'Rat Pack'" were especially fond of Shor.

The bar and restaurant had been famous since the 1930s and 1940s. It was a place where famous people mingled. For many, many years Joe DiMaggio had his own table there. Politicians and Broadway stars also mingled there.

As New York folklore would have it, famed clutch-hitting New York Yankee catcher Yogi Berra was once introduced to Ernest "Papa" Hemingway by Shor himself.

"Yogi, this is Ernest Hemingway. He's an important writer."

"What paper you with, Ernie?" asked the catcher.

"On one side of the dining room sits Earl Warren, the distinguished chief justice of the Supreme Court. On the opposite side sits Frank Costello, the notorious boss of the New York mob. Scattered at tables in between are Ava Gardner, Mickey Mantle, John O'Hara, Ed Sullivan, Rocky Graziano, Chet Huntley, Eddie Arcarro, Red Skelton, and Red Smith," recalled Frank Gifford in later years, who on that night was dining with Jackie Gleason. Gleason and Shor were barroom buddies, and the two lived an uproarious life together. It was said Gleason never paid for a meal, but that his bar tabs were legendary. Gleason's variety hour was among the highest-rated shows in the country. And legend has it that after spending an uproarious night at Shor's, Gleason once fell asleep during a negotiation with CBS executives that would have made him the highest-paid television performer in the world.

In fact, Gleason, Sinatra, and Shor went together to the famed 1951 playoff game where Bobby Thomson hit the "Shot Heard Round the World" off of Ralph Branca. In his book *Underworld,* Don Delillo alleges that Gleason was so drunk that he threw up on Sinatra's shoes.

Shor's was a men's club. Players who brought their wives too often were banned. The food was never really considered anything more than mediocre, but the bar service was incredible. What celebrities liked about Shor was that what happened at Shor's stayed at Shor's (at least until many years later).

The city was full of heroes in those days. The highest in the New York firmament was DiMaggio, the legendary Yankee Clipper. But a new cadre of stars was bursting onto the scene, including Mickey Mantle, Willie Mays, Duke Snider, Berra, Whitey Ford, Billy Martin, Phil Rizzuto, and a slew of other personalities.

Toots was a good friend of Tim Mara's. Jack also knew him. While baseball and boxing had always ruled New York's roost, the stars of the New York Giants—and there would be many of them—would start many of their infamous social rounds by meeting at Shor's before painting the town red. Their ascendancy in the city, as well as in the sporting world, was just in the offing. And one of the launching pads was Shor's.

"Toots was a passionate Giants fan who knew everything we were doing and when to dispense with the commiseration when I wasn't doing well," said Gifford.

In his autobiography Gifford related a lost weekend he and Conerly spent together right before the 1959 training camp. The two footballers and Shor spent a weekend drinking and causing a scene at one of Sinatra's Atlantic City shows. Somehow, at the end of a three-day drunken adventure, the two gridiron stars were put on a plane to arrive in Vermont in time for training camp. The two were trying to call for a cab. They were shocked when who should they see waiting for them at the little airport but the widely grinning Wellington.

"Need a ride?" he asked wryly. The dumbfounded players got into the car, and Wellington started driving. "So how was Sinatra's show?" he asked the two backseat passengers, and then he casually tossed that day's newspaper into the backseat. Their little escapade had made the papers, including a photo of the three drunken personalities slouched, eyes half closed, in the back of a limousine with an empty vodka bottle.

"How can I explain," wrote Gerald Eskanazi years later, "what it was really like? Of the after-game dinners, of the pats on the back at

Toots Shor's, of the vacations together at Grossingers, of the feelings before the game that no matter what mistakes they might make on the field, somehow, someone would come along for the Giants and make it right?"

In the 1950s, and later in the early 1960s, Mara's athletes would make their way into the highest echelons of New York celebrity. The 1950s would be a pay-off for the many years the Maras had stuck with the struggling franchise, always being seen as second-class sports citizens. In the 1950s New York City was "the City of Champions," and the Giants would rise to incredible heights of fame to take their place among the conquerors.

A HINT OF GREATNESS

Baseball, trains, and television were king. *I Love Lucy* and *The Jack LaLanne Show* were hits, and Milton Berle, Sid Caesar, Red Skelton, and Ernie Kovacs were the kings of comedy. It seemed then like Truman, MacArthur, and Eisenhower were running two-thirds of the world. Cuba was the number one resort destination. And Madison Avenue's great creation of the time was the dancing Old Gold cigarette pack.

The 1950 season was a blessing for the Giants faithful and for the NFL. Attendance would hit an all-time high in 1950, with more than 1.9 million coming to see NFL games. The league had been newly reorganized. New York now found itself in the new American Conference of the NFL, which held the Giants, the Redskins, the Eagles, the Steelers, the Chicago Cardinals, and the old powerhouse of the AAFC, the Cleveland Browns.

The death of the old AAFC brought great tidings to the Giants. They hauled in lineman Arnie Westminster, and defensive backs Tom Landry and Harmon Rowe, and safety Otto Schnellenbacher to compliment Emlen Tunnell. With this backfield, Owen unleashed the umbrella defense, which featured the two defensive ends dropping back into pass coverage while the three-deep defensive backs formed an umbrella of zone coverage, which was cutting-edge defense in those days. The defense had any number of permutations, and Howell tried to develop as many different versions as he could in an attempt to confuse opposing quarterbacks. It worked. The Giants defense bent, but rarely broke. And with Choo Choo Roberts and

Eddie Price in the backfield, Owen found a running and passing game that could compete with any team.

The former AAFC champion Cleveland Browns were led by the quarterbacking of Otto Graham and the rushing of Marion Motley. They also had a deep-threat receiver in Mac Speedie. Defensively they featured a number of stars who gave many of the league's teams fits. Twice that year, the Giants beat the Browns. But that year, for the first time, both conferences ended up in ties, and so playoffs were necessary in both conferences. New York and Cleveland met in the American Conference. The Browns beat the Giants 8–3 and went on to win the 1950 NFL championship. But it was a signal that New York was back.

One of the bright spots in 1951 was the signing of another talented running back, Kyle Rote. Rote was an All-American tailback from Southern Methodist University, and was signed by Wellington.

Rote had come by virtue of a "bonus pick." Each team was given the opportunity to pick a slip of paper out of a hat. Regardless of your finish, you picked first if you got the lucky ticket. "My brother Jack or I usually drew from the hat, but that year I said, 'Let's see if we can change our luck if Steve does the picking." Owen reached in and pulled out the winning ticket. The Giants went first, and Wellington insisted they take Rote, the Heisman runner-up that year to Ohio State halfback Vic Janowicz.

Before the draft, a reporter had asked Jack, "Who are you going to pick?" And Jack replied, "Rote." And the reporter replied, "That's ridiculous. ... Rote is the number one player in the country and he'll be picked long before your turn comes."

"Who knows?" replied Jack cheerfully. "Maybe we'll get lucky. Maybe we'll get the bonus pick," he said nonchalantly. Luck had found the Maras.

The Giants became a bridesmaid again in 1951, as the only two blemishes on their record were a pair of hard-fought losses to the Browns. The Browns finished 11–1–0 and the Giants finished 9–2–1.

"If we could only have beat those goldarn Browns, we would have been champs of everything that year," Owen said.

In 1952 Wellington drafted Gifford, another multitalented player. Gifford and Rote would be two more stars among many that would take the Giants even further. Gifford warmed up to the Maras almost instantly. A cocky, young star from Southern Cal, Gifford found the Maras fascinating and friendly. "The Giants operated like the small family business they were," he recalled. "They were a wonderful Irish family, and over the years they became family to me. I came to look on T.J. as a kind of distant grandfather, Jack as a favorite uncle, Well as a surrogate father, and Timmy [who was by now club secretary] as both brother and best friend."

In 1952 some said the Browns had deteriorated, but the fact was the rest of the NFL, especially their division, was catching up. The Giants were still at the vanguard of that group. While the Browns only managed an 8–4–0 campaign, the Giants went 7–5–0, and while they beat Cleveland twice that year, they gave up games to teams they should have beaten.

In March 1953 a suit attempting to break the logjam that prevented home games from being televised was brought against the league. Jack and Well were at the forefront of the league's policy. Jack testified in court as to how television in particular was much more damaging to gate receipts than was radio. While the Giants were becoming a lucrative business with a radio and television show, Jack told of how the team had only one sellout, and how gate receipts from one sellout game were as lucrative as their entire television contract.

"We spend a lot of money building up fan interest within a 75-mile radius of New York City. We consider that Giants territory. We want the fans to see and hear the Giants' games to arouse and keep their interest in our team," Jack told the prosecutors. "We don't want any other team televising in our territory when we are at home. For example, if the Philadelphia Eagles are playing a head-on game and televising in Trenton, 60 miles from New York, that hurts our gate, especially if we are playing just another ballgame that day."

The team was stocked with talent in 1953, so the Giants' record was particularly galling. The team finished a humbling 3–9–0 under Owen. In the last few games of the season, the team had given up on the old, strong line coach, laying down to Cleveland 62–14, and then losing in the last quarter to the champion Detroit Lions, 27–16.

It must be pointed out that the Giants were penurious at that time, and the salaries they paid, while more than some teams in the league, were woefully short for those trying to live in a city as expensive as New York. What the Maras didn't want anyone to know was that they were having money problems at the time. Not only were salaries low, the players wore the same jerseys every year. "Same with the pants," Gifford recalled later. "They looked great from a distance, but up close they looked as though they'd belonged to Jim Thorpe." Cleats were fixed over and over again. If a player wanted new cleats, he had to buy them himself. Helmets, even damaged ones, were fixed rather than replaced.

It got so bad that the Canadian Football League was able to recruit tackle Arnie Weinmeister. He was given bonuses to try to get other Giants to jump to the northern league. None did.

Gifford recalled that after the loss in the last game of the season in Detroit, "I saw a tall, silver-haired man in an elegant gray suit and black homburg striding towards me. It was the Giants' owner, old T.J. himself." Despite the horrific year, Mara cheerfully walked through the room, his head held high. He approached Gifford, extended his hand, and said, "We thank you."

"As he did that, I noticed him slip an envelope in my locker. Then he was gone," recalled Gifford. Gifford socked the envelope away and opened it later to find five $100 bills. Gifford didn't know why Mara had done it, and he didn't know if he had done it for anyone else. "But I was very moved," wrote Gifford, "and I also needed the money."

While money had been some of the problem, the on-the-field product suffered from something far simpler, and yet more delicate—chemistry. The first battle was one of morale. The new, younger kids did not fit with Owen. Owen was quite old by now, and he had been the hired hand and third brother since 1927. He was hard on his players, as he always had been in the past. But in the past he had been able to connect with them, and they in turn had confidence in him. By 1953 the distance from his generation to the current one had expanded beyond his reach. The team needed a new coach, among other things.

In retrospect, many sportswriters opined that the family was too loyal to Owen, keeping him on beyond his years and abilities. They had kept him on for sentimental reasons, and this was business. Sports were becoming way too big a business for them to be that emotionally attached. It would be the most emotionally charged decision Tim, Jack, and Well ever had to make.

"As much as the Maras—Jack, Wellington, and the late T.J.—hated to admit it, they had to agree that the gridiron parade had passed by their old warhorse," wrote Don Smith, the team's former director of publicity, many years later. "During Owen's long and successful tenure, it was unthinkable that he would be...replaced. Stout Steve was so close to T. J. Mara that neither had ever considered a signed contract necessary." Smith related how Owen was summoned upstairs by the three after a loss to Cleveland. He stomped into the office and flopped into a wicker chair. "What's up?"

There was an awkward moment—perhaps the first in the four men's lives. Jack acted as speaker. Steve was to move to the executive suite with them. A new man would coach. Who? They didn't know yet. Owen stayed out of a sense of duty to coach the season finale, and then left.

"Years after lesser owners would have replaced Steve Owen as coach, the reluctant decision was reached to pension the man who had served the team so well," wrote *New York Times* sports columnist Arthur Daley. "I want you to be the first to know," Jack said. "We're making a coaching change."

"Jack, that makes me sick at heart," Daley told Jack.

"How do you think I feel?" said Jack.

"He looked miserable," Daley later reported.

"It was the toughest thing I ever had to do. ... Steve was like family."

Owen remained bitter over the firing and refused to talk with the two brothers for many years to come. It must be said that, the Giants were willing to let him take any front-office position he might like. But Owen could not live with another man coaching his team.

JIM LEE HOWELL

When the news of Owen's firing hit the press, the most interesting headline came from the *New York Daily News*, which read, "Giants Boot Owen Upstairs, Lombardi Seen New Coach." The story reasoned: "Steve Owen, long renowned as 'the coach without a contract,' yesterday was removed.... It was learned by the *News* that president

Jack Mara is seeking the services of Vincent Lombardi." As the story went on to point out, the feeling was that Lombardi "stacks up as just the injection of 'young blood' the Giants seem to need." But as famed biographer David Maraniss pointed out, "The Maras were hesitant to put Lombardi in the head job, worried that he was lacking professional experience and unsure that he could be a disciplined leader."

The Giants really wanted celebrated West Point football coach Colonel Earl "Red" Blaik. Blaik was considered one of the best football minds in the country, and was an institution at the U.S. Military Academy. His list of graduated football stars was one of the great accomplishments of college coaching.

"In December of [1953], I met with Jack and Wellington Mara three times at the New York Athletic Club. They offered me the Giants coaching position, each time offering me a higher salary. Fantastic as the offer seemed to me, I could not bring myself to leave the Military Academy," Blaik admitted years later.

"We tried Red Blaik," Wellington said years later, "but he said he wouldn't care to leave West Point." The Maras had a good relationship with Blaik.

According to Maraniss, "When Army played at the Polo Grounds, the Maras invited the coaching staff to stay overnight as guests of the Giants and watch the pro game the next afternoon. Blaik reciprocated by inviting the Maras to West Point." The Maras would continue to have a close relationship with Blaik for years to come. At the time, he offered to be a friendly advisor, but did not want the job for himself.

"When we fired Steve, we had three assistant coaches on the team," said Wellington. They were Jim Lee Howell, Allie Sherman, and Ed Kolman. Kolman was out. All three thought they would not be re-upped, since new coaches liked to bring in their own guys. Then Howell got a telegram from Wellington asking him to stop by the Giants offices before he left town. Howell thought there might be some paperwork or documents to sign. He arrived at the offices on West Forty-second Street, on the 17th floor, and walked in to find all three Maras waiting for him. His wife sat waiting in the car, double-parked.

"Better take a seat," said Jack. "How would you like to coach the Giants?"

Howell agreed. He signed a contract within the hour, went downstairs, got in the car with his wife, and drove back to Lonoke, Arkansas, where he had a 700-acre pig farm.

The press had a field day. The basic tenor of the press could be summed up as "The penny-pinching Maras had hired a cheap local man to do a skilled man's job. A big name would have required too much—too much money, too much control, too much equipment, too much of everything to upset the little apple cart that was the Maras and their team."

"I was impressed with his character and strength," said Wellington. "In a lot of ways he reminded me of Steve."

Howell, who stood 6'6", had been dubbed the "Human Howitzer" by Grantland Rice, and was a staggeringly good defensive end out of Arkansas when he played there between 1934 and 1936. Howell had come to the Giants in 1937. He played for the Giants from 1937 to 1942 and from 1946 to 1948. In 1948 he was moved onto the coaching staff.

Howell had been a rough, tough lineman and was a favorite of Owen's. In fact, many of his philosophies were shaped by Owen's thoughts, as Howell served under Stout Steve for more than 11 years. Howell, like Owen, would be with the Maras for a great number of years—more than 36 all together, and would also replace Owen as one of the core advisors to the family for years to come.

"They are a great family," Howell said of the Maras, "starting with T. J. Mara himself. He always wanted to have the best team possible, and he certainly worked at it." He admired Jack, and then he spoke of Well. "Well has been great for football because it's his life. He was 15 years old when he signed Tuffy Leemans."

"When I came up, Well would work out with the club, he would take calisthenics, which he still does. Some people said he shouldn't be that close to the players, but I was happy to have an owner who came out to the field. If we had any problems, we didn't have to get on the phone and call him. He was interested and liked the game enough to be out there with us.... I think Well is the most knowledgeable owner in the game."

"Another side to Well Mara is trades," said Howell. Howell pointed out the constant competition with the Canadian Football League in those days.

"Let's stop the nonsense," Well said, and got Alex Webster to leave the CFL and join the Giants. It was a revolutionary move in 1955.

But while Owen influenced Howell and Howell loved his owners, he had some ideas of his own. As the owner of a 700-acre pig farm half a continent away, Howell had developed an ability to manage people much like a corporate executive, and that would be his innovation.

Now, with unfettered, "free substitution," Howell could start to play players one way, keep them fresher, and get more out of each player. And with two assistant coaches who would divide the responsibilities between offense and defense—which was necessary because the play-calling was becoming more and more complicated—Howell could count on a higher level of attention to detail. In his own way, Howell was actually closer to Jack. He was a businessman, a manager.

Howell saw his job as a man who ran a large company, and he needed managers. And Wellington had an idea where to draw his next manager from.

"DIFFERENT AS DAYLIGHT AND DARK"—VINCE LOMBARDI AND TOM LANDRY

"At our last meeting, Wellington, a Fordham classmate of Lombardi, asked if the Giants could talk to Vince about becoming an assistant on the Giants staff. I told him that I would feel a loss if Vince were to leave West Point, but that I had aided assistants to get head coaching jobs in the past and would not stand in the way of Lombardi's bettering himself," Blaik said years later. "Although they failed to realize they were getting a man with the potential to become their next head coach."

Mara called Lombardi. There was initially a misunderstanding, as Lombardi thought he was calling about the head-coaching position. Lombardi was devastated to learn the offer was for a subordinate job. Lombardi approached Blaik and told him he needed a raise or he would have to accept the Giants' offer. Blaik rebuffed Lombardi, reminding him that he was already the highest-paid assistant on the staff and topped out on the pay scale. Reluctantly, Lombardi accepted the Giants' offer. He later told intimates that if West Point had offered even $1,000 more, he would have stayed there.

There was one thing Wellington asked Lombardi to do—to visit Howell on his pig farm in Lonoke, Arkansas. Howell later admitted he would rather have kept Sherman, with whom he was familiar, as assistant coach. Lombardi was horrified by pig-farm life, but Howell won him over with an offer to run the offense entirely on his own, and by offering him freshly shot duck over rice.

As Wellington later recalled, Lombardi let out "a huge guffaw" when he returned to the Giants, offices in New York, recounting his trip to Arkansas to his future employer. "I remember him laughing about all the cow shit in Lone Okie, Arkansas," which Lombardi purposely mispronounced.

"Lombardi told me he spent as much time dodging piles of cow dung as he did talking football. He said it was the strangest interview he ever had," Wellington said.

When the 41-year-old Lombardi's hiring was announced, the Giants were handed many kudos by the local press for their vision in hiring the up-and-coming offensive genius. The genius of Lombardi was simplicity and execution. "Lombardi's philosophy was to run a half dozen basic plays, but to run them with such precision that no one could stop them," wrote sportswriter Peter Golenbock.

For the defense, Howell chose Tom Landry. Howell already knew Landry. He was still a player and, as such, he would be the All-Pro player/coach of the defense for the New York Giants at age 29.

"[Landry] designed a defense he called 'the inside 4-3' and the 'outside 4-3.' It was revolutionary because in the past everyone played man-to-man defense," wrote Golenbock. Landry would take the "umbrella defense" to a new level. Most defenses of the day tried as much as possible to line up man-on-man, driving back the offense with brute strength. "Landry's defense depended on his players knowing what the other team was going to run and stopping the lanes where the play was expected to go." Landry used his down lineman to disrupt the offensive line and to shield those offensive linemen from getting to his linebackers, who would then make the tackle.

Landry also did something else. "He made his defensive players watch game films for hours on end," wrote Golenbock. Landry looked for tendencies of any kind that would give his team the edge, whether they were body attitudes that tipped opposing players off, or tendencies of what plays they called on specific downs and distances.

There was little dissention, either from players or writers. The Giants were now armed with the best brain trust in the NFL. And, eventually, the sportswriters came around to Howell. "Mostly he is the administrator and coordinator, and that apparently is the way to do the job today," wrote Red Smith.

"If the question is about offense, Howell says, 'Ask Lombardi about that.' Defense? 'Tom Landry is the man to see,'" Joe King wrote for the *New York World Telegram*. King saw Howell's system as a "logical evolution—the pros have brought football to a peak of specialized skill."

Landry was stoic and let the many characters on defense do his shouting for him, while Lombardi was always loud and sometimes manic-depressive. Landry called him "Mr. High-Low." When the offense performed well, Lombardi could be heard throughout the training complex, singing, hollering, screaming. When the offense performed poorly, he could be sullen and depressed, chewing on Landry and Howell's ears for days at a time.

To be fair, both men were extremely competitive. While they spent much time together, discussing strategies and personnel, Howell had two competitive prima donnas on his staff who complained alternately that there was too much focus on the other guy's territory.

"I would like to say I developed them... [but] they had it when they came in. They did their jobs; you didn't have to keep after them," said Howell years later. "'They were both superb coaches—different as daylight and dark, but they were great coaches and fine people."

In 1954 the Giants went 7–5–0 under Howell in his first year, which was only good enough for third place in what was now called the NFL Eastern Conference. But fans could see a new posturing about this team. Something was happening. Something good.

But Cleveland still won the conference and the NFL championship.

WELLINGTON GETS MARRIED

Dave Klein once wrote, "Well is an enigma. He is at once friendly and secretive, affable and cool, cooperative and closed." He could exhibit a frightening temper one moment and could use a rapier wit the next. Sometimes his humorous bon mots were just funny, and sometimes they were sword-like thrusts mean to eviscerate people.

While football was on the upswing, Wellington's dating life had suffered. Long obsessed with the success of his team and an admitted homebody, in 1953, at 37 years old, Wellington was still alone. It was said that he actually considered the priesthood at one point in his life. His entire life, Wellington was a devout Catholic who normally attended 8:00 AM mass before going to work.

In 1953 Wellington met Ann T. Mumm. The two met in church when they both tried to come to the assistance of a woman who had fainted.

"It was a sporting courtship," she recalled. "While all of my friends were at the Stork Club, I was at the Fordham gym."

Ann lived at 164 East Eighty-second Street with her father, George Mumm, a widower. She was an alumnus of St. Lawrence Academy and the Berkeley School, both in New York. In 1954 Well and Ann were married at the Mara family parish, St. Ignatius Loyola Catholic Church. Ann's brother, Robert Mumm, escorted her down the aisle. Jack was Well's best man.

Eventually Well and Ann settled in the affluent suburban town of Rye, New York. The Maras would go on to have 11 children: John Kevin, Susan Ann, Timothy Christopher, Stephen Vincent, Francis Xavier, Sheila Marie, Kathleen Mary, Maureen Elizabeth, Ann Marie, Meghan Ann, and Colleen Elizabeth.

Married life proved to be the salve that Wellington needed. He went to church and then to work each day and then commuted home. He spent as much time as possible with his wife and children in the comfort of their home and at Winged Foot, where many Maras are still members of the old club today.

"Wellington dearly loved the ambiance of his father's team, jogging around the practice field in an old blue sweat suit, followed by swarms of little tow-haired Mara children," George Vecsey wrote.

Well's four sons would spend all their childhood summers as ballboys. Wellington said that days spent watching his sons running around the game, wide-eyed, just as he had when he was a little boy, were among the greatest days in his life.

In 1968 Ann ended up on a plane with Don Meredith and Pete Gent. She was returning from watching the Cleveland-Dallas play-off game on a first-class flight from Dallas to New York. The Cowboys had just gotten thumped by Cleveland, 31–20. Landry, now head coach of the Cowboys, had pulled Meredith in the third quarter and both players were upset, since they had thought there was still plenty of time to beat the Browns.

Disgusted, the two refused to take the team plane home.

"Let's just take the first plane outta here," Meredith told Gent. The two saw Gifford and started talking to him. "We sat in the last row of the first-class section of the plane to New York. Meredith was on the window and I was on the aisle, and by accident we ended up sitting next to Gifford. Giants owner Wellington Mara's wife was on the other window seat," Gent recalled.

"We sat down and Don lit up...[a] joint, handed it to me," said Gent. "I puffed on it and I handed it back to Meredith and he handed it over to Gifford, who looked at it and immediately put it out in his drink!"

They chatted with Gifford, but Ann didn't speak to them the entire flight. Considering the Maras' conservative views, one can only imagine her opinion of drugs and alcohol.

Another story about Ann also happened to concern the Dallas Cowboys. Tex Schramm "recalled when the Giants seated the families of visiting officials directly behind their own people in Yankee Stadium. Once Cowboys owner Clint Murchison was, of course, cheering for the Cowboys. Ann...had enough of this and stood up and tried to club Murchison with her purse. When this failed, she tried to have him thrown out of the stadium."

"You can't talk about Mr. Mara without talking about his wife and sons and daughters," Phil Simms said. "To see them after victories and see Mrs. Mara's face and knowing she was competitive and enjoying victories more than a lot of players, probably. Mrs. Mara complained to me after I retired about the team not winning the previous year. I said, 'Mrs. Mara, you went to the Super Bowl [recently].' She said, 'Phil, I expect to go to the Super Bowl every year.'"

Well and Ann stayed very much within a small circle of friends, and were not seen out on the town as much as his father and mother were. But the two were both very involved in their children's education and their church. Of course, they had a huge extended family, with their siblings' children and with their other extended family, the Giants.

"For years they lived in White Plains and most of their friends were Catholic doctors from their old neighborhood. ... Mara also sent tickets for every game to the rector at St. Ignatius and the faculty at Fordham. One section of seats for Giants games was known as 'Jesuit Row.'"

Ann and the kids went to the home games religiously, sitting as usual, in the sun.

In the mid-1970s head coach Bill Arnsparger asked Wellington if he could move the Giants bench below the press box.

"The visiting coaches can see our sideline signals from their seats in the press box."

"Get better signals," Wellington retorted.

Wellington Mara used to say "There are no ex-Giants, just old Giants." To him, anyone who wore Giants blue was a member of the family for life. And Ann agreed.

Many years later, Wellington would say at his enshrinement in the Pro Football Hall of Fame, "Ann pays me the supreme compliment. She supports me even when she doesn't agree with me, which of course, is very rare." This was Wellington's wry humor coming through.

On the occasion of their 50th wedding anniversary, Ann suggested they renew their vows. Sardonically, Well replied, "I wasn't aware they had run out."

Ann would say of him, many years later, "The Giants were his whole life. It was his faith, his family, and the Giants, and sometimes I wonder where the Giants came in. His players always came first to him. He did things for them that people don't even realize. I know that once-a-Giant, always-a-Giant is a cliché, but he really believed that."

THE SECOND SNEAKERS GAME

In 1955 the Giants team was stocked with even more talent, including Rosey Grier, Alex Webster, Jimmy Patton, and others. The team faltered in the first three weeks, and then the parts of the machine started to hum and the Giants made a run of it in the second half of the season. They ended at 6–5–1. Cleveland won the conference again, and then won the NFL championship as well. But good things were about to happen for the Giants.

On the afternoon of October 16, 1955, the Giants home opener was scheduled at the Polo Grounds against the Chicago Cardinals. That morning, before mass, Tim drove to see his sons at their homes in Riverdale during a monsoon-like rainstorm that had caused much damage in the metro region.

"He came up to ask, 'Should we call the game off or not?'" Wellington later told Hank Gola. "There was something else. Bert Bell had called my father and said, 'I've got two Texas oilmen who have offered $1 million for the Giants if they would move to Yankee Stadium.'"

"We never found out who they were. I always thought it might be the Murchison brothers [who eventually bought the Cowboys], but I never did know. My father said, 'You know, if we're worth $1 million in Yankee Stadium, and they don't want any part of us in the Polo Grounds, we ought to start thinking about moving to Yankee Stadium.'"

Tim, Jack, and Well refused the offer.

"Football is our business and we intend to stay in it," Jack told the press. Jack then threw in a reference to the champion horse Nashua. "If Nashua alone commanded $1,251,200, how could anyone accept only $1,000,000 for the Giants?" He was right, but at the time it was the most anyone had ever offered for a pro football franchise. It was noted at the time, "Their television-radio package is one of the most lucrative in professional football, netting an estimated $150,000 annually."

But the offer showed that professional football, and the New York Giants, were on the rise. Yankee Stadium, which was now empty following the baseball season, offered many advantages. It was larger than the Polo Grounds. It could hold more people, meaning the Maras could make more money. Also, it was a better-equipped stadium and offered the Giants a premiere showplace for their team, giving them a better vantage point from which to beat back another challenge. It proved to be a very smart move. They would begin play there in 1956.

Mara said later of the move, "We felt like we were leaving a lot of tradition behind us," but the players seemed to be energized by the move. Tim insisted Jack discuss the idea with Topping, who Tim still loathed from the days when Topping challenged the Giants' football supremacy in New York. Jack made the deal without rancor.

On the team's first day at Yankee Stadium, Gifford and some others went out to the monuments in center field. Later Gifford realized he was using Mantle's locker. This was the new heyday of sports in New York City, and it must have seemed absolutely right that Gifford and Mantle used the same locker.

"I know our players felt it was a little added incentive, that, 'We can't go out and louse up this place the way the Yankees have established it.' I think that definitely was an aura that overhung everybody," Wellington said.

The 1956 Giants started the season 6–1 and rolled to a solid 8–3–1 record. That was good enough to return them to the top of the Eastern Conference. Cleveland had fallen on hard times, and the Chicago Cardinals were the second-best team in the conference that season, finishing 7–5–0.

After a particularly galling loss to the Washington Redskins that year, a first-year reporter named Dave Klein wrote a scathing article about how the Giants had quit during the game. The article was pointed out to Big Tim. The following Sunday, after a tie against the Chicago Bears, Klein walked into the locker room to do his interviews.

"You!" screamed Tim Mara, who ran at Klein. "You get the hell outta here!" the big, ruddy Irishman screamed. Klein thought Mara was kidding, so he tried to slide his way around to another part of the room. Then Jack spotted him.

"Didn't you hear what my father said?" he screamed in front of the players. Klein walked out, waited a few minutes, and attempted to come back in. This time he was given a bum's rush by the prickly Wellington. "You heard my father and my brother. Do I have to throw you out, too?" Klein eventually left, filed his story, and worried that he might not be allowed in the locker room ever again.

The next week he showed up and caught glares from all three Maras. Eventually, when he realized there was no chair for him in the press box and the Giants weren't trying to accommodate him, he started to leave.

"Where the hell are you going?" asked T.J., who was seated, eating something.

Klein told him he was going home. "Just a minute, Smith," Mara said. "Sit down here with me. And you sit with me the rest of the season. I'm sorry I blew up.... But do me a favor. Never use the word *quit* when you write about the Giants."

"The Giants moved into Yankee Stadium this year, and once New York beat the quick-starting Chicago Cards in a midseason showdown, they easily charged down the home stretch," wrote David Neft and Richard Cohen in *The Sports Encyclopedia: Pro Football.* Rookie Sam Huff was the quarterback of the offense, playing the middle linebacker, with Landry calling the plays now from the sideline.

"Wellington Mara once said I was the kind of guy who'd kick somebody in the head in order to win," Huff said. Other new additions to the team included ex-Los Angeles Rams defensive lineman Andy Robustelli and ex-Steeler Dick Modzelewski. Tunnell and Rosey Grier also added tremendous passion to the team.

After playing five years for the Rams, Robustelli had been told that they were taking offers on his services. He was bitter. He recalled his conversation with Wellington.

"I've been talking to the Rams about you, and they're willing to trade you," Well said to Robustelli. "I know that you're 30 years old, but do you think you could play two or three more years?"

"'I'll try to play as long as I can, but I don't know how long that will be,' I told him, trying to sound calm."

"If you tell me that you can play, or at least will try to play for that long, then I think I can make a trade for you."

"'Go ahead and make the deal,' I told Well."

In that season, of 22 players voted All-Pro, the Giants had five players named, including Robustelli, Grier, and Tunnell, with Gifford and Roosevelt Brown making it on offense. Brown had been drafted in the 27th round three years earlier. Wellington had found him in the *Pittsburgh Courier,* one of the newspapers Well subscribed to trying to find talent for the team. Brown went on to make All-Pro eight times and was the Offensive Lineman of the Year in 1956. Drafted from little Morgan State, Brown would be among that small cadre of players to be with the Giants for years. His years of hard work were rewarded; eventually he became a coach and a trusted advisor.

"The Maras were fine people and they knew how to treat people right. The only thing for me to do was to do my best in return," Brown said.

By now the Giants were playing in Yankee Stadium, and Well was participating more than ever. One of Wellington's innovations was to take photographs of the opposing team's formations from high up in the stands using an instant Polaroid camera. He would then stuff the Polaroids into a sock with a rock and throw the sock down to the Giants sideline, where Lombardi or some other coach would grab it out of the air with a baseball glove. Then the coaches and players could see the opposing team's formations and address changes that needed to be made on the spot. Originally this technique was for Lombardi and the offense, but the practice was extended to the defense and Landry as well.

Conerly's wife, Perian, wrote about the practice in her book *Backseat Quarterback*. "The Giants...use on-the-spot photography in recording significant changes in [opponent's] formation. Giants vice president Wellington Mara frequently doubles as cameraman. From the highest tier he trains a Polaroid camera on the action below and drops the finished pictures down to the bench in a weighted sock." Perian admitted that for years she and other wives thought the projectiles came from hostile fans, not knowing that they came from the Giants owner.

Perian also explained in her book that, "If [a] player is assisted to the locker room or fails to return to the game in a reasonable length of time, either Jack Mara, Giants president, or Father Dudley, the unofficial team chaplain, thoughtfully seeks out the anxious wife and gives her a first-hand report."

Father Dudley was affectionately known as Father Ben. According to Gifford, Father Ben was as much a part of the Giants as the Maras, and few in the era could imagine the team without his benevolent presence. He had grown up in the same tough neighborhood in Philadelphia as Toots Shor. He was known for drinking his Manhattans straight-up, although he often switched to brandy later on in the evening. Father Ben and Shor wound many a night down together, with Shor constantly apologizing for cursing in front of the imbibing priest.

When Gifford once asked the priest if he thought it was beneficial to pray, since men on the other teams were also asking the same God for victory, Father Ben replied, "Yes, Frank, I've found that it does help to pray—particularly in the years when we have good personnel."

When Gifford was recuperating in the hospital after a crushing blow by Chuck Bednarik in 1960, it was Father Ben who came into the room and asked that it be cleared so that he could talk privately with the injured Gifford. Once the door was shut and the two were alone, Father Ben revealed that he had snuck in some booze for the two old friends to share a drink.

Father Ben was a steadying influence and a constant presence around the Giants organization. He was also among the inner circle of Mara confidants and trusted religious advisors.

On December 30, 1956, the NFL championship was at hand. The 1956 season up to that point had been charmed. New stadium. Great record. Five All-Pro players. And here in front of the Giants were the Western Conference champions, and constant NFL rivals, the Chicago Bears.

With 56,836 fans in attendance braving the late December chill, the stage was set. And it was eerily reminiscent of the 1934 championship. The winds had turned Yankee Stadium's turf to ice. The Giants' mimeograph machine in the press box had frozen. Cleats were useless.

In the week leading up to the game, T.J. made rare appearance in the locker room. The weather leading up to the game had been unusually cold. "Boys," Mara said, according to Grier, the beloved gentle Giant who was a terror on the field, "back in '34 we played the Bears for the championship in weather just as bad as this, and we nearly lost. The team went into the lockers at halftime, trailing 13–3".

Tim explained how they procured the sneakers by stealing them from the Manhattan College lockers, and how they eventually came back and won the game big.

"This year we are going to do the same thing," said the old man, "except we don't have to steal the sneakers." Mara then turned to Robustelli. "Andy, you own a sporting goods store. Can you fill an order for a good pair of sneakers for every man on the team by the end of the week?"

"You betcha, Mr. Mara," said Andy. That week, Robustelli's sporting goods shop in Cos Cob, Connecticut, received boxes of a new line of sneakers from Keds.

"On game day it was 15 degrees. Howell dispatched two players, one with cleats and one without. After their trials they came back, and Howell bellowed, 'We all go with sneakers!'"

The score was 33–7 at the half. Then Chicago switched to sneakers, too, but it was too late. The Giants won in convincing fashion, taking the NFL championship 47–7.

"All over the city that fall, players who had been ignored or made to feel inferior to their baseball counterparts were getting the sort of VIP attention that had previously been the sole province of baseball players," wrote Michael MacCambridge. While T.J. had already been a regular at Shor's, now his players were invited there, as well as to 21, Manuche's, etc. And Madison Avenue executives were drawn to the Giants as well.

The best example of this was Conerly's success. He became friendly with longtime Giants fan and, Philip Morris executive Jack Landry. Conerly was hired as one of the first Marlboro men, and worked for Philip Morris well into the 1970s. Gifford would eventually get television announcing opportunities with CBS, and eventually kicker Pat Summerall would do the same.

Gerald Eskanazi told a fascinating little side story about the 1956 championship game. It seemed after the game, "but before the long night of revelry to come, Jack Mara saw Tunnell standing by himself across the street from the stadium. Mara approached Tunnell, who was staring at the ballpark.

"'Someone should put a statue of a Giant on top of that building,'" Tunnell told Mara.

THE BIG KICK

In 1957 the Dodgers and baseball Giants played their last seasons in New York. They were headed west. For the football Giants, the 1957 campaign turned out to be a bust. Despite so much talent, they struggled to a 7–5 record. Meanwhile, a rookie running back in Cleveland had reenergized that franchise. His name was Jim Brown, and in 1957 the Cleveland Browns were the Eastern Conference champions, going on to lose the championship to the Detroit Lions. The game was televised by CBS.

"Nick Baldino, a friend of Wellington's for 60 years, remembers the day they buried a fellow Fordham man, a running back named Len Eshmont. Eshmont played for the Giants one year, in 1941, then went to San Francisco after the war and played eight [actually four] seasons with the 49ers. He died in 1957 of liver cancer," wrote Bill Pennington for the *Asbury Park Press.*

At the funeral, Wellington told Eshmont's widow that there wasn't much he could do to console her. "But if those three little girls of yours want to go to college, don't worry about a thing," the quiet owner told the grief-stricken widow.

"But God help you if you ever told anybody he did something like that for somebody," Baldino said from his home in Elberon.

In 1957 and 1958 Well was still making trades. From the mid-1950s to the early 1960's, all told, he drafted Gifford, Rote, Brown, Grier, Huff, and Jim Katcavage, and traded for, Tittle, Robustelli, Summerall, Del Shofner, Dick Lynch, and Modzelewski, shaping the powerful Giants teams of those same years.

A good example of Ann and Well's marriage and how they operated as a couple was best exemplified by a small story told by Lombardi biographer David Maraniss. In 1957 Lombardi was the highest-paid assistant in the league. The Eagles offered him the head coaching job for only slightly more money. Lombardi was desperate to go to any organization that would give him the opportunity to run his own team. He told Bell he would take the spot. But Well immediately called Lombardi, prevailing on him. He reasoned that the ownership structure was woefully undecided, and that only headaches awaited him in Philadelphia.

"You'll never get along with them. They'll never let you run the team the way you want to do it. I don't think you ought to go there," cajoled Wellington.

"No sooner had Mara hung up than the [Lombardi] phone rang again and it was Mara's wife, Ann, urging [Vince's wife] Marie to persuade her husband not to leave the Giants," wrote Maraniss. Lombardi eventually turned the Eagles, offer down.

While many Giants players of the era were very proud of that 1956 championship, most still consider the 1958 campaign to be the most memorable. As for television, the NFL had a blackout rule, meaning that it would not allow home games to be televised locally. But CBS executives were thrilled with the Giants anyway. Their biggest attraction was Giants away games, where the numbers were up by huge amounts.

The Maras, who'd struggled for decades to fill the ballpark, were understandably leery of television's draw. The prevailing thought among owners was that if you showed the home games on television, no one would come to the stadium. And being an old boxing promoter, Tim Mara believed in the gate. At that time the gate was much more lucrative than television contracts. The Giants were now averaging around 50,000 fans per game, and many of the big games were sellouts.

Be that as it may, the Giants were already making money off television. They had programs, which usually aired about midweek, showing highlights from the week's previous game. By 1958 away games were also televised. With each away game the Giants were becoming more and more popular. But if you were a fan who lived in the metro area but did not attend the game at the stadium, you had no choice—the game was only on the radio.

In a light moment before the season, Conerly and Jack sparred humorously over Conerly's contract.

"I want you to know," said Conerly, with a thick southern drawl, "that I led the entire National Football League last season in one department of play."

"Show me," scoffed Jack, handing his player the football almanac.

"Here it is," said Conerly, pointing to the book triumphantly. "Most points after a touchdown by rushing—Conerly, 1."

"That point had come more by accident than by design," wrote Arthur Daley. A bad snap on a point-after attempt had forced Conerly to run for his life. It was only by accident that he ran toward the goal line and scored a point.

⤚⤙

The 1958 season was filled with the kind of heroics that have filled numerous books.

From the very beginning, the race was on between New York and Cleveland. In a midseason showdown between the two best teams in the conference, New York edged out the Browns in Cleveland, 21–17. But New York faltered elsewhere, and they were put in the position of having to win their last two games just to tie the Browns.

In the fourth quarter, against Detroit, Conerly drove the team into the end zone in five plays, and the Giants defense held on to seal the victory 19–17. The last game of the season, thanks to scheduler Bell, was Cleveland at New York. More than 63,000 fans saw the first play, which was a heartbreaker, as Jim Brown broke through the Giants defense and ran for a 65-yard touchdown. Things looked bleak, and Cleveland continued to dominate well into the fourth quarter, holding a 10–3 lead. Conerly tied the game. Then both teams had stalled drives. A light snow that had been falling was getting worse and worse. With 4:30 left in the game, Summerall tried a 38-yard field goal and missed. The defense held in the driving snow, and the offense took the field again. They sputtered with little time left on the clock. On third down Webster dropped a wide-open pass that would have easily been a touchdown. The Giants were at midfield, fourth down.

With the last seconds ticking away and the snow almost blinding, Howell bellowed for Summerall. Everyone on the sidelines, including Summerall himself, was aghast. The fans in the stands were in shock.

Wellington, by his own admission, was up in the stadium rafters, "sitting on the phones and taking those Polaroid pictures" during the game. "That Summerall kick was the most vivid play I remember. I was sitting next to Ken Kavanaugh and Walt Yowarsky. We all said, 'He can't kick it that far! What are you doing?'"

When Summerall approached the huddle, a shocked Conerly barked into the driving snow, "What the fuck are you doing here?"

The attempt was listed as a 49-yard field goal, but almost everyone there said it was anywhere from 52 to 55 yards. The snap came, and Conerly, the best holder in the league according to Summerall, placed the ball down, laces away. Summerall struck the ball and followed through. For those in attendance, the ball seemed to hang in the air forever, as if time itself had simply stopped within the old stadium's walls. The snow made it absolutely impossible for the crowd to make it out. Where was the ball? Even Summerall himself could barely see the tops of the goal posts.

"I didn't see it go through," Summerall said. "You couldn't see that far in the snow. But I knew. You could just tell."

The ball sailed through easily and landed safely in the hands of a Giants front-office worker. The Giants had won, 13–10. They had earned a one-game playoff in one week's time against the team they had just defeated. They would go on to win the following week's divisional playoff game against the Browns, 10–0.

In the locker room after the game, T.J. showed up, as jubilant as ever. The old man walked around the room as proud as a man could be. And when asked about Summerall, he responded, "What a kick. What a kicker. But what the hell, that's what I pay him for, and I'm glad to see he earned his money today."

THE GREATEST GAME EVER PLAYED

The Giants had won the coin toss—the game would be played in New York. The next day, Wellington and the ticket manager, Harry Bachrach, were in the Giants' offices. Located now at Columbus Circle, next door to the coliseum, Maras and their staff were furiously stuffing 60,000 tickets into envelopes, preparing for an awesome run by Giants fans. According to *New York Times* sportswriter Eskanazi, "For almost an entire week the workers and visitors to 10 Columbus Circle had to wait and wait for elevators, which disgorged thousands of ticket-holders. The line stretched from the lobby, snaking outside and around Fifty-ninth Street, and curling west to Ninth Avenue."

"If we weren't thrown out then," said Wellington, "we'll never be thrown out of anyplace."

It was a tough week for Wellington. There was real worry in his life. Ann was preganant with the couple's second child. Their first child, John, also known as Jack, after Well's brother, was in St. Vincent's Hospital. He was recovering from mastoid surgery. The mastoid bone is behind the ear, and once infected, the most common treatment, especially in those days, was the removal of bone and tissue. Wellington slept in a bed next to his son each night. In the morning he awoke, went to see the team work out, then went back to Columbus Circle to sell more tickets, and then returned to the hospital. It was a brutal grind. Jack recovered, and Ann's delivery was fine. They were a happy family of four, although they would soon grow again.

The Giants were also fine. The stadium was packed, in anticipation of the final showdown of the year with the dreaded Browns.

Landry's crew of monsters were now a fashionable killing machine. And while Jim Brown was getting fat on the rest of the league, his record against the Giants was somewhat diminished. The game, although a sellout, was not a barnburner, and was in fact a less thrilling affair than the 10–0 score might indicate. Brown had only eight yards in seven attempts. While his coach, Paul Brown, had attempted to pass more often than run in an effort to throw the Giants off, the De-Fense, as it had now come to be known, had shut down one of the greatest of all runners and set up the most important NFL championship game of the century.

While the point-makers on the team—Conerly, Rote, Summerall, Gifford, and Webster—were golden boys, it was the Giants' defense that was capturing the imagination of New York. It was the favored unit of the fans. The chants when they took the field could sometimes be deafening. They were among the first defenses to take hold of the public's imagination and would go on to set the standard for Giants teams for decades to come.

This championship game would mark the beginning of the rise in popularity of the National Football League and the league's dominance over all sports on the American landscape. This is when football trumped baseball. NBC carried the game, which was played on December 28, 1958, at Yankee Stadium. It would come to be known as the Greatest Game Ever Played.

There were several reasons for that. The stadium was packed—a complete sellout. The television audience was the largest for a game up to that point. And most importantly, the game would have an exciting finish in regulation and an even bigger comeback in overtime—the first ever in NFL championship history.

There was no question that pitting Johnny Unitas and Raymond Berry against Tom Landry's defense was the premiere matchup in many fans' minds.

The Giants went up 3–0 in the first quarter, and the Colts responded with two second-quarter touchdowns, making the score 14–3, Colts. In the third quarter Mel Triplett scored on a one-yard dive, and the score was 14–10 Colts.

Now Wellington helped out from up in the stands. With his trusty Polaroid, Wellington had photographed the Colts' defense.

Studying the Colts' defense he saw "a tendency by the Colts' secondary to overshift to the strong side. Conerly called a play to capitalize on Mara's undercover work," wrote sportswriter Harry Eldridge Jr. With one minute gone in the fourth quarter, Conerly isolated Gifford in the right corner of the end zone and pinpointed a touchdown pass to make it 17–14. The Giants were now in front.

The De-Fense took the field. They held. The teams exchanged the ball back and fourth. With 2:30 to go, on fourth down, Gifford took a handoff on an outside sweep. Tackled with room to spare for the first down, confusion broke out when Big Daddy Lipscomb accidentally broke Gino Marchetti's leg in a pileup. When the ball was eventually spotted, the Giants were inches short, and the Colts regained control of the ball. The Colts moved the ball with stupefying precision. Unitas and company took the ball from their own 14-yard line and, with less than two minutes remaining, marched it down the field to the Giants, 13-yard line. With only seven clicks still left on the game clock, Colts kicker Steve Myhra's 20-yard field goal had tied the game. Overtime!

The Giants received the ball, but Lombardi's offense could not get on track and the Giants were forced to punt. Then Unitas put on another dazzling display, marching 13 plays and more than 80 yards to set up the final play.

The teams lined up on the 1-yard line. Alan Ameche crashed into the end zone, head down. The two teams fell as a massive pile straight into the arms of history. Win or lose, the game itself was breathtaking. And almost everyone who had a television set by 1958 had watched it, with some 45 million viewers, including President Eisenhower, who had been watching the game on his retreat in Gettysburg.

"This is the greatest day in the history of professional football!" Bell shouted from the commissioner's box. Heroic in defeat, the Giants were the envy of the football world.

No one put it better than Schramm, one of Wellington's most vocal adversaries, who years later said, "If you look back in history, the NFL had its largest escalation and biggest television growth period in the late 1950s and the early 1960s, and that's because the

Giants had great teams then. That's when you began to hear about the first umpteenth-million-dollar television contract."

"Pete Rozelle always told me that the reason pro football took off was because it happened just at that time, in that season, and it happened in New York," Wellington said. "If it had happened in Pittsburgh or Green Bay, it wouldn't have taken off."

"In the 1958 title game, pro football had arrived as a viable alternative to baseball, not merely as the most popular sport, but as the one that best defined America," wrote Michael MacCambridge.

A Texas millionaire was also watching. His name was Lamar Hunt. He watched the Colts-Giants game with great interest. "The '58 Colts-Giants game...in my mind, made me say, 'Well, that's it. This sport has everything. And it televises well.' And who knew what that meant?"

CHAPTER 7

A Death in the Family

DEATH OF A GIANT

In the weeks after the heartbreaking loss, the Giants coliseum offices were bowled over by a rush for next season's tickets. Tim was as jolly as he had ever been. His little storefront enterprise had finally grown up. He didn't have to hand out tickets for free any more, or even sell them at half price.

Every morning he showed up at his usual 7:00 AM only to find another dozen orders for tickets. "We're gonna sell out next year," he said over and over. Timothy James Mara had no idea how right his prediction was. By the late 1970s and early 1980s, the waiting list for Giants tickets would be 20 years—a whole generation's wait for tickets to the little $2,500 franchise he'd bought on a whim.

But Tim Mara would never see it happen. He passed away on February 16, 1959. In *The New York Times*, Arthur Daley wrote a column for his fallen friend titled, "A Pioneer Passes." Daley played up the "gay and breezy" fashion in which Tim told stories, especially about the founding of the club.

"Perhaps pro football would have succeeded without Tim Mara. But it would have been a much longer and more arduous battle," Daley wrote.

Mara was 71 years old. He had kept a losing franchise afloat for decades, building it into a perennial powerhouse. He'd won three league championships. And he'd been one of the founders who helped save the league when others wanted to close it down.

"He died on a real high," said Wellington, referring to his father's good spirits due to rising ticket sales.

147

"The National Football League will not see Tim's like again. And Tim's mark is also on his sons. He gave them love, honesty, decency, and character. The bright little newsboy of 59 years ago wrote quite a success story," wrote Arthur Daley, tim's good friend.

Wellington was 43 years old, and Jack was 51. Together, under their father's watchful eye, they had ostensibly been running the day-to-day operations for almost a decade. Tim came and went, with other obligations pressing upon him. But he was gone now. The boys were saddened, but business went on. As always, Jack ran the business, and Wellington ran the football team. And the organization, while saddened at old Tim Mara's death, moved on without too much of a skip.

MORE GOOD-BYES

There was no question about it—Lombardi was supposed to follow Howell as the next head coach of the New York Giants. But in December 1958 the Green Bay Packers approached the Giants for the express purpose of asking Lombardi to join the Packers as their next head coach.

Lombardi had a contract with a year left as the highest-paid assistant in the NFL. and still had a year left on that contract. Jack and especially Wellington did not want Lombardi to leave, but they could not hold him in good conscience. Howell had led the team to unprecedented glory. They could not replace Howell when the Giants were poised, along with a few other teams, at the top of the professional football world.

So reluctantly they let Lombardi go with this proviso: when the Giants head coaching position became open, he would be given first option on taking the job.

"For a long time pro football was a part-time job for both players and coaches. I remember Vince Lombardi, for example, working several different jobs in the off-season while he was with us. Actually, the year he decided to go to Green Bay, he had taken a position with a bank," Wellington said. "In fact, the day the Packers signed Vince, his picture appeared in the financial section of *The New York Times* underneath a small story announcing his new job as vice president of a New York bank."

And so one of the "brain trust" members was gone. And a fatal error, a miscalculation of the highest kind, maybe of hubris, had occurred.

Still, the 1959 team seemed not to miss a step. They raced to a 10–2–0 record and left the Cleveland Browns well within their wake. They were very clearly the best team in the East, both offensively and defensively. In the NFL championship they again met the Baltimore Colts. They met on December 27, 1959, at Baltimore, in front of 57,545 rabid fans. Going into the third quarter the Giants held a tenuous 9–7 lead. Suddenly the Colts exploded. Unitas ran for one touchdown and passed for another; Johnny Sample intercepted a Conerly pass and ran it back for a touchdown. The final score was 31–16, Colts.

Within weeks, assistant coach Landry was ready to tender his resignation. "After the '55 season, [Landry] had moved to Dallas in the off-season in an attempt to find a career in the real world in which he might find success," wrote sportswriter Golenbock. "Landry was at a crossroads in his life. His football salary was only $12,000 a year, and he either had to find a better paying job in football or get out of the game and go into business full time."

Rumors abounded that Landry would follow Howell as coach. But the old coach wasn't leaving, and no offer by the Giants was tendered.

"I left the Giants in the 1959 season because I was planning on leaving football all together. The money just wasn't very good, and it was pretty much a part-time job," Landry said. The former electrical engineer figured it was time to get started founding some sort of business. "The Cowboys got a franchise and asked me to be their head coach."

"We hated losing Tom, but I understood his desire to get back to Texas. Not long after he did return home, however, Bud Adams called and asked Tom if he'd be interested in coaching the Houston Oilers of the New American Football League. Now, I didn't want Tom leaving the Giants, but I was even more concerned about the rival league getting him. So I phoned Tex Schramm of the Cowboys and recommended they keep Tom in the NFL and hire him for their coach," said Wellington.

Schramm offered Landry the job, and Landry took it. Little did anyone know that Landry and Lombardi would take their rivalry to a whole new level by the mid-1960s, and that this final drain on the Giants "brain trust," would in fact be the death knell of the Giants organization's success in the years to come.

PETE ROZELLE

In January 1960 the NFL meetings were held in Miami Beach. Out of all the very important issues that needed to be addressed, the most important was the replacement of the late Bert Bell. Who would replace the longest-serving and best of the league's commissioners and presidents?

Jack and Wellington were among the contingent pressing for Marshall Leahy. Leahy was the 49ers' bright and well-liked lawyer. Several votes were taken, but the Leahy group could not muster the 75 percent necessary to carry a motion. Things got hot. The Colts' Carroll Rosenbloom and Halas of the Bears did not like Leahy or what he stood for—carrying on current NFL policies. Halas, Marshall, and Rosenbloom were strong enough to hold off each other and several other lesser organizations.

Many more ballots were taken. The owners were in a deadlock. "If Jesus Christ himself came down here, you people would still insist on Leahy!" Rosenbloom cried out after yet another deadlock. Tempers were flaring.

Wellington sat with Dan Reeves, and they eventually came up with the idea to nominate Vince Lombardi. They discussed it with Jack, and they felt Jack was the one to approach Packers president Dominic Olejniczak. From his body language Wellington and Reeves could see Olejniczak's immediate dismissal of the idea.

As they sat on the couch in the lobby of the Kenilworth Hotel, Wellington turned to Reeves and said, "Dan, it's got to be Pete."

Alvin "Pete" Rozelle was the youngest general manager in the NFL. He had taken Reeve's moribund Los Angeles Rams and turned it into a stunning business success.

Rozelle was born on March 1, 1926, and grew up in suburban Compton, California. He was an excellent athlete in high school and had served time in the navy during the war. He had been the publicist for a college football team, and then held a series of public relations jobs in Southern California. Rozelle joined the Rams in the mid-1950s and was eventually offered the general manager's job. He had a sterling reputation, and he hadn't been in the league long enough to have any real enemies.

Reeves and Wellington approached Paul Brown and Jack and the idea began to gain support. When the Maras, Brown, and Reeves confronted Rozelle with the idea of putting his name in for commissioner, Rozelle was shocked. "You've got to be kidding me! That's the most ludicrous thing I've ever heard." Unfazed, the little group went on. Wellington then approached Dan Rooney. He convinced Rooney, and Rooney agreed to talk with the Eagles's Frank McNamee.

"Great! Who the hell is Pete Rozelle?" said a weary McNamee.

"I don't really know him either, but if Well says he's okay, that's good enough for me," replied Rooney.

That evening the meeting took place and the group asked Rozelle to exit the room. They discussed the idea of Rozelle being commissioner. It was their 23rd vote. Rozelle waited in the men's room, half nauseous, washing his hands to pass the time. When he returned, he was told he was the new commissioner.

"Gentlemen, I can honestly say I come to you with clean hands."

NFL MERCHANDIZING

Wellington Mara was a smart man. While he might not have been the tremendous financial spreadsheet wizard his brother was, his eye was always on the bigger ticket items. He was clearly ahead of many men his age.

One item in particular was merchandise. Well had been one of the men behind the push for merchandising. "Before Pete Rozelle became the league's commissioner in 1960, the professional teams sold their program advertising individually, and no one sold clothing or other items with league or team insignia. Wellington Mara, the president and co-owner of the Giants, said Rozelle had come up with the idea of centralized sales," Frank Litsky wrote. Mara and Rozelle saw the opportunity.

"It was not to promote a moneymaker, but to further the image of the league," Mara said. Rozelle ended up hiring Larry

Kent to run NFL Properties. Kent was already a successful merchandiser, having promoted Roy Rogers, Dale Evans, Trigger, and their singing group the Sons of the Pioneers for 12 years. He had established Pioneer Corrals in department stores all over America.

"We formed NFL Properties to sell program advertising," said Lou Spadia, former San Francisco 49ers president. "We hired Larry Kent as the first president, and he did a fine job getting the league and team logos on T-shirts, lunch pails, anything. His goal was to get a page of NFL items in the Sears, Roebuck catalogue, and he did that."

At the time few companies, especially football teams, sold T-shirts, or anything else for that matter, with their logos on them. It was a business that did not exist before television. The original plan was to pool advertisers for stadium programs, but the idea grew.

Thus was born NFL Properties. Originally the group charged licensing fees of less than 10 percent of the retail price. The profits from the sales were shared equally among all the league's teams. In 1960 14 teams recieved $2,600 each. Kent retired in 1975. By 1999, when Kent died, each of the NFL's 30 teams earned more than $5 million each year from NFL Properties.

A NEW LEAGUE OF OWNERS

In 1960 Harry Wismer of New York, Lamar Hunt of Dallas, Barron Hilton of Los Angeles, Max Winter and William Boyer of Minneapolis, Bob Howsam of Denver, and K. S. "Bud" Adams of Houston met in a Chicago, Illinois, hotel room to start a league called the American Football League. The NFL had withstood many challengers before, but this would be the most effective group they had ever faced. Later, the AFL would also add a team in Buffalo, New York, owned by Ralph C. Wilson, and another in Boston led by Billy Sullivan. On November 22, 1959, they held their inaugural draft.

What proved so smart about this league was that in late 1960 they adopted an equal sharing policy regarding a national television contract, which the league president would negotiate on behalf of the league. Eventually Joe Foss was named commissioner of the new league for a three-year term. Foss was a veteran of World War II, where he won a Medal of Honor, and he was the former two-term governor of South Dakota.

Foss and the owners filed a deposition with the Department of Justice asking for federal antitrust action against the NFL. The flash point was the NFL's granting an expansion franchise to Texas entrepreneur Clint Murchison, challenging the AFL for supremacy in that city. By June 17, 1961, the AFL had filed a $10 million private antitrust lawsuit against the NFL.

The 1960 AFL championship game was played on Sunday, January 1, 1961, at Houston with the hometown Oilers beating the Los Angeles Chargers 24–16 to win the league's first championship.

This new league leveraged a major contract from ABC. The NFL had a real worry on its hands. But there was much more to discuss for the Maras.

The real challenge of the AFL came home when the AFL challenged three player's contracts with NFL teams. One of those teams was the New York Giants.

Charlie Flowers was from Mariana, Arkansas, and played fullback for Mississippi. He had been drafted by the New York Giants. He was the 10th pick in the 12th round of the 1959 NFL draft. What happened next should have been routine, but the AFL was pressuring the NFL on three players: LSU star Billy Cannon, Johnny Robinson, and Flowers.

Jack and Wellington could have let it go and no one would have cared. But they were NFL old guard, and they were going to fight it like old Tim would have. Flowers, however, was an incredibly honest guy, and with his "'Aw shucks, Mister'" Southern charm, he was a great story for any newspaper man. When the newspapers got a hold of Flowers, Jack, and Well—especially Well—the Maras were doomed to look bad.

"I went to New York last December and signed with the Giants. But Mr. [Wellington] Mara said: 'Son, if you don't want to play with the Giants, just say so. We don't want any player who doesn't want to be a Giant,'" Flowers told the press. The line was purely Tim's kind of salesmanship.

Wellington actually strong-armed Flowers into signing a pact near the men's room at the All-American dinner in New York. Mara was trying to sign, seal, and deliver the impressionable young man early in order, to cut off AFL interference.

"I received a contract and a good bonus check from the Giants, but I sent it all back and asked Mr. Mara to stand by his statement about not wanting anybody who didn't want to play with the Giants," said Flowers. He then added insult to injury, stating for the record, "I definitely want to play for Los Angeles. I'm plenty mad about this thing."

Wellington had sent a letter to AFL commissioner Foss to request that the Los Angeles Chargers, who had also drafted the gifted fullback, withdraw their contract.

"We have a legal contract with Flowers and will take steps necessary to enforce that contract," Jack told the press. Foss refused to assist the Giants. They went to trial.

During pretrial examinations the truth about the Flowers defection really came out and it turned out to be an inside job. Ed McKeever, the New York Giants scout who found and recommended Flowers, had in fact been paid $1,000 to turn Flowers toward the AFL. Another Giants draft pick, James Varnado, a fullback at Southern, had also been turned by McKeever. Eventually McKeever became the general manager of the Boston Patriots.

Of all the trials that the Maras had been involved in, the Flowers trial had the most action. Flowers had signed contracts with both clubs. No one was sure if he was that slippery or that naïve.

"Giants coach Jim Lee Howell was called as a witness and had to be restrained by two U.S. Marshals," wrote Jeff Miller, editor of the *Dallas Morning News*.

"You will conduct yourself as a gentleman in my court," hollered the judge at Howell. "Put your feet on the ground and restrain yourself!"

The Giants lost the trial. Wellington had agreed to keep the contract secret until after the Sugar Bowl, otherwise Flowers would have been regarded as a professional by the NCAA and been disqualified from playing. According to the judge, the player retained the right to cancel the contract until it was approved by the NFL commissioner, a common clause in all NFL contracts. Wellington had held the contract secret until after the Sugar Bowl, and by then Flowers had changed his mind.

When asked by the judge about the concealed contract from the dinner in New York, the puckish Wellington described it as a "harmless deception." The Giants lost the case and received a black eye in the press. These kinds of losses made Wellington especially bitter and would color his view completely when discussions began later on a possible merger of the leagues.

THE 1960 SEASON

"Jack always thought I was extra-liberal in paying the players," Wellington said years later. "So once we let him deal with Conerly, the last contract Conerly ever signed. I had a golf date, and Jack said, 'I'll handle him.' I always felt like Jack had a yen to see how well he'd do with Charlie in contract talks."

Well remembered the incident with laughter. "I don't remember the figures, but it was by far the biggest contract Charlie ever had, and it was more than I was prepared to give him."

"I've been dealing with the wrong brother all these years," Conerly said to Wellington some time after the contract had been signed.

The 1960 season started off strongly. In October 1960 the CBS show *The 20th Century*, narrated by Walter Cronkite, featured an episode so unique that it is easily remembered today. It was called "The Violent World of Sam Huff."

The Giants had been the first team to win a championship with a new position, created by Landry, called middle linebacker. In 1959, at the age of 25, Huff became the first NFL player to appear on the cover of *Time* magazine. Huff's personality and his unique position in football made him an instant celebrity. Chants of "Huff! Huff! Huff!" from the Giants faithful were not unusual.

Actually his name was Robert Lee Huff, and he was born in 1934, during the Great Depression, in Edna Gas, West Virginia. His father was a poor coal miner, and for Huff, football was a way to avoid following in his father's footsteps. Huff got a scholarship to the University of West Virginia. He was a 230-pound All-American lineman, but when he joined the Giants, both Lombardi and Landry thought he was too small to play the line in the pros. But Landry took a chance on Huff.

"The Violent World of Sam Huff" was a 30-minute episode in which Huff became the first player ever wired for sound during a preseason practice and an exhibition game. For the first time,

America could gain an up-close, inside look into the violent world of pro football. It was raw.

"Any time that you play football," Huff said during the show, "there is no place for nice guys. You have to be tough."

The episode was a tremendous hit, and was further evidence of football's growing popularity. It was also just the beginning of CBS's connection with the Giants. Kyle Rote, Frank Gifford, and Pat Summerall were all eventually recruited by television. Gifford and Summerall became nationally recognized television broadcasters. These relationships were forged in the glory years, when young, eager television executives in New York also decided to cash in on the cachet of these new, modern heroes.

But age was starting to catch up with one of the league's flashiest franchises. Injuries had decimated some of the biggest names, including Conerly, Katcavage, and Gifford. On November 20, 1960, the Eastern Conference came down to a showdown between Philadelphia and New York at the stadium. The Eagles were leading 17–10 when the Giants tried to tie the score late in the game. Gifford ran upfield, turned to catch a Conerly pass, and continued running upfield.

Chuck Bednarik, one of the toughest men ever to play the game, came across and hit Gifford with a crushing blow directly to his chest. Gifford's body lay completely deflated on the field. Many feared he was dead. Bednarik stood over the unconscious Gifford, swinging his arms wildly and cursing.

"Chuck knocked him right out of his shoes," said Tom Brookshier, an Eagles defensive back.

"I was celebrating," Bednarik said, "but the reason wasn't that he was down. The reason was that the hit won the game."

"It was perfectly legal," Gifford said later. "If I'd had the chance, I'd have done the same thing Chuck did." He received a concussion so serious that he would miss the rest of the season and all of the next one. It ended all chances the Giants had. They lost the game and faltered during the rest of the season. They finished 6–4–2, well out of the money.

The end of the 1960 season marked the end of Jim Lee Howell's coaching career with the Giants. He moved into player personnel. But the vacancy caused Jack and Well instant nausea. After the Maras had let Landry go to Dallas, Howell announced in a private meeting with the Maras that he would no longer coach after the 1960 season. For however mad they might have been at Howell, he was still practically family. Howell, in private, admitted to being burned out, and did not want the job at any price.

What to do? The Giants called up Olejniczak at the Green Bay Packers. Olejniczak granted them permission to talk with Lombardi about the vacancy, but only in secret. Lombardi came to New York to discuss his return, even as he was being feted by the press as Coach of the Year for his dramatic turnaround of the Green Bay franchise. In the files of the New York organization, there were documents that stated "both parties recognized his obligations in Green Bay, and it was agreed that the matter would be tabled until the completion of the 1960 NFL season."

But the 1961 season saw even more improvement in Green Bay. At one point Red Smith wrote, "They love Vincent in Green Bay and they love him in New York." Smith also said Lombardi made no attempt to "hide his homesickness" for New York. Arthur Daley of *The New York Times* and the venerable Stanley Woodward both wondered in print how Lombardi could waste his time in Green Bay while his home and the big stage awaited him in New York. The press put it on the shoulders of Jack and Well.

As Maraniss pointed out, "Lombardi's attachment to the Packers board of directors could not match the personal bond he felt toward the Maras." Lombardi vacillated all season long, while at the same time he was pressing all fronts to keep every option open. It was no secret what Lombardi had accomplished in Green Bay—and many thought there would only be more glory. He had more control in Green Bay than he could have had in New York, and his defection might prove a problem because it would give other coaches in the league ideas about renouncing their contracts and jumping to other teams, either within the NFL or to the AFL.

Wellington and Lombardi met in secret in Philadelphia before the 1961 championship game. Lombardi told his friend he had decided to stay in Green Bay.

"He said he had to fulfill his obligations there. And he also knew they had a darned good team coming back. He told me that," Well said. The Mara's had miscalculated their timing and their pull. If they wanted him, they could have had him, but the cost to themselves and the NFL would have been too great. And they hadn't counted on Lombardi's ability to turn Green Bay around so quickly.

Wellington admitted years later that it was one of the biggest mistakes of his football career, and one of the two biggest regrets of his professional life.

HELLO ALLIE—THE SECOND CHOICE

It was no secret the Giants had tried to renew their relationship with Lombardi. And when they failed to get him, the Giants knew who they would approach.

Allie Sherman was their next choice. The problem was that Sherman was also the next choice of the Pittsburgh Steelers and the Green Bay Packers. Sherman loved to tell the story of how he was approached by Lombardi in a men's room, where Lombardi told him he wanted Sherman to be his offensive coach. Sherman had been coaching in Canada for three years before returning to the Giants as a scout.

Sherman had been drafted by Greasy Neale in Philadelphia, and played between 1943 and 1947. He was a small (5'10", 160 pounds) affable Jewish kid from Brooklyn with a razor-sharp offensive mind. He was born to be a coach.

Said Sherman in 1960, "I called Well back and he made me the offer to replace [Howell]. I told him Vince had asked me to go back to Green Bay with him. ... I had ruled out Pittsburgh. So it was Green Bay or New York." I told Mara I would take the job, and I thanked Lombardi but I turned it down."

"Well told me he had made a promise to Vince," Sherman said later. "He told me he had committed himself to offer the job to Vince, but if Vince couldn't get free, I would be his only other choice. He asked me to be patient. He knew I had other offers...."

Later, while they were at the Senior Bowl in Mobile, Alabama, Wellington came to Sherman. "It looks like Vince can't get away. I'd like you to be head coach of the Giants," said Well.

"Jack Mara told me I didn't have to prove anything. I didn't have to win big to keep the job. He said they knew I was a good coach, and they were ready for a team to be built."

But Sherman thought they could win, and win now. He buried himself in his basement and watched all the films from the previous few seasons. After watching the films, he felt they needed to fill in a few blank spots. Sherman gave them a shopping list. What he wanted more than anything was a new, verteran quarterback, because Conerly was fading. He needed one speedy receiver, a cornerback, and a tight end.

"Well never tried to make a trade without my approval, not then and not later when the trades backfired. I'll give him that. He never tried to take charge," Sherman said.

Wellington went to work on Sherman's shopping list. He got a rookie split end from Los Angeles named Del Shofner. He traded for a small tight end named Joe Walton. And he brought in Erich Barnes from the Chicago Bears.

Earlier in the year San Francisco tried to shop Y.A. Tittle to the Giants, but the price was too high for Well. He didn't like Tittle in early 1961, but by August he was a big fan. Tittle played two seasons with the Baltimore Colts of the All-American Football Conference (1948–1949) and one with the Colts in the National Football League (1950). Then he played 10 seasons with the San Francisco 49ers. He had earned the respect of the entire NFL. His stats were impeccable. But the knock against him as a quarterback was that, despite all his heroics, he'd never won a championship.

Wellington accepted the trade San Francisco wanted—one of New York's best linemen, Lou Cordileone. The deal prompted a famous quote from Cordileone, who said in shock when he was told of the trade, "Me for Tittle? You mean, just me?"

It was without question one of the best series of trades in the history of the league. It would not be outclassed until Jimmy Johnson traded Herschel Walker for five players and eight draft picks decades later.

"The difference between playing for the Giants and San Francisco is that when you lost a game out there, the owners gave you the feeling you'd let them down. Here you lose a game and they're trying to console you, as though they'd let you down," Tittle would later say.

"My wife really liked Mr. Mara. He came to California to sign me after the 1961 season, when I was Player of the Year," Tittle said later. "So I had intended to really hit him hard when it came to salary negotiations. So I played it hard."

"I'm not going to play next year. I'm getting older and I'm going to retire, because it's not worth it," Tittle told Wellington. "So Wellington came to California to see me and to talk me out of retiring. Minnette [Tittle's wife] invited him to spend the night in our house in our spare bedroom."

"If I'm going to have hard-nosed negotiations, we can't have him stay in our spare bedroom," Tittle told his wife. "But that didn't work, because she liked Wellington a lot. So when he came out to talk contract, when I was going to try to play hard and tough, my wife came into the living room."

"Y.A., would you hurry up and sign that contract—we're 30 minutes late for dinner," Minnette said. And that was that.

Wellington had been stupendous, and the signing of Tittle would secure his reputation as a football genius. Shofner would go on to become a legend to many loyal Giants fans, as would Walton and Barnes. What few people realized, including Mara, was that Tittle still had three of his best seasons in him; he would prove to be one of the greatest and most revered players in Giants history even though he would only play for them for four seasons. Tittle was so great it prompted world-famous writer Irwin Shaw, a football fan, to say, "Without Tittle the Giants couldn't go from Grand Central to Times Square on the subway."

ART MODELL

Art Modell was a hotshot New York advertising executive and a lifelong New York Giants fan. He met with Jack and Well and explained he wanted to buy a team. He had artfully put together an ownership committee and submitted his financial statement. "It was a load of shit," said Modell later. But in the end the Maras worked the phones and the owners and vouched for Modell. He had leveraged anything and everything for this opportunity. In 1961 Modell bought the Cleveland Browns for $4.1 million.

This was the beginning of one of the most devoted friendships between owners—that of Wellington and Modell.

"Well was my friend for 45 years, and I never had a better friend. He was like my brother. He was a man of extraordinary character, integrity, and decency," Modell would say many years later.

SHARING THE WEALTH

In 1960 Jack had secured the most lucrative television package in the NFL, with the Giants pocketing $175,000 per year. Of the eight other teams with contracts, Pittsburgh was the lowest earner with $75,000. CBS decided to follow the formula ABC used, which was to offer one lump sum for all the NFL games and let the owners scramble over the allotted sum. Bill MacPhail, the CBS executive in charge of the deal, offered $3 million for the entire season package. Immediately the owners started to fight, and Rozelle had a brawl on his hands during his first 12 months in office.

By the 1961 annual meeting that the report of the commissioner revealed that the owners had still not come to an agreement on how the money would be divided. The challenging AFL owners had split ABC's money evenly, but the NFL owners, used to having their own deals in radio and television, were reluctant to give up control.

At the Warwick Hotel Rooney had been dispatched by a group of owners to try to convince the Mara brothers to join the plan to split the overall television monies. The Maras had been understandably reluctant—Wellington more so than Jack. This discussion had been on the table for some time, and Halas had had spirited conversations with both Jack and Wellington.

Rooney won over Jack first, who then went to work on his brother. These kinds of business issues had always been left up to Jack. But Wellington strongly resisted at first, thinking of all the years their father's other businesses had supported the team just to keep it alive. It was only in the last decade that the team had begun to make any money, and now they were giving it to others who hadn't earned it.

The Maras were conservatives. They were old-timers despite their young age. They had opposed league expansion. They were not in favor of the Dallas franchise or the Minnesota franchise, afraid that

161

expansion might lead to a diluting of product and add instability to a shored-up league.

Jack prevailed upon Wellington, discussing the good of the league and the sacrifices they would have to make to ensure the league survived. If there were no small market teams, then the same six clubs would be playing each other. Wellington knew that Jack was right. It was a point of pride—like their father, they wanted to be stewards of the NFL. They wanted to do what was in the best interest of the game. That had been their mantra all along, only this time they were putting their money where their mouth was.

At the owners meeting the next day, it was Wellington who made an impassioned speech about revenue sharing. "We should all share, I guess. Or we're going to lose some of the smaller teams down the line, and we've all stuck together."

The Maras stood to lose the most. Jack and Well were risking their personal fortunes. It was in fact both a momentous decision and the right decision. And it insured the continuation of the league, especially in the face of the AFC's challenge.

"We were able to do it because the owners thought about what was best for the league," said Rozelle years later. "The Maras in New York, Dan Reeves in Los Angeles, and George Halas in Chicago—the three dominant markets—agreed to share television equally with the others, which was a major concession. They were wise enough to see the long term and they've been rewarded. All the franchises have seen their money increase from television as a consequence and the league as a whole has remained strong. All of the franchises have remained viable and have the means to compete with the rest of the league. That's what I think sports should be."

GLORY DAYS

Wellington had found players to fill every request on Sherman's shopping list. The NFL waited to see what Sherman would do with them. The beginning proved a little shaky. Conerly was a favorite among the players, but his skills, his eyesight, and his longevity over the season were all suspect, at best. He was still a great man, but at the age of 40, he could no longer lead the team on the field for a full season.

At his first Giants camp, Tittle found the offensive unit cliquish—after all, these players had been in the trenches with each other for years. He thought they saw him as a usurper—a man who couldn't win the big one. "The Giants may have feigned cordiality to their new teammate but, for weeks, 'Yat' was the loneliest guy in town."

Tittle and Conerly shared quarterbacking duties in the beginning of the season, but it soon became clear that Tittle was more capable. The Giants offense was starting to move some, and the defense was coming back too.

The Giants raced through their schedule. By beating Philadelphia twice late in the season, they took sole possession of the Eastern Conference with an 10–3–1 record, while the Eagles finished 10–4.

The NFL championship game took place at Green Bay on December 31, 1961. The subzero conditions kept Green Bay fans away from the first championship game ever played there. Only a disappointing 39,029 showed up. The game was tied at zero going into the second quarter when Green Bay exploded for 24 points. When the game ended, the Packers had defeated the Giants 37–0.

Despite this loss, the Giants season had been a resounding success. They had split their series with Landry's Dallas team and they had lost to Lombardi's Packers, but Mara was proud of the team's effort. The fans were just as in love with the team as ever, and Tittle was named the NFL's Most Valuable Player of 1961. It was a successful campaign.

With Tittle leading the team, the 1962 squad started off by tripping over the first few games of the season, but the Giants reeled off nine straight wins to end the season and take the Eastern Conference yet again. Tittle played even better than he had the year before. He threw 33 touchdown passes for a career-high 3,224 yards. In addition Webster had been reborn. After disappointing campaigns in 1959 and 1960, he gained more than 1,200 yards from scrimmage in 1961 and 1962. With a 12–2–0 record, the Giants went to the NFL championship game with great hopes. They had been one of the biggest stories in the NFL all year, along with Lombardi's Packers.

When the Giants took the field against Green Bay on December 30, 1962, 64,892 screaming fans at Yankee Stadium applauded their hometown heroes. Lombardi's Packers were 13–1–0, led by Bart Starr, Paul Hornung, and many other stars. With 7:26 left in the third quarter, the Giants scored on a blocked punt in the end zone and made the score 10–7, Packers. But after that the Packers slowly pulled away and won 16–7.

Still, Wellington and Sherman had built a winner, and everybody was watching.

Although Sherman had been the team's second choice to run the Giants, Jack and Wellington couldn't have expected what they actually got. Sherman was considered a genius. People from all over the league—coaches, executives, and owners—paid homage to what he had accomplished. Few, if any, had anything bad to say of the job he had done bringing New York to three consecutive championships.

Sherman's contract had one year left on it when Jack and Wellington negotiated an extension. On April 23, 1963, at Mamma Leone's restaurant in New York, Jack announced a new deal, with Sherman signing a five-year pact that paid him more than $35,000 per year. In two years he had compiled a 22–5–1 record, a huge feat for a relatively new head coach. And he had been named Coach of the Year in both those years. Jack Mara's face beamed as he put his arm around the ecstatic Sherman.

FAMILY TIES

By 1963, Tim, Jack's son—who was called Timmy and later T.J. by the family—was now working within the organization. He was 28 years old and had always been Jack's pride and consternation. T.J.'s best and worst attributes were both extreme. T.J. was bright and extremely affable. He grew to live quite the playboy's life despite his father's conservative personal and religious views. "A headstrong youth, he found himself in numerous scrapes and difficulties," wrote Dave Klein, "some of which might have become even more serious had he not had the reputation of the Giants and the Mara family to fall back on."

T.J. attended the Fordham Preparatory School at Fordham University and then entered Iona College in 1958. In 1962 he became the secretary-treasurer of the Giants. He was well liked by players and coaches alike. While mercurial, like his uncle Wellington, he was now the youthful face of the family to the employees of the company. Wellington was T.J.'s godfather, a charge he took very seriously—especially after Jack's death—but not in a way Tim appreciated.

Like his Uncle Wellington, Tim grew up on the sidelines, the scion of a great sports franchise. The two actually used to room together during Giants training camp for years. Tim proved to be a great friend of star running back, Gifford, Summerall, and many of the other Giants. In fact, while many others found it difficult to navigate the waters between and his uncle in later years, Gifford was always the easy, well-loved family member who could slide in between the two. Tim, Gifford, and running back Tucker Frederickson also owned a boat together down in Florida for a while later in life.

Tim was originally engaged to be married to Nancy Maresco. Nancy's parents were the Philip Marescos of Riverdale in the Bronx. They also summered in Lake Oscawana. Nancy was an alumna of Elizabeth Seton School and attended Barry and Finch Colleges. Their engagement was announced in October 1962.

However, nuptials were announced in September 1964, when T.J. married Barbara Ann Dauphin. Dauphin was a glamorous model, whose parents formerly lived in the Bronx but now lived in Palm Springs, California. She had attended St. Catherine's Academy in the Bronx.

Jack hoped that married life would calm down his son and slow down his somewhat tempestuous lifestyle. Like his father, T.J. loved the lifestyle Winged Foot afforded. But while Jack made sure he got work done first, T.J. preferred to spend more time at the club and elsewhere. T.J. proved to be both charming and funny, as well as incredibly headstrong. His marriage was troubled from the beginning, but it would hold for a while.

T.J. did not seem interested in the everyday business of the New York Giants. "For years, when Tim should have been learning about the football business, he allowed Well to make all the decisions. He did not demand reasons and answers or offer his own ideas. He never negotiated a contract or talked to an agent," wrote Andy Robustelli, All-Pro tackle of the 1950s and 1960s teams and director of operations in later years with the Giants.

Tim was a more complicated individual than Wellington, in that he tended to do things to extremes. When he did work, as when he played an instrumental role in the team's move to New Jersey, he worked hard, and demanded a lot from those who worked around him. But his greater image was that of a playboy. He spent summers in Spring Lake and winters in Florida.

"I don't deny it," Tim said of his playboy lifestyle. "I like to play hard, but I figure if you work hard, you are entitled to play hard. I like to travel. I don't think I have to be here 12 hours every day. But I know what's happening all the time."

On the other side of the spectrum was Jack's daughter, Maura. She had graduated from Elizabeth Seton School in Yonkers and had attended Rosemont College.

She was an avid Giants fan: "As a child I sat in one of the field boxes that were set up directly behind the Giants' bench in the Polo Grounds. One could actually reach out and touch the players." Whenever old Doc Sweeney would have to stitch up a slashed Giant or tape a sprained ankle or knee, "Grandma would make me cover my ears."

Jack would take T.J. and Maura with him on some away games. "When the Giants took the trains to games in Philadelphia and Washington, I had meals with the players in the dining car. The thrill...remains with me still," she said years later.

"I remember training camps...and one plane ride to Cleveland when the team charter lost an engine. Bobby Gaiters, a diminutive running back, came rushing through the cabin shouting, 'Captain says some of you big guys will have to jump.'"

In 1962 Maura was with the promotion and publicity department of the Society for the Propagation of the Faith. In September 1963 the engagement of Maura Barclay Mara to Richard J. Concannon was announced in *The New York Times*. Richard hailed from Massapequa Park, Long Island. He had attended St. John's College and, like Jack, had passed the New York bar exam. Unlike Jack, he actually practiced law as a working lawyer, with Kelley, Drye, Newhall, Maginnes & Warren in New York, having graduated from St. John's Law School in 1958. Concannon was a steady, purposeful young man. He specialized in litigation and health care. He became a member of the New York State Task Force on Life and the Law at its formation in 1984. He was also a legal consultant to the archdiocese of New York and a member of the Cardinal's Committee of the Laity. He published and spoke extensively on legal issues related to medical ethics. He steadily advanced at his practice, making partner, and to this day is still with what is now known as Kelley, Drye & Warren in New York City. Some of his clients have included New York Medical College, Continental Illinois National Bank & Trust Company of Chicago, Brooklyn Doctors Hospital, and New York Hospital. He was also a trustee of Marymount Manhattan College of New York City between 1975 and 1984.

"Of course, there is a less serious side to my addiction to the Giants," Maura once said. "One Monday morning after an especially grueling loss to the Redskins under Coach George Allen, I checked into the hospital for minor surgery. When it was time to leave, the young resident who discharged me announced, "Mrs. Concannon, if I knew you better, I'd tell you what you said about George Allen while you were under anesthesia.'"

On July 23, 1963, Lizette Barclay Mara died in Spring Lake, New Jersey, at her summer residence. She was 75 years old. Lizette had remained very active in the Roman Catholic church charities up until her death. She had been the director of the McMahon Memorial Temporary Shelter and the Lady of Charity of the Catholic Charities Volunteer Bureau.

Jack and Wellington were very much shaken by her death, as they had been when their father died. Luckily, they had each other to lean on. By that time Well's family had swelled to 10 children.

HALL OF FAME

On September 7, 1963, the sparkling and modern 19,000-square-foot, two-building Pro Football Hall of Fame in Canton, Ohio, was officially opened. The facility would hold busts of famous contributors to the game. Among the inaugural class in 1963 were Sammy Baugh, Bert Bell, Joe Carr, Dutch Clark, Red Grange, George Halas, Mel Hein, Pete Henry, Cal Hubbard, Don Hutson, Curly Lambeau, George Preston Marshall, Blood McNally, Bronko Nagurski, Ernie Nevers, and Jim Thorpe. And Timothy J. Mara.

Wellington and Jack attended the festivities. Jack received a copy of McNally's new book on football. McNally signed it, "Johnny Blood, John V. McNally, Best regards from us both!"

Jack was there to accept the induction on behalf of his father. Tim's presenter was Arthur Daley of *The New York Times*. Daley said:

> Tim Mara provided the great stage pro football had to have: New York City. Tim used to say the New York Giants were founded by a combination of brute strength and ignorance. In his whimsical way he added that the players provided brute strength and he himself had supplied the ignorance. The smiling Irishman was half right: the players did supply the brute strength, but Tim was smart, shrewd, courageous, and unswerving in the pursuit of his objective. Others had attempted to sell the game to the big city but they had been gypsy-like. In 1925, when Timothy James Mara established the Giants, he had to build more than a team he had to create fans. He set high standards, he insisted upon a major-league operation, full-time coaches and players, high-caliber competition. He realized the league needed New York as much as the city needed the league, time and again he pulled them together. He left a many-towered self monument, a football manned metropolis, a prospering league, and most of all the greatest dynasty in all sport—the New York Giants.

Then Jack took the stand:

> Thank you, Arthur. Distinguished guests, ladies, and gentlemen. This Sunday the New York Football Giants, and Mara family, start their 39th year in the National Football League, and during this time

> we've had our share of victories and defeats, our high
> spots and our low spots, but I don't think that any-
> thing can compare to the honor and the thrill that I
> feel now to accept this for my father. Thank you.

Jack was overwhelmed by his emotions. He cut his speech short. "Just think,"" Jack said, standing in front of a bust of his father at the Hall of Fame. "My son and all of Well's kids will be able to come out here and know their grandfather was so famous. I hope they'll remember me with the same respect. I never felt myself equal to Dad."

THE TICKET TO SUCCESS

Despite the emotional ups and downs of the previous few years, the 1963 season got off to an incredible start. The Giants were sold out. For the first game of the 1963 season, Harry Bachrach guessed he might have been able to sell around 90,000 tickets if the stadium had been big enough. Some in the organization thought it could have been much more.

Even Joan Sherman, Allie's wife, and Ann Mara confirmed for the newspapers that friends had been calling for weeks, but that no tickets had been available since the end of the previous season.

"We're going nuts turning away orders," said a spokesman for McBride's, a ticket agency. What were people doing? They were going to Connecticut. The antenna in Hartford made it possible for people to watch the games on television there.

"These Giants games out of Hartford are the greatest thing to this region's motel business," said A.O. Samuels, president of the New Englander Motor Hotels in Danbury, Westport, and Greenwich. The article also cited the Stratford Motor Inn, where 3,000 fans had congregated to see the championship game on televi- sion. Stratford had several groups that had reserved rooms for all seven Giants home games.

The Giants tripped to a 3–2 record before exploding for eight wins in their next nine games and taking the Eastern Conference. Tittle had a tremendous year. He threw 36 touchdown passes— even more than he had in his previous two years—had a 60.2

percent completion average, and won the NFL Player of the Year Award again. Gifford and Shofner also had incredible years, and the defense performed stoutly.

On November 22, 1963, President John Fitzgerald Kennedy was assassinated in Dallas. Rozelle decided to play the NFL games as scheduled. The AFL cancelled its slate of games. Rozelle admitted afterward that it had been a mistake. Giants fans wrote in to the local papers, mostly outraged by the NFL's decision.

"One woman caller who said she had been going to Giants games regularly for 30 years said: 'I certainly won't go to this game. Neither will my husband. And I will not sell or give away my seats so someone else can use them.'" And another Giants box holder said, "Tell Rozelle and Mara we couldn't care less about tomorrow's game. It's deplorable it's being played."

Wellington was against it. Being a company man, he would not balk in public, but he admitted years later that he and Cleveland Browns' owner Art Modell strenuously objected to playing the games. According to Mara, Modell had urged Rozelle not to play the weekend games.

Wellington recalled defensive lineman Robustelli asking him, "Why are we playing these games?" Mara could only shrug.

Writer Stanley Cohen attended that weekend's Giants versus St. Louis Cardinals battle, for first place at Yankee Stadium. He recalled singing the national anthem, "singing full out for the first time perhaps since grade school assembly.... We sang it that way until the end, and then, in place of the customary applause that signaled the start of the game, there was only silence."

As MacCambridge noted, Norman Mailer attended the game with George Plimpton, "the two writers sitting silently for much of the contest, feeling the natural sadness." Over the coming weeks the game regained some of its luster, and while some anger lingered, the season resumed its brilliance for the Giants.

The Giants' traditional foe, the Cleveland Browns, had finished one game out of the money. The Giants went 11–3–0 and Cleveland went 10–4–0. This set up a classic duel between the Giants and the Monsters of the Midway—the Chicago Bears—who finished 11–1–2.

The game was played on December 29, 1963, in front of 45,801 of the Chicago faithful. It was eight degrees outside when the two teams took the field at Wrigley Field.

Gifford took in a 14-yard touchdown pass from Tittle in the first quarter, and then Chicago answered with a two-yard touchdown run themselves. Then the Giants put up a 13-yard field goal to take a 10-7 lead into halftime. In the third quarter a Tittle screen pass was intercepted and run back to the New York 14-yard line. Three plays later Chicago plunged across the goal line again. Tittle passed valiantly, attempting to bring New York back. Chicago's defense was aggressive, forcing Tittle's third and fourth interceptions of the day and sealing Chicago's hard-fought 14–10 victory. However, a devastating tackle by Larry Morris left Tittle with an injured knee. But Tittle would not be denied. Battered, he put forth a heroic effort.

Though they did not know it then, Jack and Well were at the end of one of the best dynasties in professional football. From 1954 to 1964 the Giants had been perennial contenders, and often flashed incredible brilliance.

A BROTHER RETURNS

Steve Owen returned to coaching in 1955, working at Baylor, and then as a line coach with the Philadelphia Eagles. His last job had been with the Syracuse Storers of the United League. It was the hardest farewell the Mara family had ever experienced. Owen always remained bitter. For nearly 10 years he refused to talk to either brother.

Author Fredrick Exley wrote a fascinating work of autobiographical fiction titled *A Fan's Notes*. The book's quasifictional hero was a Giants fan. In the book he ruminated on Owen's fate. "It was Owen who over the years kept bringing me back to life's hard fact of famelessness," wrote Exley. "I heard of Owen from time to time, that he was coaching somewhere in Canada—perhaps at Winnipeg or Saskatchewan. Wherever, it must have seemed to him the sunless, the glacial side of the moon. Owen unquestionably came to see the irony of his fate."

In 1963 Jack found out Owen was in financial straights and called the old coach. Would he want a job with the Giants? In December

1963 the Maras convinced Owen to return to the Giants as a team scout. Jack advanced Owen some money. Owen died on May 17, 1964, at the age of 66, before he could once again serve the Giants. It had personally pained Jack that Owen had been away so long.

"I was glad Steve was back where he belonged before the end. He was never meant to leave the Giants," Jack confided to Daley.

THE CRASH OF 1964

On a calm day in early 1964 Jack Mara stormed into team publicist Don Smith's office and said gruffly, "They've gone too far."

"What is it?" asked Smith.

"They've traded Huff!" replied Jack.

During the off-season, Sherman and Well had traded away Huff and Dick Modzelewski.

"On paper it's a good trade," Jack said. "But have you thought about the reaction of the fans? This might be one to forget about. We might just want to let Sam retire."

"Jack was right, but I didn't see it," Sherman said later. "I know now I made a mistake."

They were looking for ways to get younger, but the two new players, both cheaper, also proved completely inferior to their older, stouter departed counterparts. Rosey Grier had also already been traded, in another effort to get younger. And on top of that, Tittle finally showed his age, as did Gifford, Webster, Shofner, and Robustelli.

The team was a straight-out disaster. In one season they had gone from perennial powerhouse to patsy. They finished dead last in the Eastern Conference with a record of 2–10–2. In the first game of the season they were absolutely decimated by Philadelphia, 38–7. It didn't get much better than that the rest of the year.

They had traded away talent that was still worth something. Huff, a crowd favorite, in a denounced move, went to play for four more productive years for the hated Washington Redskins. Grier went on to star in another great defensive line, the famed Fearsome Foursome of the Los Angeles Rams, which featured Merlin Olsen, Grier, Deacon Jones, and Lamar Lundy.

In 1976 famed sportswriter Gerald Eskanazi asked Wellington if he agreed with the deals that broke up those championship teams.

"Obviously I did, because I could have stopped any one of those deals. But I didn't sense the era was ending." [Unfortunately, the nucleus of the team's stars was aging, and trades brought in no noteworthy talent. Some of the stars were lost to retirement, and others were given away in bad trades.]

The Giants were broken, and further events were about to throw them, and Wellington, into a tailspin.

NOW CRACKS A NOBLE HEART

If the 1964 season was not enough of a sign of the change in fortunes of the Maras's football team, January 22, 1965, certainly was a quick preview of two ships that were about to pass in the night.

Jack and Wellington held a press conference at Mamma Leone's restaurant to announce the retirement of Tittle. "This is the moment I have dreaded," Tittle said. "I don't want to come back and be a mediocre football player again. I was one last fall." He also made a crack about knowing he was too old when one of his younger teammates asked him if he could date Tittle's daughter. The gathered press laughed...and then they raced out of there.

Only a few hours later, the Jets also hosted a press conference. Theirs was at Toots Shor's, and they were announcing the signing of that son of Pennsylvania, by way of Alabama, Joe Namath, who had just signed a record $400,000 contract. This was a small, but significant, moment between the two franchises. One was about to head into what sportswriters and fans would eventually call "the Wilderness Years," while the other team, and their flamboyant quarterback, were headed for immortal glory.

Regardless of this event, WNEW radio expressed interest in airing Giants games for the upcoming season. Tim Mara recalled his father saying, "We are going over there and we're going to tell them the price is $50,000." Tim said that Jack was shocked when he got it. It was the most lucrative radio deal in the NFL.

Around April 1965, Jack's doctors discovered a tumor. It was colon cancer. One of the first people he told was his close friend Daley, the sportswriter from the *Times*. Helen and Jack showed up at the Daley's' doorstep for a planned luncheon. The two men watched a baseball game and shared a few beers. During the meal, Jack announced he was undergoing an operation to see if doctors could arrest the cancer's advance.

"I've straightened out my financial affairs, and I am at peace with my God," Jack told them. "There's nothing else I can do but resign myself to whatever God wishes."

"His religion was his strength. He was a good man, kind, generous, and thoughtful," wrote Daley months later. "He had all the virtues. On top of that he had a glowing personality, a quick smile, and a ready quip that drew people to him, high and low. Everyone liked Jack Mara."

During the course of May and June, as spring was turning into summer, Jack underwent treatments. It was no good. The cancer had spread like wildfire.

In late June, Vince and Marie Lombardi were at their son's wedding rehearsal dinner, in Minot, North Dakota, when news hit them that Jack was in fact dying of his cancer. Time was short. Marie was dabbing her eyes all night. When asked why, she said she was crying for Jack.

Jack Mara died at Memorial Hospital in New York City on June 29, 1965. He was 57 years old. He had been the president of the Football Giants for 31 years.

The Giants were having a rookie camp when news hit that Jack had died. Emlen Tunnell, now a coach, sat on the steps at Fordham University, buried his head in his knees, and started to cry. A priest walked by.

"Would it be all right, Father," he said, "if I went in the chapel and lit a candle for Jack Mara?"

One obituary opined, "Mr. Mara gave away a lot of bonuses to people whose time with the Giants had passed, former players, coaches, and sportswriters." A team official who refused to be named said, "Nobody can ever know how many people Jack helped out."

"[Frank Gifford] had just arrived in Hawaii on a long-delayed vacation that he really looked forward to, Wellington said "when he got there he heard Jack had died. When he heard that, he got on the next plane back to New York. He said, 'If it weren't for Jack

Mara, I would never have gotten to New York. I would never have gotten to Hawaii in the first place.' There's really nothing he would ask me to do that I wouldn't do."

"Like his father Tim before him, Jack represented the fine family tradition and spirit that carried the league through it difficult, formative years," said Rozelle. "I feel a deep personal loss, but all of sports has lost one whose extremely high principles and ethics gave it immeasurable dignity."

New York City Mayor Robert Wagner sent the family a telegram calling Jack a "leading figure in the sports life of our city and our nation."

Jack's funeral was held at the family's church, St. Ignatius Loyola Roman Catholic Church, on Park Avenue and Eighty-fourth Street. The mass was celebrated by Father Ben, as well as Archbishop Fulton J. Sheen of New York and the Most Reverend James J. Hogan, of Trenton, New Jersey.

"The pews were filled with the famous at Jack's funeral," wrote Dave Klein. Rozelle, Halas, Modell, and executives from every other team came from across the country to pay their respects. Gifford, Rote, Strong, and Webster were among the many players present. Mayor Wagner also attended. So did more than 500 other people. The church was packed, with more mourners outside. As one article pointed out, a throng of everyday people who piled into the back of the church and spilled out onto the sidewalk. The Giants faithful had shown up for their fallen prince. They had come to share in a celebration of the man who guided their Sundays after the churches had let out. It did not have the curiosity seekers that make so many celebrity funerals a fiasco. Instead it was a solemn event. It was a good-bye to a very popular and successful man who was respected by many. It was laying to rest a prince of the city.

"As I left his room in Memorial Hospital for the last time," wrote Daley later, "I kept thinking of the farewell that Horatio uttered at the death of his cherished friend, Hamlet, 'Now cracks a noble heart. Goodnight, sweet prince, and flights of angels sing thee to thy rest!'"

175

PART II

1965–2005

CHAPTER 8

The Wilderness Years

ALONE

A small article appeared in the newspapers a few days later, announcing that Wellington Mara was now the president of the New York Football Giants. Timothy J. Mara, Jack's son, was named vice president and treasurer. Raymond J. Walsh, the former GM, was named secretary. No new GM was named. It felt most unnatural to Wellington. He was in a fog. He was 49 years old, and he was alone.

In the last seven years he had lost his father, his mother, and his brother. While he still had Ann and the kids at home, at the office he was truly alone. The Giants had been a family business by his own admission.

"The family atmosphere just worked out naturally," Wellington once said. "We were a real family organization. There was my father, Jack, and myself. And that was like Howell, Landry, and Lombardi. I used to handle the personnel, and Jack handled the business side."

"Jack was always the boss," he had once said.

Now, the laughter and humor that were supplied by Tim and Jack, their quick quips, their howling laughter, the Irish brogue, the funny jokes, were nothing more than memories. Wellington, who used humor more like a weapon than as a leveler, could not maintain their boisterous men's club atmosphere.

In running a family business, for better or worse, there is a layer of management and above that is the family. The family could have conspiratorial conversations, discussing this employee or that. They could discuss business practices and decisions, as they all shared the same sense of values. They had the same goals—keep it profitable and keep it going. Who could Well confide in now? Who were his conspiratorial cohorts now?

What was Wellington to do? With all due respect, he was not prepared to be the president. He had very much stayed away from the running of the business. The facts and figures could be overwhelming. And they would be. These were never his strong suits anyway. While he was consulted on and informed of Tim and Jack's decisions, he trusted their counsel and felt relieved not to have to deal with that portion of the business.

On the other hand, he generally ran the show on talent and had done extremely well at it up until now. No single person between the late 1930s and the early 1960s could boast any larger number of superstars than he had either drafted, discovered, or resurrected. But his father and brother, who could speak up without fear of retribution or reprisal when his choices became too wild, were now gone. They were his conservative safeguard against hubris. Now what?

On many levels, from 1965 to 1983, these were in fact "the Wilderness Years," as many sportswriters and fans have called them. But there is a deeper meaning one can glean from this very apropos moniker, for they applied to the business of the Giants and to Wellington himself

Wellington was easily overwhelmed by trying to take up his personnel responsibilities as well as responsibilities that were formerly his brother's. As the Giants grew in the 1950s and early 1960s, the value had easily increased. At the time of Jack's death, the franchise was estimated to be worth $10 million. The budgets were significantly different from what they were when the family had just started out. Stadium fees, ticketing, stadium concessions, apparel fees, taxes, payrolls, television and radio deals, program costs, and the list of needs and responsibilities from his brother's side were numerous. In the past these were neither his cares nor his worries.

Added to this were the many important issues the league was facing as a whole which included a challenge to football supremacy from a crosstown rival league franchise. As an elder statesman at this point in his still-young career, Wellington was asked to join and head committees that were crucial to the league's survival. This put further strain on his abilities to meet his now doubled responsibilities.

And to whom could he turn? Who could he trust to run the monetary side of his business? Who could he turn control of the business over to? He could not bring in a complete outsider. And he did not choose to turn to his nephew.

Scouting was another problem. While he had been the franchise's secret weapon for many years, other teams were developing complex scouting systems, attempting to find new ways to scout and recruit players. With new teams and new methods, the playing field was becoming more competitive. The Giants on the field had always been innovators; from Owen to Landry and Lombardi, the Giants had succeeded by out-thinking the problem—or outworking it. The irony was that, as innovative as the organization had been, their scouting was not nearly as good now as it was then.

And to some extent, the Giants had gotten lucky. And any truly successful organization does have its run-ins with that shady lady who comes and goes without anyone knowing her movements. The Giants had pulled more than a few rabbits out of the hat. And as all cycles go, especially sports franchise cycles, the Giants were certainly due for a downturn in luck, the kind any sports organization eventually experiences. But between mediocre scouting, wasted draft choices that went bust, and trades that went sour, the Giants were about to spiral completely out of control.

The other thing that many players and coaches accused Wellington of later was hiring only company men. He had a vision of the Giants as the IBM of the football world. But in truth, many thought he was letting his personal beliefs interfere with his hirings and firings. If you weren't a "Mara man," meaning you weren't conservative in your viewpoints and your politics, then you were not welcomed by Well himself. This was never confirmed by Wellington, but some of his personnel moves seemed to confirm a pattern, especially in the early years after Jack's death. Is it any coincidence these were also during the most rebellious years of the 20th century? The Giants, under general manager George Young, would eventually develop a test given to players to make sure they had personal discipline and some sense of emotional and mental maturity. A few gifted or highly touted players were allowed through that did not reach these watermarks. It must be pointed out that New York especially was a playground that catered to wealthy young men with newfound fame. The Giants worked hard to find those players they thought would not fall into the trap of being more interested in the distractions than the business at hand.

Divided responsibilities led to a lack of focus. It was hard enough running the personnel side of a flagship franchise. It was a full-time job. So was running the fiscal side of such an endeavor. Wellington was dividing his focus. He was only spending half the time he had before on personnel because he was being drawn away by the fiscal duties. He was performing the fiscal duties only half as well as Jack, and he was devoting less time to them than Jack had.

This was now a multimillion-dollar franchise, and it had outgrown any models he had personally experienced to cope with the demands of such a huge enterprise. This is where Wellington's personality flaws—and there were plenty—truly kicked in.

The model the new breed of NFL owners used was to hire professional accountants and money managers to run teams, as well as a whole series of professional football executives. Rozelle had been the prototype professional football executive, running the business of a multimillionaire.

Wellington could not bring himself to do this. To him, it seems, the new breed of owners appeared gauche. Maybe he was still numb after the loss of his brother. What is clear is that he failed, when the opportunity confronted him, to change with gusto and adapt, using successful business models available to him from the sports world or from the world of business. He had been a personnel guy his whole life—he was not an entrepreneur. He was not a businessman, like his father and brother. In all fairness to him, this was how he was raised, and this was how he coped.

Other drains on Wellington, whether he admitted it or not, were his wife, Ann, and their growing children. This is not a cheap shot against Ann, who proved to be a willing and game tycoon's wife in public and who was always ready with a smile and a can-do attitude. However, one has to consider that at 49 years of age, maybe Wellington would have liked to spend more time with his wife and children. He was at the time in his life when many men slow down, and especially successful ones like to take advantage of their success. Travel. Buy themselves expensive toys. Diversion at that stage of life is not unusual or undeserved. Also, one must assume by the number of children (11 in total) and lifestyle they led that Wellington and Ann were happily married, or at least very compatible.

Wellington faced a crossroads in 1965, but he tried to confront it by himself. He threw himself into his work, pacing the quieter offices that he and his family had shared. Depression and confusion must have taken a grip on him. Like a man who stands on a beach and tries to stop a wave from hitting the shore, Mara was overwhelmed, and either couldn't or wouldn't admit it. He refused to accept the new ideas that were infiltrating the upperechelon of high-end, professional sports management, afraid he might give up the familial atmosphere (which would also come under fire later on) he and his father and brother had worked so hard to create.

The fans would remain loyal throughout these years. Some critics would grumble that the Maras were just counting the money in this era. By 1965, despite their grotesque showing in 1964, the Giants were nearly sold out. And in the coming years the fans kept buying tickets, hoping their team might resurrect itself. In those years, the Giants were certainly bringing in lots of money. And in the coming years, Wellington would help the franchise make even more. So it was not out of fiduciary trouble that the Giants were lacking, unlike some other struggling clubs in the NFL.

In 1976 Gerald Eskenazi, of *The New York Times* interviewed Mara for a book he was doing about the "Old Giants" of the "glory years." Wellington made an interesting admission that spoke volumes. "You know, when Jack died," Well said. "Well, we haven't done much since. I really think the problem was that it took me too long to realize I couldn't do both jobs."

"People said we were cheap and didn't care if we won, because all our games were sold out," Mara told *The New York Times* in 2001, recalling the 1970s. "That got under my skin. We weren't cheap. We were just stupid. We made a lot of poor personnel decisions on the football field. That's why we lost."

It would take the 10 years before Well would come to that admission, and another 10 years to bring the team back from the doldrums.

AFL MERGER TALKS

By Thanksgiving of 1965 the NFL and AFL were on a collision course. Both leagues were competing for top-flight rookies. Now AFL team owners were starting to feel the pain. The defending AFL champion San Diego Chargers were not making money. Rookies were getting contracts for well above $100,000. It got so crazy, AFL and NFL teams were fighting among their own league's teams, scrapping for players. And there didn't seem to be any end in sight.

In the beginning many of the owners wanted to do to the AFL what they had done to other up-start leagues—crush them. But unlike other up-starts the AFL was made up of generally wily or well-financed owners who understood the business and who could see the cash at the end of the rainbow if they could keep their expenses in line. And the AFL had a television contract every bit as lucrative as the NFL's.

Back-channel negotiations had been going on since as early as 1959. Lamar Hunt and Halas seemed to get along, and they talked on many occasions. By 1965 there had been intense negotiations between NFL team owner Carroll Rosenbloom (of the Rams) and AFL team owner Ralph Wilson (of the Bills). Eventually Rosenbloom, Schramm, and Modell met with Wilson. The NFL had made it clear that it would not accept all the teams, that some of the teams would have to move to different cities, and that there would be a one-time fee paid by the AFL to the NFL if a merger was to occur.

"My original plan was to get Oakland out of Oakland and the New York Jets out of New York," Tex Schramm said. But by 1966 these scenarios seemed unabtainable. The Raiders and Jets had been successful, and their AFL brethren stood beside them.

Schramm talked to Rozelle and felt he could strike the deal. Rozelle said he would have to get the blessing of the Giants and the 49ers before he could go ahead. Schramm called Wellington first.

Neither Louis Spadia, the 49ers general manager (who represented the colorful Morabito sisters), nor Mara received this news warmly, but they said they would keep an open mind in the interest of the league. Eventually Schramm and Hunt negotiated on May 3, 1966. The deal was put forth—$18 million as a fee, with $2 million going to each NFL team. It seemed like things were moving forward.

But a wrench was thrown into the works by Wellington. At Winged Foot Country Club, Well was lunching with Fred Corcoran, agent of Buffalo placekicker Pete Gogolak. Corcoran was a Winged Foot member, and happened to tell Wellington that Gogolak was available. Gogolak had been the Bills' second-leading scorer, but his contract had expired, and Wellington wanted him. Corcoran spat out the price—$96,000. Mara said Okay. Gogolak became the highest-paid kicker in NFL history. The only problem with this was that there had been a gentleman's understanding that the two league's would not try to steal each other's star veterans. Wellington's signing was a declaration of war against the AFL and those who would make friends with them.

The Giants had not yet released this bombshell by the time the next owners meeting took place in Washington, D.C., on May 16. Rozelle started off the meeting by making an announcement about Well's signing. Rozelle announced it with some amount of relish. Those who had been secretly negotiating were furious.

"This is a disgrace!" Lombardi lashed out at Rozelle and Mara. He was fuming. "Wellington, I can't believe that you would do something like this, to put us all in jeopardy!"

"Goddammit!" roared Rosenbloom. Schramm was also furious. So was Ralph Wilson when he found out a day or two later. But Al Davis, Oakland Raiders owner and AFL commissioner, was thrilled. The AFL would return the favor in a matter of days, offering contracts to a dozen stars in the NFL. Wellington had precipitated a war.

But he also got his hand in the merger negotiations. A small panel consisting of Schramm, Lombardi, Rosenbloom, Bidwill, and Mara was put together. Spadia was furious. The league, including his friend Lombardi, was stabbing him in the back.

Mara put his arm around his friend, Spadia, and said, "It was bad enough when the enemy was shooting at us. Now we've got our friends shooting at us too."

In actuality, all the teams but those in New York and San Francisco wanted the merger. But none of those NFL teams begrudged Spadia and Mara their anger and suspicion, particularly the Giants, who had bled so much money and fended off so many attacks over the years. Rozelle did not want the merger. He was eventually strong-armed into it, although he would come out on top as the commissioner of the newly merged league.

Wellington had been shrewd in this deal. He admitted later that he knew what he was doing and had already considered the outcome. He would play hardball, and when he asked his price, they would pay. It was a forgone conclusion that he could not get the newly popular Jets out of town, especially when his recent teams had been mediocre. "If I try to get the Jets to move," he told his fellow owners at the time, "I'd be crucified." And he was right.

Rozelle had to fly out and meet with Josephine and Jane Morabito. The ladies were mad, and they were known to be tough negotiators. Wellington had gotten $10 million. They wanted $10 million too. Rozelle said he could not get that money, so the ladies pressed for advantages. They would be able to continue their rivalry with the Rams, despite the Raiders. They would get first dibs on home dates, and the Raiders would have to play away games those weeks.

The NFL owners capitulated. They would divide the AFL's fee money between the two clubs. Spadia would get $8 million and Mara would get a one-time fee of $10 million. The payout would be stretched over 20 years. Per the agreement, over the 20 years each AFL club would pay $2 million.

Mara held firm. He wanted something else. He wanted the first draft pick in the next draft, no exceptions. The NFL owners threw that in, too.

Wellington found out years later that Sonny Werblin, the owner of the New York Jets, had told Hunt that he would have moved the team if that had been a stipulation of the league merger. But it was supposed to be the last thing to be thrown on the table—the trump card. The AFL never had to use it. Wellington hadn't pressed hard enough.

BROADWAY JOE

"Joe was the colorful rogue," wrote Clyde Bolton of the *Birmingham News* about Namath. "But Tucker was the All-American boy you wanted your daughter to marry." Tucker was Tucker Frederickson. Frederickson and Namath were linked by fate. Namath had beaten Frederickson when the two were in college. Namath won their showdown with his team, the University of Alabama, beating

Auburn 21–14. Despite Tucker's heroic 117 yards on 22 carries, Namath recovered from a mediocre first half and threw the game-winning touchdown.

Namath and Frederickson were both available in the 1965 NFL and AFL drafts. Mara was interested in Namath, but the rumor going around the league was that the Oilers would take him. Mara was intrigued by Namath, but he did not want to get into a bidding war for the young quarterback's services. He could not hope to compete and he didn't want to throw away a pick. According to author Jeff Miller, Wellington said, "They were giving people oil wells and gas stations at the time." After the Gogolak signing, this seemed slightly insincere. Maybe it was sour grapes. Also, Frederickson was a better fit with the Troy Donahue "golden boy" image that New York had cultivated with such glamorous players as Gifford and Rote. Frederickson seemed like the natural choice, according to Namath biographer Mark Kriegel. The assumption seems right on.

The fact was, they concentrated on Frederickson and had him signed up before the draft went down. The draft was chock-a-block with future stars and Hall of Famers, including Dick Butkus and Gale Sayers (both taken by Chicago), and Fred Biletnikoff (Oakland).

The Oilers had traded their pick to the New York Jets. Sonny Werblin liked Namath very much, and he did not stop until Namath was signed.

The Jets were originally christened the New York Titans, which was supposed to be a play on the Giants, name. No one went to see their games at the old Polo Grounds, despite surprisingly even performances. The team was founded by Harry Wismer, who eventually had to be bailed out by Werblin and Leon Hess, an oil tycoon, who renamed the team the New York Jets and moved them to the newly opened Shea Stadium.

Namath came to be known as Broadway Joe and Joe Willie. He was tall, lean, and handsome. He was a ladies' man who wore fur coats on the city streets and on the sidelines. He was an instant attraction in New York. And his passing skills and teammates helped to bring New York some excellent records.

In 1966 the Jets finished 6–6–2, and in 1967 they finished 8–5–1—both respectable records that outshone the Giants, records of the same period. In 1968 they went 11–3–0 and won Super Bowl III. In 1969 they fell short of defending their title, but finished 10–4–0.

Regardless, Namath was the 1970s and Mickey Mantle all rolled into one. He was always seen out about town, and was often seen hawking something on television. He was tall, dark, and handsome and women loved him. The feeling was mutual.

The fact of the matter was, the Giants were only mediocre during this same period. This made life difficult for Wellington. While he was drafting, hiring, and firing, this renegade group was winning a Super Bowl and had Giants fans frothing.

Jets fans could taunt with Namath, Matt Snell, and George Sauer as their current stars. And the Giants fans could say they *used* to have Conerly, Tittle, Gifford, and Huff, but those guys couldn't win football games any longer. Wellington was losing the publicity war, and he knew it.

AH, WILDERNESS

In an effort to show there would be continuity, and that the Giants were sure of the future, Wellington tore up Sherman's contract again and inked him to a 10-year commitment.

"The most important thing that we could do was to get the best leadership possible on the field," Mara told the press. "That's why we have given Al a new contract." It would be a day Well would rue for the rest of his career.

"I gave Allie a long contract because I felt the most important part of the operation was the head coach," Wellington told Eskanazi years later. "I felt he was the best man available and I had secured that end of the business for 10 years. I gave him a contract from 1965 to 1974."

Sherman's 1965 team gave a lot of false hope to the fans. The team finished 7–7–0, tied with the Dallas Cowboys for second place in the Eastern Conference. The savior was Earl Morrall, a quarterback who had come to the Giants from the Detroit Lions. Morrall threw 22 touchdowns that season, and great hopes were raised for the 1966 season. Tucker Frederickson carried most of the load on the ground, and the defense showed up just enough to make them solid.

However the 1966 season proved to be one of the absolutely lowest points in the history of the team, when they finished with a disgraceful 1–12–1 record. Frederickson was out all year with an injury and Morrall was sidelined for half the season with injuries as well.

In 1967 Wellington traded for one of the most exciting quarterbacks in the league: Fran Tarkenton. Tarkenton's unorthodox style of scrambling and throwing made him difficult to defend against, and sometimes hard to play with. But in Homer Jones, a speedy end, Tarkenton found a new mate to play pass-and-catch with and the two developed into a dangerous combo.

Jim Finks and Bud Grant of the Minnesota Vikings had traded Tarkenton, a six-year veteran quaterback, to the Giants for a first- and second-round choice in 1967, a first-round choice in '68 and a second-round choice in '69. (Incidentally, Minnesota used the Giants' picks thusly: Clinton Jones and Bob Grim in '67, Ron Yary in '68, and Ed White in '69.)

Wellington called it "our most expensive trade."

Tarkenton, in his first Minnesota game ever, came off the bench as a rookie and fired four touchdown passes and ran for a fifth in a big upset of the Chicago Bears. However his style was so unorthodox that Coach Norm Van Brocklin was sometimes critical of his biggest star. Still, the game was such a huge deal that writers in New York wrote about it for months.

The Giants now had a star quarterback who could be compared to Namath. However, as Larry Fox of the *New York Daily News* pointed out, "Unlike bachelor Joe, Tarkenton is married to his college sweetheart and has a two-year-old daughter—and has two good knees."

"A scrambler out of the University of Georgia," wrote Fox, "Tarkenton shocked the Giants' brass by showing up at their offices wearing an olive gold sports jacket, paisley tie, television blue shirt with a monogrammed cuff, and tremendous green cuff links."

Tarkenton had a mixed relationship with the Giants. In the end, he was one of the new breed of NFL players, and wasn't really all that far off from Namath. His style was unorthodox. He wore colorful clothing. He played to his own tune. And ultimately this bothered Mara and frustrated the Giants coaches.

In 1967 author Elliot Asinof was given unprecedented access to write about one week in the life of a football team. Wellington had been incredibly reluctant, but in the end he, gave his consent.

After a 34–7 shellacking in Chicago, Sherman greeted his staff the next morning.

"'Well, you've had all night, damn it. You guys better have some ideas ready,' Sherman came on like gangbusters in obvious mockery of his own bitterness," wrote Asinof.

"The question is: Do you think they're putting out? Are they trying? Are they trying?" asked Sherman of his coaching staff. On his staff then were Tunnell, Roosevelt Brown, Alex Webster, and others. The problem was emblematic of these years. Each coach tried to speak up about their unit's successes, but no one could put a finger on it but Sherman himself.

Webster criticized Frederickson. Tunnell defended him. And then another coach defended him, reminding Sherman that they'd gotten a lot out of the banged-up former superstar.

"I wish this club had a real tough leader," said Sherman. "An angry physical man. We used to have them on each unit. Guys who were drivers. Guys who demanded that everyone put out. And if they found one of them dogging it, they would take him outside and really punish him. They did it to each other all week long. No slacking permitted, damn it. Then, at 1:35 PM Sunday they'd be blood brothers out there."

That was no longer the case. Still, the Tarkenton and Jones touchdown duo helped the Giants climb back to mediocrity at 7–7–0. Tarkenton threw 29 touchdowns that year. Lombardi's Packers won the championship, beating Landry's Cowboys.

Lombardi's Packers went on to the first ever AFL-NFL World Championship Game, which later came to be known as the Super Bowl. On January 15, 1967, at the Los Angeles Memorial Coliseum, the National Football League champion Green Bay Packers defeated the American Football League champion Kansas City Chiefs, 35–10. Before the game, Wellington, who'd flown a whole group of New York reporters to the super event, slipped Lombardi a note that read, "This is a war, and we cannot think of anyone better equipped to carry our standard into battle than you."

In 1968 the Dallas Cowboys went 12–2–0, and the Giants finished second with 7–7–0. Tarkenton and Jones were still an effective combo, but the backs were slow, and the defense was still a hodge-podge. Meanwhile Lombardi and Landry were squaring off against each other in the NFL championship game, which the Packers won 21–17. After that, the Packers went on to take the second Super Bowl 33–14 against the Oakland Raiders.

On a less-public stage, Wellington continued to be true to himself. In 1968 Fred Bessette of Clifton Park, New York, wrote to Wellington. He and his wife had been on the waiting list for season tickets for almost a decade and still were no closer to getting two season tickets. Wellington wrote back saying there was nothing he could do this year, but Bessette should write again the following year. Bessette did, and eight days later two season tickets arrived by mail—Section 127, Row 1, seats 1 and 2.

"He was a wonderful man. I'm one of the many people he touched," Bessette told the press many years later.

GOOD-BYE, ALLIE

"Good-bye, Allie! Good-bye, Allie!" The chant became common during the 1968 season.

"Good-bye, Allie, good-bye, Allie," the fans sang to the tune of "Good Night, Ladies." "We hate to see you go."

The Giants had not really won between 1964 and 1968. Sherman's record in his later five years was a woeful 24–43–3. In his first three years he had 33 victories. There was no doubt Sherman could coach, but maybe he had been there too long. Maybe the talent wasn't as good. But there was no discussing it. The fans had had enough and they wanted a change.

When Sherman had the talent, he had produced, but the first-round draft picks weren't working out. The Giants also hadn't discovered any diamonds in the rough. However they did have stars such as Tarkenton and Homer Jones, who racked up 1,000 yards for three straight seasons. But in 1967 and 1968 the teams had achieved nothing better than 7–7.

Sherman hosted an "Ask Allie" call-in radio show on WNEW. Things got so bad in 1966 that *The New York Times* ran an article "titled, "Answer-Man Sherman Suffers Giants' Critics Gladly on Radio."

Dave Anderson of *The New York Times* wrote at the end of the 1966 season, "While the players unpeeled dirt-smudged tape as if they could not get it off fast enough, Wellington Mara...talked yesterday about the front office's game plan for 1967, as if it could not arrive fast enough."

The Giants had the second pick, and were looking at Steve Spurrier from the University of Florida and Bob Griese of Purdue. Well said that he was sending Sherman to scout both players immediately. Instead, Wellington and Sherman traded for what they thought was a sure thing—Tarkenton.

At the end of the 1966 season, during a horrific loss to Landry's Dallas Cowboys, the first of many signs for Mara and Sherman appeared in an article titled, "Next Year is Today" reading:

> Good-bye Allie
> We Love Ya'
> But
> Sorry 'Bout That.

In 1966 Wellington stuck by his coach, saying his feelings toward Sherman "were the same as before the season started." But the shine on Sherman was wearing off fast. Many felt he should never have gotten the 10-year contract. The pressure was on.

With the 1968 club putting up a second 7–7–0 record, Sherman was on his last legs. "Allie believed the team was never going to be good enough to win the whole championship. He said we'd never be better than second best. I think he felt that maybe they were jaded or had gone as far as they could go," Wellington said later.

During the last several home games at the stadium, banners and chants grew more and more omnipresent. Enormous banners read "Good-bye Allie!" and the growing chant became even louder.

In the summer of 1969 former Dallas Cowboys receiver Pete Gent came to New York after he had been waived by Landry.

Gifford got Gent a tryout with the Giants. The Giants were eager to see the old—but renowned—receiver. His visit was brief. "He saw Coach Allie Sherman as incompetent, hated Fran Tarkenton, whom he called 'one of the worst people in the world I ever met,' and after he called Giants owner Wellington Mara 'crazy,' his football career came to a sudden end," wrote sportswriter Golenbock.

In 1969 the Giants agreed to a preseason exhibition game in New Haven, Connecticut, against the New York Jets. For Wellington, the game was personal. All the games were personal for Well, but he especially wanted the Giants to beat the AFL, Jets. The defending Super Bowl champion Jets blew the Giants out, winning 37–14 in front of 75,000, most of whom were Giants fans.

"Well Mara reacted as though someone close to him had died," wrote Dave Klein. According to Klein, Mara missed a whole week of training camp, for the first and only time since the war, because he needed time to think. For Wellington to lose to the up-start AFL darlings, the Jets, was a personal insult.

Wellington allegedly called it "the most humiliating day of my life."

The Giants lost all four preseason games. "I really didn't decide until the night of the Montreal game," said Wellington. He was sitting in the stands in Montreal with Art Rooney, who asked Wellington what was wrong, and Well confided for the first time what his feelings were about the Giants coach. After the final loss of the preseason, Wellington flew home with the team. "I couldn't sleep. Allie was my friend, just as Steve Owen had been my father's friend. But I really couldn't see any other choice. There was no way out."

The next morning, Well asked Sherman to stop by his house before going to work. Sherman suspected what was coming. Wellington gave him the bad news. "I feel like I should fire myself, too," Well said to Sherman. "I haven't been any help to you these last years. Maybe the day will come soon when we can both sit in the stands on Sundays and watch the team play."

Sherman was angry because Wellington would certainly not fire himself. But the job had grown too big. "Once Jack died and the NFL got so big and complicated, it became clear Well couldn't handle it all by himself. He knew it too, but Well is the kind of man who moves slowly, who takes a long time to make up his mind," Sherman said. Sherman admitted that Wellington had never forced any trades or draft picks on him. Still, "I never thought he would do what he did," said Sherman.

"Either Al was going to have a nervous breakdown or I was," Mara said later.

"Sure he got screwed," an unidentified head coach told Klein. "If they tried to give me the kind of garbage they gave him and passed off as professional football players, I'd have quit. But he couldn't quit. His ego insisted that he could make winners out of garbage."

"Wellington Mara yielded to intense pressure from the fans," wrote Daley. "He did it with considerable reluctance because he knew Allie had one of the brightest minds in the football industry. But the respect that little Allie had once elicited from the hulking brutes under his command had slipped away as the losing record sent team morale spinning downhill with it."

"I expect Allie and I will be two of the highest-paid spectators in Yankee Stadium," Wellington joked about the situation with the press. Wellington agreed to eat Sherman's contract for the remaining years, as long as he did not work for another NFL team or any other football franchise. He never did, and collected every paycheck due him until the contract was paid out. He and Wellington would remain on speaking terms and stayed friends until Wellington's death.

THE NEW NFL: AFC VERSUS NFC

The 1969 owners meetings had a huge black cloud hovering overhead. And that cloud took the form of a question: who was going to move over to the newly formed AFC? No franchise wanted to do it, but it had generally been understood and agreed that for the good of the NFL as a whole, some of the old franchises had to move over to add legitimacy and stability.

"It would emasculate the NFL if the Browns were to leave," Modell said. Rozelle told the owners they would be there until three teams were chosen in order to make two 13-team conferences.

"Oh, hell, we're going to be here forever," grumbled Rosenbloom. However, the deadlock was broken when Modell, who had been diagnosed with a bleeding ulcer prior to the meeting, was taken to the hospital. Later that night, Art and Dan Rooney and Wellington visited him there.

In his hospital bed, Modell announced he would move to the AFC "if my friend Art Rooney will come with me, and if I can have the blessing of my dear friend Well."

"Now wait just a minute..." started Dan.

"Now Danny," said Art. "Not so fast."

"Dan, don't become agitated. Just wait and see where this goes," Wellington quietly told the younger Rooney. The older Rooney was instantly drawn to the new AFC Central Division.

"Wellington was a mentor for me and a counsel I could call on. I remember when the Steelers were asked to join the American Football Conference. I was very reluctant to become part of the AFC and was upset at the prospects," Said Dan Rooney, years later.

"It worked out for the best and was very successful for the Steelers. He was there to help and offer advice that could work for the league and anyone who might need assistance. During most of Wellington's years with the team, the New York Giants had great teams and played terrific games, winning championships. The Rooney family has been friends of the Maras for four generations. We've had excellent times together," Art Rooney said.

Thus Cleveland and the Steelers went over to the AFC Central, where they were reunited with famous Browns coach Paul Brown. Ironically, Colts left for the AFC East to be linked in the same division as the New York Jets, who had beaten them in Super Bowl III.

FATHER'S LITTLE DIVIDEND

In April 1971 Wellington was added to the Fordham University Hall of Fame along with Hank Borowy (who pitched in three World Series, including two for the Yankees, and continued his career with the Cubs, the Phillies, the Tigers, and the Pirates); Zev Graham (a former football star with the Akron Bulldogs and a successful metropolitan high school coach); and Ed Kelleher (a former Fordham University basketball coach who had compiled a 211–97 career record and whose teams had only lost nine times between 1924 and 1929). Frankie Frisch, the "'Fordham Flash," was one of the Hall's original inductees, and he attended Wellington's induction dinner.

On June 23, 1971, the newest Mara brought forth by Wellington and Ann was born. She was named Meghan. And upon her birth, President Richard Millhouse Nixon called the Mara house to congratulate Well and Ann on their most recent addition to the household. Only problem was, neither Well nor Ann was home.

Well was at the hospital picking Ann up to bring her and Meghan home. And all the other kids were at day camp, except for Susan, the second oldest. The phone rang in their Rye, New York, home, and 15-year-old Susan answered.

"I thought it was just someone who wanted my father," Susan said. She told the caller he wasn't home, and wouldn't return for at least an hour. She then heard the secretary tell the president that Wellington wasn't home. The secretary told Susan that the president would talk to her instead. Nixon was a famous sports fanatic, especially where football was concerned. Nixon was so obsessed, he once asked infamous control freak and Redskins head coach George Allen to run a play that he, Nixon, had devised himself.

"I thought it was a friend playing a joke," Susan said later. "I had to believe it. It was his voice. I heard it. I was amazed."

Susan talked with the president for almost 10 minutes. The stunned Susan failed to ask Nixon even one question. It seemed Nixon steered the conversation. "I was too excited," she said. He asked her questions about the Giants and about the Mara family. "He told me that my mother should have another baby so we could field our own football team," the excited girl related.

On July 4th weekend, 1971, Wellington, Tim, and Laura dedicated a new charity, founded with the help of the Archdiocese of New York, called the John V. Mara Catholic Youth camp in Putnam Valley, New York. Named for Jack, the camp was opened for boys between the ages of nine and 15. The camp's ideals were to place emphasis on the major organized sports, including football, basketball, baseball, and swimming.

Cardinal Cooke, the archbishop of New York, dedicated and consecrated the grounds in a ceremony. Also in attendance were Ann, Concannon, Tunnell, Carl "Spider" Lockhart, Frederickson, Joe Morrison, and Bob Duhon.

MARANOIA

"The [1971] season was a bummer from every conceivable angle," Tarkenton said later. During that disastrous season, defensive end Freddie Dryer approached Tarkenton.

"Frannie, you're not going to believe what'll be in the newspaper this afternoon," Dryer said. Dryer had gone to Larry Merchant of the *New York Post* and thrown up his guts about the season to the sportswriter. Dryer had coughed up everything to Merchant, relating the disasters, the bungles, and the player distempers. He criticized the coaching and the management.

Merchant published this explosive series under the banner headline: "Maranoia."

In the third installment, Merchant started his diatribe with the following: "The season was not a total disaster for the Giants. Bob Tucker led the league in catches. Wellington Mara led the league in speeches." Merchant referred to an inside view of the "management chaos," and how Mara's speeches were a source of derision among the players. Merchant referred to a recent speech the players had gotten from Mara, which Dryer referred to as, "the usual mumbling, unintelligible garbage." Mara had attempted small, individual conversations with many of his best players. These attempts to draw his young team closer to him only repulsed them more, according to the insider.

Merchant also named a number of players, including Tarkenton, Dryer, Lockhart, and Jim Kanicki, who "want out now." Merchant derided Wellington for attending practices in his sweat suit, running around the team track, watching the team, and for his long-lasting loyalty to the men who surrounded him in the upper echelons of the organization. Merchant noted that "players aren't necessarily the fonts of all wisdom in these matters," and ran a quote from the insider who claimed that the team, for the rest of the decade, would not beat the Cowboys, the Redskins, or the Eagles.

"Poor Wellington Mara. He is a man in future shock. His code of old-fashioned loyalty and Boy Scout morality, however virtuous, is irrelevant in modern football," Merchant opined.

It must be noted that football in general was somewhat under siege during the halcyon days of the counterculture. From the rebellion of the 1960s to the "me" generation (as satirist Tom Wolfe anointed it) of the

1970s, football's militaristic and gladiatorial overtones made it a target of even its own insiders. The ultimate anti establishment icons were Gent, Rick Sortun, and Dave Meggyesy, all of whom played the game and lampooned football's machismo, taking cheap shots at the game's foibles in print. An executive, it seemed, was always fair game, which is always true in sports but even more so in that era. An executive was seen as an extension of the clichéd American power culture. Tarkenton and Dryer were also a part of this group of players who became rebellious. But their intentions, their aims, of being successful professionals cannot be discounted. And both eventually were leaders on Super Bowl teams.

"I happened to have a friend on the staff, a coach, who kept me informed from time to time on what was happening in the bureau-cracy," wrote Tarkenton. "When the series came out, the inside organization thought I was the source, the tipster. ... The consterna-tion inside the Giants organization and the team over the articles and all the losing was now pretty unanimous."

Regardless, Tarkenton's life with the Giants was over and he knew it. Not that Tarkenton's experience with the Giants had ever been good to begin with. Despite some accomplishments on the field, his negotia-tions with Wellington had always been difficult at best.

One year Tarkenton could not come to a satisfactory conclusion in his contract negotiations. And Wellington told him, rather than play a preseason game, maybe Tarkenton should go home. So he did. When Wellington found out, he told the media that Tarkenton had retired.

Then Gifford called Tarkenton. Though Gifford was retired from football, he and Tarkenton were good friends.

"Why doesn't Wellington call me himself?" Tarkenton asked Gifford.

"You know Well; he wouldn't do that," Gifford retorted.

"It was part of the tableau some executives and personnel heads like to arrange in their dealings with their performers. Wellington would call it protocol," Tarkenton wrote later. And when the two finally reached an agreement, the Giants announced that Tarkenton had recapitulated, despite the fact that he had never actually retired. The times had changed, and like many of his generation, he found it difficult dealing with those baby boomers that would not play by the old rules.

After the Maranoia articles appeared, and after the failure of the 1971 season, Tarkenton approached the executives, including Wellington, and told them that he had nothing but respect for them, but "I just don't think you've got the organization here, Wellington. And I don't think you have the players to win." Tarkenton was asking to be traded. And he took a staggering pay cut to leave New York to go back to Minnesota. He was prepared to earn less and win more, rather than be well paid and lose.

"Both of us believed we were being reasonable men, pursuing ends we thought could be equally beneficial to player, team, and management," reasoned Tarkenton.

Bob Tucker took a slightly different viewpoint.

"It was abysmal—the coaches were unprofessional," said Tucker. Eventually he complained loudly enough to be traded—also to the Minnesota Vikings. Wellington had called his friend Jim Finks. While Finks missed some players from his New York years, it "was like I'd died and gone to heaven. I was back in the football business. ... It was thrilling. The Giants had been so bush league." Ironically, Tucker, who was essentially blacklisted by Wellington, keeps a place near Giants Stadium.

Dryer went public a year later, when he was playing for the Rams. Merchant again quoted the ex-Giants player. "It was tough sitting on the bench, especially the way the Giants were going. I thought they were just doing a good patch job. They're living in a dreamland. Wellington Mara would give a dozen little reasons why we weren't winning," Dryer criticized, "and the amazing thing was he really believed it."

MORE DARK YEARS

Well's next choice of personnel was unexpected. He hired "Big Red," Alex Webster, to be the next coach of the team.

"Of all the assistant coaches, Alex has had the least experience. But he could be an inspiring influence on a ballclub whose morale has ebbed," Wellington said. "He loves the game, he loves the team, and his popularity will go a long way toward giving everyone a lift."

But things only got worse. The Giants went 6–8–0 in 1969. The next season showed some promise. The Giants now had a solid running back in Ron Johnson, and the defense was anchored by Dryer and Lockhart. They achieved a record of 9–5–0, and they would have won the division had they defeated the Los Angeles Rams on the season's final Sunday, but they were drubbed 31–3. It would be their best record until 1981. The records for the next three years were 4–10–0 in 1971, 8–6–0 in 1972, and a woeful 2–11–1 in 1973.

By the beginning of the 1972 season, Tarkenton and Dryer were gone. "Once they were the New York Football Giants' most flamboyant players—Fran Tarkenton, the inventive quarterback, and Fred Dryer, half beach boy, half defensive end," wrote Dave Anderson.

"But shortly after the 1971 season they were banished by Wellington Mara, primarily because the Giants owner considered each too individualistic for the Giants' corporate image," wrote Anderson. Dryer went on to fame, along with Merlin Olsen in Los Angeles on the Rams. Tarkenton went on to three Super Bowl appearances. This story was not lost on New York sportswriters.

The Giants had traded away Dryer and Tarkenton and received Norm Snead, Bob Grim, Vin Clements, Eldridge Small, Larry Jacobsen, and Brad Van Pelt. As Anderson wrote, "In the NFL, six sometimes is less than two."

By December 1973, Webster was dispirited. "The Webster rapport with his hired hands diminished, and he even found himself challenging [running back] Charlie Evans to a fistfight," wrote Daley. "Discontent always spreads when a team loses, and Alex found himself unable to motivate his heroes."

Webster was a solid leader, but he was at the mercy of the same bad player personnel decisions that Sherman had been. Webster's tenure included a long list of disasters, punctuated by brilliant games by Tarkenton and others. It was another period of utter futility.

"At midseason I started thinking that I'd need a new coach. I had the feeling twice during the season that Alex didn't have the answers and that he stayed on only because he didn't want to leave me holding the bag," Well said.

"[Webster] dropped a bombshell without warning during a press luncheon," Daley wrote. "He had tipped off Mara the night before in a phone call to Philadelphia, where the Giants boss was attending a gathering of talent scouts…it will be a total housecleaning.… It has to be a complete break with the past." For Daley, a longtime Mara confidant, to write something this strong was an indication of how low the franchise had fallen.

The personnel area was a disaster. And in the press, Wellington started taking the hits for poor moves.

"Mistakes in personnel evaluation and management operation—requisites for success in any competitive business—may be more to blame for the fall of the New York Giants than the inefficiency of coach Alex Webster," opined Neil Amdur in *The New York Times*.

"Unless other sweeping administrative changes are instituted," wrote Amdur, "such as the hiring of a strong general manager with broad powers related to personnel and the college player draft, the Giants could be headed for their own energy crisis in the coming years."

"According to some assistants, Webster continued to contact, confer, and confide in Mara for game decisions on fourth-down gambles and field goals, much to the dismay of colleagues and some players," continued Amdur.

"The man is one of God's greatest people," an assistant told Amdur, "but he doesn't have any idea of what it takes to play winning football today. He just won't let go."

Mara was a jumble of contradictions. He paid huge prices for Tarkenton, Ron Johnson, and Randy Johnson, some of the highest-paid players of the day (some of whom eventually performed back-up rolls), and yet he let them train at the rundown Roosevelt Stadium, or trek to the Yale Bowl for some games, or train in the confines of their Jersey City training facilities.

Amdur also cited the fact that Tim Mara, Jack's son, was riding in an air-conditioned limousine in Los Angeles, California, alongside the unairconditioned Giants bus. "That's good for morale," one coach said. "The Giants are teaching player loyalty, but where is the management loyalty to the players?"

Wellington, by the early 1970s, was already being seen as an anachronism. And the "family" atmosphere the Giants had built for years was now seen as a negative. Where players in the 1940s and 1950s saw playing for the New York management as a positive, by the early 1970s they were called "paternalistic."

Statements from Wellington, such as, "Next to my own family, I care most about the Giants family," were now considered laughable. Players were resentful of this attitude. The paternal feeling the Maras had worn as their badge of honor was now scene as a target in the new counterculture and political times of the 1960s and 1970s.

"Wellington's sense of his role and the franchise was rooted largely in that first season after Fordham that had begun it all," wrote David Harris, author of *The League: The Rise and Decline of the NFL*.

As Ross Wetzsteon wrote in *Sport* magazine, "Wellington's greatest virtue, his loyalty to the Giants family, had turned into his tragic flaw. He inherited a noble tradition and served it well—precisely at the time that that tradition was becoming outdated. He kept players who were no longer producing.... Loyalty had been the key to the Giants, success; it became the crux of their failure."

The Giants were cited as being years behind in scouting and draft day coordination, and they had an inability to find what was necessary to compete in the new market. Essentially, Wellington was running the team in the same way he and his brother had been running it in the 1940s and 1950s. Where he had been an innovator then, he was a dinosaur now.

"I just hope he stays out of it," one NFL coach said. "He's not drafting a Boy Scout troop, but football players. And that's what the Giants need now—players, leaders. Lots of 'em."

"Can the Giants restructure themselves? Or will a new coach and/or general manager simply serve at the whim of Mara, an owner whose sincere pride often conflicts with the pragmatism necessary to survive in pro football.?" asked sportswriter Neil Madur.

To be sure, the Giants had thrown away their draft picks:

1961—No First Round Pick
1963—No First Round Pick
1967—No First Round Pick
1968—No First Round Pick
1973—No First Round Pick
1975—No First Round Pick

These first round picks had been thrown away in trades meant to camouflage problems in the now. They had been wasted. The worst of these was the 1975 draft pick. Because of the horrendous performance of the team in the previous season, the Giants had the first pick in the NFL draft. Wellington traded that pick to Schramm of the Dallas Cowboys for journeyman quarterback Craig Morton.

"Morton's problem with the Giants was that the New York line was a sieve, and so the immobile Morton spent much of his time on his back as the Giants finished at the bottom of the NFL," wrote sportswriter Golenbock. And Dallas? They walked away with Randy White out of the University of Maryland, who went on to become a Super Bowl MVP. This is the kind of short-sightedness that was driving the Giants into the ground. It was pure, out-and-out panic by Wellington and his hand-picked "family."

And what of the players they did get in the first round in those years when they kept their picks? In the 10 picks they did draft, the Giants got one year of All-Pro play from Frederickson before he hurt his knees, they traded away Dryer, and the rest were busts of various kinds:

1962—Jerry Hillebrand, LB, Colorado
1964—Joe Don Looney, RB, Oklahoma
1965—Tucker Frederickson, RB, Auburn
1966—Francis Peay, T, Missouri
1969—Fred Dryer, DE, San Diego State
1970—Jim Files, LB, Oklahoma
1971—Rocky Thompson, RB, West Texas State
1972—Eldridge Small, DB, Texas A&I
1972—Larry Jacobsen, DT, Nebraska
1974—John Hicks, G, Ohio State

As incredibly productive and imaginative as he had been between the late 1930s and 1963 regarding personnel, in a 15-year period Wellington had laid a Giant egg. He had reversed the trends he helped create.

Wellington was fighting the green-eyed monster. As the Jets had prospered, Wellington pressed harder and harder, making as many moves as he could to try to find the quick fixes. He admitted it years later.

"I think the Jets coming in when they did contributed to our bad years, because we tried to do everything for the short term rather than the long haul—we'd trade a draft choice for a player, figuring he'd give us one or two good years. We didn't want to accept how the public might react if we had a bad year or two or three," Well said. Wellington was sure his fans would revolt and go to the Jets.

"In other words, it was a question of misplaced pride. The fans would have stuck with us anyhow. They did stick with us through all the bad years," Well said.

But if fans thought Wellington was merely an owner who had a love for his team, they did not know Wellington. Robustelli wrote that Wellington was obsessed by his team and its performance.

"Losing cut him like a sharp knife, and if Giants fans think that they suffered through the lean years, they have no idea how much Well Mara agonized over his team's failures," wrote Robustelli. "I almost gag when people tell me he cared only about making money, and not winning. Money has always been secondary to winning with him."

Robustelli also described how Wellington had agonized about raising ticket prices during those years. He didn't feel right charging more for teams that were not earning the fan's money. In fact, the Giants made only modest profits during the lean years.

CHAPTER 9

The Struggle

THE RETURN OF ANDY ROBUSTELLI

Wellington wanted to show conviction, and he wanted to show that the Giants were taking bold steps. They wanted to telegraph to the Giants faithful that bold moves would put things under control. Wellington hired a general manager who would hire his own coach, as most NFL teams were now run.

"When he succeeded Jack as president, Wellington thought he could continue to specialize in that area and allow Tim to take over the business side; as club president, Well would continue to oversee as necessary. Those plans fell apart when everyone in the organization turned to Wellington to solve every problem," wrote Andy Robustelli.

Wellington and Jack's son, Tim, were running the organization. They would make the choice together. Jim Finks, a former Canadian League executive who had turned around the Minnesota Vikings, was their first choice, but that did not happen. Andy Robustelli had been chatting with Tim and Richard Concannon, Tim's brother-in-law, discussing the problems of the Giants and the organization.

"Those conversations were casual," said Robustelli.

Robustelli continued to meet with Tim and Concannon. Tim went over and over conversations so as to prepare Robustelli, who would then showcase himself to Concannon. Tim had a little something extra on his side of the ownership role: he spoke for his mother, Helen Mara Nugent, Jack's widow, who had remarried a well-known and tremendously successful stockbroker, Robert Nugent.

205

And Robustelli had to get the approval of Concannon, who was there because of his wife's shares. Helen and Maura both trusted Concannon to counterbalance Tim's mercurial brashness.

On December 17, 1973, Wellington Mara announced Robustelli as the new head of operations for the New York Football Giants. According to Wellington, Robustelli, who was now a Hall of Fame player, had "full authority."

"I wouldn't be here if I didn't have the full authority to get the ballclub where it should be," Robustelli told the press. "Wellington Mara gave me his word I'll have full authority."

Mara stood in the back of the room, watching the festivities as the press peppered Robustelli with question after question. "I won't have any decrease in responsibility," Mara told the press, "but I will have a decrease in duties."

Reporters touched on a tender subject when they asked if Wellington's children would be allowed to wander around as they had in the past.

"I told Well there'd be times I won't want the kids in there, and he told me, 'Whatever you say,'" Robustelli told the group. But the "family" issue overall was a big question.

Wellington's children were a scary subject with the owner. They were scurrying about the place all the time, some players felt, but no one would say anything. A story about a union rep and Mara on the subject of the Giants family was infamously related in *Sports Illustrated*. In 1971 defensive end Bob Lurtsema, who was also a union rep for the players association, was cornered by Wellington. Mara was feeling like he was losing touch with his players. He asked Lurtsema to conduct an informal poll among his teammates regarding his rapport with his players. When the two met a week later, Mara insisted the player hold nothing back.

"He asked for an honest report," the end told *Sports Illustrated*, "and I gave it to him, both barrels."

"Lurtsema was a good defensive lineman and a popular figure in the locker room. Lurtsema tends to be direct," Fran Tarkenton remembered.

"You have no rapport with the players and the Giants family image is not there. There is no question about it," the end told

From left to right: Steve Owen (coach), Jack Mara (president), Tim Mara (founder), and Wellington (secretary) in the late 1930s. Owen was a member of the Mara family inner circle for many years. His firing in the 1950s was an emotional blow to the family as well as to Owen. They reconciled before Owen's death. PHOTO COURTESY OF RICHARD WHITTINGHAM.

From left to right: Wellington, the ubiquitous Father Dudley, Tim Mara, legendary saloon keeper Toots Shor, and Jack Mara. The three Mara men formed a powerful triumvirate, and at their peak they had strong connections to many of the city's social, economic, and political circles. PHOTO COURTESY OF THE PRO FOOTBALL HALL OF FAME.

Jim Lee Howell was Owen's protégé. First a player and then a coach, Howell replaced Owen as the key football man within the Mara inner circle. He was the first modern head coach to divide his staff into offensive and defensive coordinators, and he hired Vince Lombardi, Tom Landry, and Allie Sherman. Like Owen, Howell would be with the organization for decades. PHOTO COURTESY OF AP/WIDE WORLD PHOTOS.

The New York Football Giants participate in a practice in the late 1950s. Offensive coordinator Vince Lombardi, in a dark baseball cap, looks on as Wellington stands toward the back in his trademark baggy gray sweat suit. Unlike other owners, Mara consistently attended practices; he rarely interfered. PHOTO COURTESY OF GETTY IMAGES.

At Yankee Stadium on November 17, 1957, Wellington the innovator was photographed as
he photographed the game. An early owner of the instant camera, Wellington was the first to
use the new technology during competition. He would photograph the opposing defense,
develop the photo, and then put the photo in a sock weighted with a stone. Then he'd heave the
sock directly to the Giants sideline, where Lombardi or another assistant would catch it with
a baseball glove and study the photos, looking for anything that might help them gain an
edge. Wellington was also the first to film football games and practices for coaching purposes.
PHOTO COURTESY OF THE NEW YORK DAILY NEWS.

Wellington Mara and NFL Commissioner Pete Rozelle in San Francisco in January 1981. Wellington spearheaded Rozelle's nomination. Wellington also championed television revenue-sharing and NFL licensing, and he led the fight against the labor union. He spent so much time at the NFL offices that some Giants insiders frowned on Mara's frequent absences.
PHOTO COURTESY OF AP/WIDE WORLD PHOTOS.

Wellington hands the trophy over to Bill Parcells after the Giants defeated the Denver Broncos 39–20 in Super Bowl XXI in Pasadena, California, on January 25, 1987. In the midst of their feud, Wellington and Tim refused to share the victory stand. Despite the rift between the Maras, Parcells remained close with both men through the years.
PHOTO COURTESY OF AP/WIDE WORLD PHOTOS.

George Young, the hardworking general manager, was hired as a result of Tim's pressure to relieve Wellington of his personnel control. Young's arrival brought success and proved to be the turning point in the franchise's fortunes. PHOTO COURTESY OF AP/WIDE WORLD PHOTOS.

Wellington is all smiles after being inducted into the Pro Football Hall of Fame on July 26, 1997. He is part of the only father-and-son team ever to be inducted into the Hall. He was introduced by longtime family friend and confidant Frank Gifford. PHOTO COURTESY OF AP/WIDE WORLD PHOTOS.

Executive Vice President John Mara (left), Wellington's oldest son, stands with his father and new coach Jim Fassel as they watch drills in the practice bubble on January 5, 2001, in East Rutherford. John's ascension could only come about after Tim and Wellington sold their shares. PHOTO COURTESY OF AP/WIDE WORLD PHOTOS.

Ann Mara stands beside her husband on January 14, 2001, at Giants Stadium on the day the Giants beat the Vikings 41–0 in the NFC championship game. PHOTO COURTESY OF GETTY IMAGES.

Surrounded by family, Ann Mara leaves St. Patrick's Cathedral in New York after Wellington's funeral on October 28, 2005. The funeral drew thousands of respectful mourners and a who's who of sports and political figures. PHOTO COURTESY OF AP/WIDE WORLD PHOTOS.

Kate Mara sings the national anthem on October 30, 2005—the first NFL Sunday after her grandfather's burial. Behind her stands the throng of Wellington and Ann's grandchildren. The Giants beat their longtime rival, the Washington Redskins, 36–0 in their late owner's honor. Kate is a successful actress, with substantial television and screen credits to her name, and is one of the many accomplished grandchildren in the Mara clan. PHOTO COURTESY OF AP/WIDE WORLD PHOTOS.

Mara. Mara sat back, asked a few more questions, and then thanked the player.

"At least you gave me an honest answer," said Well.

Lurtsema was cut from the roster only hours later. Wellington swore he knew nothing of the plans to cut him, but that seems highly unlikely, and many local reporters at the time agreed.

"You're damned right I am bitter," Lurtsema said later. "I hope someday I can come back and haunt them, after playing five years and just getting dumped," he told the press. In fact, Lurtsema went on to play with Tarkenton for the Vikings for five seasons (appearing in Super Bowls VIII and IX) and played with the Seattle Seahawks for two more, retiring in 1977.

Dave Anderson pointed out that "the selection of Robustelli...was in keeping with the Mara tradition of hiring within the 'family.'"

Robustelli earned some points with Wellington when he told the press that the Giants would not be permitting long hair on the team. "I'll be struggling like hell to get some of it cut," Robustelli said.

But as an old friend told *Sport* magazine, "Wellington believed that the extended family system could still work in the modern era, and without his father or Jack around to fall back on, he brought in Andy not so much as a general manager as a kind of surrogate older brother."

One general manager of another NFL franchise said, "Football had changed dramatically in the years since Robustelli had played. He tried to build the kind of team he remembered from the glory days, the days when the defense would come off the field and tell the offense, 'Just hold 'em til, we get back.' Instead of turning the franchise around, he set it back another five to 10 years."

Another unidentified general manager said, "Football was moving from the patriarchal era of the Halases and Rooneys and Maras into a highly sophisticated sport, and the Giants were remaining a family operation."

"In retrospect I didn't really know or realize how far behind we were as an organization," Robustelli wrote years later. "We needed to overhaul the entire organization. But I realized it had to be done within the framework of its president, who wanted to be loyal and faithful to certain people, as well as a vice president who had similar loyalties. Clean house? No way!"

THE WAR YEARS: TIM AND WELL, 1969–1977

"[Tim and Dick] were seeking someone to do their bidding and make their half of the ownership more dominant," wrote Robustelli in his autobiography in the 1980s. "I began to see some of the things that took place to push Well aside. By taking the job as director of operations, I felt I could equalize the involvement of everyone—Tim, Well, and myself—in our respective areas, helping to strike a good balance." As Robustelli pointed out, Tim, "would do almost anything to get Well out of the decision-making process.

"This Machiavellian atmosphere smothered us throughout most of my tenure as director of operations, seriously impeding the team's resurgence. Tim's side of the ownership thought first about how it could control every move, rather than how the moves could help the team."

The pull on Wellington continued. He was doing slightly less on operations and finance, but he was doing league work now, too. "I was doing a lot of league work on the labor committee, and we had a conference call one day to pick a new chairman for the committee," Wellington stated. "I was still signing players back then, and partway through the meeting I had to get off the phone to finalize a contract. I got back on an hour later and asked everybody how we were doing."

"Fine; you're the new chairman," said one of the other owners.

At one league meeting, Al Davis, "Carroll's boy," raked Wellington over the coals as not being part of the modern day owners' cabal. Robustelli asked Wellington when he would consider putting the Maras' interests ahead of the league's.

"That's the way I am. I still have a feeling for the league, and the league needs us to try to convert those people to seeing we're all in this together and that the future of the game is in our hands," Well said.

Robustelli disagreed. He asked Well when he would start to play the game by the same rules as many other owners did. "You're not going to convert them," Robustelli said.

"I think what I am doing is correct."

At the time, his fellow owners and executives had mixed reviews of Wellington.

"He's from the old school..."

"A stubborn Irishman with good instincts..."

"He's a staunch league man..."

"He gets on his high horse and preaches sometimes. He's also a little goofy..."

"Something of a wimp..."

Yet among NFL owners, his franchise was among the most envied. One must assume that some of the unattributed quotes may have been sour grapes. One of the things they most envied was his new stadium—not so much the building, as the deal that he and Tim had negotiated. In the war years of the New York Giants, it was the last of two or three things he and Tim would ever flat-out agree on.

The feud was beginning—a blood feud between Tim and Wellington. By 1975 Tim was 39 years old. He would only get angrier each year as his uncle's outdated ways continued to drag the franchise down.

"I really don't remember when the team went bad so quickly. I guess it was tough to replace all those old stars. Wasn't it about that time that Dick Lynch's ankle went bad?" said Tim sarcastically.

In fact, years later, Tim realized he hadn't spoken to his uncle since the two argued in a parking lot over the distribution of the family's comp tickets while the two were attempting to leave for an away game.

According to more unnamed sources, Wellington as team president was performing the day-to-day duties of the president's office. According to Robustelli, who obviously must be counted as a Wellington friend, Tim and his side "did little to alleviate" any organizational problems. "Tim and his group allowed Wellington to make all of the decisions and do all of the work and then blamed him when they went wrong."

Tim wanted to try new ways and his uncle did not. But it was apparent, even to Wellington, that his way was not working. As sportswriter Ross Wetzsteon wrote, "Here [Wellington] was getting it from all sides about remaining a mom-and-pop organization in the age of the supermarket, and now his own family was suddenly joining the chorus."

"Temperament, lifestyle, and values all contribute to their feud, but it goes deeper than that," said an unidentified friend. "It's in their blood."

Mostly at issue was Tim's lifestyle. While he remained largely out of public view when it came to managing the Giants, that was about the quietest part of his life. Mostly, Tim was well known in every hot spot on the Upper East Side of New York, one of its most affluent areas. The clubs were filled with women who came from wealthy families and who went to Smith, Vassar, and a number of well-known women's colleges. Tim also hung out at well-known bars where sportswriters like Mike Lupica and numerous sports world hangers-on hung out.

Tim was loud. He would tell anybody who cared to listen that he owned half of the NFL Giants. Some thought him a charming rogue. Others looked on him as the family's black sheep.

"Of course, from Wellington's perspective," wrote Wetzsteon, "anyone with a credit card was living in the fast lane."

"I think Wellington wears a tie with his pajamas," one family friend said. "And as for Tim, when it comes to wine, women, and song, his only failure is that he can't hold a tune."

"Wellington was prepared to make changes," a friend told Wetzsteon. "He isn't a stubborn man, he knew what had to be done. But the fact that it was Tim got his back up. He resisted not because he thought Tim's ideas were wrong, but simply because they were Tim's."

"It's too bad we had to go through it, but I am happy with the results. ... It just proved what I said was right," Tim said later. "We had to get someone in here who knew what he was doing. ... It's just too bad some people had to be offended by what happened. "There has to be a system that you adhere to; that's why I fought so hard for what I believed in back in 1979. I just thought things had passed us by. ... It took a little while. ... We had to decide on resolutions by which we would run the team. The results have made up for any of the early problems we might have had in getting things started," Time continued.

It seems Tim's instincts were right, but few wanted him to actually run the team—especially Wellington. And what frustrated Tim further was that he had to placate his mother, sister, and brother-in-law, while Wellington only had to answer to himself.

"I thought we spent too much money and were just not getting any results," Tim said. "We always went out and got something, but it was always something stupid. We brought in Larry Csonka and all those guys from the WFL. I can't even remember their names. They didn't help much."

Tim's disloyalty was the most unforgivable slight in his uncle's eyes. Wellington had literally sat on the sidelines for years while his father and brother ran the team. With his sense of patriarchy, Wellington must have seen Tim's abuses as nothing less than treason against the king. No matter the amount of ignominy he would have to suffer, Well would fight Tim with his every last breath, and Tim would return the favor.

Much like Lyndon Baines Johnson and Robert F. Kennedy, Well and Tim were just two dogs that did not like each other. They didn't seem to need a reason to fight. But for many years they simply refused to talk or in many cases even acknowledge one another.

FRANK GIFFORD GOES TO CANTON

In January 1977 the Pro Football Hall of Fame announced that year's inductees. Among the honorees were Forrest Gregg, Gale Sayers, Bart Starr, Bill Willis, and Frank Gifford. A player must wait five years after retirement before they become eligible for induction, and Gifford had waited six years beyond that.

He had made seven pro-bowl appearances at three different positions: playing defensive back, halfback, and flanker. And he had been Player of the Year in 1956, the year the Giants won the championship.

"I was certainly aware that [election] might not happen. Players are so much better today. Each year they are better than before, and as you move down the line, you know there are others who will be seriously considered," Gifford said.

Of all the people possible, Gifford chose Wellington to introduce him at the induction ceremony. Well spoke eloquently of his former star player and friend.

"For me, for 25 years Frank Gifford has personified the son every father dreams of, the player every coach dreams of, the father a son would cherish. I like the man," Wellington told the crowd. "In speaking of Frank Gifford in any of these facets of his life, it's necessary to speak in terms of humility, versatility, and excellence."

Wellington then went on to recall the Chuck Bednarik hit without using the Eagles standout's name. He referred to Gifford, supine on the field of Yankee Stadium. "You thought he might die, you knew he would never play again, but he didn't die, and he played again, and how he played." Wellington then praised him again: "Frank has a very special place in the minds and the hearts of the Giants and the Mara family. When he announced his retirement in March 1965, my brother Jack, who was then president of the Giants, said Frank was one of the greatest players who ever played for the Giants."

In fact, Jack had quipped at the time, "The Giants loss is CBS's gain." Wellington recalled how Gifford had switched planes in Hawaii to return for Jack's funeral, quoting Gifford when he said, "If it hadn't been for Jack Mara, I would have never gotten to Hawaii in the first place."

Wellington finished, saying, "Frank, as you join this distinguished company, I am sure that your place will be where it has always been—in the forefront. Because as Jack Mara said, even among stars, you are a standout."

Gifford started off his acceptance speech thanking people from early in his life. When it came to football, the first person he remembered was Lombardi.

"I had a lot of great coaches, one man in particular. Marie Lombardi is sharing these steps today.... Vince...meant a great deal to my life, in fact turned my football life around for me, and it was one of the great privileges any player could have to play and know and perhaps even more than to play for him to know a man of Vince Lombardi's caliber."

Frank went on to thank his wife and kids and some others. And then he came to the Maras. "Anyone who knows me personally knows the depth of feeling not in terms of gratitude but the deep feeling that I have for the entire Mara family. Wellington's father signed me to my first contract, or at least advised Wellington, I am told. I was very close to Well's brother, Jack, as I am with the entire family and Jack's son, T.J., who is here with us today. They have my undying gratitude and, of course, my undying love."

MEADOWLANDS MOVE

The Giants were the forerunners of the league in developing super stadiums and super stadium packages. The turn from gypsy franchise to sports complex was a fascinating game the Maras played out with Mayor John Lindsay and former AFL enemy Sonny Werblin.

Werblin had been forced out of the New York Jets. But he reemerged a few years later promoting a plan to put in a state-of-the-art sports complex in the swamps of New Jersey, directly across from the Lincoln Tunnel. Werblin's visionary complex needed a home team to anchor the 76,000-seat stadium. The Giants were the first team he approached. Werblin and Well were now friendly, and Wellington told Werblin that he was "receptive to a possible move." Giants Stadium would be a key component of the proposed Meadowlands Sports Complex.

"We're interested, but not committed," Wellington told the press in early May 1971 about moving to New Jersey.

"It's a thorny thing," said Mike Burke, who represented the Yankees, "and I am not pretending that it isn't, especially when the city has a dire need of funds in so many areas. It may sound self-serving, but someone must declare his faith in the future of the city."

The Maras were negotiating with the city and Lindsay and at the same time with Werblin. The state of New Jersey would pay for the stadium through a bond issue act. The new stadium complex would feature "theater-style seats, two instant replay boards, a two-story press box, and 72 luxury boxes." The Giants would pay for and own the suites, which they in turn could rent out to the top 100 corporations in New York and New Jersey.

Sports Illustrated also pointed out that the Giants would "get free office space, free watchmen, free maintenance staff, free cops, free scoreboard crew, free insurance, free water, free heating, free electricity, free sewage and waste disposal, and free transportation for all fans who have to park more than a quarter of a mile away. The Giants pay only for the PA announcer and their phone calls. The Giants also get 25 percent of parking fees, 400 free parking spaces, 50 percent of concessions, all advertising in program and souvenir books...all memberships in the stadium club, all radio and TV revenue, and up to 2,700 free tickets per game."

By September 1971, the Maras had played off the city against New Jersey and come up with one of the biggest sweetheart deals any sports organization ever got. Wellington and Tim signed for a lease on a new stadium.

"The football Giants bought their bus ticket to Jersey yesterday," wrote Larry Fox in the *New York Daily News*.

"We're moving, but we're not leaving. ... Each stadium was the most famous of its era, but every family dreams of the day when it can move into its own home and go away from its in-laws, no matter how great the in-laws have been to live with...and our relations with the Yankees have been great," Wellington told the press. "If you have a seat at Yankee Stadium, you will have a better one in Giants Stadium, and 10,000 to 15,000 of you who don't have seats in Yankee Stadium will have one in Giants Stadium."

"The Giants have sold every available seat for the last 15 years," commentator Howard Cosell bellowed in a vicious tirade against Rozelle and the Giants.

They were called "the Hackensack Giants" by an offended *Newsweek* magazine.

And another David Harris cited the *New York Post* as having asked: "What else can you expect from the son of a bookmaker...an Irishman named Wellington?"

Wellington, tremendously wounded, retorted to the *Post*, "I'll tell you what you can expect. You can expect that anything he says or writes may be repeated, aloud, in your own home, in front of your children. You can believe he was taught to love and respect all mankind—but to fear no man. And you can believe that his two abiding ambitions are that he pass on to his family the true richness of the inheritance he received from his father the bookmaker—the knowledge and love and fear of God—and, second, that the Giants win the Super Bowl."

"The new Giants Stadium will be 6.9 miles from Times Square," Rozelle had to testify in Washington about the proposed move. "Yankee Stadium is 6.6 miles. The same fans will have tickets. Some will have a somewhat longer bus ride, but others will have a shorter ride."

According to Harris, the city fought what he called a "rear guard action" against the New Jersey sports complex. This was especially devious, and showed what the term "playing with the big boys" really meant.

"New York bankers were told quietly that if they bought bonds, they would no longer receive any city or state business. Sonny Werblin had to overcome strong opposition. Fortunately, the banks and businesses of New Jersey stepped in," Harris wrote.

By November 1973 Governor William T. Cahill was gone and a new governor, Brendan T. Byrne, told Mara and the press that he might have to renegotiate the stadium agreement. Mara said the East Rutherford stadium was "by far the best deal I've heard of, and we are still enthusiastic about moving there." While the Giants approved 12 extensions because of delays in financing and approval in New Jersey, they were committed by that point. However, Mara pointed out to the press that Yankee Stadium still wanted them back, and any further delays might prove to be the tipping point. Byrne eventually made it happen.

Since the bond issue was completely subscribed, "no public money was spent," Mara said later, "and the investment made out like gangbusters."

Mara's pitting of two entities, two cities, against each other became the textbook blueprint for other sports owners, both in the NFL and in other sports.

Unlike with the Dodgers and baseball Giants in the 1950s, who moved for sweetheart deals to another part of the country, the Giants had moved only a couple of miles, but had taken advantage of the geographics advantages and didn't have to give up their fan base. The important thing to understand was that moving teams became an opportunity for sports franchises to cash in on new stadiums and whatever benefits they could collect as well. It had been done before, but never so successfully as in the 1970s. The state of New Jersey realized the incredible monetary draw the franchise would be to the state, and Mara's move presaged a whole new era of movement—something, ironically, he would be against.

To be sure, Mara was part of a push in that period. This was an initiative that Rozelle had instigated, pressing to get new, sparkling homes for his franchises, including Detroit, Buffalo, New Orleans, and New York. Not to mention Dallas, New England, and Kansas City.

Also, like it or not, the Giants had always been second-class citizens, both at the Polo Grounds and at Yankee Stadium. The baseball teams always got first privileges, and sometimes made life for their football brethren difficult, not allowing preseason games at

Yankee Stadium or insisting on away games early in the season, etc. The Giants would now have a new home—a football stadium— where they would be the primary team. And if other events would be hosted there, they would be scheduled around the Giants.

The Giants were summarily evicted. The city insisted that construction would have to begin on October 1, 1973, in order for the stadium to open up newly renovated for the 1976 season. Dave Anderson of *The New York Times* quoted an unnamed, highly placed city official as saying, "We're not going to do the Giants any favors. We're going to throw them out as soon as the Yankees' season ends."

Indeed, the NFL released its season schedule without indicating the place for the Giants home dates. Rozelle stepped in and lifted the television blackout on the condition that the Yale Bowl Corporation agreed. Rozelle had helped his friend. The blackout was lifted for all teams by 1973.

While Wellington fought the war in the press, Tim spent most of his energies planning, along with the Sports Authority, one of the most advanced stadium complexes in the NFL. He was a major force in the move. Tim knew everyone at the Sports Authority, and could make things happen there. It was his rebirth in the organization. His many late nights there, his heroic effort to get the stadium ready for the first big game, would only make him more anxious in the coming years.

Still, there were other concerns. The move proved to be very costly in the short term. On September 23, 1973, the Giants played their last game at Yankee Stadium. Numerous delays occurred at the new sports complex, and so at the start of the 1974 season the complex was not yet ready. In 1974 the Giants played at the Yale Bowl, in New Haven, and in 1975 they found themselves playing at Shea Stadium, before Giants Stadium was finally available in 1976. This era of movement and chaos led Red Smith to call them the "New York–New Haven–Long Island–New Jersey Giants."

According to Richard Whittingham, a Giants historian, "They were the most highly visible orphans in the NFL, and it apparently had a deleterious effect on the players."

And the records reflected that. In 1974, under new coach Bill Arnsparger (who had helped build a dynasty in Miami), with Craig

Morton at the controls, the Giants went 2–12–0, and in 1975 they went 5–9–0.

THE NFL VERSUS THE PLAYERS UNION

In 1971 Edward R. Garvey was made the executive director of the National Football League Player's Association (NFLPA). Born in Burlington, Wisconsin, he graduated from the University of Wisconsin. He then spent two years in the U.S. Army and later returned to his old college to earn a law degree. After graduating, he took a spot in the Minneapolis law firm of Lindquist and Vennum, whose largest client was the National Football League's players' union, for which he became counsel. Garvey would go on to serve as executive director until 1983. And he would lead two players' strikes (1974 and 1982), poking holes through Rozelle's league, often citing antitrust legislation.

John Mackey, the former head of the players union, had been a tight end on Rosenbloom's Baltimore Colts. Mackey hired Garvey. In 1971 Garvey met with the owners to discuss free agency, which was something the owners had been fighting over. This was supposed to be "an olive branch discussion," according to Rozelle.

"He was a bright young man," Wellington said afterward, "and he was extremely conciliatory."

Appearances were deceiving. The day after the olive branch discussions, the NFLPA filed *Mackey v. NFL* in Minneapolis Federal District Court. In 1974 the NFL appointed Wellington chairman of the NFL's management council. Garvey looked on Mara as a symbol of everything that was wrong with the current NFL. He was old guard. And the NFL sent Wellington into battle knowing exactly what message they were sending. There was no mistaking what each side was saying to the other. For all the negatives Wellington may have carried, in these tough negotiations he was the man who was sent to deliver the blow. It was also a thankless job, and whoever took the spot would get smeared by the talented Garvey. Mara was up for it.

On March 16, 1974, NFLPA President Bill Curry opened with statements Wellington found "encouraging," but after Ed Garvey read a two-page prepared statement, Mara was appalled. Garvey wanted to basically emasculate the office of the NFL commissioner, and brought up a host of other issues. Wellington responded, "Individually and collectively, these demands reflect only one thesis —that the experience of generations is worthless, that a structure that has evolved through the years should be torn down and replaced by nothing. You have given us a list for the nongoverning of professional football. They are accompanied by monetary demands which, although still far from complete, we estimate would cost the clubs $100,000,000 more this year. We do not say that our system is the only system. ... We do not even say that it is necessarily the best system for maintaining the high popularity of professional football. What we do say is that it is a system that has worked. ... With all the conviction at my command, I urge you to reexamine your values."

By April 4, 1974, the management council had a formal response to the union's proposals, arguing against "a demolition of the structure which has taken the National Football League more than 50 years to build, with no organization proposed to take its place. That's not freedom; rather, it is freedom to do as you please. ... We draw the line at a system with no rules, and we cannot be asked to bid against ourselves in altering a structure with which we have no major complaint."

There is no mistaking Wellington's voice in this response. To him, Garvey's outrageous proposals must have seemed like the worst kind of heresy, and was a complete antithesis of Mara's personal beliefs. Wellington believed in the past because he was one of the architects of the very rules he was defending. Wellington would make this a game fight.

The NFLPA threatened a strike. San Diego Chargers owner Gene Klein and Wellington were the two most stalwart owners. "I never really believed it would happen. The relationship between an owner and a player should be a lot different than the usual employer/employee relationship. Their demands were so outrageous I could only respond with disbelief and indignation," Wellington said.

On July 11 Mara called his players together during training camp. He addressed them with a very serious tenor in his voice. He told the team that if a strike was called, he would play the season with rookies and retired players. "We must operate," Well said.

By the rules of the National Labor Relations Act, the NFLPA was granted controlled access to NFL training camps. Mara insisted he have his own representatives attend any recruiting sessions, etc. "That's my football team," Mara told the press. "You wouldn't walk out of your store and leave the cash register unattended."

Harris of the *Times,* described Mara's stance as 'the strongest and most definitive' of any owner in the league." The players did go out on strike during training camp in 1974.

The trial began on February 3, 1975. The trial was before a single judge, not a jury. There were two lawyers for the NFLPA and there were nine for the NFL. The trial would take 55 days of actual court time, and there would be 63 witnesses who would give 12,000 pages of testimony. It would take up a huge amount of time. Testimony and rebuttals continued on until July 19, the last day of the trial.

A decision had not yet been handed down by the time the 1975 season started up, and negotiations between the NFLPA and the NFL had reached a stalemate. By December 28 the owners had a meeting wherein Rosenbloom attacked Rozelle, something many of the other owners were weary of. All of them were really worried about *Mackey v. NFL,* not Rosenbloom's vituperative, flailing attack on the relatively popular Rozelle. After growing tired of this useless show trial by Rosenbloom, Wellington jumped up and suggested the crowd break for lunch. Wellington said he just "wanted to break the spell."

After lunch, Mara was still "looking for something to break the mood." Well had found what he thought was a humorous cartoon. It was something Wellington had found on one of the labor lawyers' office walls. It "depicted a cowboy, having been tossed over a cliff by his horse, holding onto a flimsy bush over the lip of the precipice. Above him, another cowboy was assessing the situation. 'Hang on, old boy!' he shouted."

Mara passed the cartoon to Halas first, and then it got passed around from owner to owner.

"Everyone laughed," Wellington said. "I broke the ice."

What happened next Wellington called a "catastrophe." The judge had found in favor of the NFLPA. The NFL immediately appealed.

The appeals decision came down on October 18, 1976. Wellington was at the NFL management's council's offices in Manhattan when the news was announced.

"It was another loss," Mara said.

"This is not just a victory, but a great victory," said Ted Kheel, one of the labor lawyers.

"Everyone laughed at him and called him captain of the *Titanic*," Mara remembered, "but I soon saw his point. Garvey analyzed the appeals court decision and saw that he should start consolidating his gains."

Garvey had fought on two principles: antilabor laws and antitrust laws. The court said that the union would not be able to find its answers in a ruling; instead it would need to use collective bargaining, according to the law. A negotiating committee between the NFL's attorneys and Garvey commenced.

Garvey had made enough progress that the NFL knew it needed to find some leeway. In January and February 1977 the two sides continued to negotiate. On February 16, 1977, an accord was reached. Wellington was replaced by the NFL owners of the management council in June 1977.

Wellington had served a purpose for the owners, but he had also dedicated a lot of time to the cause. He had fought the good fight, but he wasn't paying attention to the Giants' business—not as much as he needed to. Maybe he would have said that the league's needs came before those of the Giants', but by this time Giants fans were growing increasingly angry.

Regardless, he was subsequently placed on the arbitration committee with Gene Upshaw. And when the first case came up on a salary dispute, the group found unanimously in favor of the player.

In 1975 the *New York Daily News* ran an article by Norm Miller titled, "How Long Can Giants Fans Wait for Revival?" In it he wrote, "How long is Wellington Mara willing to wait? ... It is nearly two years since Mara phased himself out of the direct operation of the Giants...if there's been any progress, it's been hard to discern."

In December the *News* ran a photo of bundled up fans watching a Giants game in the snow, with a banner under them that read in bold letters, "IMPEACH MARA."

MIRACLE OF THE MEADOWLANDS

The new Giants Stadium hosted its first game on October 11, 1976. It was a beautiful October day, with 76,000 Giants fans screaming for victory. The Giants had a decent defense, headed by stalwart defensive linemen John Mendenhall and George Martin and linebackers Brad Van Pelt and Harry Carson. It was the year of the bicentennial, and the Giants were in the 52nd year of their existence. And for the first time in those 52 years, the Giants would host their first home game in their own stadium.

The offense starred retread Larry Csonka, newly returned from the World Football League. When the Giants took Csonka, they technically did not owe anything to the Dolphins, whom he had left to join the now-defunct renegade league. Well, who had a reputation for doing the right thing, insisted that the Giants relinquish two third-round draft choices.

In an effort to make sure the contractors would be given enough time to prepare the stadium for the big opening home game, the Giants, first four games were scheduled on the road. Coming into the game the 0–4 Giants faced the 4–0, Landry-led Dallas Cowboys.

This was the opening sentence in Norm Miller's coverage the next day: "A large banner held aloft by a fan immediately after the Cowboys had driven 65 yards to their first touchdown with the game seven minutes old told the story of the Giants' housewarming flop yesterday: 'Brand-New Stadium, Same Old Giants.'"

"The fans were ready to play today," said Coach Arnsparger sarcastically after the game. That it was Landry's Cowboys added all the more to the sting of the loss. Arnsparger went 0–7 before the now-desperate Well fired him and hired John McVay, who had coached at Memphis in the WFL. McVay led the team to a 3–4 record and, despite a 3–11 finish, gave hope to the fans for the next season.

It must be pointed out that Morton would be traded in early 1977 to the Denver Broncos. He would take the Broncos to the Super Bowl that season. This turned out to be more of an indictment of the New York franchise than of Morton's performance in Denver.

At this point the players felt cursed, and morale was at an all-time new low. During the summer, John Mendenhall said, "I'm looking forward to the season to see what disappointments it will bring."

And Harry Carson said, "To be a Giant is to always feel sad underneath."

In 1977 the Giants took Joe Pisarcik from the Canadian Football League and made him their quarterback. With a decent defense, a porous offensive line, and erratic play at the skill positions, the Giants proved that their mediocrity was no fluke when they finished 5–9 under McVay.

The highlight of the 1977 New York Giants season was Gifford's election to the Hall of Fame. Gifford was now one of the larger-than-life figures of ABC's *Monday Night Football,* where he was the straight man in a circus headed by both Cosell and Dandy Don Meredith.

In 1978 the league increased the number of regular season games from 14 to 16. And in that same year the Giants picked up veteran offensive lineman Jim Clack from the Pittsburgh Steelers. Clack was from a small town and had been happy in Pittsburgh. The fact that the Giants were a family-run team, like the Steelers, comforted him. "My first day there Mr. Mara came down and he talked more about Mr. Rooney than anything else," he said. That helped smooth the way right away. Clack became team captain for three years.

The Giants were 5–6 going into a showdown with the Philadelphia Eagles on November 19.

With under a minute left, the Giants were leading 17–12. The Giants were running out the clock against their divisional rivals. They were going to be 6–6, leaving Giants fans with momentary hopes of a winning season.

"When the play came from the sidelines, most of the offensive unit, Pisarcik included, questioned it," wrote Miller for the *New York Daily News.* Why not just fall on the ball? "What followed was a thousand-to-one shot for any gambler," Miller wrote. It became as infamous as Franco Harris's catch had been miraculous. It was called "the Miracle of the Meadowlands," and would be seen by many NFL players, owners, sportswriters, and fans as the epitome of what the Giants had come to symbolize.

Pisarcik began his cadence. The ball was hiked, Csonka missed the handoff, and history was about to be made. Philadelphia defensive back Herman Edwards saw the ball skittering across the stadium turf, so he scooped it up and ran for the end zone. It was a 26-yard fumble return for a touchdown. The Giants had snatched failure from the jaws of victory, losing with less than 20 seconds remaining, 19–17. The Eagles headed for the playoffs, and the Giants headed for 6–10.

"I remember the fumble against the Eagles only too well. Andy Robustelli and I were sitting in a booth next to the coaches that game, and as time was running out we heard one of the coaches screaming over the telephone insisting that they run a play rather than falling on the ball. He kept calling for the play. It was an indication to me that the guy in a position we depended on had just lost it. He made a terrible error, and the next thing we knew the Eagles had scored the winning touchdown." The Giants' coach, Bob Gibson, was fired the next day.

Worse than the fumble was its aftermath. "We went back into the locker room and everybody just started arguing with each other," said Clack. He pointed out that in Pittsburgh this kind of reaction would not have been tolerated by the players themselves. "I went to the phone and called my agent saying I wanted to be traded," Clack said. However he stayed through the 1981 season.

The newspapers ran stories of a bonfire that built by season-ticket holders burning their tickets.

Three weeks later a small plane flew over the stadium. And each time it passed by, the fans screamed and jeered and applauded. The small plane, hired by a fan, trailed a banner that read, "15 years of lousy football...we've had enough." Eventually the crowd in the stadium began to chant, "We've had enough! We've had enough! We've had enough!"

So had Tim. And so had Wellington.

More importantly, so had the league.

CHAPTER 10

That Championship Season

MR. ROZELLE AND MR. YOUNG

Before the end of the 1978 season the New York press was already talking about the Giants getting a new coach. When asked if he had heard the Giants were looking for a new coach, Wellington answered cryptically, "Oh yes, I've heard about it."

With the end of the 1978 season, Andy Robustelli offered his resignation on December 31, 1978. "During my five seasons as director of operations, the games played behind the games played on Sunday were far tougher and costlier to the franchise than anything that ever happened on the field," Robustelli wrote later. "Like the games on the field, there were soon two teams in our office."

Robustelli said he had intended all along to return to his five-office travel business, which was very successful in Stamford, Connecticut. This may be true, but Robustelli never mentioned it in any of his press conferences. He never indicated that his Giants job was of a temporary nature. Yet he insists that he tried to instigate discussions about his successors in late 1977. And there was no doubt he saw Tim as a disturbing force.

"Tim simply wouldn't sit down in meetings and join Well and me in decision-making discussions. Often he sat mute...and then came back the next day with his repetitive 'my mother and sister don't think...' or 'we don't think...' line. After a while I knew that he was probably not getting his advice from his mother and sister but probably his brother-in-law and some of his friends on the outside," said Robustelli.

"Those were some tough years," Tim said later. "We weren't winning, we didn't have good players, there were just a lot of things that went wrong. ... And after Andy Robustelli resigned for the end of the "78 season, I had a concept of how we should try and run things for the future. ... Simply, I didn't feel we had to lose."

Robustelli had offered the names of Bobby Beathard, the personnel director at Miami; Jan Van Duser, league executive; and Terry Bledsoe, an assistant director of operations for the NFL.

"What made this year so hard to accept was the knowledge that we were losing Andy," Wellington said.

Tim had decided he had had it. To his own credit, he knew he was not qualified to run a franchise, and wanted a professional executive to make things right. Wellington, as usual, had his own ideas. Wellington and Tim had reached a new low.

"The poison of their feud spread throughout the entire system," a former assistant revealed. "Things had bumbled along under Wellington and Andy, but now? Either Wellington or Tim had to give in, and neither one would. It wasn't so much chaos as paralysis."

"Suffice it to say there were severe and bitter fights, but it's nobody's concern except the family's," Wellington said.

"Sure, it was a rudderless ship—I think that's what it's called—and there was some unpleasantness, shall we say, but it got blown way out of proportion by the press," said Tim.

"I have not excluded the possibility of a public or private buyout of the Giants to solve their ridiculous disputes," said an irritated Governor Brendan Byrne. "The sports complex is a first-class, professional operation and New Jersey had expected a similarly professional performance from the Giants."

When confronted by the press about the feud, Tim said, "That's true, but...nothing has happened to jeopardize the smooth functioning of the organization. ... I can't see how this can hurt us any more. We've been in the cellar five of the last six years; how much worse can we get?"

In the early 1980s the oldest living Giants player, John Alexander, who was 89 years old, came to a Giants game and was fêted by press and fans alike. The press wanted a photograph of Alexander with the owners. Instead Alexander walked away with two photos: one of him with Wellington and another with Tim.

When Well and Tim passed each other in the hallway, they stared coolly past one another. Every Wednesday morning there was a board of directors meeting. Conversations were cold, calm, and quick. They did not even watch games together. Wellington used to watch from the owner's box while Tim paced the press box. It was alleged they even fought about what pencils to buy. And workers were still wincing in 1991 about the double memos they'd have to send, one to Well and one to Tim, about the purchasing of sundry items, right down to light bulbs.

They could not agree on who would be the next head coach. As soon as one threw out a name, the other immediately nixed it.

Tim insisted on Redskins coach George Allen. This was meant to be a real suggestion as well as a complete insult to Wellington. Allen was a control freak who had been fired twice because he had frustrated owners who wanted to tinker with their expensive play toys. But Wellington was a professional personnel man, even if his glory days were past. Allen wouldn't want Well anywhere near the team. And he had beaten the Giants 11 times in a row while with Washington, which made the insult all the more hurtful.

Said Tim, "My own choice, based on his winning record, is George Allen. George called me two weeks ago. I explained our situation to him and that we had to pick a director of operations first. He said he would welcome the opportunity to be interviewed for the coaching job. He understands he would only be the coach here and if he's just a coach, I think he would be a very good choice.

"I feel we should interview about 10 candidates," Tim told the press.

Wellington had called Dan Reeves and asked him to come up to New York for an interview. Reeves's interview was supposed to be confidential. No one was to know. No one.

This became one of the most difficult moments in Well and Tim's relationship, and was precipitated by a rather devious Wellington.

"Mr. Mara told me not to tell anyone they were talking to me," Reeves said. "When I got back to Dallas, Tim Mara called and asked if I'd been up there for an interview. I told him no." But there was a problem. "I didn't know that Mr. Mara had told Tim

227

about it. I take coaching pretty well. He told me not to tell anyone, so I didn't. But a good relationship doesn't start off with people lying to each other."

At one press conference, Tim was asked what he thought of the Dan Reeves interview. Tim said, "I heard rumors that Reeves came here, but when I called him to ask about it, he told me he was looking at oil wells in Texas."

"I got a call from Tom Landry," Tim later explained, "who explained to me that Reeves was very embarrassed but that Well had asked him to please keep their meeting confidential. I explained to Tom that I understood Reeves' position. This wasn't the first time Well has done something like that." Tim said that Wellington had done several things "behind my back."

Tim had also suggested Gil Brandt of the Cowboys, Don Klosterman of the Los Angeles Rams, and Joe Thomas, who had been the general manager for the Baltimore Colts, the Miami Dolphins, and the San Francisco 49ers. Well had suggested Reeves and Darryl Rogers of Michigan State University. Other names that were brought up in print were Joe Paterno of Penn State, John Robinson of USC, Bill Walsh of Stanford, Hank Stram of CBS and formerly of Kansas City and New Orleans, Johnny Majors of Tennessee, Frank Burns of Rutgers, Bo Schembechler of Michigan, and George Young of the Miami Dolphins.

At one point, one Giants player reportedly said to another, "Hear the latest rumor? The next coach is John Mara," referring to Well's oldest son.

Terry Bledsoe had been hired during 1978 as assistant operations director under Robustelli. Wellington and Robustelli had made the case from the beginning that Bledsoe would not be the new director, but would be the deputy underneath the new man. According to Mara and Robustelli, Bledsoe was the first Giants executive of the modern era of football at the Giants.

Tim blasted Bledsoe in the newspapers in order to make it clear that he and his side of the Giants slate did not approve of Bledsoe as the new director of operations. Tim had insisted that when Bledsoe was hired in May 1978, it had been done behind his back. Tim wrote to Rozelle that as half owner, he did not approve the move. Rozelle tried at the time, like Pontius Pilate, to wash his hands of it. But to no avail, it would seem later.

"Tim Mara has agreed to waive the objections raised in his letter of May 17 relative to this contract upon the understanding that Terry's duties as an employee will not be appreciably altered nor will he be signed to a new contract or extension without board approval in accordance with bylaw procedures now being developed," Rozelle wrote Wellington.

"I wrote that I represented 50 percent of the stock in the team and that Terry Bledsoe was not what we needed to get out of the rut," Tim said. Tim assured Rozelle that his uncle was determined to move Bledsoe up to Robustelli's old position.

Wellington called Bledsoe, a former NFL management council executive and former sportswriter, "one of the brightest young executives in sports."

"I told Terry myself that it was not anything personal, but that I felt we should get a topflight director of operations when Andy retired," Tim told Michael Katz of *The New York Times*.

They were at a stalemate. Then Rozelle stepped in. Several owners were very concerned, including Well's friend Art Modell and Dallas Cowboys executive Tex Schramm. Schramm wanted the league to be strong in New York. "That city has the largest media concentration, the largest television market, and you need a good team in New York. It hurts our league when the Giants and the Jets aren't strong," reasoned Schramm. "If you look back in history, the NFL had its largest escalation and biggest television growth period in the late 1950s and the early 1960s, and that was because the Giants had great teams then. ... You couldn't get tickets to Giants games. I don't care what anybody says, it all happens in New York. That's where the market is. ..." Many owners were watching Rozelle.

Rozelle indeed stepped in and promised to help stem the problem. Both Well and Tim presented lists to Rozelle. He reviewed them and talked over all the names with each. He promised to make something happen. Rozelle would make both Tim and Well sign a document, which still resides at the NFL league offices, in which both agreed to give up power for the good of the team. As president, Wellington's only real power was to vote for the organization at league meetings or to appoint someone to do so in his stead. The agreement allowed Tim's faction even less.

"The fact that [Tim's] decision-making capacity was also lessened by the agreement with the league meant nothing because they [Tim's faction] never wanted to get involved anyhow," Robustelli wrote. Tim had a press conference and promised there would be a man in the position by February 1, 1979. The deadline came and went and nothing happened. And that's when the Maras' feud finally went public.

What happened next was best figured out many years later by Jerry Izenberg in his research and interviewing for his book *No Medals for Trying*. Apparently, as Tim told Jerry Izenberg years later, he and Wellington had agreed on league office executive Jan Van Duser.

"What I think happened," Tim told Izenberg, "is that [Van Duser] worked in the city and every day the papers were filled with this battle and he must have taken one look at the headlines and said, "Who needs this? Thank you but no thank you!'"

Wellington then acted. "I called Bobby Beathard, then the Redskins general manager, and he endorsed George Young without reservation. ... So I called Pete and he said to me, 'What do we do now?' And I said, 'You make sure that George Young's name is on that list.' They [Tim, Richard, Maura, and other's in Tim's group] didn't know about my phone call."

"I had known of George through work he had done in NFL scouting meetings. I had seen him in action, I had read his reports, and I thought he was very good. But I told Pete that I didn't think Tim would go for him, especially if it was someone I recommended or liked," Wellington said. Rozelle sold Tim on Young. In Young, Rozelle had found a man with an accomplished professional background, who was well respected around the league.

In the meantime Roselle had called legendary Notre Dame coach Ara Parseghian, who immediately rejected the offer.

"I started to get anxious about the whole thing. I felt we were losing our shot at hiring a good coach—Bill Walsh and John Robinson were among those available—and so I held a press conference and announced I was going to hire a coach first," Well said.

Wellington held his renegade press conference on February 8, 1979, without telling Tim's group. As president he could do this, but given the tenor of the times, it was meant to provoke. The meeting was highly attended.

One of Wellington's incendiary comments was, "As president I have the full decision-making responsibility." The press was in shock. "And then all hell broke loose," said Wellington later.

Tim called a second press conference to refute Wellington's statements.

"I want to have a winner. Well wants to have a winner his way, but Well's way has had us in the cellar the last 15 years," Tim said.

Said Well, "Tim walked into the room shortly after I spoke and basically said, 'No, you're not.' Pete was at a tennis tournament with Pat Summerall down in Florida when the news broke, and he called me immediately. And I told him it was time he recommended George Young to us."

Wellington's press conference, while it seemed reckless from the outside, was calculated. The deadlines had come and gone, and coaches were being hired by other teams. His nephew was determined to prove to everyone that his uncle couldn't move without him, and Rozelle and Summerall were playing tennis.

"I thought that as a result of the difficult time we were having in agreeing on a general manager and the delay it was going to cause us, we would lose our top choices for a new coach. They probably would not be available by the time a general manager was hired. I was afraid we would end up with a second-rate coach," Wellington said.

Wellington knew exactly what he was doing.

"It seems we've been growing further apart," Tim told the press.

Rozelle returned and pressed both sides. They were to choose between Frank Ryan, current Yale athletics director, or Young. Rozelle wanted it cleaned up by Valentine's Day.

"I had Frank Gifford check Young out for me. He called Bobby Beathard and got a glowing report, and he told me that he was definitely the man," Pete told Tim.

Young seemed worth meeting. From Rozelle's perspective, the situation must have seemed surreal—caught between a well-known erstwhile owner who suddenly demanded accountability and an out-dated legend who refused to change the direction of the club.

"I saw my first one in 1942," Young said of seeing his first of many Giants games as a young boy. "I was also at the 1956 champi-onship game that they won against the Bears. I remember when we beat Green Bay badly in the last game of the 1986 season, they announced that the last time the Giants had scored more than 50 points in a game was against the Colts in 1950. I was there too."

On February 14, 1979, Rozelle flew Young into New York.

"Now we go on Wednesday to the Drake Hotel and we interview Young for two hours. We're impressed and we go to Rozelle's office," Tim told Izenberg.

"I only brought the suit I was wearing when I came up," Young revealed later. Young was at the Drake Hotel under the fictitious name of Wayne Rosen, who was actually Rozelle's driver. Young was interviewed by both Well and Tim separately at the NFL offices. Young had played tackle at Bucknell and then became a history teacher in Baltimore. He had even taught the man named Boogie who eventually became one of the main characters in the movie *Diner*. While in Baltimore, he befriended Don Shula. He started working for the Colts not long after, and then followed Shula to Miami. He had gone from scout to offensive line to player personnel. He had become an experienced NFL executive. But wasn't he afraid to step in between the feuding Maras?

Said Young, "I had worked for Carroll Rosenbloom, Joe Thomas, Bob Irsay, and Joe Robbie, so I knew a little bit about these situations. Compared to those guys, the Maras were choir boys."

Young would have the authority to hire and fire. Friends of Well or Tim were open game. Those that relied on office politics instead of job competency were soon let go. Young overhauled the organization in a way no one had since Tim Mara had fired more than half the team.

Ross Wetzsteon wrote of Young, "Young exudes a Sidney Greenstreet composure; he is exactly the kind of person you would want around when tempers flare."

"Now remember, the press conference is scheduled for that night. We're sitting there and we have to go over the new resolutions about how the club shall be governed and who has right of first refusal in the event of a stockholder's death and things like that. I also placed the football operations in the hands of whoever would get the general manager's job," Tim said years later.

The agreement was for five years. The salary for the general manager was agreed upon. At 2:45 PM, Young was asked back to the NFL offices. He spoke with Rozelle and then with the Maras again. They offered him the job.

It took Young "about half a second" to say yes. "This was a flagship franchise, a very special job, and a terrific opportunity for me," Young said.

Young spoke to his wife (it was Valentine's Day, after all) and spoke to Robbie, the Dolphin's owner.

"So George is in the other room and we're dotting the i's and crossing the t's," remembered Tim. "Now it's like 7:00 PM and nobody is left in the league offices, so Pete walks over to a typewriter and he starts to type out the press release for that night. It's probably the first one he wrote in 25 years and the last one he ever wrote. While he's writing, he suddenly looks up and says, 'This is a great way to spend today. It's my wedding anniversary.'"

The four then went over to Gallagher's Steakhouse for the press conference.

"The war between the Maras came to an abrupt truce last night," wrote Bill Madden for the *New York Daily News*, "when the Giants co-owners plucked George Young from the Dolphins organization as the surprise choice to run their football operations....he was offered the job of refurbishing the Giants franchise from its present chaotic condition."

"He must be the only person in the world who can command the respect of both Wellington and Tim on a day-to-day basis," said an insider. "He's a little more firm with Tim than he is with Wellington, but he gives both the impression they have major input into all decisions. They don't really, but the important thing is that he makes them think they do."

"I wanted George to inform me of any major player or coaching moves. And I wanted to feel free to give my opinion," Wellington said later. "I still went to practice and kept in touch with what was going on personnel wise. But George was the one making the decisions."

"I imagine it gets tough for George at times, but he has very broad shoulders," Wellington said years later.

Wellington stated in a letter to Rozelle that he now understood the insistence that one person own a majority of a team in order to avoid such situations. "I regard it as a personal tragedy that our club provide proof of the wisdom of that rule," Well was quoted as saying in *The New York Times* in January 1987.

Young wasted no time. He hired 37-year-old Ray Perkins to be the next coach of the New York Giants on February 22, 1979. And in May, maybe most importantly, Young took the biggest risk any general manager ever took when the Giants drafted an unknown quarterback named Phil Simms from tiny Morehead State with their first pick in the draft. The boo-birds were out in full force. Why not Kellen Winslow? Why not Charles Alexander? What most fans didn't know was that Simms had been rated highly by several teams, and would probably not have lasted past the second round.

The 1979 season began with hope and, despite a 6–10–0 record, ended with hope. The Giants had several All-Pros, including Van Pelt, Carson, and punter Dave Jennings. And the unknown quarterback finished second for All-NFL Rookie honors. There was the chance something could change.

TURNAROUND

The 1980 season was a major disappointment. Simms showed patches of brilliance, but also played behind a sieve of a line, and was often injured. Carson and Brian Kelley had knee injuries and running back Doug Kotar was also injured.

For the 1981 season the Giants brought in first-round draft pick Lawrence Taylor, a linebacker from North Carolina. He instantly became one of the highest-paid rookies in the league. And then there was the midseason arrival of running back Rob Carpenter from the Houston Oilers. Carpenter brought consistency and power to the New York Giants, and Taylor proved to be that once-in-a-lifetime player that changes the history of a position. Along with Van Pelt, Kelley, and Carson, the Giants linebacking corps was considered one of the best in pro football.

However the most important signing of 1981 was of a struggling, journeyman defensive coach named Bill Parcells. Parcells had been with the club in 1979 and then left. He had been rehired and told by Perkins to run the defense. On looking back, Parcells said, "[Lawrence and I] came riding in to clean up the town, a couple of guys from an old Western."

That's a bit of a misstatement. Lawrence would go on to become one of the greatest linebackers in the history of the game, but there were a lot of good players on that defense, including Jim Burt, Byron Hunt, Mark Haynes, George Martin, and Gary Jeter. But Parcells did an excellent job of mixing and matching his parts. He drove his unit hard, and the defensive unit, which had been awful the year before, was shaping up into one of the better units in the NFL. The fans soon warmed to the group.

Through it all Wellington was always there. "He was a tremendous owner. I didn't want to come to New York when I was drafted," said Carson, years later. "But coming and finally understanding the rich history and tradition of the organization really gave me an appreciation for playing with the Giants. The thing that stands out in my mind about Wellington Mara was, even though he was the owner, he was like a player. After every game, he was the first one to come into the locker room. After a win you'd see a big, broad smile on his face and he'd congratulate every player. After a loss he'd come around and tell the players to hold their head up. He was one of us."

The Giants went into their last game of the season in December 1981 with a record of 8–7. With a win they would qualify for the playoffs (with a little help). The Jets, who had beat the Giants earlier in the season, would have to beat Green Bay to secure the Giants a spot in the playoffs. The biggest problem, however, was that the Giants were playing the 12–3 Dallas Cowboys at Giants Stadium.

With Simms sidelined due to a separated shoulder, Scott Brunner was at quarterback. Not surprisingly, the Giants struggled against the Dallas Cowboys. However, the Cowboys were also struggling. The Giants had been seeing signs of improvement in recent matches against Dallas. These matches were usually close, with the Cowboys pulling it out with a field goal or a last-minute touchdown.

On a Saturday afternoon, on December 19, 1981, the game began. Halfway into the game, in the metro region a slow snowfall would begin, as if fate had finally picked up a magic Gotham snowglobe and given it a little shake. Ask any Giants fan alive—there was a sense of magic in the air that day. Thousands of silent hopes from the Giants faithful, hoping this might be the day of deliverance went up into the snowy skies that day.

By 1981 New York was on the comeback, and about to enjoy one of its greatest golden eras. The city had, like the Giants, lain dormant for 15 years, bottoming out with the famous *Daily News* headline, "Ford to City: Drop Dead!" Punk rockers were making it at CBGBs, and investment bankers were making it at Solomon Brothers. John Lennon had been assassinated in the city, but there was no denying, New York was suddenly shaking off a weird slumber and was ready to turn a new corner. And now so were the Giants.

The weather was 25 degrees, and a 20-mile-an-hour wind created a windchill around zero. In the first half New York held the vaunted Cowboys to 41 yards of total offense. Unfortunately, two long Giants drives fizzled into two missed field goals.

In the third quarter the Giants and Cowboys traded touchdowns. Then Brunner threw an interception and the Cowboys went up 10–7. After failing to convert a third down, the Giants punted back to the Cowboys. On a Cowboys drive in the fourth quarter, Tony Dorsett fumbled the ball on the Dallas 45 and defensive end Martin recovered it. With less than 30 seconds remaining, Joe Danelo kicked a 40-yard field goal that tied the game, 10–10. The Cowboys hadn't pulled this one out yet. The Giants were going to overtime.

It was an ugly, tense overtime. Taylor stripped Dorsett of the ball and the Giants ended up with a 33-yard field-goal attempt. But the ball bounced off one of the uprights. The Cowboys got control back, but several plays later Hunt intercepted a Danny White pass and ran the ball back to the Dallas 24-yard line. The offense stalled, and Danelo lined up a 35-yard field goal. He struck the ball, and it sailed through the uprights.

This was possibly the most important game in the second 50 years of the Giants organization. This was the game where the organization broke through whatever it was that was holding both the team and fans back. While the later Super Bowl appearances were of momentous meaning for the organization, this win, which could mean their first playoff appearance in 18 years, combined with the rebuffing of

Landry's dominant Cowboys, was a statement. No matter their performance in the playoffs that year, simply breaking back into the postseason was everything.

On Sunday, December 20, the Giants family gathered again. Players, coaches, office staff, and their families gathered in the Giants Stadium press box to watch the Jets play Green Bay. The Maras and Young had put out a huge buffet with an open bar. As defensive back Beasley Reece told *Sports Illustrated*, "Kids were running around all over the place. Everyone was trying to play it loose...but I can assure you that all eyes were glued to that TV set...but until the Jets went ahead 28–3, I couldn't tell you if it was roast beef or coleslaw.... That's how tight I was."

The Jets won and the Giants were in the playoffs for the first time in 18 years. The Giants next had to go to Philadelphia. On December 27, 1981, the Giants "got defense," wrote Mike Lupica of the New York *Daily News*, "because these gritty, dreaming Giants always give you defense." But what 71,611 fans didn't expect was 161 yards of Rob Carpenter and three touchdown passes from Scott Brunner in a 27–21 playoff victory. "Try to remember all the days across all the years when a Giants running back played a game quite like this," wrote Lupica.

After this victory the Giants went to San Francisco. There the team was outclassed by a better, more advanced organization that would go on to dethrone the Cowboys and take the first of five championships. The game teetered early, but too many breaks went against the Giants. San Francisco won 38–24.

But the season had been a huge success. And the Giants had proven they could compete again. And Giants fans were thrilled.

୧୨୬

Young would draft some premiere talent, duplicating Wellington's feats. Between 1981 and 1993, Young would draft:

Phil Simms, QB, round 1, 1979
Lawrence Taylor, LB, round 1, 1981
Joe Morris, RB, round 2, 1982
Carl Banks, LB, round 1, 1984
William Roberts, OT, round 2, 1984

Mark Bavaro, TE, round 4, 1985
Howard Cross, TE, round 6, 1989
David Meggett, RB, round 5, 1989
Michael Strahan, DE, round 2, 1993
Jessie Armstead, LB, round 8, 1993

The turnaround was in full swing, and Young was going to deliver. But there was still going to be some stumbling along the way. In the strike-shortened season of 1982 the Giants went 4–5–0 and finished 10ᵗʰ in their conference. Again, Simms was hurt and Brunner filled in. Kotar retired. And the Giants took a big step back.

However, the program experienced its biggest setback on December 15, 1982, when Ray Perkins announced his decision to leave the Giants to head the sidelines of the University of Alabama. Who would Young pick now? And would Wellington or Tim object?

MR. PARCELLS

Young knew immediately who he wanted to replace Perkins. Wellington was at the owner's meeting in Dallas. Young called him first. And then he called Tim. The Maras agreed.

"George told me that he wanted to name Bill Parcells the next coach. And he told me he wanted to name him the same day that Ray Perkins made his announcement so there wouldn't be weeks of speculation as to who was going to be the next coach," Tim said.

"I grew up a Giants fan and I recall being as young as 10 and watching the *New York Giants Football Huddle* on television with Marty Glickman. I started going to games when they were still playing at the Polo Grounds," Parcells related. I remember one against the Steelers.... I was at the Cleveland game in 1958 when Pat Summerall kicked that field goal for the win, sitting in the right-field bleachers at Yankee Stadium. And I'll never forget the overtime loss to the Colts a couple of weeks later. I had gone ice-skating with a bunch of friends of mine. They were all on the ice, and I was sitting in the car listening on the radio."

Parcells wanted to be a players coach, but it didn't work. In 1983 the Giants finished 3–12–1. After the phenomenal success of the 1981 season, it was a bitter disappointment. And the off-season that year was difficult. Three of the Giants top linebackers wanted out. Simms basically told the management, in a somewhat public way, "play me or trade me." The general malaise seemed to start to regain a grip on the Giants team.

Most notably, Young was upset. And there were rumors Parcells was not long for the Giants world. Young had not liked the results of the season, and it was Wellington that was alleged to have saved his job. But there was no doubt Young had been thinking over Parcells's early departure.

Jimmy "the Greek" Snyder, the famed analyst for CBS's *The NFL Today* game day football show, said on the air that University of Miami coach Howard Schnellenberger had been approached by the Giants to replace Parcells. Snyder said that Schnellenberger was flattered, but he already had a handshake agreement to go to the USFL's New Jersey Generals, owned by Donald Trump.

Schnellenberger had apparently scheduled a news conference. The Associated Press reached Schnellenberger's wife, who claimed she did not know anything. Trump denied that Schnellenberger was commited to his team.

"Schnellenberger, whose Hurricanes faced Nebraska in the Orange Bowl on January 2, said matters had never reached that point, although those teams and several others had talked to him," Frank Litsky wrote in *The New York Times.*

"After listening to them, I told them that my desire was to move this football program along and try to win the national championship," said the 49-year-old coach.

Young angrily refused to comment on the CBS story.

"Bill is the coach," was all Young would say. But it lit a fire under Parcells.

"It took the threat of losing my job to get me to say, 'I'm doing this my way,'" Parcells admitted later. He got rid of those players he thought were holding the team back, even those who had talent but who had too much attitude or were critical of the team and coaching staff.

৯৯৯

On March 20, 1984, Wellington was voted the president of the National Football Conference. This would be another drain on his time, but with the qualified Young running things, it might be just the diversion he required.

From 1971 until 1977 he was chairman of the executive committee of the NFL management council, the labor arm of the NFL, where
he and the league lawyers battled and negotiated with Ed Garvey. It
was under Mara's leadership that the league achieved five years of labor
peace from 1977 to 1982. Mara succeeded the late Halas as president
of the NFC in 1984. Mara also served as a member of the Hall of Fame
committee and continued to serve on the executive committee of the
management council. Wellington succeeded Vince Lombardi, after his
death, as a member of the competition committee. He served as president of the National Football Conference from 1984 to 2005.

At this point it was jokingly stated that Wellington was now
tending to his mail. In fact, he tried to respond to as many requests
as was possible that came to the organization. He and his brother
before him had always tried to be good about answering the mail,
no matter how mundane the issue might be. He also spent time on
television issues and public relations. This kind of personal touch
was what helped the Maras build their loyal following. And of course
he liked to watch practice and hang around the locker room with the
trainers and players. He also enjoyed horse racing, especially later in
life. Early on, his father and brother would drag him out to the racetrack, but it was apparent young Wellington's mind never really left
the field of play. In later years he became much fonder of escaping
to the racetrack's peace and quiet, and of course for a little betting
action. He enjoyed playing 1–6 daily double. Meanwhile, it was
alleged Tim was reduced to overseeing player and business parking
spaces and comp tickets in the Giants organization.

Tall and thin, Tim often skulked around the Giants offices. He
often seemed preoccupied, "wearing clubby sports jackets or turtleneck
sweaters, looking to keep busy." At times he almost seemed bored. "He
once revised the parking regulations for the staff, notifying all concerned an hour before a home game, sending secretaries and players
alike into the club lot to jockey their vehicles into the proper spaces."
He was alleged to have had Marty Schottenheimer's car towed during
a Sunday home game because it was improperly parked. According to
Will McDonough, it was rumored that in February 1984 Tim wanted
to let Young and Parcells go and replace them with Schnellenberger,
whom he still wanted to run the organization.

From the late 1950s to the end of his life, Wellington's game-day routine changed little. On Sundays he went to 8:00 AM mass and returned to have a big breakfast. After that he left for the stadium. "I try to get to the stadium by 10:00. I walk through the dressing room, maybe check with the trainers about something—possibly an injured player, who's going to be available and who isn't. I like to walk through the dressing room so the people see that I'm there. I keep remembering Michael Burke told me when he was running the Yankees. He had come from farming stock in Ireland, and he said his grandfather's favorite saying was, 'There's no fertilizer like the farmer's footsteps.'

"I'm not a glad hander. I don't go up to a player and say, 'Have a good day.' I'm just there, that's all. I almost never go out on the field before a game. Once in a while if it's a special opponent we're playing, I'll go over and say hello—like to a Parcells, maybe a John Fox, someone like that. But mostly I stay away. I don't believe in fraternizing the day of a game," Well said.

However, Mara, as usual, was playing down his role. Mara, like his father, from whom he had learned his manners, often thanked the players after the game. Wellington was no stranger to the locker room. He would be saying "Thank you," to each of the players, either patting them on the back or shaking their hands.

His father had done that, too. Wellington made sure he did it as often as possible. Tim did it, too, on home games. It was the only time many employees saw the two in the same room, when the men would walk through the locker rooms thanking the players after a win or loss. There was no mistaking it: Tim very much loved the team. The difference was that Wellington lived with his team day in and day out, and had for more than 60 years at that time.

"He did not own the team in order to get on the 6:00 news or the back page of the tabloids or to buy his way into the power circles of the city," wrote George Vecsey. "He owned the Giants because they were a family business, like a farm stand or a shoe-repair shop."

By the mid-1980s Wellington was very much considered what other owners and sportswriters referred to as "the old guard." Their numbers were dwindling. Of the owners who were entrenched before Rozelle became commissioner, Halas and Rosenbloom were dead. Billy Bidwill had adopted the new ways and the Packers were, at the time, considered on the fringes of football. The last two holdouts were the Maras and the Rooneys. And for them the situation was getting harder and harder.

"We're people who use football for our primary income and we're getting crowded like the corner grocery faced with a supermarket across the street. Greater capitalization is required," Mara said. "I don't know how to cope with the rise in salaries, the rise in operating expenses. The new owners now are people who've been successful in other areas. They don't depend on football for money. Many of the great fortunes have now come to the game. They're better at business than the founding fathers, but when someone isn't interested in the bottom line at the end of the year, it sets the salary standards for all the others." The Rooneys agreed with Mara's statement.

In 1984 the Giants went 9–7, and there was tangible improvement. Simms was now a commanding starter, Taylor continued to wreak awful havoc over NFL offenses, and the defense continued to impress with authority.

New York traveled to Los Angeles on December 23, 1984, and beat the Rams 16–13 in the NFC wild-card playoff game. The next week, at San Francisco, the Giants scored a field goal and a touchdown in the second quarter to cut the San Francisco lead to 14–10. But before the end of the half, Joe Montana took the wind out of the Giants' sails when he connected with Freddie Solomon to make the score 21–10, which wound up being the final count.

While perhaps 1981 had been a fluke, people were now getting the sense that the Giants were ready to actually turn the corner.

In 1985 the Giants went to the playoffs again. Despite their 10–6 record, they could not take the division, as Landry's Dallas Cowboys swept the season's series with the Giants, giving the Cowboys the tie-breaker.

This time San Francisco came to the Meadowlands, and the Giants won 17–3. However, in their next game, the Giants went to Chicago to play the eventual Super Bowl winners, the Chicago Bears coached by Mike Ditka. Losing 21–0, the end of the season was a bitter defeat because the team failed to score, and the game, which had stayed close for a while, was a great disappointment. But still, many people liked the rising New York Giants. They would like them even more the next year.

Wellington spoke to the press. He explained that the Giants had been competitive for 22 games in 1985, including the preseason and the 49ers playoff game. "Go back to last year," Mara told the press. "The Bears lost to the 49ers, 23–0, for the NFC title. If they can improve that much, we can, too. You're certainly not satisfied unless you're number one. But let's face it. Only four teams went further than we did. And a lot of our young players haven't reached their potential."

THE PROMISED LAND ONCE AGAIN

In the mid-1980s another challenger had presented itself in the form of the United States Football League, a springtime professional football league. By May the USFL and the NFL were headed into U.S. District Court, with the USFL claiming damages of more than $1.3 billion. The USFL claimed that the NFL had conspired to keep the USFL from jumping to a fall schedule because it had exclusive contracts for stadiums and television. Trump, the well-known real estate mogul and owner of the New Jersey Generals, was the most vocal of the USFL executives. Davis and Mara, among others, were scheduled to testify. Davis, of course, would testify on the USFL's behalf.

In the highlight of the trial, Davis spoke out against the power of the NFL and lamented the demise of the Oakland Invaders, a team struggling to make it in the absence of Davis's Raiders, who had abandoned the city for Los Angeles.

"All that stuff about the Invaders," scoffed Mara. "What's that got to do with the price of potatoes?"

"At least in Los Angeles he was fighting for his own franchise," Art Modell said. "I could respect that, but I can't respect this."

What was more at stake in this era, beyond beating the USFL, was the possibility that some of the older families in the NFL might have to sell their franchises. This was a very real threat to the Maras, the McCaskeys, and the Rooneys. Even Wellington admitted after the danger passed, "We would have had to sell the team."

The USFL was awarded $1, which was seen as a rebuke by the jury to the league. After a decision was announced, Rozelle was asked if the NFL would merge or assume the eight remaining USFL teams. "I would not anticipate a merger," Rozelle said, nodding toward Wellington, who stood next to him.

"Nor do I," said Wellington, firmly.

Trump claimed the USFL had gained a huge moral victory, but many of the other USFL owners saw the verdict as a death sentence.

"The verdict sounded like a compromise, which our attorneys say is not uncommon when there is a deadlocked jury," Wellington said in his role as NFC president. "The jury found us innocent of tampering with the networks. Specifically ABC and ESPN. Apparently all they found was that we were successful in business, and by being successful we caused ourselves damages of $1.... I am most pleased with the complete vindication of Pete Rozelle as opposed to Donald Trump. I'm glad we won out against people like Howard Cosell, Al Davis, Ed Garvey, and Donald Trump."

When asked what he thought might be the fate of the USFL, Well answered, "I don't know. That's their problem." The USFL folded.

Tim and John Mara—Wellington's oldest son and a lawyer in New York City—were also relieved. John told the press, "The team is the family business. It is not just a plaything or something we do for the sake of ego.... Many football teams face the possibility of not making a great deal of money. For family owned teams, that would present a big problem because this is our primary source of income." John admitted that if the Giants ever reached the point where the organization no longer was able to make enough money to support the family, it would have to be sold. "I just can't imagine what life would be like without it."

"It's a problem," Tim said. "But with an organization that is properly run, we should be able to survive."

As to the feud between Well and Tim, John once said, "Do I think we'll ever sit down together for Thanksgiving dinner or Christmas? I'd have to say no, probably not. But I really don't think the situation is that bad. It's been seven or eight years since that thing became public, and just because we don't get along socially does not mean it affects the running of the team. I think too much is made of the feud. But I guess when a team loses, people look for reasons. ... I definitely do not think the feud has affected the team on the field."

"I don't think the family problems have hindered the running of the team. And credit to that must go to George," Wellington said.

"George has done his job very diplomatically, and very well," Tim concurred.

☙❧

The real controversy of 1986 was the Mara family's decision to sell the subsidiary company, Stadium Operating Corporation, which controlled luxury-box rentals. The Maras wanted to spin off the small company, which controlled 67 of the 72 suites in Giants Stadium. The principal buyer was Thomas D. O'Malley, who was a vice president with Solomon Brothers and a resident of Greenwich, Connecticut, a suburb very near Mara's home.

The reason this became a political issue was that the New Jersey Sports and Exposition Authority took the Maras to court to block the sale. Although the Authority owned the stadium, the Giants, under their agreement, owned the luxury boxes. This was never the issue. The Authority had tried to negotiate for the suites, but had failed to offer a price the Maras would agree to. Each box's value, for one season, was around $40,000, and total rents from the boxes generally ran about $2.7 million. The remaining five boxes would stay split, three for the Mara family and two for the Authority. The Maras earned somewhere between $10 million and $20 million from the sale of the boxes. O'Malley, owner and CEO of Argus Investments, Inc., in Stamford, Connecticut, also later bought the rights to lease the luxury boxes at Mile High Stadium in Denver.

The season started off ominously, with a 31–28 loss to the Dallas Cowboys in the Giants, first game of the season. But they won their next five games before dropping a 17–12 score at Seattle. They then won their next nine games, including a win over the Cowboys and two over Washington, to finish the season 14–2–0. They were to the NFL that year what the Bears had been the year before—the dominant team everyone thought would win it all.

The Giants first playoff matchup was against the San Francisco 49ers. The first play of the game was not for the faint of heart. Rice took a pass from Montana and raced down the field. Only yards from the goal line, he fumbled the ball completely untouched by another

245

man, and the Giants recovered the ball in their own end zone. The Giants were a juggernaut, and they rolled over the 49ers, 49–3.

Next to show up at Giants Stadium was the wild-card entry Washington Redskins. The Redskins had beaten the Los Angeles Rams in Washington and then the Chicago Bears, on the road, to earn this spot. They were an excellent team, and this was the NFC showdown. Many analysts thought that the winner of this game would win the Super Bowl. The stadium was packed with 76,600 screaming fans.

Wellington Mara had seen it all before. And he had certainly seen all but a few of the Redskins-Giants games early in the history of the rivalry. "We need George Preston Marshall and his raccoon coat," said Well. The Giants overwhelmed the Redskins 17–0 to earn their first Super Bowl, which would be held in Pasadena, California, that year. After the NFC championship, Wellington, all smiles, walked around the locker room thanking the players.

"Bill Parcells wasn't the easiest man for a front office to get along with. The late George Young found that out as the Giants' GM," Peter King of *Sports Illustrated* later wrote. "But Mara really liked Parcells. He liked the way he ran the team, how he got the most out of his players and how he was able to get truants like Lawrence Taylor to produce at their max. And Parcells, in turn, respected the heck out of Mara. He reminded him of his speak-softly dad. Not once in 10 years as a coach or assistant did Parcells go to practice without seeing Mara there."

In Pasadena Wellington showed up wearing his "practice hat," the same rumpled fisherman's hat he'd worn for years. He had been to every Super Bowl as a spectator, and now he was here with his team. "I just want to see how things are done," Well said, almost apologetically.

"This was as warm a sight as is likely to emerge from this Super Bowl: Wellington Mara, 70 years old, hat flopping over his forehead, finally getting to stand on the edges of a Super Bowl workout by his beloved Giants," wrote Vecsey.

Vecsey pointed out that some owners threw wild, loud parties for their friends and hangers-on, and hoped to draw television coverage. "Wellington Mara's place was with the Giants, somewhere behind the trainers and the ballboys and the priests and the coaches," wrote

Vecsey. "He was always there for the steaming practices in July; no sense in changing patterns for the Super Bowl."

"I always said the Giants would make the Super Bowl," Mara told the press wryly. "I just didn't know if I'd still be around."

In the Super Bowl, John Elway led the Broncos to a 10–9 halftime lead, despite Elway being tackled in the end zone by Martin before the end of the half. The Giants had had their chances but were trailing. However in the fourth quarter, whatever doubts anyone had were absolutely obliterated as the Giants rolled up 30 points to Denver's 10, which they scored after the Giants had already salted the game away. The Giants beat the Broncos 39–10.

Simms had been almost perfect in leading the offense, completing 22 of 25 passes, and was named the MVP of the game. And the Giants had won their first league title since 1956. Thirty years.

The feud between Wellington and Tim was not dispelled by the victory. For the Lombardi Trophy presentation from Rozelle to the coach and owners, it was only Parcells and Wellington up on the platform.

"Your father, Timothy J. Mara, founded the Giants in 1925 and the first season you were a nine-year-old ballboy. Ever since that time I think the Giants have been both a business and a love to the Mara family," Rozelle said before handing over the silver trophy.

Mara recounted the other Giants teams that had won and called the current team a "great bunch of men!" Tim never took the podium. "We're co-owners, but Well's the president," Tim said. "I understand." It was a classy move by Tim.

A day after the game, Ann Mara told the press it was the first time she had slept well in over a month.

"It was great," Wellington said of accepting the trophy, "but I tried to be professional about it and remember it was great to win our other championships, too."

It was difficult for many to understand, but Wellington had seen every single championship game.

"To the people on the inside of the organization, it's just as big as it was back then. But there's more outside pressures that you try to shield the players from now," Well said. One sensed in Mara an attempt not to show up his players from the past, some of whom were still under his employ, such as Jim Lee Howell, who was a consultant to the team.

After that championship, Dave Anderson wrote about the fact that there was still some dissatisfaction among fans who were angry with the Maras for taking so long. Maybe the Maras were just counting the money?

"In actuality, nobody cared more about winning than the co-owners, especially Wellington Mara, for whom the Giants have been a life's work. And if both Maras hadn't cared about winning, they would have sold the club for millions. ... In pro football, Mara is a grand old name again," concluded Anderson.

Giants fans back in New York were elated. Lynn Mara Shivek had gained her middle name due to her parents' devotion to the team during the year of her birth, 1956.

"I've watched the Giants all my life. I've been to Yankee Stadium, the Yale Bowl, wherever," she said.

The game was broadcast into the New York Film Critics Circle annual banquet on two televisions at Sardis.

At Manny's in Moonachie, New Jersey, a dentist married his dental hygienist during the halftime show.

"We were Super Bowl champions. ... Like Parcells said, now that the Giants have finally won the championship, all the ghosts can be buried. The ghosts with names like Tittle, Conerly, Robustelli, Huff, Gifford, Rote, and all the rest," said defensive star Leonard Marshall. "I am thankful of all the love these guys have shown me, and they've set a standard for today and for future generations of Giants. I'm honored to be a part of it all."

There would be no ticker-tape parade. New York Mayor Ed Koch had seen to that. Since the Giants no longer had the classic N.Y. on their helmets and played in New Jersey, Koch saw them as a "foreign team," and said the city would not pay for a ticker-tape parade.

A letter to the editor was published in *The New York Times* in which Bob Rosenbaum of Summit, New Jersey, chided the haggling mayor, writing, "Come on, Ed! Wellington Mara is not Walter O'Malley. We all live in the same place together."

Wellington countered that they would hold a celebration with their fans at Giants Stadium. Before the Super Bowl, Koch made a peace offering by sending 12 cases of New York's Great Western

Champagne, donated by Seagram's. "Even if we can't shower you with 'ticker tape' as the champions of football, at least New York will give you the opportunity to shower each other with good champagne," Koch said. The mayor wasn't even in the city. He was in Warsaw. When told that the Maras would choose a celebration at Giants Stadium, Koch told the Warsaw press, "I'm told that Wellington Mara says they prefer to walk around Giants Stadium."

The players flew back to New York on one plane and the family and guests flew back on another. "The team had a huge pillow fight on the plane. We were grown men, but there was no alcohol allowed and we had to do something to let out our feelings. So we had this pillow fight and I remember Wellington Mara...got hit on the back of the head a few times. But he just flipped 'em back to us so we could keep going," tackle Karl Nelson remembered.

At the after party at Giants Stadium, Wellington chatted with many of the old timers. "Charlie Conerly told me, 'I was so into that game. I was so excited,' and Ken Kavanaugh, who coached the receivers on that 1956 team, asked me, 'Where is Simms, I've got to tell him how great he was.'" Wellington was amazed at their reactions.

For Tim and Wellington, the season had brought only a widening of their rift.

In one article, Tim said he was "taking a more active role" and "overseeing the operation," but when pressed for specifics, he would demure.

"Because of the feud, Tim Mara never developed any kind of persona, and it would be pointless to judge his potential," wrote Vecsey.

Robustelli had published a scathing attack on Tim in his autobiography, which was published during the season. "[Tim] has been credited—incorrectly I might add—with being responsible for much of the team's success in the mid-1980s. Nothing could be further from the truth."

In all fairness to Tim, under him the Giants might indeed have won sometime in the future, but his prodding had forced a change that had brought about the new regime. And in all fairness to Wellington, he had seen the team through their greatest highs and their lowest lows. Both wanted success. Who could imagine the pain of a great personnel man who could not pull his team together when it most needed him? What other team had gone to the NFL championship six out of eight years? It would be impossible to imagine the incredible pain Wellington must have suffered as a result of those years spent in the wilderness. But that pain must have made this championship feel even better.

But still Tim and Wellington would not talk.

In the mid-1980s it got so bad that Wellington had Venetian blinds installed between the two owners' luxury suites. Tim one-upped him by erecting wood paneling. Wellington left the blinds on his side. Gifford, a man who was friends with both men (he had been Tim's contemporary and friend; Wellington was his oldest friend and mentor), could not get the two to reconcile after the 1986 Super Bowl.

Sadly, Wellington and Tim did not talk to each other at their own party. It was further evidence that their rift was in fact permanent. "What's it been, eight years now? ... It's been so long, actually, that you take it for granted. After it's been going on so long, it becomes part of your life. You know how it is," Tim said in January 1987. "The stories published lately have been pretty accurate. No one could go too wrong with what's been written." Wellington mostly stonewalled the press on the issue throughout his life.

❧

After the Super Bowl hysteria died down, the Atlanta Falcons attempted to steal Parcells from the Giants with the help of Parcells's agent, Robert Fraley. The Falcon's had released coach Dan Henning at the end of the season.

Fraley had called Rozelle after Young denied him the right to talk to Parcells about a position with the Falcons. Parcells was in the middle of a four-year pact with the Giants. Rankin Smith Jr., the Falcon's president, denied Parcells was on their short list. Rozelle ended it immediately over Fraley's objections. The Giants had said no, and that was where it ended. Fraley asked Rozelle to intervene. "I told the agent, 'Nope, that's it,'" said Rozelle.

JOHN MARA

John Mara was the first-born child of Wellington and Ann Mara. Like his father and his cousin Tim, John spent his summers as a ballboy at Giants training camp. He also attended many of the same schools they had attended—Boston College and, like his uncle Jack, Fordham Law.

"I really didn't decide to go to [Fordham] Law School until my senior year," said John.

He was married in 1980 to Denise F. Walker, and had four children by 1986.

Walter had attended Boston College and was a special education teacher and educational coordinator at the Essex School in East Orange, New Jersey. John and Denise were married at the Roman Catholic Church of the Resurrection in Rye, New York. Timothy C. Mara was John's best man, and five of John's sisters were bridesmaids.

John did not join the Giants organization immediately. He practiced law with the firm of Shea & Gould (among whose clients were also counted the New Jersey Generals of the USFL) in New York City.

"He's intelligent, always done well in school and in the legal business," Wellington told the press in 1986. "Although he hasn't been exposed as much to the team as I was at his age, I see he has a feeling about the team and the same kind of values I had on how it should be run. I can see a lot of myself in him, but I think every father likes to see that in his oldest son."

"I thought it would be interesting and somewhat challenging to practice law, and I like it a lot," said John. He did not want to go straight to the Giants and be known as the "old man's son," but wanted to go out and prove himself as a successful executive first.

The idea was that John would eventually take his father's place at the table in board meetings. Neither Wellington nor John had a timeline. "I'd prefer to make the move while my father is still there. That's certainly something I have hoped for all my life, to work with him. ... I don't know if I would meet resistance from the other side of the family."

"I have given retirement some thought. I feel healthy.... I have seen a lot of friends and acquaintances who have retired and do not relish that lifestyle," Wellington said.

And of course, there was still Tim to consider. "I would like to be president. But I think the way we are set up, we could run the organization without a president. ... We all meet every Wednesday and go over the week's matters, and have seen how well that works," Tim said.

Like his father, John attended all games, home and away, and was a quiet presence in the locker room after every game.

THE CANCER SCARE

In 1987, Karl Nelson, the Giants excellent offensive tackle, was diagnosed with cancer. He was placed on injured reserve as he began his treatments. Nelson was the fourth player to be diagnosed with cancer in the 13 years since the Giants had moved to East Rutherford. Most notably, well-liked and successful running back Doug Kotar had died of an inoperable brain tumor in 1983. In 1986 John Tuggle, another Giants running back, had died after several years of treatment for a rare cancer of the blood vessels, called angiosarcoma. Also, in 1980 linebacker Dan Lloyd had been successfully treated for lymphocytic lymphoma and had since moved to California, where he was coaching.

There were many concerns. No team in the league had experienced such a run of cancer ever. Nelson's case was the final straw. Was it just coincidence? Was it the stadium area? Was it something else?

On August 29, 1987, the state of New Jersey announced a comprehensive environmental investigation of the stadium area. They tested air, water, and soil quality to confirm that this was not a cause of the cancer. Doctors stated at the beginning of the study that since all four cases were different types of cancers, they did not think they would turn anything up. But there were murmurs among fans and players alike—was there something wrong? The New Jersey Sports and Exhibition Authority and the New York Football Giants both wanted the study done, if for no other reason than to dispel worries by players and workers at other areas within the sports complex that something was wrong.

Wellington sent a letter to all the players and office workers, reassuring them about the stadium environment and saying the Giants would do anything to help the state complete its investigation.

"We think the department of Environmental Protection and the Federal Environmental Protection Administration ought to go in there and see what's going on," said Kenneth Brown, director of a 30-member environmental group known as the Environmental Federation. "What we hear about the Giants players are the same kinds of things we often hear from residents and factory workers who are exposed for a time to toxic elements and then report cases of cancer. It's a real legitimate concern."

"I think an environmental study is warranted, if only to ease the minds of the players and the people who work here everyday," said safety Kenny Hill.

In the meantime, Nelson was going through cancer treatment. The Maras had a car drive Nelson's wife back and forth to the hospital every day. Young had asked Nelson's wife, Heidi, not to discuss Karl's condition with anyone, but Heidi, a feisty woman, said "I grew up here and I have lots of friends and family here. And I have the right to tell anybody I want to tell." While she said, "The Giants were good to us," she would do what she thought best for herself and Karl.

Nelson's chemotherapist, Dr. David J. Wolf, sent him from New York Hospital across the street to Sloan-Kettering. Politically, it was not a good move to send a semifamous patient to another hospital.

But the fight over Nelson's treatment had started early. "There had been a fight over who would get the case," Nelson said. "Wellington Mara…had his guy and Tim…had his guy. Don't get me wrong. Each had my best interests at heart. And I have to say right here that the Giants were great to me. They paid all the bills. I got private rooms and, if insurance didn't cover it, they paid the difference. They even paid all the deductibles and I didn't know they were going to do that. I ran up a total of $170,000 in bills for the radiation and chemo treatments, and the Giants paid for everything that insurance didn't."

Things got a little uncomfortable for Nelson during the 1987 players strike, but the Maras were incredibly generous. They insisted they pay Nelson's salary through the strike to make sure he and his family would not be any further affected. "I apologize to you guys," Nelson said during one of the first NFLPA players meetings during the strike, "but the Maras have decided to pay me during the strike. And I'm in a little different situation." According to Nelson, his fellow players were very understanding.

Nelson overcame his cancer and came back to play in spots in the 1988 season. But the cancer resurfaced in January 1989. Nelson had to undergo more serious treatment. He was kept on as an employee by the Maras for the entire time, though they could have terminated him during his contract and left him to the vagaries of an insurance policy's long-term care clause. Nelson lost his hair and went through severe chemotherapy. But today he is a cancer survivor. He officially retired in December 1989. The Giants had moved him from roster to assistant coach, though the most he could do was show up once a day and help Fred Hoaglin, the offensive line coach. Nelson admitted he was not a good coach.

When Nelson left he was a little depressed because he had been with the organization so long that the players he had played with were gone, and there were few friends to see him off.

Brad Benson had retired. Chris Godfrey was gone, and Billy Ard was in Green Bay. "I announced my retirement at the team's weekly press luncheon. I got to thank the Maras and the Giants. I acknowledged that they'd done anything I'd ever asked and had really taken care of me."

It was also revealed later that Kotar, Lloyd, and Tuggle had remained on full salary throughout their treatments as well and that the Giants had done as much for them as they had for Nelson.

The state investigation, meanwhile, had proven inconclusive, as many suspected it would. There was no evidence of any toxicity. The study cost the state more than $50,000.

AFTERMATH

The 1987 season was a wash. The NFL experienced a major strike, the second in six seasons. Television revenues were part of the cause—the networks were being squeezed to their highest limits; players saw the extra millions of dollars, and suddenly decided they would not wait for the trickle-down version of those dollars. The new NFLPA president, Gene Upshaw, former guard of the Oakland Raiders, was the most vociferous NFLPA president yet, in true Raiders form.

When the strike started, the NFL played the games using scabs. NFL owners got it from all sides. Vecsey called it "Brand X Football" and wrote, "The people who go to these fraudulent games deserve what they get." The Giants replacements were especially atrocious. "The strike produces a feeling of 'a plague on both your houses.' Others characterized it as 'millionaires fighting with billionaires,'" continued Vecsey. Few could fault either the players or the owners, but they would have to come to some negotiation. And eventually they did...but it was too late. The Giants season was over; they finished 6–9–0 and could only look forward to the next season.

Just before the 1988 season got underway, Art Rooney, Tim's long-time friend, died. He was buried on August 27. There were 1,000 attendees, his five sons and their families, including Wellington, Rozelle, Hess, Art Modell, Schramm, Davis, Hugh Culverhouse, Mike McCaskey, Billy Sullivan, and Ralph Wilson. Former players included Jack Ham, Mel Blount, Lynn Swann, Larry Brown, and Andy Russell.

Just that April, Wellington had joined Art and the rest of the Rooneys at the Kentucky Derby along with New Jersey Governor Thomas Kean. That year, Eugene V. Klein, better known as Gene Klein, former San Diego Chargers owner, and Davis had a horse named Winning Colors. Winning Colors was trained by horse racing's biggest star, D. Wayne Lukas, and ridden by famed jockey Gary Stevens. The horse had been bred by Echo Valley Horse Farm. She broke to the front early and took the race, making her only the third filly ever to win the Kentucky Derby. The NFL contingent was thrilled. Other than to Super Bowls the Steelers played in, "I enjoy it more than any other trip," Rooney told the press.

Rooney had tired of the league meetings, leaving more and more of the running of the team in his son's hands. Rooney once said, "It was more fun then," of the league meetings in the old days with Bell. "Things were slower. The pressure wasn't as great. You didn't make money. You were always facing the crisis of another day's rent."

"He longed for the day when league meetings were an hour of business and two days of cards and horses," wrote Rooney biographer Andrew O'Toole. "He missed sportsmen like Mara, Bidwill, and Marshall; businessmen who placed personal interests above the greater good had replaced their like."

Art Rooney had bought the Steelers in 1933 and had spent countless hours with Tim, Jack, and Well. And Dan Rooney and Well were good friends—both from Irish Catholic families. Art was buried at St. Peter's Roman Catholic Church in Pittsburgh.

"If we were to bury Art from another church," said Vincent M. Leonard, the retired bishop of Pittsburgh, "I don't think he'd go."

It was a loss of another longtime family friend. Still, the Maras and the Rooneys would continue to be good friends.

In 1988 the Giants finished 10–6, but did not make the playoffs. They finished tied with Buddy Ryan's Philadelphia Eagles, but the Eagles held the tiebreaker. The Giants might have taken the division if they had won their last game. But in a game that must have truly angered Mara, as well as all Giants fans, on the last Sunday of the season the 10–5 Giants lost to the 7–7–1 New York Jets. Former Giants player Joe Walton was now head coach of the Jets, and his team was elated at their toppling of their more successful crosstown rivals. The loss would scar the Giants organization for years to come.

Another blow hit the Mara family when Joseph C. Nugent, the second husband of Jack's widow, Helen Phelan Mara Nugent, died on December 6, 1988. He was 85 years old. He was survived by his son, Joseph C. Jr. of Fairhaven, New Jersey; two daughters, Barbara Bovers and Constance McQuade, both of Manhattan; two brothers, Paul of Penn Yan, New York, and Thomas of Northport, Long Island; 14 grandchildren and seven great-grandchildren. Tim, Maura, and Richard comforted Helen.

THE OLD GUARD AND THE NEW COMMISSIONER

On March 22, 1989, Rozelle announced he was going to resign as NFL commissioner. He had been commissioner for 29 years, and he had created, in many different ways, the NFL that exists today. He transformed it from a secondary sport into a league that now easily challenged baseball for the nation's heart.

But there had been rumors. He was tired. He was overwhelmed. The owners wanted more power, and Rozelle had, over the years, centralized some of that power. Just 2½ months prior to his announcement, in January, a report had surfaced in a major article titled "Owners Contend Rozelle Is Slowing." In it, an unidentified owner, who described himself as a friend, told Michael Janofsky of *The New York Times*, "This has been a brutal, brutal decade. There is no question in my mind it has slowed him down. There has been enormous pressure on him, and I've seen the fire leave his belly." Not one owner who was interviewed publicly had anything bad to say, but it was clear that the article presaged some discontent within the NFL owners' ranks.

Wellington defended his friend, saying, "I haven't seen much visible evidence of a slow down."

But in fact, Mara and Modell had been two of the five owners who had met sometime in February or March 1988 in Phoenix, Arizona, because they were "troubled enough over the increasing weight of Rozelle's responsibilities to discuss the matter in a private meeting." Hess, Schramm, and Rooney were the other owners. These were among the strongest and most influential owners in the league. This was Rozelle's inner circle, with whom he had consulted during his tenure. These were the men who counseled him, and whom he counseled.

"Rozelle heard of the meeting shortly after it had ended. ... One owner who did not attend the meeting described it as having been 'secret, very hush, hush,'" wrote Janofsky.

The message was clear—Rozelle, in effect, was out. And Wellington had something to do with it.

Wellington and Lamar Hunt were the cochairmen of the search committee to select a new commissioner. Other committee members included Modell, owner of the Cleveland Browns; Robert Parins, president of the Green Bay Packers; Dan Rooney, owner of the Pittsburgh Steelers; and Ralph Wilson, owner of the Buffalo Bills. All 28 teams would be given the opportunity to mail in names for possible successors. There was some consternation among the owners that Rozelle had picked the search committee members rather than allowing a vote by all the owners.

"We formed the committee based on long-term dedication to the league," Mara told the press. "The idea is to have people who have experience and can draw on that, realizing the mistakes and successes of the past and trying, most importantly, not to duplicate the mistakes."

Possible successors right off the bat included Jack Kemp, former Bills quarterback and the secretary of Housing and Urban Development; Peter Ueberroth, former baseball commissioner and organizer of the 1984 Los Angeles summer Olympics; Paul Tagliabue, a Washington lawyer who had helped Rozelle many times; and Vernon Jordan, the former president of the National Urban League.

The biggest issue on the table was whether to replace Rozelle with two people or one. Most owners were very much against a "two-headed camel," as Schramm referred to it.

"We have one president of the United States," Wellington said. "The important thing is for the top guy to be able to turn to the right people to get the proper administration."

"The more we look at it, the more amazing it is that Pete Rozelle was able to do what he did," Mara said in another interview about the search. "Any new commissioner coming in, one of the first few questions has got to be, 'What about labor?'" It was obvious that the owners were concerned about the possibility of more strikes, and wanted to avoid another costly war.

"In football, we'll have a strong head man and two, maybe three, deputies.... Who he is is more important than what he is," Mara concluded, saying that the next commissioner did not need to be a lawyer. Few newspapers failed to mention that Mara was once again at the vortex of the commissioner search, noting that he was again influencing the hiring of this most important individual.

In May 1989 the owners met in New Orleans and more names surfaced, including Finks, general manager of the New Orleans Saints; Roone Arledge, the president of ABC News; retired army general Pete Dawkins; Lowell Perry, the head of the NFL charities, and others.

Only one thing was clear to everyone. With so many choices, the election of the new commissioner was going to be a bigger dogfight than the one that had resulted in Rozelle's election in 1960, on the 23rd ballot.

When asked about this possibility, Wellington replied, "There's nothing wrong with good, honest infighting."

He would rue his words.

Finks proved to be the early front-runner in the press, and more and more owners voiced their consternation over the process, although few would allow their names to be printed next to their quotes. To be named commissioner of the NFL the candidate would need to receive 19 owner votes out of 28. On June 6, at a meeting in Chicago, Finks found a bloc of 11 owners were steadfastly against him. His name was nominated several times, and the vote came up the same each time—17 for and 11 against. Hunt, Mara, Rooney, and Modell led the charge for Finks. Oil baron and Wellington's close personal friend Hess was also with them. But Dallas, Philadelphia, San Francisco, Seattle, Indianapolis, Tampa Bay, Los Angeles, Denver, and New England all abstained each time Finks's name was brought up.

The vote was not so much against Finks as it was against Rozelle's inner circle. It was the new league against the old guard, and Mara was seen as the prototypical old guard. Eddie DeBartolo of the San Francisco 49ers, Norman Braman of the Philadelphia Eagles, Jerry Jones of the Dallas Cowboys, and Mike Lynn of the Minnesota Vikings were part of the new generation of owners that were leading the charge against the old guard.

Denver's Pat Bowlen also joined this cabal of new owners, which became known as the Chicago 11, who were worried about cronyism. The new commissioner could not pick up the gauntlet Rozelle had abandoned. Finks was seen as an extension of hostilities toward the NFLPA. Many were concerned that Finks was just a continuation of Old Guard policies. The owners wanted a new outlook for the league and for labor confrontations. They wanted someone to work with Upshaw and not antagonize him. DeBartolo and Lynn were dispatched to pepper the commission with questions as to why and how Finks had become its sole offering.

"The selection process was flawed from the beginning. This will expand it," Bowlen told the press on July 15, 1989.

Eventually, Mara and Modell offered a compromise. A new search committee would be formed in exchange for the dissolving of the Chicago 11 bloc. The session was long and grueling, but the compromise was eventually embraced.

The new committee was comprised of Mara, Hunt, Ken Behring of the Seattle Seahawks, Davis of the Los Angeles Raiders, Jack Kent Cooke of the Washington Redskins, and Lynn. By August 4, 1989, the new committee had met again in Chicago and interviewed five new candidates. Among the new list of candidates were Paul Tagliabue, the NFL's Washington counsel; Robert Mulcahy, president and chief of the New Jersey Sports and Exposition Authority; Willie Davis, former star of the Green Bay Packers; Paul Kirk, former Democratic Party chairman; and Finks.

Then leaks about disagreements between the owners started to make their way into the newspapers again. Among other tidbits was Wellington's writing to Hugh Culverhouse Jr. denying that the committee met secretly with Finks as part of a larger ploy to name "their own man." This was one of only dozens of letters that were flying back and forth between team offices.

By October 8 Mara had told all the committee members and all the owners to be prepared to stay through the rest of the next week, if necessary, to resolve the issue. On October 25 Dan Rooney chaired one of the meetings, now held in Cleveland. And the smoke was clearing. Art and Well were staunchly behind Finks. Pat Bowlen and Lynn preferred Tagliabue. In the first two votes, Tagliabue led Finks 15–11.

In Cleveland on October 26 Tagliabue won the election and was announced as commissioner. Both he and Finks were well qualified for the position, but Tagliabue was seen as a little more of an insider, someone who already had working knowledge of the NFL offices. And Finks's candidacy was weakened becasue he was aligned solely with the old guard, if for no other reason. The vote was clearly a rebuke of Modell and Mara, dished out because a great many owners felt that they had been purposely ignored.

In a compromise, the new owners allowed that Finks could be number two at the NFL offices. But Finks, when phoned by Modell and Well, flatly refused the offer.

"I thought it would be a dream team if we could get the two together," Mara told the press. "But when we found it wasn't possible, we also felt it would be a detriment to the league to keep fighting this battle."

The new breed of owners was pressing the league in a new direction. Mara, Modell, McCaskey (grandson of Bears founder Halas), and Rooney were being squeezed by the new owners, such as Victor Kiam (Patriots), Jones, Bowlen, and others. But now the league had a new issue. It wasn't just NFL vs. NFLPA, which was not going to go away; but was there a gap between the new owners and the old guard? Bowlen didn't think so.

"What we might have learned out of this as much as anything else is that for all 28 teams, from Wellington Mara to Jerry Jones, it is very important that we meet more often. That could make a tremendous difference in everything," Bowlen said.

ANOTHER RING

While the appointment of a new commissioner spilled over into the 1989 season, another small story hit the newspapers, and an old friend was welcomed back.

In 1989 the Dallas Cowboys were bought by Jones. Landry, who had taken the Dallas Cowboys to 12 conference championship games and five Super Bowls and was now called America's coach, was fired in favor of a new coach, Jimmy Johnson.

Wellington invited his old friend to be his guest for the Cowboys-Giants December 16 showdown. It would be the first Dallas game Landry would attend since his firing in February. "I know New York has got to win the game, but then I will not root against the Cowboys," Landry said. It was the first time he was not involved in football since piloting B-17 bombers in World War II. The two sat in Wellington's box and watched the game.

In 1989, spurred by their horrific experience of the year before, the Giants roared to a 12–4 record, second best in the NFL. On January 7, 1990, the Giants faced the NFC wild-card team, the Los Angeles Rams. The Giants dominated the first half in virtually every category, including time of possession and yards gained, but due to a fumble near their own end zone, the Giants went into half-time down 7–6. The Giants dominated the game in the second half as well, and scored a touchdown, but the Rams put up two field goals and tied the game, forcing overtime. Rams quarterback Jim Everett connected with Willie Anderson on a 30-yard touchdown pass. Anderson caught the ball, sprinted for the end zone, and then jogged into the players' exit with the Giants fans' hearts. The stadium was almost silent as fans exited the stadium. It was one of the most devastating losses in Giants history.

In 1990 the Giants had a banner regular season. Phil Simms was on top of his game, and Taylor, though slower, was still an incredible warrior. Parcells had tapped former St. Louis Cardinals star running back O.J. Anderson—a grizzled veteran who had restarted his career with the Giants. He would be the team's workhorse in 1990.

The team went 13–3 with the league's leading defense. The Bears went 11–5 under Mike Ditka, and San Francisco finished 14–2. The Giants would have to go the rest of the way without Simms, who was injured with two weeks to go in the regular season. Backup Jeff Hostetler would quarterback the team in his place. The Bears came to Giants Stadium and lost 31–3, the same weekend that San Francisco beat Washington 28–10. Now the Giants would have to go to the West Coast and play for the NFC championship. The 49ers were fighting for an unprecedented third-straight Super Bowl championship. Not too many analysts gave the Giants a chance. Even if they made it to the championship game against San Francisco, it was assumed that the travel and the two-time world champions would defeat them.

The game was a seesaw battle, and at halftime the teams went into the locker room tied 6–6. San Francisco then scored a touchdown and the Giants answered with a Matt Bahr field goal. The 49ers were ahead 13–9 with one quarter to go. In the fourth quarter a Giants drive stalled and ended with another field goal, making the score 13–12. The Giants defense had been valiant all day, knocking down magical 49ers quarterback Joe Montana. The 49ers were running the ball, trying to squeeze the clock for time, when nose guard Jim Burt stuck his head into 49ers running back Roger Craig's arm, forcing the ball out. Lawrence Taylor alertly picked up the fumble and secured another chance for the Giants with 2:36 left. Bahr kicked a 42-yard field goal as time expired, and the Giants secured a 15–13 victory. It was one of the greatest wins in Giants history.

In January 1991 the coming ground war against Iraq, which everyone anticipated, cast a mighty and patriotic shadow across the Super Bowl proceedings. Whitney Houston, who performed the national anthem, went on to make it one of her best-selling records ever. Security for this event was the most intense ever used at a sporting event in the United States up to that point.

Super Bowl XXV was hosted in Tampa, Florida, on January 27, 1991, and matched the Giants, the league's best defense, against the Buffalo Bills and their supercharged no-huddle offense. The Giants were considered underdogs. The Giants scored 10 points in the first half in front of the 73,813 fans that came to see the game, but the Bills defense proved to be the difference before the first half ended, as they scored a safety on quarterback Jeff Hostetler. In the third quarter the Giants responded with a nine minute, 29 second, 75-yard drive that culminated with a one-yard Anderson plunge. Anderson would go on to be named game MVP for his 102 yards on the ground. It was at this time that the brilliance of Parcells's game plan became apparent. The Giants were dominating the time of possession, keeping the high-powered Bills offense off the field. And when the Giants defense was on the field, defensive coordinator Bill Belichick's confusing and brutalizing defense hurt the Bills offense with brutal hitting and tackling. The Bills responded in the beginning of the fourth quarter with a drive of their own, and scored on a Thurman Thomas 31-yard touchdown run, taking a 19-17 lead. The Giants then responded with another long drive, but it finally stalled and Matt Bahr kicked a 21-yard field goal to bring the score to 20–19 with 7:20 left. With a little more than two minutes left, the Bills began a drive that marched the ball down the field and brought it to the New York 29. Then came Bills kicker Scott Norwood with eight seconds left on the clock.

As Norwood lined up the kick, Ann Mara rubbed her rosary beads, all the while whispering for Scott Norwood to miss. The stadium held its collective breath as Norwood's kick sailed through the dark sky. Wide right. The Giants had won against all odds.

"Bill Parcells is the best coach the Giants ever had," Tim told the press after the game.

Wellington and Parcells also had a formidable relationship. "Theirs was a relationship few people ever saw or knew about. Parcells owned horses and had a love-hate relationship with them, as all horsemen do. One day he told Mara this one particular horse was good, but wait till you see the one I've got in the barn," wrote King of *Sports Illustrated.*

"That's what they all say,"' Mara said. Then the Giants training camp moved nearer to Albany a few years later. The exit from the New York Thruway was near the Saratoga Race Course. According to King, Parcells dropped a note to Mara telling him he knew the real reason the Giants had moved 120 miles north. "Don't tell anyone," Mara wrote back.

"Mara knew Parcells was superstitious and believed if you saw a penny on the ground, heads up, it was good luck; a tails-up penny was to be avoided at all costs," wrote King. "And so sometimes, when he went down to the locker room to get dressed for practice, Parcells would find a penny, heads up, in his locker. Mara's work."

Sadly, as was their tradition in the last Super Bowl, Wellington and Tim did not share the podium. In fact, things had been brewing before the team's stellar run that would dramatically change the direction of the organization for the next 20 years.

MONEY, MONEY, MONEY

Despite their Super Bowl appearances, the Giants lost approximately $6.7 million between 1986 and 1989 per financial statements released as part of an antitrust lawsuit brought by a group of players against the league:

1986	lost $7,000
1987	lost $1.4 million
1988	lost $4.2 million
1989	lost $1.09 million

Team officials and executives remained well paid, though, including some of the highest salaries in the league in some cases. Parcells saw his salary increase from $140,000 in 1983 to $725,000 in 1990, making him one of the highest-paid coaches in the NFL. And Young, who earned $94,000 in 1981, earned $441,250 in 1990. After Super Bowl XXI Parcells earned a bonus of $280,000 and Young collected a $246,000 bonus as well. This clearly shows the Giants weren't pinching pennies in the new era.

One of the surprises of the financial statements was that defensive coordinator Bill Belichick ($175,000 per year) and offensive coordinator Ron Erhardt ($183,500 per year) both made more in salary than Wellington and Tim Mara. Tim and Well each collected salaries of $150,000 from 1982 to 1990.

In all, the Giants paid their coaches $2,309,043 in salary in 1990, with every staff member making more than $100,000 except Charlie Weis, who earned $95,375 as a first-year assistant special teams coach.

"I feel right now, if there is a problem, we are our own worst enemy. The individual clubs have increased the costs to where they are today. We all overreacted to [the USFL effect on] the 1984 draft," Tim said. "I believe football and all sports are a prime form of entertainment and there will always be a need for them. ... If we continue to do our homework, I don't foresee any problem in maintaining a successful operation."

However, the Giants made more than the league average in 1986, earning $36 million in revenues. By contrast, the 49ers had made only $31.4 million in 1989, the year of their fourth Super Bowl, when they lost a total of $14 million.

These kinds of numbers, however, can be misleading. Plenty of owner-executives take low salaries but take out bonuses, loans, and profits in cash and in other ways. Lifestyle packages can be added to the company's bottom line, such as dues to country clubs and professional organizations; in the Maras' case, that might have included their Winged Foot and New York Athletic Club fees. A portion of their entertainment expenses were also probably written off. Leasing of cars and other luxury items can also be written off to the company. Some companies tend to do these kinds of things in their highest grossing years so as not to penalize the company in subsequent, less successful years. Gauging the success of an organization by judging those things can be misleading. While many of the top-line expenses were released, many of the others that would give a much more accurate picture of the Maras' lifestyles were not released.

265

If anything, the news comforted fans and sportswriters who felt the Giants might be tightening the cash flow in order to take as much profit as possible out of the organization. The released documents proved the organization was paying top dollar to its staff in order to keep them. These expenses may have been suggested by Young, but would have had to have been approved by both Wellington and Tim.

A GIANT EMBARRASSMENT

There is no doubt that Wellington Mara was undeniably wound up in his faith and in his church. The Mara family was and remains today one of the largest contributing groups to the Catholic church in the metro region, as well as being wonderful and devoted backers of some religiously affiliated charities and organizations dedicated to good works. There is no denying the family's dedication to helping the less fortunate.

They are also on record as being affiliated with many conservative politicians, including state and federal congressmen and senators, as well as governors and presidential candidates. No one is sure when Wellington broke from his father's Democratic political leanings, but he was a dedicated conservative. This was in the decade that saw the United States raise such conservative icons as Ronald Reagan, George H. W. Bush, Pat Robertson, and many more.

Anna Quindlen, one of the op-ed writers for *The New York Times,* wrote a blistering attack on Wellington on January 24, 1991, when she published "Offensive Play." "Sunday, the Super Bowl will be played in Tampa Bay and so, inevitably, my thoughts turn to abortion," Quindlen began her barrage.

Wellington and six players from that Super Bowl team had made a film wherein they were interviewed on passing, blocking, and their opposition to a woman's right to an abortion. "It's a bizarre juxtaposition that might be reminiscent of *Saturday Night Live* if it weren't so offensive," Quindlen wrote.

The movie was called *Champions for Life.* Wellington produced the 10-minute movie with Robustelli. The players involved included Mark Bavaro, Martin, Phil McConkey, Chris Godfrey, and Jim Burt. Some quotes from the movie included:

Bavaro: "At the end of the game, all the Giants players left the field champions. Now with the abortion death squads allowed to run rampant through our country, I wonder how many future champions will be killed before they see the light of day."

Martin: "I hope and pray that the Supreme Court has begun to turn the tide against the legalized destruction of babies allowed by the *Roe v. Wade* decision. That infamous decision said that unborn babies have no rights, just as the shameful Dred Scott decision said that black people have no rights."

Simms: "When I woke up the next morning and read those statistics in the paper, I was very pleased and proud. But there was another statistic in the paper that morning that didn't get the same coverage the Super Bowl got. I guess they thought it wasn't very important. It was just a little item that stated there are an average of 4,400 babies killed every day by abortion."

The film was distributed by American Life League, an antiabortion group based in Virginia. They sent out hundreds of promotional videos around the country to like-minded antiabortion organizations. The Archdiocese of Los Angeles alone bought almost 300 copies, including some to be shown in schools.

Wellington himself was quoted as saying, "The church has never changed its teachings on the sanctity of human life—it didn't make up a rule for the convenience of a particular time, like a rule at a country club, as the governor would have us believe." Mara was referring to New York Governor Mario M. Cuomo.

"Mr. Mara remains co-owner of the team, and he remains devoted to this cause," wrote Quindlen. "He may envision…another 10-minute sermonette linking athletic prowess and moral superiority. It's his right to do that. I just think it's out of bounds."

Regardless of the correctness of either side's position, the idea of a sports organization entering the realm of politics was seen as a huge faux pas, especially by the other owners and league executives. It was a political agenda that should not have been linked to a sports franchise. Wellington wanted to use his notoriety to help a cause he believed in. While there is nothing wrong with backing up one's beliefs, the abortion issue is so touchy that many in the sports industry felt that his push was inappropriate.

267

Sports Illustrated titled its coverage of the story "A Giant Embarrassment." The article related, "No matter how one feels about abortion, it's hard not to be repulsed by the video's inflammatory language. Apart from questions of taste, there's one further objection that should be raised...no women are heard from in the video. In fact, women aren't even mentioned," citing Quindlen's previously published editorial.

Wellington was impassioned in his belief. "We live in an age when mankind, in its arrogance, seeks to abrogate to itself the right to limit or to deny life to the afflicted and the unborn. That is the challenge of our generation. The challenge and the shame. It is a challenge that must be met, a shame that must be expiated," wrote Wellington. "It cannot be met by act of Congress alone but by the will of the people, motivated by the informed youth of America who reassert the values that were the cornerstones of the foundation of our country and who want to embrace again the sovereignty and beneficence of God. That is the capability of Life Athletes, to give the youth of America the ultimate means with which to confront and vanquish the culture of death which threatens them."

Mara never gave up on these values. "In later years, Mr. Mara struck a finer balance. The strident activism of Champions for Life gave way to the temperate, values-based advocacy of Life Athletes. Mr. Mara quietly continued his work for a cause to which he was deeply and sincerely committed. But he was too considerate—and too smart—to shove that work in the faces of the many customers who disagreed with him," wrote Chris Godfrey.

Wellington was a donor to Life Athletes, an organization founded by Godfrey, one of the stalwarts of the 1986 Super Bowl offensive line. The conservative club's mantra was: "Virtue. Abstinence. Respect life." The Life Athletes commitment included:

1. I will try to do what is right, even when it is difficult.
2. I will give myself only to that special person I marry as my partner for life.
3. I will respect the lives of others, especially the unborn and the aged.
4. I will not quit or make excuses when I fail. I will try again.

Godfrey was a devotee of Wellington, writing, "In a cynical world that seems to know the cost of everything and the value of nothing, Wellington Mara helped us appreciate the important things, namely faith, family, friends, and life itself."

"We've written a curriculum that is going into schools," Godfrey said. "Right now it's going into Catholic schools. Archbishop Edward Egan has directed that it be used in all schools' religious instruction.... It cites a lot of Catholic authorities. We are working on a curriculum for other schools. Most of our members are religious of some type, most of them are Protestant or evangelical. ... Everybody that is a Life Athlete is pro-life."

In 2002 Well was honored by the organization Life Athletes. But this time it was a much more low-key affair.

ART MODELL AND BOB TISCH

"Bob, we now hear that Tim Mara is serious about selling his 50 percent of the team," Modell said. He was speaking to former postmaster general Robert Tisch. "Would you be interested?"

"I was pretty well set to get the Baltimore franchise when Art Modell called me," Tisch said in later years. He had been trying to get a franchise in Baltimore. New York's gain was about to be Baltimore's loss.

Preston Robert Tisch, along with his brother Laurence Tisch, ran the Loews Corporation. Together they had made millions of dollars as turnaround specialists. He was born on April 29, 1926, in Brooklyn, New York.

Tisch attended DeWitt Clinton High School in the Bronx for one year before changing to Erasmus Hall High School in Brooklyn to finish his high school education. He then went to Bucknell University, but left to join the army. He served in the army from 1943 to 1945. He came back and went to Michigan, where he took a B.A. in economics. He was married to Joan Hyman in 1948 and had two sons, Steven and Jonathan, and a daughter, Laurie.

In late 1990 Wellington had gone to Modell and Modell knew Tisch. "The Giants came into my life last November. Wellington and I had lunch and I heard there was a possibility Helen was selling," Tisch said.

Tisch and Tim talked, and they shook hands and closed the deal. Tim, Maura, and Helen were to receive $75 million, making the New York Giants, at the time, the second most valuable sports franchise in North America behind the Yankees, and approximately tied with the Cowboys and the Bears. They were supposed to have closed the deal sometime before New Year's Day, 1991, but there was a problem. The team kept winning.

"Tim's sister Maura was a big fan and Timmy kept saying, 'Bob, Maura won't sell the team as long as we're in the hunt for the Super Bowl,'" Tisch said. "I had a handshake deal, but I didn't have a firm agreement, but I said, 'Timmy, I can't blame her. I understand. We'll talk again next week.' But each week they would win a playoff game. They never anticipated being in the Super Bowl in '91."

Tisch said he attended Super Bowl XXV, in Tampa, "as the owner-in-waiting." Tim, Well, Art, Helen, and Maura knew, but no one else did.

Tim, Maura, and Dick Concannon had considered selling the team in 1984 and 1986, obviously each time hoping to take advantage of the team's rising fortunes to maximize their value when they sold. "But this one was the first one we seriously considered. I just felt at this point in my life the time was right," Tim said at the time.

༜

Many in the league and within the team were glad Tim sold. They would have been glad if either side had sold. There was no denying there would be relief within the organization now.

"Well and I will get along fine," Tisch told the press. A friend of Rozelle's, Tisch was welcomed readily by the other NFL owners.

Tim's group had walked away with $75 million before taxes and estate penalties.

"It highlights again the problems of family ownership of teams in this league," Young told the press. "What we pay the players has forced prices up so high we're forcing the family ownerships out.

Some have said the team was sold because of the feud. It had nothing to do with the feud. It's a private family business decision."

But even at the end, the Maras refused to talk to one another.

"At the closing we had them in two different rooms," Tisch
later revealed. "In one room, Maura Concannon asked me,
'What's happening in Plan B of the draft?' I said, 'Wait a minute,
Maura.' I went next door to Well Mara and asked him, 'What's
happening with Plan B of the draft?' I went back and told her."

"I'm looking forward to 10 good years of football," Tisch
told Wellington.

"Then you'll have to go through 30 years of football,"
responded Wellington.

It was done. The most famous family feud in the world of professional sports was over. The family schism was complete. And
now the Giants, for the first time in the organization's history, was
not wholly owned by the Maras. It seemed almost incomprehensi-
ble. To many fans and sports executives, they just assumed the two
would go on struggling with each other into history. Though the
management feud was over, the Giants were about to have
new struggles.

The lasting moment of the entire event was Maura Mara
Concannon's editorial for *The New York Times,* which she wrote in
February 1991.

"Fifty years of a life brushed aside in a tidy 10-word headline:
"Robert Tisch Agrees to Buy 50 percent of the Champion Giants."
What the headline fails to say is that somewhere lost in talk of the
uncle and the nephew is the sister who grieves for the end of a fairy
tale filled with giants..." wrote Mrs. Concannon.

"Since childhood I have traveled each hard-fought yard with
these Giants...

"My father, Jack, then 17, handled one of the sideline
markers. ... Steve Owen, who would coach the Giants for the first 15
years of my life, was operating under the only contract he would ever
have: a handshake.

"When college beckoned, I chose a school that was 'geograph-
ically desirable,' that is, with a Sunday morning express train that
got me home in time for kickoffs. If the Giants were 'away,' Mother

Mary George would unlock the darkened administration building, which housed the campus television set, and I would watch in a deserted classroom."

Like other fans, Maura used the other media to keep up with the Giants as much as possible. "During the season I am consumed with a need for information. When not tuned in to Mike and the Mad Dog, I pore over the daily sports pages and three weeklies devoted to the Giants. I start worrying about game-day weather on Tuesdays, when the the first five-day forecasts appear on the evening news," wrote Maura. "But thousands of loyal Giants fans follow a similar, crazed routine. It is the strength of my emotional bond to the team that has worried others—and, at times, me.

"The decision to sell my family's stock in the New York Football Giants has been a heartbreaking one for me. But eventually it was inevitable. Football has always been my family's sole business, albeit a passion as well, not a toy or a tax shelter. As one of the last mom-and-pop owners in the league, there are no shopping centers, pizza parlors, or hotels to bail us out when million-dollar lawsuits, salaries, and estate taxes threaten.

"Much has been made of the Mara family feud, but it is a painful fact of life that has taken its toll. My brother Tim, whom I hope most people realize led us not only to the Meadowlands but to the promised land of two Super Bowls, probably put it best: 'The business of football isn't fun anymore.'

"I will always be a part of the family who 'bleed and sweat and yell and exult' for the Giants. But perhaps—and only perhaps—I may one day attain just a hint of detachment, and when we lose I will not despair. Sundays will mark the end of my week, but not the end of my world.

"I have called my life with the Giants a fairy tale, and so it has been. Which is why I was not altogether surprised that my story should end with a glass slipper—the one that fit Matt Bahr but was a shade too small for Scott Norwood."

PARCELLS LEAVES

Tisch's welcome to the New York Giants was the defection of his star coach. Parcells had decided he wanted out. Parcells's poor health and other factors notwithstanding, his agent was again talking to other clubs, including Tampa Bay.

The Maras denied that Parcells was available. "He's under contract to the Giants. So if he's going to coach, he will coach for the Giants," Tim had told the press before he announced the sale of his half of the club.

When Parcells made the announcement in May 1991 that he was leaving, it should have been a shock to no one. He'd said halfway through the season that if they won the Super Bowl, he was gone. But there had been other reasons he was leaving, not the least of which was the difficult relationship he was having with the front office and the departure of Tim Mara, with whom Parcells was much closer (in age and friendship) than he was to Well. When Parcells was angry with something, he would go to Tim sometimes instead of Young. Parcells called Tim his go-to guy.

Parcells was reluctant to negotiate, and Young was too callused to woo and pursue his star coach. And with the sale to Tisch pending the NFL owners' voting approval, Parcells's contract negotiations were put on hold. There were too many negatives.

As to his negotiations with the team, Parcells said, "They're treating me like a player." This was a Young miscalculation. As to his health, Parcells said, "I drink coffee. I smoke regularly. I'm 30 pounds overweight. Real smart." And in fact, Parcells did have serious health concerns.

Also, he had his agent, Fraley, whispering in his ear that the Giants, with aging stars, would be all downhill. If he stayed, his reputation would be tarnished, just like Al Arbour. Arbour had won four championships for the Islanders, but was bounced years later when he couldn't win without his stars. If Parcells quit now, eventually he would be able to write his own ticket. Parcells would be able to apply for a job as general manager and head coach.

"He's an unsettled guy. I expect him to be back as our coach," Wellington told the press.

Tisch echoed Well, saying, "His negotiations will probably start next week."

The New York Times summed up the situation best when Dave Anderson wrote, "By not wanting to negotiate, Bill Parcells wanted to leave. To show that he didn't deserve to be treated like a player in contract negotiations. To avert the uncertainty of Bob Tisch's influence. To eliminate being a victim if the Giants struggle. To assure his stature and his price for the opportunity that will develop at Tampa Bay, if not elsewhere. And most of all, to build a Super Bowl contender with his imprint."

With Parcells gone, in May the Giants had nowhere to turn. Defensive genius Belichick had taken the head job with Cleveland. Young turned to Ray Handley, who not a month before had been the running backs coach. It was the biggest mistake of Young's career. With a decent core of players, Handley would lead the Giants to some of the worst seasons in the team's history. In 1991 the Giants went 8–8–0, and in 1992 they went 6–10–0. By the end of Handley's run the team had become a circus, and Parcells's departure was the reason why.

In January 1993 Tom Coughlin spurned Young's entreaty to take the head coaching job at the Giants. Parcells was still available. And the press wondered why the Giants would not rehire Parcells. In fact, it was revealed years later that Parcells had called Wellington and asked him about the opening. But this much became apparent: Parcells didn't want to work with Young and Young didn't want to work with Parcells.

CHAPTER 11

A New Beginning

JOHN JOINS THE GIANTS

With the departure of Tim, Bob Tisch and Well agreed to bring Wellington's son John on board. John Mara's ascension was announced by Tisch. John joined the team as executive vice president and general counsel.

"It was one of the things I was very anxious to attain before I agreed to the [sale of 50 percent of the team to Tisch]," Wellington told the press. "It did not take a great amount of negotiating with Bob.... This makes it possible for one of my boys to play an important role with the team and to be in a position to move in as my successor. This sort of removes me one notch from the day-to-day operations. I'll still be involved, but if I feel like staying home one day, now I know I can do it."

"I couldn't imagine Tim welcoming me with open arms," John said. "The sale certainly facilitated this move."

By this time, John had spent nine years with Shea & Gould. Holding down a full-time executive position did not leave him much time to stay involved with the team, "although I did talk to my father almost on a daily basis to try to keep up with things."

"I plan to be a visible owner, but I don't have any particular changes in mind," John said.

Many had foreseen the possibility of Tim and John someday working together. Now John was in, and it was clear that the Maras would be involved with the Giants for years to come. But in the future, who would he be dealing with on the other side?

FREE AGENCY REDUX

The NFL management council that had helped construct the player free agency agreement that expired in 1987 consisted of Jack Donlan, Hugh Culverhouse of the Tampa Bay Buccaneers, Tex Schramm of the Dallas Cowboys, and Joe Robbie of the Miami Dolphins. The NFL was now ready to face yet another confrontation with the NFLPA, and a new group needed to be picked.

Wellington, Dan Rooney, Tagliabue, and Harold Henderson, an NFL lawyer, were now chosen to try to deal with this problem. The irony of this was rich.

The players once again went to Minneapolis Federal District Court, this time to fight Plan B free agency. [Plan B was a restrictive, limited version of free agency. It allowed a team to protect numerous players and greatly hindered a player's ability to market his services.] During the course of the court case, the players' union and the NFL continued to have a dialogue to try to solve their differences with Gene Upshaw and NFLPA lawyer Jim Quinn.

The NFLPA ostensibly won in September 1992, with Mark Collins, a Giants player, one of those whose name was on the complaint. A jury found that Plan B free agency violated antitrust laws. The litigation before the court judged four of the eight complaints worthy of damages. But the other four did not merit any damages.

Collins was happy. He was awarded $178,000, which was to be trebled, according to U.S. antitrust laws. Wellington struck a more even-keel position, saying, "The jury obviously thought Plan B was fair in some cases and not in others. In four of the eight cases they said Plan B wasn't just. It's not a question of we won and they lost. Both sides gained something they wanted and lost something they wanted. It looked like an invitation to us to come up with another system."

Eventually, the approval of a new contract went to a group of seven, which included Tagliabue; Wellington; John Shaw, executive vice president of the Los Angeles Rams; Jack Kent Cooke, owner of the Washington Redskins; Al Davis of the Los Angeles Raiders; Pat Bowlen of the Denver Broncos; and Mike Brown of the Cincinnati Bengals.

Essentially, the owners granted a new kind of free agency in exchange for a salary cap, not unlike the NBA. With Tisch bringing his ways of making money to the organization, Wellington was back at the NFL offices.

GOOD-BYE, MR. SIMMS

Ray Handley had been a bust in more ways than one. And by the end of his tenure, the Giants, a proud franchise only two years earlier, were a sheer disaster with little hope, despite still having more than half the roster that had recently won a Super Bowl.

Handley was released after a 6–10 season in 1992. A large number of names were bandied about as potential replacements. The Dallas Cowboys defensive coordinator Dave Wannstedt's was one. On January 7, 1993, Young interviewed Wannstedt for the Giants job. Wannstedt chose to go to the Bears instead. Young's choice for the job, however, was Tom Coughlin, a former assistant of Parcells and now head coach at Boston College. However, after much wooing by Young, who talked Coughlin up to Mara and Tisch, Coughlin spurned Young, preferring to stay in Boston.

Mike Ditka and Buddy Ryan were also mentioned in passing, but not seriously considered. So were Ray Rhodes and Vince Tobin. But the biggest name available on the market was a man named Bill Parcells.

But Young would not even call Parcells. Young had felt betrayed by Parcells's desertion in early 1991 and refused to discuss Parcells as a possible candidate. Behind closed doors he was vehemently opposed to Parcells, citing in particular Parcells's and his agent's threats to leave the franchise after each Super Bowl win.

"Young waited for Wannstedt, the Bears' president, Mike McCaskey, went after him. McCaskey hurried to Dallas and offered Wannstedt the job. He took it. Even with the Cowboys preparing for Super Bowl XXVII yesterday, the Bears named Wannstedt their successor to Mike Ditka," Dave Anderson wrote in *The New York Times*. "By waiting instead of acting, Young committed pro football's deadliest sin, on or off the field: he got outhustled."

Then Parcells was gone, hired by Bob Kraft of the New England Patriots. At the press conference, Parcells was asked about the Giants.

"The Maras are the two men responsible for what Bill Parcells has," the Patriots' new coach said, referring to Wellington Mara and

Tim Mara, the Giants' co-owners during Parcells's eight seasons as their coach. "There'll always be a warm place in my heart for them."

"Parcells didn't mention a place in his heart for George Young, the Giants' general manager," wrote Anderson, "who never even phoned to explain why he wasn't being considered for the job…"

Dan Reeves, who was recently relieved of his head coaching duties in Denver after many successful years, was hired. Wellington liked and respected Reeves.

❧

"May I have your attention for a minute? I just heard a report that Phil Simms is on his way to San Diego. Let me say this as emphatically as I can: Phil Simms is not being traded. Not this year, not last year, or in the 20th century. To San Diego or to anyplace else. Period. Okay?"

This was it. With this little announcement, Wellington left the pressroom as quickly as he had appeared. In August 1992 this was the statement of the co-owner of the New York Giants. "I've heard too many reports, too many rumors flying around from everywhere. I wanted to lay it all to rest. The guy is staying," Wellington said afterward to another reporter.

Mark Bavaro, the talented tight end, was now with the Browns. When Bavaro was unceremoniously released, Wellington had "quietly increased the battered tight end's severance payments," reported Anderson.

With Dan Reeves and Simms at the controls, the Giants made one of the most improbable runs in football. The 1993 season was one of those years that gives fans great memories, but may result in confusion for subsequent seasons. In 1993 Reeves rejuvenated the core of the team, mixed in some new bodies, and made an incredible run. The Giants assembled an 11–4–0 record going into the last game of the season. The Cowboys, now resurrected by Jimmy Johnson and fearsome as defending Super Bowl champions, came into Giants Stadium for one of the most memorable last games of the season in franchise history. Simms, running back Rodney Hampton, and the offense played brilliantly. And the Giants defense played valiantly. It was a playoff atmosphere. The winner of this game would have home-field advantage throughout the NFC playoffs. The loser would become the wild-card team, and would have to travel the following week.

The Giants played a spirited game, and the contest went into overtime. But it was Dallas's Emmitt Smith's incredible performance with a separated shoulder that resulted in a 16–13 overtime loss for the Giants.

The Giants were the wild-card team. They won their first-round game 17–10 over the Minnesota Vikings. The Giants were looking good. But the team had a short week and had to fly to San Francisco, where they lost 44–3. It was their worst performance of the year. It was also Lawrence Taylor's last game. And as it turned out, Simms's, also.

One of Simms's finest years was 1993. He completed a career high 61.8 percent of his passes. He played in all 16 games, threw for more than 3,000 yards, 19 touchdowns, and only nine interceptions. And to make things even better, Simms, Hampton, and offensive linemen Jumbo Elliott and Bart Oates made the Pro Bowl.

One of those many moments that went unreported in Mara's life also occurred in 1993. Always known as a thoughtful and generous owner, when the Giants played Seattle that year Wellington invited Hall of Fame end Red Badgro to the game to sit in the owner's box. Badgro was older than Wellington, and was treated with as much respect as possible by Mara. These kinds of gestures were common in Wellington's life.

Often there were stories of disgruntled or petitioning fans, who, for example, asked for seats under the overhang as they got older . Or seats for families who'd lost loved ones or needed special access. These were Wellington's people, and he took care of their requests, as did all the Maras, whenever possible. This was a family trait shared by Tim, Jack, T.J., Wellington, and Wellington's children, which made the fans so loyal from the start.

☙❧

In June 1994 Simms was working out in the weight room when Reeves summoned Simms to his office. Simms assumed he wanted him to sign some footballs. Instead, Reeves told Simms the ugly news. Between the discussion on his recently repaired shoulder and salary cap issues, Simms was being released. Reeves and Young both spun the release as best they could.

Wellington, however, was furious. They had just unceremoniously released the best career quarterback the Giants had ever had. In an unprecedented move, Wellington held his own press conference. He began the press conference saying that he wasn't sure how long he could control his emotions. Actually fighting back tears, Wellington, a man who had released hundreds of players in his long career, fought with his emotions, calling it "a day of overwhelming sadness." Mara said that he disagreed with Young and Reeves and spoke admiringly of Simms. But he also said he would support the decision they had made. Then, in an emotional state, he left the podium.

The moment was the crystallization of a number of things. "In the days leading up to the decision to cut Simms, several owners said Mara tried to find ways to keep him or, they said, at least try to pay Simms his $2.5 million salary," wrote Mike Freeman in *The New York Times*. Essentially, Mara was trying to find Simms a golden parachute. But all such machinations counted against the salary cap. Even placing him on injured reserve would still count against the cap.

Wellington was bitter for a number of reasons. Firstly, the cap was forcing a situation. Secondly, Simms's salary was a large one and was a bad bottom-line hit on the team. According to the bylaws he'd signed with Tim and with the Tisches, Wellington, for all his posturing, could not single-handedly overrule Young and Reeves even if he wanted to.

"This is not the case of an owner who has lost touch. ... The game has changed drastically over the decades since Mara has been involved, and by all accounts Mara has stayed one step ahead. He is a progressive and trusted owner who remains heavily involved with the league," wrote Freeman.

"I think Wellington may be the most dedicated owner I know," an owner who asked not to be identified told Freeman. "I think he wanted to do everything he could for Phil because the two are so close. And I think he also feels that the longime players aren't treated right."

In 1994 the team suffered without Simms, as Kent Graham and Dave Brown tried to steer the ship. The team started off with three wins, but then suffered a seven-game losing streak, which they righted with a six-game winning streak to end the season 9–7. Many wondered what the Giants would have achieved with Simms at the helm. But Young and Reeves were determined to move forward for the sake of the organization.

Years later, Wellington said, "I was convinced it was a mistake at the time, but I went along with it. I was not happy about it at all."

"I have rarely seen him so distraught," wife Ann said. "He felt close to Phil and he was upset. That was probably one of the saddest days of his life. He thinks the team let Phil go too early."

ANOTHER DEATH IN THE FAMILY

January 1995 started with bad news. Jim Lee Howell died on January 4. He had played on four division championship teams and coached three other conference championship teams, including the NFL champions in 1956. He was 80 years old. He had fallen and broken his hip three years earlier and suffered to the end. Wellington was emotional about the loss. Howell had stayed on with the Giants until 1986 in some capacity, and without exaggeration had become like a brother to Wellington.

With a sentimental sense of humor, Wellington recalled Howell's most famous quote about his own coaching abilities: "I just blow up the footballs and keep order."

On February 22, 1995, Jim Katcavage died of a heart attack. He was 60 years old. One of the greatest New York Giants defensive linemen, who played on one of the top five defensive lines of all time, had passed away. Robustelli spoke warmly of his old line mate. And Wellington remembered Katcavage as "one of our greatest defensive ends," and reminded the press of the year when Katcavage had played the entire season with a broken collarbone.

But the biggest single loss was that of Timothy J. Mara. On June 2, 1995, Tim, Jack's son, was dead at 59 years old. Tim had spent a great amount of time in Jupiter, Florida, where he golfed and sailed and fished. And he had increased his involvement in charitable causes. He sponsored a charitable golf tournament and remained in close touch with both Gifford and Parcells. He returned to New York every fall to follow the team. But he had contracted Hodgkins disease.

In 1994 Frank Gifford brought the uncle and the suffering nephew together. "They hadn't been communicating. They had totally different lifestyles," Gifford told the press. The two met at Gifford's Manhattan office. Gifford occupied a special place within the Mara clan. He remained tight with Tim and Wellington both. Both trusted him as someone who could appreciate their predicament and whose discretion could be counted upon. Pressed by Gifford, the two discussed the team. They discussed the distant past, Giants games won and lost, like the two longtime fans they were. They discussed the present Giants, old players, and family memories.

"It was a very cordial meeting, something both of them wanted," Gifford said. "The two shook hands. They never really got around to talking about what had happened in the past. But they talked about the team, about many things.... I think it would have taken awhile, primarily because their lifestyles were so different. But I think they would have gotten back to being what a family should be again if Tim hadn't gotten ill."

Wellington had a mass said for his stricken nephew at St. Patrick's Cathedral when he first learned Tim had Hodgkins disease.

"Tim was a very, very caring person," Young told the press. "He did a great deal for people who couldn't do anything for him." According to Young, it was always a race between Wellington and Tim to help anyone in the Giants organization. It was revealed at this time that Tim had given thousands of dollars to each Giants employee when he sold his interest in the Giants.

"I am going to miss him a lot. He was one of my pals," Parcells, now the New England coach, said. "Most of what I have is because of the Mara family, Wellington and Tim. I talked with Tim two or three times a week. We remained very close."

Once again, the Mara clan gathered to honor one of their lost family members at St. Ignatius Loyola Church, on Eighty-fourth Street. By now its ranks had swelled. Though its founders were seemingly gone, Wellington and Ann alone had filled its ranks as never before with their 11 children with their assorted spouses and children. Maura and Dick and their three daughters were there, as was Helen Mara Nugent, wife to Jack, mother of T.J.

"A death in the family is a very personal thing," Wellington told the press. "I would ask people to respect my privacy at this time."

WELL AND JERRY

Jerry Jones had bought the Cowboys and their stadium for $150 million in 1989. He was one of the new breed of owners who was looking to make money and get camera time, at the expense of anyone. He was seen as brash and rude and smart.

But a stunt he pulled September 6, 1995, put him on a collision course with Wellington and the league. The Giants and Cowboys were scheduled to play a *Monday Night Football* game at Giants Stadium that night. The Giants had also planned to honor Simms by retiring his No. 11 at halftime. The Cowboys made an announcement before the game that they had made an exclusive seven-year apparel deal with Nike. Jones had made deals with Nike and Pepsi, which flew directly in the face of the league-negotiated deals with Reebok and Coke. The Cowboys beat the Giants 35–0. Jones's Cowboys were in the middle of an incredible run of championships, and it seemed Jones knew how to succeed in the NFL.

Asked why he had chosen to announce the deal during Simms's night, he replied unthinkingly, "We knew the nation would be looking."

Jones's deal was a renegade move, because all apparel deals were supposed to be made through the NFL league offices alone.

"After the dust settles, a lot of people will see the merits of letting clubs control their own destinies," said Jones.

One of Jones's most outspoken critics was none other than Wellington. "He seems to be forgetting that you are only as strong as your weakest link," Well told the press.

"I am for pooling money and helping the disadvantaged teams that have tried, that have gone to work.... I just believe that if we had an incentive, we could do it better." Jones countered.

By making his statement so brazenly, he had slapped the old guard and the commissioner right in the face, à la Al Davis, the Raiders controversial owner. Robert Kraft of the New England Patriots had fielded a similar deal but kept the unique contract a quiet affair, trying to stay under the radar. Jones, whose team was flying high with each week's new success, thought that teams should be free to make their own deals and control their own destinies. This flew directly against what had made the NFL so uniquely successful. Even Kraft, who was also a renegade, was afraid of Jones's fiery brand of manifest destiny.

"I don't think he has the concept of what it means to be a member of a team," Mara told the press. "When you do something to enhance yourself at the expense of your team, you hurt the team.... He looks like he wants to share other people's revenue, but not his."

The NFLPA also drew from the pool of collective licensing, and the NFLPA executives were very concerned with Jones's rogue actions.

"Wellington Mara has long loathed Jerry Jones, so vindicated with a victory over Dallas [in 1994] at the Meadowlands that the genteel Giants co-owner spoke shockingly out of school, sniffing, 'It's nice to see arrogance humbled,'" wrote William Rhoden.

At a subsequent owner's meeting, Jones spoke up. Jones was proud that the Cowboys sold more merchandise than any other team. Jones wanted a deal that each team should be able to keep a substantial portion of its own licensing fees. It was, in his mind, only fair that the teams generating the largest incomes get to keep a larger percentage of the revenue. He thought he should get more revenue since his Cowboys were driving sales.

Allegedly, Wellington, Modell, and Rooney were not happy with this line of thinking. This was not the team thinking of the early 1960s that had made football the premiere sport in America. But some of the newer owners were intrigued by Jones's speech. He was encouraging free market economy. If the weaker teams lost revenue, they should move to a town that would better support them or sell out. Jones's tough love was seen as the law of the jungle. That which does not kill you makes you stronger.

Wellington responded, "I think we are starting to have a problem here, and many of my fellow owners who have been around for a long time are getting a little nervous. The NFL has been a goose that lays golden eggs for a long time, and the key to its success is that we have always been able to subdue our own selfish interests for the good of the league."

Jones burst out in nervous laughter, but no one else was laughing. All the other owners were hanging on Wellington's every word.

They wanted to hear what the old man had to say. He did not speak often in meetings.

"I am willing to accept the offer that Mr. Jones has put on the table," Well told his NFL brethren, "as long as he agrees to a similar condition of mine. If each team is to be rewarded for its success in one area of our business, then we should all be rewarded accordingly. My proposal is to divide the league's television revenue in a similar manner, based on the television ratings for each team's market area. I have reviewed last year's ratings throughout the country. It looks like Mr. Hess [Jets owner Leon Hess] and I will be dividing about 20 percent of the NFL's television revenue. The remaining 80 percent will be divided accordingly, and Mr. Jones might want to note that there are 21 NFL cities that generate more viewers than the Dallas–Forth Worth area." Mara sat down and the discussion wound down. The talk of dividing revenues was tabled.

HOLDING ON

An odd story ran in several regional newspapers in November 1995. It was about the precautions the Maras were taking to beat the estate taxes so that the family could retain their stake in the Giants franchise after Wellington's death. In such a case, the Maras faced a brutal 55 percent federal estate tax. After the death of Joe Robbie, the owner of the Miami Dolphins, the Robbie family had found themselves wanting to hang on to the Dolphins, but instead were forced to sell in order to pay the 55 percent of their father's holdings. Wellington wanted to be able to avoid that for his family. It was John, with his legal background and connections, who helped lead the charge.

"It will be hard to keep control and pay the taxes...." John told the press. However, the Maras had worked out a number of scenarios, hoping they would enable the surviving children to hold onto their father's business. In 1997 the Giants were estimated to be worth $175 million, and the Mara's ownership accounted for $87.5 million. "The estate laws are so severe. I think we've done some careful planning, which we believe will allow us to carry on control of the organization," John said, thus ensuring Mara involvement well into the next century.

The biggest hurdle was that Wellington's main business was the Giants. NFL owners who owned multiple companies, like the Tischs, could draw income from other sources or sell off other assets to keep their NFL franchise. On Wellington's death, the family would owe the federal government more than $40 million—cash they would not have unless they sold the team. At the same time, there were at least six other NFL franchise owners that were looking at similar circumstances, including Art Modell. Modell had done something different. In his move to Baltimore, he had been paid a bonus by the city. Modell never touched the bonus, and he set up the money so that it could be used to pay off the estate taxes in the case of his demise.

Estate taxes in the United States generally prevent the passing on of wealth in the form of one lump sum to another generation. Although legions of lawyers have spent millions of hours to find or create loopholes, the system was created generations ago to prevent the United States from falling into a haves-and-have-nots caste system.

What technique the Maras used was not disclosed. They may have left the team in Ann Mara's name, thus they would not have to pay taxes until her passing. The more likely scenario was a tax loophole in section 6166 of the tax code. In this scenario the family sets up a payment plan with the Internal Revenue Service for the debt to be paid off over a specific period of time, which could be as long as 14 years and nine months. While there are some interest rates that are applied as penalties, many wealthy estates get around the law by such methods. Or they might have bundled such a package with a very large life insurance policy, or some combination of the above.

Regardless, Wellington was planning for his survivors to take over and for continuity to be maintained.

REEVES, PARCELLS, AND FASSEL

In 1995 Reeves went 5–11–0 and in 1996 he finished 6–10–0. And as Giants fans had sung for Sherman, they also sang for Reeves. Young relieved Reeves of his job.

Who would the Giants hire next? Again, there was speculation. Many names came and went. Parcells left the Patriots after the 1996 season. He ended up with the New York Jets. Leon Hess, the longtime owner of the Jets, made the bold move of tapping another team's coach. After much posturing between Hess and Patriots owner Robert Kraft, they negotiated an agreement for Parcells. But

Parcells's return to New York was bittersweet—for Giants fans as well as for Wellington and Parcells. Parcells had wanted to leave the Patriots, with whom he was fighting, and return to the Giants.

Mike Freeman revealed in *The New York Times* years later that Parcells had called Wellington directly. This was before he began talks with the Jets. He had gone around Young's back because he knew Young did not want him.

Parcells told Mara that he wished to return to the organization and the Giants family. Wellington and Tisch were both willing. But again, Young said no. It was the second time that Parcells had tried to rejoin the team. He had wanted back in after Ray Handley's disastrous 1992 campaign, but Young proved to be the obstacle then, too.

"The one thing you learn when you've been doing this as long as I have is that nothing surprises you," Young said later about the Parcells rumors. "There are a lot of things going on around here, and while those things may surprise some people, they don't surprise me." Young hesitated. "It wouldn't surprise me if I was here next season, it wouldn't surprise me if I was not. I may not be wanted here anymore."

Asked if he would quit if Parcells was hired, Young said, "No comment.... But what do you think?"

Young argued that it was apparent Parcells would not honor a long-term contract. Parcells was rejected, and instead the team hired Jim Fassel, an offensive coordinator under Handley for the Giants in 1992, and also a quarterback coach who had worked with John Elway. He could groom a new quarterback in Simms's absence and lead the team into a new era. In 1997 Fassel led the team to a 10–5–1 record, with Danny Kanell at quarterback and Charles Way running hard. And 1998 saw the team finish 8–8–0, in desperate need of a quarterback.

HELEN MARA NUGENT

St. Ignatius Loyola by this time had seen its share of milestones in the history of the Mara family. Indeed, it had seen baptisms and weddings aplenty by 1997.

On February 21, 1997, the beloved wife of the late Joseph C. Nugent and John V. Mara, Helen Phelan Mara Nugent, died. Her wake was held at Frank E. Campbell's funeral home, and the funeral mass was on February 25 at St. Ignatius Loyola. Gathered again were Wellington and his family, Maura and her family, and Helen's great-grandchildren.

Maura had had three daughters. Christine Concannon had gone to Holy Cross College and was a network buyer at Young & Rubicam, one of New York's most prestigious advertising agencies. In 1992, when she was 25 years old, she wed David Ehrlich Geithner, and they had two children, Peter and Claire.

Kathleen Mara Concannon had gone to St. Michael's College and received a master's degree from Lesley College. She went on to become a schoolteacher at the Chapin School of New York. In 1994, when she was 27, she married David Anderson, a sales representative for Anheuser-Busch.

Sheila Concannon went to Providence College. In October 1997 she married Joseph Taylor Melvin III, known as Taylor, a marketing officer at the North Carolina Trust Company in Greensboro, North Carolina. Taylor's father was the chairman of First Home Federal, a bank in Greensboro, and president of the Joseph M. Bryan Foundation of greater Greensboro, a charity that focused on public education.

Both Sheila and Kathleen had been married at St. Ignatius Loyola.

Wellington and Ann, John and his wife and family, and the rest of Wellington's children attended. Wellington was now, for all intents and purposes, the patriarch of a large network of cousins and relations. Though some of those relationships might have been strained, there was nowhere that Maura's daughters went that their heritage as members of the Giants family wasn't whispered.

Well could not help but know his position. He was now the only link to the Mara past. He was the only link to Jack Dempsey, Gene Tunney, Steve Owen, and a whole series of golden eras that no longer existed. If he drew sadness from it, he never said so in public. But for the rest of his life, he was the soft-spoken historian of Giants history, if not sometimes a little sarcastic. But this did little to keep him from his decades-old routines.

THE HALL OF FAME
In 1997 Wellington was elected to the Pro Football Hall of Fame. He was elected alongside Don Shula, Mike Webster, and Mike Haynes. His election made him and Tim Mara the only father and son elected to the Hall of Fame.

"Naturally I'm very honored and surprised at my election to the Hall of Fame," Mara said. "I don't feel like I've ever been one to make or contribute to the headlines. I guess my chief qualification is longevity."

"Three things are important in Wellington's life," Young said. "His family and religion, the Giants, and Giants fans. Whatever he does, he's thinking about them all the time."

At Canton, Wellington chose none other than Gifford to introduce him.

"Right up front I'd like to say Wellington Mara's election to the Hall of Fame is so long overdue. He and the Mara family have played a decisive role in helping to guide the National Football League for over 70 years. Well and his family were a dominant presence in this league long before the sellout crowds, huge television and multimillion-dollar player contracts, and Super Bowls," Gifford said. "The league's growth, popularity, its phenomenal financial success, have paralleled Well's lifetime commitment to the game." Gifford spoke of the years in which Well and the Maras led the league quietly from behind the scenes. Then he spoke from personal experience.

First he asked the entire Mara clan to stand. Eleven children and multitudes of spouses and grandchildren and other in-laws stood up. "That's an awful lot of off-season," Gifford joked.

Gifford referred to the Giants family, made up of "former players and coaches and their wives and children. I can't tell you, and Well would kill me if I did, how many times some member of that extended family has needed help and Well has been there. I know, because he has been there for me."

Gifford mentioned that during his playing career, Wellington was always fair in his contract dealings, and indeed, was so trustworthy, Gifford said there were some contracts he was sent that he never bothered to sign. He just showed up and played and got paid. He called Well decent and honest.

Gifford then made mention that Well had been his presenter in 1977, and spoke of the nice quote about Gifford being the son every father would want to have. "I don't know about that, Well. I'd just like to say to you…you are the father every son would be blessed to have, the brother any man could want, and certainly the best friend anyone could ever have."

Wellington then took the podium. First, he thanked everyone, including Gifford and those assembled. Then he said, "First of all, my wife and sweetheart, Ann Mara. Ann pays me the supreme compliment. She supports me even when she doesn't agree with me, which of course, is very rare. We also have, and they have already stood up, we have 11 children, nine spouses, one hopeful fiancée, and 12 grandchildren here. At home, on our taxi squad, we have 16 more grandchildren."

After the chuckles and applause, Well got down to serious matters. He thanked all those responsible on the election committee for his recognition, but then he demurred. "I overwhelmingly feel that I come to you as a surrogate—someone who takes the place of someone else. If it hadn't been for his untimely death some 30-odd years ago, Jack Mara would certainly have taken his place alongside our father long ago to form the first father-son team in the Hall of Fame. For it was Jack, together with Dan Reeves of the Rams and George Halas of the Bears, who cast what I think is the most important vote that was ever cast in the National Football League." Wellington pointed out that it was the sacrifices of these three teams that enabled Pete Rozelle to pool the league's clout and extract more money than anyone thought possible to establish the NFL. "Unhappily, their selfless vision is too little shared by many who today benefit from their rewards."

Then Wellington referred to his father and brother, who he said "laid down the standards and principles according to which he wanted the new family business to be operated. In his time, Jack practiced and embellished those standards and principles far beyond any abilities of mine. I accept this honor today as acknowledgement of my stewardship over that legacy of decency which they handed to me and which I, in turn, hope to hand over to that taxi squad and others."

This is truly the crux of the man. He believed in his family and his God. And he believed in what he owed to those who went before him. Wellington had never intended to be president of the Giants. It was not his goal or his desire. He drew immense pride from being the president of the New York Football Giants. But it is safe to discern from the thousands of miles of ink spilled in the history and lore of the Giants that Well would have given up his chair if Jack could have lived longer.

In becoming the historian of the franchise, Well had also become the historian of the family. And from that he drew both great joy and great sadness—joy from the position and from his immediate and Giants family, sadness in the many friends and family who had passed. He was the last of his kind—the only link to the past—and he knew it.

ANOTHER GIANT LOSS

In 1997 the Giants were crowned champions of the NFC East. Young told the press that Coach Fassel was "the right man at this time" as far as the Giants were concerned.

"He knows how to motivate the players," Wellington added. "He took a big chance when he told Kanell he had to play well in the first half in Philadelphia, but it worked out," continued Well, referring to quarterback Danny Kanell. Wellington added that the division title was "just as sweet as the last one," referring to the 1990 title. He admitted he had not expected it.

But the 1997 campaign ended bitterly for the Giants. With a tremendous lead going into the fourth quarter of a home divisional playoff game against the Vikings, the team suffered a major meltdown. The Giants had easily dominated most of the game, but in the fourth quarter the team gave up 13 points amid bickering and infighting that took place on the field during the game. Minnesota won. But the season had clearly been a success.

Amid all this, Parcells was leaving the Patriots and moving to the Jets, having failed to return to the Giants once again. And now, it seemed, his former adversary was leaving, too.

Young was retiring from active football operations and moving to the NFL offices. However, there had been talk that the new world of the NFL had passed Young by, as it had Wellington. The game had grown and he hadn't.

"You heard it everywhere—at league meetings, at the camps of the Giants' chief division rivals, and just in passing," Thomas George wrote in *The New York Times*. "George Young has lost it. What a dinosaur!"

"Sure, I heard the talk about George, everybody did, but I don't know that he had to be vindicated," Charlie Casserly, the Redskins' general manager, said. "He already built two Super Bowl championship teams that have left their mark in New York sports history."

Obviously, the division championship had quieted some of that talk, but the truth was that Young was getting too old to shoulder the responsibilities of a major franchise. He was still a respected personnel man, but the game in fact had changed, just as it had for Wellington, and Young needed to step aside.

"We have a very young team and most of these players are signed for at least a couple of years. I'd say that George has made a couple of good decisions there. George is full of football knowledge and he has patience. We have not always agreed, but I always yield to his thoughts," Wellington told the press. But the vote of confidence was short lived—Young was gone.

Young had been with the Giants for 19 years. He had led the team to two Super Bowl titles, four NFC East championships, and eight playoff appearances. He was 67 years old, and had been involved in sports of one kind or another for 52 years. He was leaving the Giants to join the NFL offices.

"My whole life has been winning and losing football games. It's going to be tough to deal with when they kick off the football in the first game of the next season, but I'll have to deal with it," Young told the press. "My heart tells me to stay, but my head tells me it's the right time to do something I can be happy with for a while. The club is in good hands. The timing is best for the organization and the timing is best for me."

Parcells, now the Jets coach, issued a statement, saying of Young: "The Giants are losing a great football man. George is the man responsible for returning stability and credibility to the organization and a man to whom I am personally grateful for the opportunity that he extended to me and the support that he gave while I was the coach there."

"We couldn't agree on anything," Wellington said of the decision he and his nephew Tim made to hire Young. "We did on George."

Ernie Accorsi, the Giants' assistant general manager since 1994 and a former top football executive for the Cleveland Browns and the Baltimore Colts, became the new Giants general manager. Rick Donohue, who was the Giants' assistant director of player personnel, took over as assistant general manager.

"Hopefully, I'll do things with the dignity this franchise has always done things," Accorsi told the press. "And I hope someday I can pass this organization on to someone in the same condition that George presented it to me."

In all the press coverage, accolades by Wellington were oddly absent. It can be assumed that there were two primary factors. The first is that Wellington wanted to let Young have his shining moment in the sun. Young had indeed left the team significantly better than he had found it, and the press hailed him as the great reconstructionist, having revived one of the great franchises in sports. However, another point must also be made: the release of Simms was still something that smarted, and that had put a small gulf between Young and Well.

❧⌘

In early 1998 Dallas Cowboys owner Jones had led the NFL television talks and had produced a record contract for the NFL. Brash, annoying, and highly successful, Jones had squeezed the most lucrative sports television contract in media history from television executives. The contract virtually guaranteed each NFL team approximately $80 million per year. In 1993 each club had received $53 million, which was up from $41 million the previous year.

"It's new money now," Wellington told the press, "but soon it'll just be part of every club's budget."

Mara recalled how 20 years earlier Rozelle told the NFL owners how the television money would come rolling. Shaking his head, Wellington said, "George [Halas] told us, 'I hope we don't live up to our income too soon.'"

Wellington was more interested in how the new salaries would creep up as well, which was a worry of many owners. "'I think a soft cap would be a disaster for us. I think our cap isn't hard enough," said Wellington.

Many wondered if the discrepancy between rich players and poor players would continue. Wellington was one of them. "I worry that certain teams with large cash reserves who have already spent a lot on free agents by prorating bonuses—cash over the cap—I worry that they could distance themselves even further. That's a threat to competitive balance," Mara said.

On the good side, however, was the fact that after a series of tough negotiations, the NFL and the NFLPA had agreed to extend the contract between them to 2003. Football, and the Giants, stood in good stead. With the new money, the succession of the company in place, and the accord with the NFLPA, it seemed the road ahead would be smooth for a while. And with Wellington's and Tim's squabbles over, and Young and Parcells's battles behind them, the Giants could focus on football going into the new century.

But Wellington was opposed to one section of the negotiated labor settlement. And he was willing to lead a cabal of owners to defeat it. One owner, anonymously, told *The New York Times,* "Wellington is strongly opposed to one part of this agreement and in turn, the entire thing. When Wellington talks, people listen. He will swing votes, and a week from now we could be back at the negotiating table with the union. Wellington, single-handedly, could kill this deal. He commands that much respect."

Wellington was opposed to the guaranteed contract provision of the tentative agreement. As Mike Freeman explained, "If a player who has been in the league five years or more and makes the active roster but is later cut, he still receives his full salary for that year. That, in effect, makes the contract guaranteed, something new for the NFL."

At the NFL owners meetings in Orlando, Florida, on March 22, 1998, Wellington stepped up to the microphone and made an impassioned plea to his fellow owners not to vote for this new extension.

"The situation was much tighter—and more dramatic—than was publicly made known. After what one owner described as an incredible speech by Mara, an unofficial poll was taken, and it was determined that there were only 22 votes in support of the agreement," wrote Freeman. "In order to pass, 23 of the 30 owners had to vote for it. But after some rallying by supporters of the extension, the official vote was taken, and at that point a small number of owners changed their votes."

Wellington remained the only one steadfastly against the deal. Al Davis abstained from voting. The labor pact was passed 28–1. But Wellington had sidetracked the owners meeting significantly. He had almost killed the deal.

FRIENDS AND HOBBIES

Wellington moved easily in and out of New York society. He was not the social whirling dervish his parents had been, but Wellington did indeed get around. He went to boxing, racing, basketball, and baseball events. In his older age he seemed to appreciate the horses his father and brother had loved so much. In his youth, even when he was at the track, his mind was on football matters. He was obsessed. Now, with an older man's maturity, he could enjoy the horses and relished their beauty and speed. He spent many summers, as his father did, in Saratoga, betting races and taking in the scenery—at least until training camp began. However, the allure of thoroughbreds speeding around an oval had its power over him. In 1991 he was spotted, AWOL from a Giants training camp, betting a double or two at Saratoga.

In November 1995 New York Jets owner Leon Hess, Wellington, and Tim Rooney enjoyed an evening's worth of fun at the Meadowlands racetrack in East Rutherford, New Jersey. Well and Hess attended the races as fans, betting and having a jocular time. Rooney had a horse he was watching intently, a filly named Alina Gatto. She ran sixth in her race. Even into the early 2000s, Well invited Parcells to Saratoga to spend some time up there with him.

And Well always liked a rousing sporting event. In September 1998, with the football season underway, Wellington found time to take in a baseball game. Wellington was invited by New York Yankees owner George Steinbrenner to attend the first game of the American League playoffs. Wellington had been a Yankees fan in his youth, despite his father's hatred for Dan Topping, a former Yankees owner, and had been to the stadium many times to watch Ruth, Gehrig, DiMaggio, Whitey Ford, Mantle, and others. On September 27,

1998, he was invited to share the booth with John McMullen, the owner of the New Jersey Devils; Rupert Murdoch, chairman of the Fox News Corporation; Allen H. Neuharth, former chairman of Gannett, Inc.; actor Kevin Costner; and Phil Rizzuto, the former star shortstop and announcer for the Yankees.

The 1998 season was a bit of a disappointment for the Giants, with revolving quarterbacks and other issues. The Giants were somewhat lackluster, which, after the 1997 campaign, was a downturn. Despite a horrific 3–7 start, the team ended up with an 8–8 record and finished out of the hunt for a playoff berth in the last week of the season. But the one bright spot was on December 20, 1998, when the Giants beat the Kansas City Chiefs to win their 1,000th game. The team presented both Wellington and Tisch with game balls commemorating the win.

In 1998 Welington became a member of Legatus, a Catholic organization founded by Domino's Pizza founder Thomas S. Monaghan. The mission of Legatus espouses, "To study, live and spread the Faith in our business, professional and personal lives." Having sold the majority of his holdings in Domino's, Monaghan was determined to use some of his monies to stop abortion and spread the word of Catholicism through business, media, and funding of schools throughout the elementary, middle, and college levels.

Other celebrities who also participated in Legatus included Frank A. Olson, the chief executive of the Hertz Corporation; Harry J. Longwell, an Exxon Corporation senior vice president; and former Dallas Cowboy–turned–Texas–businessman Roger Staubach.

Some had spurned the organization, including former Coca-Cola chairman Roberto C. Goizueta, who felt that mixing religion and business might create unwanted political associations that could affect the popularity of Coke's brand. Wellington had already experienced this kind of backlash, and so he kept his affiliation to a personal level, and did not attempt any other media attention regarding his membership. But it is significant that Wellington did continue to involve himself with groups and organizations that appealed to his Catholic and political convictions. He was a participant in a way that many people are not.

His religious convictions remained stronger than ever, and his commitment and participation in things Catholic remained as fervent as ever.

Wellington was a Fordham alumnus (a Jesuit school) and "long-time friend of the University," Joseph M. McShane, S.J., president of Fordham said. "As a son of Fordham, his name will always be recalled with sincere fondness and admiration for a life reflective of the Jesuit principles of charity and compassion."

Wellington was honored during the university's 160th anniversary celebration on March 25, 2002. He was one of the inaugural recipients of the Fordham Founder's Award. O'Hare S.J. presented Mara with the award, which recognizes individuals whose lives reflect the highest aspirations of the university's defining traditions as an institution dedicated to wisdom and learning in the service of others.

"The Fordham community is fortunate to have had the opportunity to share in Mr. Mara's life and to have been able to express its gratitude with the Founder's Award," said John Tognino, chairman of the Fordham University Board of Trustees. "I have been a Giants ticket holder for 42 years, and as a youngster, I can vividly remember watching the Giants practice at Fordham's Rose Hill campus and seeing Wellington Mara on the sidelines attentively watching everything."

A generous supporter of Fordham University and its football program, Mara had instituted the Mara Family Award to honor a Fordham alumnus who makes an outstanding contribution to the program. Presentations of these awards were hosted at the annual Fordham Gridiron Club Dinner, held at the New York Athletic Club.

"I saw firsthand Mr. Mara's love for Fordham, our coaches, and above all, our student-athletes," said university athletics director Frank McLaughlin.

Wellington was on the board of trustees of St. Patrick's Cathedral. He had joined as a trustee in 1993. He served the cathedral "with great distinction and dedication," holding such offices as vice president and chairman of the executive committee and also serving on all the standing committees of the board. He spent much time with Cardinal Egan and Monsignor James K. Vaughey, executive director.

"Wellington Mara never ceased to champion the noble causes that sprang from his faith," said Cardinal Egan. "He wanted young people, especially those who lived in the most distressed areas of our community, to have an opportunity to participate in athletics so as to learn the lessons that only fair play can teach. To this end he sponsored camps for children and youth in the summer and programs of the Catholic Youth Organization throughout the year. Thus, literally thousands of youngsters benefited mightily from his concern for them and his generosity."

"Catholicism was a driving force in Mara's life, inspiring him to attend morning mass seven days a week, 52 weeks a year, until the cancer and the radiation kept him home," wrote Ian O'Connor of *The Journal News.* "The owner would often walk the bowels of Giants Stadium saying the rosary, but he didn't believe in praying for a winning total on the Sunday board."

"His idea of a good day," said son Frank, "was going to 8:00 AM mass, going to work, and getting home by 6:00 PM to have dinner with his family. He didn't care if anyone ever recognized him. My father was the most humble person in the world."

He was also a contributor and trustee, along with his son John, of the School of the Holy Child in Rye, New York. According to Elizabeth T. Marren, chair of the board, and Ann F. Sullivan, head of the school, "Wellington Mara's commitment to the Catholic Church and faith-based education has inspired his family's generosity to many Catholic schools, including School of the Holy Child. We are grateful to Wellington Mara and his family."

His commitment to Catholic hospitals was also strong. He was very involved in the Saint Vincent Catholic Medical Centers (SVCMC). According to chairman Alfred E. Smith IV and foundation president Mark G. Ackermann, Mara was a "beloved supporter of St. Vincent's Westchester/Manhattan, founder of the John V. Mara Cancer Research Center at St. Vincent's Hospital, and creator of the annual New York Giants Kickoff Luncheon."

Wellington, a member of the board of trustees of Saint Vincent Catholic Medical Centers, was called a "dear friend and dedicated benefactor," and "whose leadership and generosity greatly advanced the mission of SVCMC and the development of Catholic health care in New York," wrote Edward V. Lahey Jr., chair, and Richard J. Boyle, president and CEO.

Wellington's side of the family had no monopoly on charity. Maura had taken up where her mother left off and also belonged and gave to many charities, often volunteering her time as well. In the Mara tradition, many of these causes were religiously affiliated, but not always. Tim also was involved in philanthropy, and a small celebrity golf tournament in Palm Beach, Florida, bears his name to this day (the Tim Mara Restauranteur's Golf Classic). That tournament donates its proceeds to the local Boys and Girls Clubs of Palm Beach County. Jim Palmer, Ron Erhardt, Tucker Frederickson, Leonard Marshall, Mike Schmidt, and many others have donated their time to this event.

And, of course, for the rest of his life, Well, along with other Mara family members, took part in the Catholic Youth Organization's John V. Mara Award, which was established by Wellington and Helen in Jack's honor the year after his death. This award was given every year, even through the war years, through the auspices of the CYO. Many famous individuals received the award, some of whom were affiliated with the Giants. Awardees have included Brian Trottier, Rusty Staub, Mike Jarvis, Lombardi, Al Leiter, John Franco, and Yogi Berra.

The Putnam Valley CYO also sponsored the John V. Mara Camp, which operated in the summers. In 2002 the camp was refurbished. According to the *Putnam County News and Reporter,* "The volunteers came from every type of organization, including Putnam Valley High School, the Putnam Valley branch of the Mahopac National Bank, and other local companies. They painted cabins, built decks, tilled the soil for a farm, built shelters for animals, repaired doors and screens, and performed many other tasks needed to get the Putnam Valley CYO John V. Mara Camp ready for the summer."

❧

In May 1999 Wellington was asked to give the eulogy for his good friend and fellow owner Leon Hess. The two were cut from the same cloth. Hess was a quiet man, whose many charitable actions were kept behind closed doors, and who did great things for small people who could not afford to give back anything more than a thanks.

"When I worked for the New York Jets, I had the opportunity to meet Mr. Mara on a number of occasions. He was good friends with our owner, Leon Hess, and it was always a treat to listen to Mr. Mara and Mr. Hess discuss their teams, the league, and the old times," wrote Pat Kirwin of NFL.com. "My most memorable moment was a night at the Meadowlands racetrack when both men shared football stories and some interest in how the other was doing after each race. They truly enjoyed each other's company, and watching them went a long way for me in understanding what makes the NFL great. It was an honor and a privilege to be at that table that night."

Hess sat with Mara during Giants-Jets games. Mara once said, "Leon would turn to me and say, 'I just hope we don't get embarrassed today.' I always hoped for more than that."

"He never ceases to amaze me," said Pepper Johnson of Hess. Johnson played for both the Jets and the Giants, and likened Hess to Wellington. "He reminds me so much of Wellington Mara because they care. They don't say much. When they do say stuff and do stuff, you know it comes from the heart."

"As a man of quiet dignity, Leon Hess would probably have been embarrassed by all the attention," wrote Anderson. "But deep down, he surely would have enjoyed it, as he had basking in his Jets owner's box at Giants Stadium during the closing minutes of the playoff victory over the Jacksonville Jaguars last January."

"He loved the fans, even the ones who had reviled him," Wellington said during his eulogy. "But now those same fans stood and cheered him. He gave them the thumbs-up sign and said, 'This is thrilling.' A provident God had given him a sweet thrill before He took him from us."

"I remember going to Leon Hess's funeral and hearing [Well] speak, and he spoke without a note for like 10 or 12 minutes. I can't remember some things from two or three minutes ago. And here's a guy in his eighties, and it was awesome," said Robert Kraft, owner of the New England Patriots, years later.

"I have lost a very close friend and the NFL has lost one of its most beloved and respected leaders. Leon Hess was a man who was deeply devoted to his family, friends, and team. He was a great friend to the Mara family and we will miss him very much," Mara told the press.

WELLINGTON AND LT

Lawrence Taylor did not get off on the best foot with the New York Giants. After his third season, in 1983, Taylor met with Donald Trump. After awing Taylor with his immense office and a video about his rise to wealth and riches, Trump offered Taylor a contract to play for the USFL.

"Well, I still have three years and an option left on my Giants contract," Taylor said.

"I don't care. I want to do a futures contract with you," Trump told Taylor. Trump offered Taylor a $4 million contract for five years, with a $1 million signing bonus. Lawrence signed then and there. When Taylor told his agent, he was shocked. The agent told Taylor, "You got screwed." Eventually the Giants agreed to pay $1.75 million to buy out Trump's contract, to which Trump agreed. And the Giants guaranteed Taylor a six-year deal worth more than $5.5 million.

In August 1999 the most controversial figure ever inducted in to the Pro Football Hall of Fame took the podium. His name was Lawrence Taylor. It is almost impossible to estimate the value and impact Taylor had on the New York Giants, or on professional football in general. As a Giants player, he had helped to raise the fallen franchise and place it atop the football world. And there was little coincidence that professional football experienced unprecedented television ratings in the years he played, and that, playing in the nation's media capital, his impact on the sport was worth, if extrapolated out, billions of dollars.

Taylor was placed in an outpatient treatment program for his cocaine addiction around 1985, and was directed Dr. Joel Goldberg toward Wellington's friend Charlie Stucky. Stucky was a recovering alcoholic, and was considered a good example for Taylor. Taylor would meet with Stucky, who was also a huge Giants fan, three times a week. "Wellington Mara is one of those rare owners who cares about the person, not only as a commodity," Taylor wrote in his autobiography with Steve Serby. "Mr. Mara made it loud and clear that I would have to be serious about my rehab program this time."

But Taylor's off-the-field problems made him a target for media malcontents and naysayers. During his playing days he was suspended several times for addictions to alcohol, cocaine, and crack, and for involvement with prostitution. In September 1988 Taylor admitted for the first time publicly that he had an addiction problem. The players, coaches, and organization got behind him. Not only was he one of the most valuable players on the team, but he was also universally well liked among his peers, who respected his intensity, his knowledge of the game, and his fortitude.

On August 15, 1988, Taylor failed a drug test and was suspended for 30 days. It was the first time Taylor's off-the-field antics would hurt the team, but it would not be the last. The most valiant of gladiators had fallen. His excessive use of alcohol while partying had led to addictions much stronger, and resulted in a pull he could not resist.

On March 24, 1989, at 3:30 AM, Taylor was found asleep in his car on the Garden State Parkway in New Jersey. While no drugs were found in a urine sample taken by police, he was arrested for drunken driving after failing a Breathalyzer test.

"We owe it to Lawrence Taylor to be as hard on him as we possibly can," came the tough-love message from Wellington. There were times, Taylor later admitted, that phone calls from friends and family were not enough to pull him out of his addiction's grasp. Not even a call from Wellington himself. But to his credit, long after Taylor's game days were over and his employment by the club had ended, Wellington never gave up on Taylor.

"He has helped a million players and you may never know who they are because he won't talk about it. He really worries about L.T. To this day he's trying so much to help him straighten out his life," said Ann Mara.

On October 10, 1994, during a *Monday Night Football* game, the New York Giants honored Taylor, retiring his jersey on national television. "You know I should be nervous, but I'm not because I'm in my house," Taylor told the crowd. And then he praised and thanked his owner and friend, Wellington, "for always being there for me like a father." In ending his short speech, he said, "Without you guys here there would have been a Lawrence Taylor, but there wouldn't have been an L.T. Thank you very much." He received a standing ovation from 76,000 people jamming the stands.

Taylor had another major fall on May 3, 1996, while attending a celebrity golf tournament in Myrtle Beach, South Carolina.

Police there said he tried to buy $100 worth of crack from under-cover agents.

Then in October 1998 Taylor went to St. Petersburg Beach, Florida, to play in another celebrity pro-am event. While there he was arrested at 2:00 AM in his hotel room for possession of $50 worth of crack cocaine and possession of numerous devices used for crack cocaine. Taylor left the Pinellas County Jail after posting $15,500 bail.

Taylor railed at the local police, who he said had been harassing him all day.

"The Giants have tried to do the best they could to help him," George Young told the press. "They tried to help him help himself. Wellington Mara and Bob Tisch have been very sensitive to that. ... They've helped him at different times, including since he retired."

"I know some of his former teammates have been worried about him, too. It's a great sadness," Young added.

Taylor himself admitted that this was the toughest foe he had ever come across, saying, "You may stay clean for 30 years, but you're still close to it, and will always be an addict."

His addiction had reached its nadir with Taylor's South Carolina arrest. Leonard Marshall told the press, "In order for Lawrence to get it all back together, he needs some life-threatening experience to bring him back to us, back to his roots. When he comes back, his friends will be waiting." Wellington Mara could be counted among those friends. On October 22, 1998, Taylor entered rehabilitation for a 30- to 60-day program.

"The Giants have paid for several stints to such clinics for Taylor since he retired," wrote Mike Freeman of *The New York Times*. "The team, especially the owner Wellington Mara, and many of Taylor's close friends remain very concerned about his health."

The New York metro region clinic where Taylor stayed charged approximately $250 per day. A 30-day stay was estimated to cost at least $7,500, which Taylor definitely did not have. Taylor, who'd made mil-lions for himself and his family and millions for the league, was broke. He had squandered his money on bad investments, high living, and alcohol, drugs, and prostitutes.

"Wellington Mara, as he had previously, came to the aid of Lawrence Taylor, the former Giants linebacker, by paying for Taylor's latest stay in a drug-rehabilitation clinic, according to several people close to Taylor. It is at least the second time Mara has paid for Taylor's drug counseling since Taylor retired after the 1993 season," wrote Freeman.

During his induction into the Hall of Fame, Taylor thanked Parcells and Young, his former wife, family, and many others. Wellington was among those he thanked. "There's another man who was very important. You talk about the George Halases, you talk about the Paul Browns, you talk about all the great owners in this league. ... Let me tell you something, you're committing an injustice if you don't talk about Wellington Mara. ... He stood behind me for a lot of years on the field and off the field. Without him, I would probably not be here today. So I want to thank Wellington Mara for his kindness and generosity. Thank you, Wellington."

ONE MORE TIME

The highlight of the 1999 season was the trip the team took for their final preseason game, against the Baltimore Ravens, in Baltimore. The team took a train.

"The team boarded a special-excursion train from Manhattan to Baltimore. It was the first time, according to the team owner, Wellington Mara, that the Giants went by train to a game since 1963, when the team opened the regular season at Baltimore against the Colts. Mara also remembered that the Giants won, 37–28," wrote Bill Pennington.

"Mara's wife, Ann, said she thought the team had taken trains to Philadelphia or Washington for games since then," Pennington continued, "but certainly not in the last quarter century or more."

"It should be good for us and kind of fun," Coach Fassel told the press. "We've got our own train with a few cars, and first-class accommodations. Guys will be able to get up and move around. I think it'll be a special experience. It's two hours. I can't think of a better way for us to get this done."

The train ride turned out to be the highlight of the season. The 1999 Giants fell to 7–9. [That year, in a controversial trade, the Giants brought in veteran quarterback Kerry Collins. Though successful on the field in Carolina, Collins's bad lifestyle choices offended several African American teammates. His arrival nonetheless signaled a huge shift for the better for the organization.]

On April 5, 2000, the New York Giants unveiled a new uniform. However, it wasn't so new. The team had retrofitted the team uniform designs of the late 1950s and early 1960s for this new era. Most importantly, the *GIANTS* logo that had been on the helmet was replaced by the lowercase *ny* that had been the hallmark of the franchise for most of its history.

"By simply placing a lowercase *ny* on the helmet where the word *Giants* had been stenciled for nearly 25 years, New York's oldest professional football team returned yesterday to those thrilling days of yesteryear.... Thus, the new pants are gray instead of white and the home jerseys are a deeper shade of blue. Just like in the old days," wrote the effusive Gerald Eskanazi.

"We've been thinking about doing this since 1994, the year we wore one of those throwback uniforms," Mara said. "I know we'll get some backlash. But we're not trying to make a political statement. It's the logo I grew up with. We don't look at it as a geographical boundary."

"Each year our equipment manager would give him [Well] the new apparel for the season and it would always wind up in the same place, stuck in the back of his closet and out would come the same old and battered outfits," John Mara related years later. "When we changed our logo several years ago back to the traditional lower case *ny,* he actually started wearing some of the shirts that he had worn the last time we had used that logo more than 25 years before. 'I knew they would come back,' he said."

In 2000 the Giants drafted Heisman-winning running back Ron Dayne. Wellington was still involved in the draft process, although he did not make the final decisions. But he was unafraid to offer his opinions. "He loved participating in the draft meetings. It was his favorite time of year," John said years later. "Day after day, he would sit there as reports were read on every prospect. No matter how remote they were, he didn't want to miss anything, and he loved interacting with our scouts. He identified with them because he had been one himself for so many years."

With the addition of Dayne and Tiki Barber, the powerful new Giants running attack nicknamed "Thunder and Lightning" seemed grounded. It was a make-or-break year for Coach Jim Fassel. After back-to-back losses at midseason at home to St. Louis and Detroit, the Giants fell to 7–4. Rumors began to swell about the team and the coach's future. It was that then the aggravated and angry Fassel snapped at the press and famously gave his, "I'm moving my chips to the center of the table," speech.

It was Fassel's defining moment as a Giants coach. In the press conference after the Detroit game, Fassel told the press, "This team will be in the playoffs." In fact, he guaranteed it. Kerry Collins, Barber, Dayne, Michael Strahan, Jessie Armstead, Mike Barrow, Jason Sehorn, Ike Hilliard, Amani Toomer, and the rest of the team responded to what seemed to be a challenge by their head coach. They won their remaining five games, achieved a record of 12–4, and won a bye in the playoffs.

The Giants first opponent in the playoffs was the divisional rival Philadelphia Eagles. The Giants won the home game 20–10. With Minnesota's victory in their playoff game against New Orleans, the Giants would host the Vikings in the NFC championship game in New York. The Giants knew they would have their hands full with fearsome Vikings quarterback Dante Culpepper and receiver Randy Moss. Many people thought the healthy Vikings offense would overwhelm the Giants defense for the NFC crown.

But the game was a Giants blowout. At 2:13 into the game, the Giants were up 14–0 and never looked back, winning 41–0. It was without question the most dominating performance by any team in NFL history in an NFC championship game. The Giants gained 380 yards in the air and 518 yards overall. It was complete domination.

After the game Wellington came into the locker room to congratulate his players. In the ebullient moment, Wellington told his team, "This team was referred to as the worst team ever to win the home-field advantage in the National Football League. And today, on our field of painted mud, we proved we're the worst team ever to win the NFC championship. In two weeks we're going to try to become the worst team ever to win the Super Bowl."

The team cheered and the press ate it up. For Wellington this was a great thrill. He would get a chance to share the moment with Robert Tisch.

"We had breakfast one morning at the Regency and put it together, just the three of us," Mara said of a lunch with Tisch and Art Modell. "When Bob and I first met, he said, 'All I want to do is get 10 years of fun out of this,' and I said, 'That means you'll have to be in it for 30 years.' We laughed about it, but Sunday night [after the NFC championship game victory] I told him, 'This is one of those 10.'"

Mara referred to Modell for two reasons. Modell, who had introduced Well and Tisch, was now going to be his opponent in the Super Bowl. Modell had moved his team to Baltimore. As a part of the deal, he had to leave the name and history of the Cleveland Browns in Cleveland. His operation would be counted as an expansion team. Mara had helped his friend get approval for the move. Now the two close friends would face each other in one of the world's premiere sporting events.

"Mara was one of Modell's staunchest supporters when Modell moved the franchise to Baltimore in 1996, renaming it the Ravens and replacing the Colts, who had moved to Indianapolis in 1984," reported Bruce Lowitt of the *St. Petersburg Times.*

"I didn't like to see a team move from Cleveland, but I didn't desert Art," Well said. "I understood there were other forces in the city that were making things hard for him there."

"It was very unfairly portrayed," Mara said of Modell's move. "The politicians in Cleveland thought he'd never move. He did a lot of things for the city of Cleveland. He took over that rundown stadium and spent a lot of his own money redoing it. He put all those boxes in and sold the boxes not just for his games but for the Indians. They never would have been able to sell it on their own."

"The thanks he got was [Cleveland] built a great new baseball park, a great new arena for indoor sports. I think the crowning blow was the Rock and Roll Hall of Fame. When they put all those things ahead of him, he did what I think should have been done." Browns fans did not agree. In fact, at the time the Ravens appeared in the

Super Bowl, the most popular T-shirt in downtown Cleveland read, "Modell Still Stinks." The fans were the ones to file a motion with the league, insisting that Modell leave the Browns' team name, colors, and history there until a new franchise could be put together. And Modell moved to Baltimore.

Modell's Ravens were losers in the first three seasons. Then they improved to 8–8 and their fifth season they went to the Super Bowl. In the spring of 2000 Modell sold 49 percent of the team for $272 million to Stephen Bisciotti. Bisciotti had an option to take over the team in 2004. The cost of carrying an NFL team had grown to be too much for Modell.

Modell had long been a Giants season ticket holder, and still was in 2000. The Modell family has many interests in New York City. The famous sporting goods store Modell's was originally owned by Modell's father, but had since been sold to his uncle. "I think [Art] may be our largest season ticket holder," Mara said. With a smile, he added, "I don't think he got any in the lottery this time."

"I'm delighted to play [the Ravens]. I think it means a lot to him to be in [the Super Bowl]. You don't hesitate to beat your friends, and I'm sure he's happy to be playing us, keeping it in the family, so to speak," Wellington told the press.

Wellington was 84 years old and had 34 grandchildren, who ranged from college students to infants. When asked how many he would bring to the Super Bowl, Wellington responded, "The eligibility stands at age 10, but I can't tell you how many [are] above and below 10. I'd have to work that out."

The Giants had appeared in numerous championship games. This, Super Bowl XXXV, would likely be Well's last, and he thoroughly enjoyed it. It was his 17th NFL championship game. When asked what the difference was between some of the others and this one, he chortled, "When I first was around the team, it was like they were all my big brothers, then my contemporaries. Pretty soon, I was like their father. Now I'm their grandfather."

Wellington relished the chance of facing Modell in the championship game. He was very happy for his friend, who had been denied the championship game twice by John Elway's famous drives against his vaunted Browns teams. Well and Modell had been close friends since 1961.

"We liked a lot of the same things," Mara said. "We laugh at the same jokes, mostly his. We grew on one another. We talk several times a week about whatever happens to come up."

The two were compared by Giants General Manager Ernie Accorsi, who had built the three Browns teams that had gone to the AFC championship game after the 1986, 1987, and 1989 seasons. "Art is a man about town. He does and watches all kinds of things," said Accorsi. "Wellington is all football. He likes to watch the offensive line."

"Wellington Mara and Art Modell already rank among the legendary owners in sports," NFL commissioner Paul Tagliabue said. "Their personal friendship reflects the unique structure that has been the foundation of the NFL's success. They are tremendous competitors on the field but work closely together off the field for the overall good of the league."

"It's safe to say that Wellington's actions in revenue sharing stabilized the league," said Pittsburgh's Dan Rooney. "His counsel is always wise and to the point. Art's contribution was in television."

"Wellington Mara is the National Football League," Modell said. "He is the man everyone attempts to emulate, follow, walk in his shoes. He is a man of integrity, honor, and a competitive man. If the Hall of Fame gives out oak-leaf clusters, he should get one."

"I asked Mara if he would settle for just one more championship in his lifetime," wrote Ian O'Connor of *The Journal News*.

"Why do I have to settle for just one more?" Wellington said. "I'll take my chances."

The press coverage kept painting a portrait of Mara as the grand old man of the game. He soon tired of it, and quipped to a reporter, "To be perfectly honest, the patriarch stuff is starting to wear a little thin." He paused and then grinned. "Considering the alternative, however, I'll accept it."

The game pitted New York's balanced attack against Baltimore's incredible defense, which was compared, quite justifiably, with the 1985 Bears and some of the other great defensive teams. The Ravens featured star linebacker Ray Lewis, running back Jamal Lewis, and quarterback Trent Dilfer. The half ended with the game still close, 10–0 Ravens. But the Giants struggled against the suffocating defense of the Ravens, and lost 34–7.

SEPTEMBER 11, 2001

It was a beautiful Tuesday morning with bright blue skies and a wonderful temperature. It was the kind of day that makes sad people suddenly feel happy for a moment by just looking outside. That all ended when two massive jets packed with people and fuel slammed into the twin towers of the World Trade Center.

Wellington had been 25 years old when Pearl Harbor was attacked on December 7, 1941, a day the Giants played football at the Polo Grounds.

And he was at practice in November 1963 when President John Fitzgerald Kennedy was assassinated. Mara saw the NFL play their scheduled games two days after the assassination. Defensive lineman Andy Robustelli had protested to Wellington, asking, "Why are we playing these games?" In 2001 Wellington told the press that playing the weekend after September 11 would have been tougher.

"The same feeling is here," Mara said. "The players are human, especially our players and the Jets because they can just look out and see that smoke."

When Fassell told the players that the NFL's games had been cancelled for that Sunday, guard Glenn Parker said, "None of us wanted to be out there. When he came and told us, it was a relief."

Many players told the press they hoped to get involved somehow in the relief efforts.

"Even if it's high-fiving them and letting them know we support them," defensive back Jason Sehorn said of supporting rescue efforts and workers.

Wellington, John, Fassel, and the entire team, as well as all teams in the NFL, supported the commissioner's efforts.

"I don't know if I would have played," defensive end Michael Strahan said. "At this point money is not important; keep the money. This is life. This is respect for everybody over there. I don't think anybody in New York cares about football now, including us as players. It's not really important. The right decision was made."

"How can you sit in the stadium and enjoy a football game, and wherever you are sitting, you look and see smoke," said Pro-Bowl offensive tackle Lomas Brown. "It just would not have been right."

Wellington said he had been reluctant to press Commissioner Tagliabue "because I felt that my judgments were being flawed by emotion by looking out and seeing that the World Trade Center isn't there."

"There has been some criticism of the commissioner that he didn't come up with a solution when the bombs are still falling," Wellington said of Commissioner Taglibue. "I think Paul's hallmark has always been 'You get it quick or you get it right.' He's always preferred to get it right and I think he has gotten it right this time."

Wellington had taken part in all three of the NFL-wide conference calls on the Wednesday and Thursday of that week. Most of the teams supported the decision, but one or two clubs that went unidentified didn't agree with it.

"If they made the decision themselves, it would have been different," said Mara.

"I think anything would have been desirable, preferable, to playing the games this weekend the way the players felt," Mara said. "I was at a very tender age at that time and I didn't know where Pearl Harbor was. But I know where the World Trade Center was."

"I saw the post-Kennedy syndrome, if you want to call it that. That was very difficult. And I would think it would be even more so now because you have the constant reminder of the smoke," Wellington said.

NFL spokesman Joe Browne had announced on Tuesday that the Giants, regardless of the league's decision, would have had the option to take a bye in light of the attack.

Tagliabue had offered the Giants the option of moving the scheduled game to an away game at Green Bay, or delaying the game to later in the season, or taking a bye.

Mara had been prepared "to take the bye had the commissioner not called off this weekend's games."

"We would not have moved it," Mara said. "We would not have played."

⌘

That fall, on November 26, 2001, a special event was held at Mickey Mantle's restaurant. United Cerebral Palsy of New York City hosted the 11th Annual Sports & Entertainment Fantasy Auction.

Special guests of that evening were the members of the New York Giants NFL championship teams. Billed as "The Golden Years" special reunion, it was led by former Coach Sherman and included Wellington, Gifford, Robustelli, Erich Barnes, Rosie Brown, Kyle Rote, Dick Lynch, and Joe Walton. Gene Michael, vice president of major league scouting for the New York Yankees, was also honored as the UCP/NYC Sportsman of the Year.

The team struggled to 5–4–0 by midseason but then fell apart, losing five of their last seven games to finish 7–9–0. They had allowed 321 points for the season and scored only 294. Toomer had a 1,000-plus-yard season receiving and Barber had more than 1,500 total yards from scrimmage. But the highlight of the season was when Brett Favre fell down when Strahan broke through the line to attain the league's single-season sack record. Many thought Strahan's record suspect because they suspected Favre helped Strahan with the mark after the game was out of reach of the Giants. Regardless of the record, Strahan was the best pass rusher of his generation.

Wellington remained as active as ever. Dave Klein hosts an e-Giants website, and wrote the following about Well:

> One year a subscriber wrote to E-GIANTS to say his best friend was dying and that his hero had been Wellington Mara. He inquired whether I could intercede on his friend's behalf for a note from the man. I did. The letter, written on two full sheets of stationery, arrived within days in the man's hospital room. His wife said he was overjoyed, incredulous, and he asked her to frame it. She did that day. The next day he died,

and the framed, hand-written letter stood on his coffin during the funeral. It went inside the coffin when he was interred. That's the kind of man Wellington could be. There are lots of stories like that, so numerous that a separate book would be needed to catalog them all.

Over the years, hundreds of fans have mentioned that they met Wellington Mara and were enormously impressed with his genuine delight at shaking their hands. At training camp, outside the stadium, on the golf course, in restaurants and public places, they all went to him and he responded warmly to all of them.

A STAR-STUDDED EVENING

In 2002 Parcells was again available. He was, however, not destined to come to the Giants. Instead, he met with Jerry Jones. Parcells said Jones called him on December 17, 2002, and they met the next day. The two met at a New Jersey airport. Parcells, Jones, and Jones's associates spent three hours in a private room at the airport. They then talked for another two hours aboard Jones's private plane.

When Parcells took the Dallas job, coaching the rival Cowboys, Mara wrote him a note that said, "Good luck...to a point." And he taped a penny, heads-up, to the note, knowing Parcells's penchant for picking up only heads-up coins, which he takes for a sign of good luck.

The 2002 season was something to cheer about. Fassel turned the previous season's disappointments around, and the team finished with a 10–6–0 record. The offense scored 320 points and the defense was third best in the league in total points given up with 279. Strahan and rookie tight end Jeremy Shockey were both voted to the Pro Bowl.

The team had built a comfortable lead in their divisional playoff game versus the San Francisco 49ers. But the 49ers came back, and won the game 39–38 in San Francisco. It was a disappointing end to a wonderful season.

In 2003 Gifford and Wellington's wife Ann planned a huge surprise for the 79-year-old owner. Along with the help of co-CEO Tisch, John Mara, and the team's publicity department, the Giants would hold a once-in-a-lifetime get together. They invited every living New York Giants player they could find to a special dinner, scheduled at Tavern on the Green, on September 6, 2003.

"At the Tavern on the Green, we had a wonderful time with the help of John and members of the family and some other players. We found a lot of the former players around the league, many of them we had not heard from in a long time, and we brought them all to New York." Many had not been heard from or seen in years. There were 85 former players who attended. It was a surprise birthday party for the owner, who'd been with the Giants since the team's inception.

Well did not want to go anywhere that evening. A homebody by nature, Wellington was feeling under the weather and wished to stay home and nurse his health, with the upcoming game facing the Los Angeles Rams at the stadium the next day. However, Gifford implored Wellington to go to Manhattan. Gifford made up a story that Frank's wife, Kathie Lee, was being honored at a dinner. "And since Wellington and Ann Mara were the only family they had in the area, Frank said they simply had to attend. So Mara reluctantly put on a suit and headed to the famed restaurant," wrote team writer Michael Eisen.

"Frank told me the party was for his wife, Kathie Lee," Mara said, "but if anyone but Frank had asked me to go, I wouldn't have gone."

"We tried to keep it a secret, because I think he would have been reluctant," Gifford said. "He's done something for almost every Giant I've ever known. And you've never heard him say anything about it. He just doesn't like being in the forefront. But he's touched every one of these guys' lives, including mine, and their families."

"We made a little bit of a mistake because it was September 6, the night before the season opener. Ann was my coconspirator and had convinced him that he was coming to the Tavern on the Green for something totally different. And he was one grumpy camper," Gifford said. [Wellington complained bitterly to Ann during the ride over to see the Giffords.]

"He hasn't spoken to me since we left," she told Gifford when they walked in at around 6:40 PM.

"But we walked into the patio on the Tavern on the Green and Well looked around and the first person he saw was Lawrence Taylor. Then he saw Sam Huff, then he saw Andy Robustelli, and then he saw Y. A.

Tittle. And then he looked around and he saw John Amberg, and he saw Cutter Thompson. He had no idea what it was all about and then all of a sudden it sunk in."

Then Mara smiled broadly and joked, "I hope they know I'm leaving early." The crowd laughed.

Attendees included current NFL Commissioner Tagliabue, Simms, Taylor, Hostetler, Harry Carson, Tittle, Huff, Robustelli, Rosie Brown (who has been with the Giants for 50 years, now serving as a scout), Alex Webster, Bavaro, Matt Bahr, Billy Stribling, Bob Peviani, Joe Wellborn, Summerall, Ken McAfee, Bob Schnelker, Erich Barnes, Frederickson, Earl Morrall, Greg Larson, Brian Kelley, Dave Jennings, Brad Van Pelt, Billy Taylor, Bill Ard, Bart Oates, Karl Nelson, Chris Godfrey, Joe Morris, Phil McConkey, Jim Burt, Howard Cross, Corey Widmer, Brad Daluiso, Brian Williams, and many others, both past and present. Even longtime trainer Johnny Johnson was there, who, Mara joked, "had probably taped every male ankle in the room."

"Julius 'Whitey' Horai, known around the Giants as 'The Commissioner,' a man who has performed a million duties in 50 years with the organization," wrote Eisen, was also thanked by Mr. Mara. Also in attendance were 10 of Well's 11 children and the vast majority of his 37 grandchildren.

"I haven't slept in nights," Ann said. "I was so nervous I would give it away, or somebody else would. Then I started feeling guilty, wondering if I should tell him ahead of time. I thought that would spoil it. Let him see everybody. Then today he said, 'I really shouldn't be going in there tonight. If it wasn't for Frank and Kathie Lee, there's no way I'd go into New York.' I said, 'You'll feel better later.'"

"It was a beautiful night and a beautiful night for Wellington Mara because what I remember about that night is each of the players got up to say a few words and said that he had touched each and every one of their lives. Many of them it was an economic way, but for many more of them, it was just being there at the right time," said Gifford.

During the evening, many of the players told stories about Wellington.

"Huff told a story about his contract negotiations with Mara," wrote Eisen, "who could be extremely tough in those situations."

"We won the world championship my first year [1956] and I made rookie defensive player of the year at middle linebacker," Huff said. "I was making $7,500 at the time. When I was here you dealt with Mr. Mara. And I wanted to deal with Jack, his brother. Wellington said, 'He deals with the offense; you have to deal with me.' I said, 'I want to deal with the same guy Charlie Conerly and Frank Gifford deal with.' He said, 'You're dealing with me.' I said, 'Yes, sir.' He said, 'Here's your raise—$500.' I said, 'Five hundred dollars.' He said, 'Sam, I think you're worth it.'"

Tittle told a similarly funny story. Well turned toward general manager Accorsi, saying, "Ernie, if I'm as tough as they say I am, I guess I'll take over [contract] negotiations." They all laughed.

"To see all these people that he hasn't seen in years that he is so fond of, it's going to be great memories for him," Ann said.

Taylor also spoke, emotionally and from the heart about his former owner and friend.

"Wellington has been there for me throughout the years," Taylor said. "I've had my problems. But while I played ball and after ball was over, he was always there. He never told me what to do. He'd say, 'You know what you have to do.' He'd never sit there and say, 'You can't do this' or 'You can't do that.' He was always ready to help me. I will always, always appreciate that."

"I do appreciate this night," said Mara. "When I think about it, it kind of scares me to think how close I came to not coming."

"I'm at a little disadvantage tonight, because this was a surprise," Well said. "Having given away seven daughters in marriage—without giving them away—I haven't had time to prepare anything. I have nothing stored in my head. But there's a lot stored in my heart because if I've touched the lives of every one of you guys, you have certainly touched mine."

The mind boggles at Well's opportunity to visit with so many people from throughout his life, sharing jokes and old stories, watching the various players from across so many eras, swapping stories. This was like revisiting his entire life. It was a summation of his family's efforts and the good feelings they had engendered throughout the years. Few people get this kind of opportunity in life, and Wellington and his family were appreciative on many levels.

"I know he enjoyed it. But I think we enjoyed it even more," Gifford said later. "The one common thing we all had was that he had done something for all of us. A lot of it came out that night when we got together. That was Wellington. He did something for everyone; he touched everyone he ever came in contact with. Some of us were blessed because we had more contact than others."

"This was a great night for our family," said John Mara. "A lot of us had tears in our eyes. It's something he never would have put up with if he knew about it in advance. That's why it had to be a surprise. He doesn't like being the center of attention. He was so touched by seeing some of these players that he hadn't seen, in some cases in 30 years. It was a night that we'll never forget."

THE MARA CLAN

Wellington and Ann Mara had 11 children, including John Kevin, Susan Ann, Timothy Christopher, Stephen Vincent, Francis Xavier, Sheila Marie, Kathleen Mary, Maureen Elizabeth, Ann Marie, Meghan Ann, and Colleen Elizabeth. The Maras also have 40 grandchildren.

Wellington was happily obsessed with his family. His children's and his grandchildren's physical and spiritual welfare were always of paramount concern. And almost all the children and grandchildren also worked at the summer training camps, something Wellington immensely enjoyed. "The most fun I think was when my sons were very young and were first putting their toes in the water. It was fun seeing their reaction compared to what I remembered from when I was young. Now I have the same thing with the grandsons. There are all kinds of different reactions...."

John is currently the co-CEO of the New York Football Giants. He is not the only Mara within the organization. Chris Mara is the vice president of player evaluation and Francis X. Mara is director of promotions.

෴

Timothy Christopher Mara, better known as Chris, was born on March 11, 1957, in New York City. He graduated from Iona Prep in

New Rochelle, New York. At Iona he played football and was a standout defensive back, winning All–Catholic High School Athletic Association recognition after his senior year.

He attended Springfield College, where he played football and golf. He later transferred to Boston College, where he earned a BA in the Arts and Sciences. Like many of the Mara siblings, Chris spent many summers working at Giants training camps. During his collegiate years he worked with broadcast teams from both CBS-TV and NBC-TV during the regular football season.

Chris Mara first started working for the Giants in 1979. From 1979 to 1994 he worked as a scout in the player personnel department and was one of the staffers who helped build the two Super Bowl champion teams in 1986 and 1990.

Between 1994 and 2001 he operated an independent scouting service for NFL teams called ProRate, Inc. Fifteen NFL franchises subscribed to his company's reports. Chris then spent the 2001 and 2002 seasons as the president and general manager of the New Jersey Gladiators of the Arena Football League, where he dealt mostly with player personnel and contract negotiations.

He turned the Gladiators around. The team struggled during his first year, but improved in 2002 when they posted a 9–5 record, claiming the AFL Eastern Division crown, and Chris took the team to the playoffs for the first time in franchise history.

He rejoined the Giants on July 29, 2003, as the vice president of player personnel. He is married to the former Kathleen Rooney, and the couple has four children—Daniel, Kate, Patricia, and Connor. Kathleen is the grandchild of Art Rooney, of the Pittsburgh Steelers. This was the cementing of the two clans into the next millennium.

Chris and Kathleen were married on January 18, 1981. They were married several days after burying her uncle, Dan Rooney, one of the famed five Rooney sons.

Kathleen's father is Tim Rooney, the president of Yonkers Raceway and brother of Dan Rooney, former president of the Pittsburgh Steelers.

"The reason he's named Tim," says Art Rooney, "is that the time I had my big score at Empire City in Saratoga before parimutuel betting, one of the bookmakers I was betting with was Tim Mara, who was Wellington's father. I told him, 'I'm never going to let you forget this day; I'm naming my new son Tim after you.'"

In November 2004 Chris and Kathleen's son Daniel Christopher Mara, one of Wellington's 40 grandchildren, was married to Mairin Porpora of Huntington, New York.

Daniel was a first-year law student at Fordham University at the time. Daniel met Mairin at Boston College, where they both attended school as undergraduates.

Mairin is a computer teacher at the exclusive Rye Country Day School in Rye, New York. Her father was a managing director of William O'Neil & Company, a securities research and trading services firm, for which he directed New York Stock Exchange floor operations. Her mother was a member of the school board in Cold Spring Harbor.

ॐ

Francis X. Mara is the director of promotions for the New York Giants. Francis graduated from the Iona Preparatory School and Fairfield University. He began as an assistant to his father in the 1980s. Francis married Lynn Marie Hattrick on June 20, 1987. Lynn grew in Southampton, Long Island. A freelance artist, Lynn graduated from Marymount University of Virginia. Her father, William J. Hattrick, was a first vice president of E. F. Hutton & Company in its Riverhead, Long Island, office and mayor of the Village of Southampton.

Frank has a bit of his Uncle Jack in him. He is a golfer, and is reputed to be a fair one. He also has a son named Sean. Sean is currently a highly touted quarterback for Iona Prep. It has been rumored that Sean has gotten some pretty good looks from schools like Northwestern, Rutgers, and Syracuse.

"Wellington Mara had been as much a fixture on the hill overlooking the Iona Prep field as he was at Giants Stadium. His spot was under the two big pine trees, along with a small army of family members, at the school where several generations of Mara boys

319

have been educated," wrote Wayne Coffey for the *New York Daily News*.

෧๏๙

Susan Ann Mara, the little girl who spoke to President Nixon, attended the exclusive Convent of the Sacred School Heart in Greenwich, Connecticut. She then attended Boston College. She also received an MS in education from Fordham University.

She married John Robert McDonnell Jr., who was then an associate with J&W Seligman & Company, a member of the New York Stock Exchange. McDonnell graduated from the Canterbury School and St. Anselm's College in Manchester, New Hampshire. His grandfather, the late Peter McDonnell, was a member of the defunct brokerage house of McDonnell & Company.

The two were married at St. Ignatius Loyola Roman Catholic Church in New York on July 24, 1982. Sheila Mara was maid of honor for her sister and Peter McDonnell was best man for his brother.

Susan McDonnell is a member of Federated Conservationists of Westchester County.

෧๏๙

Steven Vincent Mara also graduated from Iona Prep, and then attended and graduated from Stonehill College. He was a specialist clerk with Francis R. Santangelo and Company, a New York brokerage firm on the American Stock Exchange. On March 12, 1983, he married Nancy Ellen Cassidy, who grew up in Larchmont, New York. She attended the School of the Holy Child in Rye and Sweet Briar College. Nancy was active at Iona Prep, where their son Stephen was part of the class of 2005. As a class parent, Nancy helped arrange for special events, including an appearance by Charles Way on behalf of the United Way.

Known as Steve, Steven Vincent is the president and a founding partner for Mara Capital. He is the firm's chief broker. Ultimately, Steve was responsible for the firm's daily activities at the New York Stock Exchange.

In 1982 he joined Spear, Leads, and Kellogg as a specialist on the AMEX when Francis R. Santangelo was acquired by that company.

In 1987 Steve opened his own sole proprietorship on the American Stock Exchange as an option market maker. He then moved to the New York Stock Exchange in 1992 as the president of Stephen V. Mara Sole Proprietorship, a traditional two-dollar brokerage, before founding Mara Capital in January of 2004. Steve is a member of the board of directors of Mara Capital, LLC.

∾∾

Sheila Marie Mara graduated from the Convent of the Sacred Heart School in Greenwich, Connecticut, and Manhattanville College. She married Ryan John Durkin, who grew up in Tiverton, Rhode Island. They were married on May 29, 1987, at the Roman Catholic Church of the Resurrection in Rye by the Reverend Kenneth B. Moore, a chaplain of the New York Giants football team.

Ryan Durkin graduated from the University of Rhode Island, and was a pre-owned car manager at the Griffin Ford dealership in Greenwich. His father was a distributor in Providence, Rhode Island, for Arnold Bakers, Inc.

∾∾

Kathleen Mary Mara, who goes by Kathleen or Kathy, graduated from Boston College and was an assistant merchandiser in the Halston division of Tropic-Tex International, a clothing manufacturer in New York. On May 12, 1996, she married Mark Warren Morehouse of Helena, Montana. The Reverend Mark Connolly performed the ceremony at the Roman Catholic Church of the Resurrection in Rye.

Mr. Morehouse graduated from the U.S. Military Academy. His father was the superintendent of Lewis and Clark County's public schools in Helena.

Mark was president, USMA class of 1983, and was later named Fort Benning Office of the Infantry School secretary and a project officer before his release from the army. Mark later became a vice president in government bond sales at Lehman Brothers, the New York investment bank. In 1997 and 1998 he worked for Deutsche Bank Securities in New York City as a sales representative for institutional U.S. government securities. In 1999 he went to work at Garban LLC in New York City as a broker in U.S. agency securities.

Kathleen and Mark currently live in Alexandria, Virginia. Mark is the legislative director for the Honorable U.S. Representative Jim Kolbe (R-AZ), who is serving his 11th term.

෨ᆢᅇ

Maureen Elizabeth Mara graduated from the Convent of the Sacred Heart School in Greenwich, Connecticut, and Boston College. Maureen was a production assistant at CBS Sports in New York.

She married Douglas Allen Brown of Southborough, Massachusetts on July 1, 1988, at the Roman Catholic Church of the Resurrection in Rye. The Reverend John McCarthy performed the ceremony.

Douglas graduated from St. Mark's School in Southborough and Boston College. His father taught mathematics and coached football, hockey, and lacrosse at St. Mark's.

Doug Brown was a member of the 1997 and 1998 back-to-back Stanley Cup champion Detroit Red Wings. He played right wing for 16 years in the NHL. He played for the New Jersey Devils from 1986 to 1993, the Pittsburgh Penguins from 1993 to 1994, and the Detroit Red Wings from 1994 to 2002.

Brown, brother of Greg Brown, was considered one of the better right wings in the NHL. Following Detroit's second Cup win he was claimed in the expansion draft by the Nashville Predators. Detroit responded immediately, sending Petr Sykora and two draft choices to Nashville in order to retain Brown's services. His consistent play helped the Wings remain competitive entering the 2001–2002 season.

He currently enjoys coaching youth hockey in Detroit.

෨ᆢᅇ

Ann Marie Mara graduated from Marymount University. She was a sales representative for Saks Fifth Avenue in New York. She married Timothy Burke Cacase of New Rochelle, New York, on March 5, 1983.

Reverend John J. McCarthy performed the Roman Catholic ceremony at the Church of the Resurrection in Rye, New York.

Mr. Cacase was the treasurer of the CRS Group, a company that owns and operates restaurants in New Rochelle. His mother is a registered nurse at New Rochelle Medical Center.

కాం

Meghan Ann Mara graduated from William Smith College and received a master's degree in elementary education from Fordham University. Until June 2000 she was a teacher at the Ridgeway Nursery School in White Plains and a field hockey and lacrosse coach at the Convent of the Sacred Heart School.

On June 23, 2000, at the age of 28, she married Charles Rogers Brennan, a son of Mr. and Mrs. Martin Brennan Jr. of Bloomfield Hills, Michigan. The Reverend John E. McCarthy performed the ceremony at the Roman Catholic Church of the Resurrection.

Mr. Brennan, then 30, was a bond salesman in Cleveland for McDonald Investments. He graduated from Boston College. His father was the founder and president of Brennan Development, a construction company in Troy, Michigan.

Meghan was the last bride Wellington had to give away.

కాం

Colleen Elizabeth Mara was an assistant buyer for women's accessories at Saks Fifth Avenue in New York. She was married to Michael Colin McLane, a son of Mr. and Mrs. R. Bruce McLane of Westfield, New Jersey, on May 30, 1998. Monsignor Donald Prior performed the ceremony at the Roman Catholic Church of the Resurrection. Colleen was then 24 years old.

Both Colleen and Michael graduated from Boston College.

Mr. McLane, who was 28, was the owner of the McLane Group, a corporate investigation and security company that he founded in New York. His father, who was the company's chairman, retired as a police officer in the 17th precinct of Manhattan. The bridegroom's mother, Judith A. McLane, retired as the head nurse in the neurology department at St. Vincent's Hospital and Medical Center in New York.

NOW CRACKS ANOTHER NOBLE HEART

The 2003 season was a disappointment. As the fans had sung for Sherman, Handley, and Reeves, so they now sang for Fassel. But Fassel had done an excellent job, as had Sherman and Reeves. But while Wellington might have possessed more patience, the fans did not. And so Fassel, who the classy fans cheered on his last home game, was released. And after a roundabout of names, the job was given to Tom Coughlin.

Coughlin was a Boston College man. He was a strict disciplinarian. Coughlin was the man Wellington wanted, and Ernie Accorsi agreed with him. Coughlin was among the best coaches available. However, the first year's results did not show this, as the players and the coaching staff took a year to get used to each other. The first season produced a bitterly disappointing 4–12 record.

"One time...after the Giants won their first game under Tom Coughlin, the coach who had caused such an uproar with his stern rules, Mr. Mara walked up to me and asked how the filly was doing," wrote Bill Pennington of the *Asbury Park Press*.

"The filly?" asked Pennington.

"You know, Lady H," insisted Wellington.

"I was at a loss for words. Here was this man whose new coach was being vilified daily in the papers, whose players were making mutinous noises, whose fans were beginning to think their team would never win again, and he wanted to talk about a horse that was owned by some friends of his, a promising filly who had just recently injured herself during a morning workout," wrote Pennington.

The horse, it turned out, was owned by Charlie and Marianne Hess in partnership with Norma Hess, Leon's widow. ... They had known each other for 15 years, and Wellington always sat in the Hess's box on Opening Day at Monmouth Park and on Haskell Day.

"More often than that, if Wellington could sneak away for another day at the track. He loved the racetrack. It was in his blood. Football may have been his first love, but horse racing and boxing weren't far behind. He was a product of his time, a time when racing and boxing meant something, especially to the son of a bookmaker."

In 2004 Wellington and Ann celebrated their 50th wedding anniversary. They celebrated the event with a ceremony at St. Patrick's Cathedral.

"My mother asked him if they could renew their vows. He was very reluctant at first," remembered John.

"The original ones haven't expired yet, have they?" Wellington smartly replied to Ann.

"Of course, he went along with it, but when Cardinal Egan asked him during the ceremony, 'Will you accept children lovingly from God?' the look on his face seemed to say, 'Your Eminence, I think that ship sailed a long time ago.'"

Unfortunately, while Ann and Wellington's resolve was strong, 2004 produced a dismal 6–10 record for the team. They had sprinted to a 5–2 mark with a new starter at quarterback, the aged pro Kurt Warner. But the Giants stumbled for two more games, and then Coughlin made the decision to start rookie Eli Manning, who they hoped would be the star to ignite the team. It proved a disastrous move in what could have been a salvageable season, but the future was Manning, and it was important to start his training right away. They lost eight games in a row before taking the last game of the season against the division rival Dallas Cowboys.

Many hoped that Manning would mature, and by coming into his own take advantage of the many weapons the Giants possessed, including Jeremy Shockey, Barber, and Toomer. During the intervening months, Accorsi added Plaxico Burress, who would compliment Toomer. The Giants should have had a stellar attack.

When Wellington was asked about his number one pick, Eli Manning, Mara said, "I'm always hopeful, but never optimistic." Then he quickly added that Manning "had a really successful training camp, much better than Phil Simms had in his first year."

In early May the 88-year-old Wellington underwent an operation at Sloan-Kettering Cancer Center in New York City to remove cancerous lymph nodes under his left arm and in his neck. He stayed in the hospital for five days. It was decided that Wellington would undergo radiation treatments, but would not have to face chemotherapy. Wellington had been dealing with nodes relating to skin cancer for approximately 25 years.

That summer, as training camp approached with Wellington's health failing, it was obvious his diminished health would show. And there was the possibility that he might not be up to attending all the sessions as he almost always had in the past. Reporters would wonder where the ubiquitous owner was.

On June 1, 2005, the team officially announced that Wellington had cancer. The announcement was the final two paragraphs of a three-page publicity release.

"It doesn't appear to have metastasized anywhere else," John Mara said. "But they'll do a little radiation just to be safe, and his prognosis is very good."

The announcement about Mara's illness was made 10 months after Tisch's inoperable brain cancer had also been disclosed. Tisch had been receiving treatment since 2004 in his battle against cancer.

In June the Giants had a three-day mini camp, and Wellington, looking frail and weak, attended both of the practices that first Wednesday. He sat watching the practice sitting down in a shaded golf cart, watching the offensive linemen working the blocking dummies. Jeremy Shockey was one of the first players to greet the stricken owner.

"During the afternoon practice he was more animated, standing alongside his son and wearing a blue Giants cap while watching players go through drills," wrote Richard Lezin Jones in *The New York Times*.

Wellington had insisted that he would be out of the hospital and back at the office in time for the mini camp. It was what got him out of bed.

"It was a big day for him," John said. "He was looking forward to it...it was his schedule, not the doctor's."

Reporters wanted to question the ailing patriarch. He shook a few of their hands, but he pointed a thumb in the direction of his son John Mara and said with his usual smiling smirk, "This is my publicity man."

"It's been a slow process, but he seems like he gets a little better every day," John said. "He's frustrated that he hasn't gotten better as quickly as he would have liked. But he's 88 years old."

General manager Accorsi also made himself available to the press. Referring to Tisch and Wellington, Accorsi said, "Both guys reassure us by their presence anyway." "Bob is doing really well, and there is such admiration for Mr. Mara."

"When I came into the league 35 years ago and I went to my first league meeting, there were about five or six of them; they're all gone now—Mr. Halas, Paul Brown, Mr. Rooney, and, of course, Mr. Mara," Accorsi said. "The galaxies are dwindling. You just try to savor every moment with these people."

On July 29, during training camp, the Giants held a picnic. Co-owner Tisch, who was 79 years old, made an appearance telling reporters he felt "fine." Just as noticeable was the absence of Wellington, who was undergoing radiation treatment and unable to attend.

Mara, however, was still his old irascible self. "During his 89th and final birthday party in August, he summoned a couple of his teenage grandsons, kids serving as ballboys during training camp, after hearing word that their dorm rooms had been left a mess," wrote Ian O'Connor of *The Journal News*.

"If I hear one more report that you're not taking care of your rooms," Well told his grandchildren, "it's the last time you'll ever go to camp."

"You've never seen kids' jaws drop so fast," son Frank Mara recalled.

Wellington's health began to fail gradually over the course of the summer and into the fall. He would have a good day here and there, but his health in fact was failing.

By October Wellington had entered the hospital again. He received numerous visitors. One visitor was Dan Rooney, owner of the Pittsburgh Steelers. The 73-year-old Steelers owner greeted his old friend, wishing to see him one last time so he could say good-bye. He also wanted to say thank you for all the years of advice and friendship.

"Your team is really good," Rooney told Mara. Well laughed. "He said they were," Rooney told the press. Mara shortly fell back asleep.

Even as his grip on this life was slipping, there was nothing Well loved more than his family and his Giants. Players visited, too, including Barber, Shockey, and Strahan, among many.

Bishop William McCormack, Wellington's Park Avenue boyhood friend, visited Mara everyday at Memorial Sloan-Kettering over the final month of his old friend's life. Neither Wellington nor the bishop spoke much. Instead, they found strength in each other's company. Old friends don't need to talk that much. "It was a faith experience for me just to be in his presence," the bishop says.

After almost a month at Sloan-Kettering, Wellington was sent home. There was nothing more the doctors could do for the failing owner. He would go home to Rye, New York, and take comfort in his final days, surrounded by those he loved and in the place he loved.

Ronnie Barnes, the Giants' vice president of medical services, who had been with the organization for a great number of years, looked after Wellington personally during his final days. Both during Wellington's stay at the hospital and at home, Barnes was ubiquitous.

"Ronnie Barnes, who my mother refers to as her 12th child, spent night after night and many days in my father's hospital room taking care of him," John said.

"Is Ronnie coming tonight?" Wellington would ask.

"Of course, the answer was always yes, and my father's face would light up when Ronnie walked into the room. We joked with Ronnie that one of the reasons he did this was because so many of the nurses kept trying to slip him their phone numbers at the hospital, but that really wasn't the reason."

"Nobody asked Ronnie Barnes to spend these nights in the hospital. He wanted to be there," wrote Mike Lupica for the New York Daily News. "He was 24 when he first came to the Giants. Then he was an assistant trainer and before long he was one of the most respected figures in his field. The Ronnie Barnes African American Resource Center is now part of the Joyner Library at East Carolina. He has written books on sports medicine. It all started because Mr. Mara and the Giants gave him a chance, the same kind of chance Parcells has always talked about. ... Ronnie Barnes, a Giant for life, would be there now for Wellington Mara."

"Ronnie, why are you so good to me?" the frail old man asked.

"Because, Mr. Mara, you've been so good to me," Barnes replied.

"Nobody took better care of him and there was no one that he trusted more," John said in his eulogy for his father. "Ronnie, my family can never thank you enough."

Peter King wrote in *Sports Illustrated* in late October, "Think good thoughts, or pray, or do whatever you do for Wellington Mara, the Giants' 89-year-old patriarch, who is home ailing, battling cancer. Mara is as close to a flawless and guileless man as I've met in this world."

࿔

"Where am I?" asked Wellington.

"You're home," said the nurse, referring to the home Mara kept just off the Westchester Country Club greens for decades.

"What day is it?" Mara wanted to know.

"Sunday," she answered. "Do you want to watch the game?"

This was how Wellington Mara's day started on the last Sunday of his life.

He answered in his own inimitable way, saying, "I don't want to lose."

Daughter Susan called her brother Frank at the stadium. Frank relayed the message to Coach Tom Coughlin through PR man Pat Hanlon before the team took the field to play the Broncos.

"And that's what happened," Frank told Ian O'Connor, sportswriter for *The Journal News,* the day his father died. "I was right behind the goal post when Jason Elam made that kick. It was going down the middle, then it suddenly started heading right. It stayed right. That was divine intervention there."

"Wellington Mara would open his eyes in time to take in the winning drive, to watch Eli Manning honor his potential as the Giants' next big star. This was all the football Mara needed to see and feel. He was back asleep by the time his players were chanting his nickname, 'Duke...Duke...Duke,' in the winning locker room," wrote O'Connor. The Giants had won 24–23.

That Monday, Barber and Shockey had come to visit. Well was not awake. They took a moment of silence at his bedside and visited with Ann. While all the other players called Wellington "Mr. Mara, only Shockey, the sometimes troublemaking, sometimes playmaking tight end, called him by his nickname to his face. Shockey addressed Wellington as "Duke," and Wellington welcomed it.

"I will be there when you get there," Wellington said to John during one of their last hospital visits.

࿇

On the morning of October 25, 2005, Wellington was surrounded by his wife, Ann, their 11 children, a couple of their spouses, and a couple of his nurses. Then he spoke his final words.

"Make sure you take care of your mother," Mara told his kids. "Make sure you take care of each other."

"He didn't want to leave until he knew we could handle it," Frank said. "Until he knew his wife of 51 years would be taken care of."

And with that, the patriarch of the Mara family and the Giants organization passed away. He had been the oldest living sports franchise owner in North America. He had seen and accomplished more than any other owner in all of professional sports. He and his father, brother, nephew, and sons had kept one of the flagship franchises strong in the media capital of the Western world. Together, along with players and coaches, he had fought off countless challenges and in the meantime had found endless amounts of energy to pour back into the fans and the city he loved.

A veteran of World War II, he had witnessed the assassination of JFK, the bombing of the World Trade Center, and 17 Giants NFL championship appearances. He had provided limitless advice and effort on behalf of the NFL. And with him had gone class, grace, respect, and his years of wisdom.

The patriarch was gone.

࿇

Accolades immediately started to flow in the media, in such a way that Wellington himself would have scoffed at due to his own humble self-image.

330

"I hate to say it, but I don't think they make 'em like that any-more," Marianne Hess said on Wellington's passing.

Mrs. Hess, sister-in-law of Leon Hess's widow, told the story about Wellington and Ann coming out of a theater on Broadway. It was pouring outside, and Well stood there in the rain, trying to hail a cab. A police officer on the nearest corner recognized the Giants owner, stopped traffic, and hailed him a cab. The officer thanked Wellington for a lifetime's worth of wonderful football.

"Wellington was amazed by that," Marianne said. "He never assumed that anyone would know who he was or think that he was anything special."

"And he would treat everyone the same way," added her husband Charlie Hess, brother of Leon, "whether you were a doorman or the president of a bank."

"Somewhere, Mara is probably smiling in his shy (and sly) way about all the praise heaped upon him over the last few days, especially kind words from the likes of Daniel Snyder, Jerry Jones, and George Steinbrenner, whose ownership style was the antithesis of his," wrote Dave Goldberg for the *Canadian Press*.

Jones, in fact, said, "Wellington Mara was someone whom I admired and respected for his love of his family, this sport, and the New York Giants. The National Football League has lost one of its fathers—a wonderful man whose contributions will be remembered for generations to come."

"There was never a more decent, honorable, and respected man in sports than Wellington Mara," the owner of the New York Yankees, George Steinbrenner, announced. "His lifelong love of the Giants was surpassed only by his love of his family. But, then, the Giants were his family too."

"Wellington Mara represented the heart and soul of the National Football League. He was a man of deep conviction who stood as a bea-con of integrity. His passions were many—his family and faith, the Giants, the NFL, and his community. He was an unparalleled leader in many different arenas," said NFL Commissioner Paul Tagliabue. "He always ensured that the Giants were one of the premier franchises in sports, but he kept the interests of the league at the forefront. When Well Mara stood to speak at a league meeting, the room would become silent with anticipation because all of us knew we were going to hear profound insights born of eight decades of league experience."

"Wellington Mara was a special person," said Dan Rooney. "He brought dignity to everyone he touched. He loved his wife, Ann, and his wonderful family. He truly was a Giant in the NFL and in life. ... He meant so much in forming the foundation and standards of the National Football League. He was kind to all and treated everyone with class. His integrity was in the forefront in every action and decision he made. His contributions to the NFL are second to none" Wellington was a mentor for me and a counsel I could call on.... He was there to help and offer advice that could work for the league and anyone who might need assistance. ... Our relationship has been meaningful and enjoyable and the games have been fun. We will all miss Wellington Mara as we celebrate his wonderful life. God bless and keep him."

"Wellington Mara was truly one of the NFL's founding fathers. He was a man of vision and led with integrity," said San Diego Chargers owner Alex G. Spanos. "He was one of the most unselfish individuals the NFL has ever known. He is without a doubt one of the key reasons the NFL is the most successful and popular sports league. He always put the league's interests first, even ahead of his own team. Back in the early 1960s he could have fought to keep the lucrative New York market to himself, but he saw the big picture and supported league-wide revenue sharing. For that reason, the league and pro football is what it is today. More than anything, he was a great family man for his wife, children, and grandchildren, as well as a good friend to my family."

"Wellington Mara was a second father to me and to everyone in this organization," said Accorsi "I knew him for 33 years and worked for him for 12. I never came to work without looking to him for guidance, for wisdom, and, especially, for inspiration. I tried to savor every moment that I ever spent with him and never for a second took that privilege for granted...he was the moral conscience of the National Football League. He now joins the pantheon of incredible men who made this league what it has become: George Halas, Pete Rozelle, Art Rooney, Paul Brown, Leon Hess, Vince Lombardi, all of whom left us with a feeling of emptiness with their passing."

"One of the things I miss the most this year is seeing him at every practice, sitting on that golf chair he always had. There was always a certain level of accountability, even in practice, because we always knew he was watching us," said running back Barber. "And after games, you'd walk into the locker room and he'd be standing right there to shake your hand, win or lose. That was one of the true moving feelings about playing for the New York Giants, having your accountability given to you as soon as you walked into that locker room."

"He was an integral part of the foundation of this league, part of the fabric of the game. I feel privileged that I knew him, and honored that he made me feel so welcome into the league. When we reflect on all he did for others and for the game, we'll also remember his dignity, his class, his manner, his kind ways, and his great family," said the new owner of the Baltimore Ravens Steve Biscotti.

"The finest values of society and professional football were all represented by Wellington Mara," said Pat Bowlen, owner of the Denver Broncos. His dignity, faith, and loyalty to our sport and to what America itself represents were of the highest order. Wellington Mara was an icon, and while his loss diminishes all of us, everyone who knew or was influenced by him is better for it."

"When George Young passed away, everybody looked at him as a brilliant general manager. I looked at him more as a person. I feel the same way about Mr. Mara," said former linebacker Harry Carson. "He was a tremendous owner. I didn't want to come to New York when I was drafted. But coming and finally understanding the rich history and tradition of the organization really gave me an appreciation for playing with the Giants. The thing that stands out in my mind about Wellington Mara was, even though he was the owner, he was like a player. After every game, he was the first one to come into the locker room. After a win, you'd see a big, broad smile on his face and he'd congratulate every player. After a loss, he'd come around and tell the players to hold their head up. He was one of us."

"My relationship with Mr. Mara was probably a little different than a lot of others. As captain, we found ourselves in some situations together and I was privy to his generosity with other people. Those are the stories that a lot of people would never hear.

"For example, the situation with Doug Kotar, and Mr. Mara taking care of his medical bills," continued Carson. "You could definitely tell that his players loved him."

"As we got older I told him, 'No longer can I say you're a great father figure. You're my friend, and the dearest one I've ever had," said Gifford. "He was extraordinary. ... He was very happy in his faith, he had 11 children and 40 grandchildren, and his children are just like he is. He had everything everyone tries to have. He had what we all strive for. He was honest, decent, kind, thoughtful—all those words people usually just get up and spout. But they were real with him."

"I remember every moment that we ever spent together.... He was always there. When we were on the field, he was always standing on the side. Our football team wanted to see him there. A lot of football teams don't want to see the owner around. But the Giants did," said Hall of Famer Sam Huff. "He was the man. You never thought about him being the owner. When you think about what he produced—Vince Lombardi, Tom Landry, all the great players and great guys he traded for, like Y. A. Tittle—it was just such an experience playing for the Giants. It was an honor that you could never forget. ... I can't imagine him not being there. I never met a finer man than him. I can't imagine him not being there."

"Whenever the Giants came to FedEx Field, I would find him and talk to him. He was like a father. A lot of my teammates felt the same way," Huff continued. "What Wellington did for the National Football League: he was the savior of the NFL. You wouldn't have 32 teams today if it wasn't for Wellington Mara. He made more contributions to the league than anybody—even more than the three commissioners."

"We have lost the conscience of the league," said Art Modell upon his friend's death. "Well was my friend for 45 years, and I never had a better friend. He was like my brother. He was a man of extraordinary character, integrity, and decency. He was a kind man who rarely spoke in anger, never used profanity, and was never unkind toward anyone. Personally, this is very, very sad, but it is also a sad day for anyone associated with football. We have lost a giant."

Bill Parcells said, "To anyone who's ever been a Giant, this is the saddest of days. Well Mara was a wonderful and generous man. He was a major influence in my life, and I was proud to have him as a friend."

"He had so many great stories, I wanted him to write a book," said former head coach Reeves. "Of course he was so humble, he said, 'I don't need to write one; I don't deserve one.' But if he did it for no one else, he should do it for his grandkids, because he had so many great memories and great stories that would be great for all of us to know about. He was just a great man. I can't say enough good things about it. He was one of the real true gentlemen I ever met in the National Football League."

Sherman said, "Wellington Mara dedicated himself to the most important things in his life: his family, his faith, and the entire Giants organization. This will always be his legacy.... I greatly admired Wellington on both a personal and professional level. He possessed a remarkable ability to understand and unite people, which, combined with his acumen for business, made him one of the great architects of the professional football industry."

"Mr. Mara was right. You don't appreciate it until you quit, but there is no such thing as ex-Giants, there are just old Giants. Since I quit playing, I appreciate that a lot more," said former quarterback and current national television personality Simms. "He was from an era where there were certain men who handled themselves differently than everybody else. I don't know if you can be that person anymore in this day and age. I don't know if society would let you be like him."

Daniel M. Snyder, owner of the Washington Redskins, said, "Wellington Mara was a dear friend, and football fans everywhere mourn his passing. Throughout my tenure as an NFL owner he was an invaluable advisor in person and in our many phone calls. As a Hall of Fame owner and backbone of the league, he shaped the sport we all love so dearly."

"He was always there to help me, even when I wasn't willing to help myself," said Lawrence Taylor. "I considered Wellington a friend. He never reprimanded me. When I was doing something wrong, he would tell me. But he was always one of the best men I've ever been around."

Countless others chimed in with wonderful stories and accolades too numerous to reprint. News of Mara's death reached all the way around the world; his passing was reported as far away as the *International Herald Tribune, The Times of India,* and the *Taipei Times.* Others who issued statements included: Tom Coughlin, Fassel, Joe Gibbs (coach of the Washington Redskins), Jerry Richardson (owner of the Carolina Panthers), Robustelli, Marty Schottenheimer, Tittle, Ralph Wilson (owner of the Buffalo Bills), and many others.

რთ

The family received friends on October 26 and 27 at the Frank Campbell Funeral Home in Manhattan at Madison Avenue and Eighty-first Street. The public was invited on Thursday from 5:00–7:00 PM. The funeral mass was scheduled for Friday at 10:00 AM at St. Patrick's Cathedral, Fifth Avenue and Fifty-first Street.

In lieu of flowers, the Mara family asked that donations be made in Mr. Mara's memory to numerous organizations, including Boys Hope Girls Hope, a charity in Bridgeton; Missouri; Life Athletes; the John V. Mara Cancer Research Center at St. Vincent's Hospital; and the Memorial Sloan-Kettering Cancer Center.

Early the morning of the funeral, Tom and Judy Coughlin visited the Mara family at the funeral home where Wellington Mara had been waked.

At 10:00, a bagpiper entered St. Patrick's Cathedral ahead of the coffin that carried Wellington Mara into the church he helped run for more than a decade, playing the song "Amazing Grace." The black, elegant coffin was carried to the church's doorstep.

"The family followed the casket down the cathedral's long center aisle. Mara's wife of 51 years, Ann, held hands with her two oldest sons, John and Chris. The altar was decorated with four bouquets of red roses, two on either side," wrote Michael Eisen.

The 2,200 seats available at St. Patrick's were filled. And outside at least a 1,000 or more filled the sidewalks. Fans, everyday people looking to pay their respects, also lined the steps and sidewalk outside the Fiftieth Street cathedral. In attendance were former New York City Mayor Rudolph Giuliani, former head of the New York Stock

Exchange Richard Grasso, NFL commissioner Tagliabue, Art Modell, Tim Rooney, Gifford, Parcells, Robustelli, Upshaw, John Madden, Pat Summerall, Notre Dame coach Charlie Weis, Willie Brown, Simms, Phil McConkey, Harry Carson, Mark Bavaro, Dave Brown, Jerry Jones, Jim Irsay, Robert Kraft, Lamar Hunt, Ralph Wilson, Mike Brown, Arthur Blank, Dan Snyder, Tom Benson, Zygi Wilf, Mike McCaskey, Randy Lerner, Carolina Panthers coach John Fox, Cleveland Browns coach Romeo Crennel, Bill Belichick, Karl Nelson, and Bart Oates, among many, many other notables.

Front-office executives included: Bob Harlan of the Packers, Art Rooney of the Steelers, Bill Polian of the Colts, Carl Peterson of the Chiefs, John Shaw of the Rams, Tom Donahoe of the Bills, Mike Bidwill of the Cardinals, and Matt Millen of the Lions. The daughter of the late commissioner Pete Rozelle, Anne Marie Bratton, also attended, as well as former Congressman Jack Kemp.

Indianapolis Colts President Bill Polian said, "I had the unfortunate duty of having to attend.... Wellington Mara's funeral on Friday in New York. It was very moving. On the one hand, sad; on the other hand, a very, very moving experience honoring the life of a man who meant so much to the National Football League and so much to New York City."

"The presence of NFL coaches from around the league, just two days before their Sunday games, spoke volumes about the level of regard for Mara," observed a story from the Associated Press. "Owners from at least another dozen franchises came to mourn, further evidence of his standing as the league's senior owner."

Barber led the current team into the cathedral alongside the casket, opposite the family. Other notable teammates present included Manning, Shockey, Toomer, and Strahan.

"This was not merely a funeral for a beloved owner of a beloved New York team. This was a sports state funeral, the state being the National Football League. Its executives and club owners were there. So were the current Giants coaches and players along with dozens of former Giants coaches and players. So were many Giants parishioners who had simply stopped by. 'Our customers,' as Mara called them," said *The New York Times*.

"The current Giants players were already inside, and so were so many former Giants, players and coaches, all these tough football guys coming here to say good-bye to Mr. Mara. But out here at 10:00 in the morning, behind the blue barriers on both sides of the street, the bagpipes and drums getting louder as they got closer, you saw something else. You saw the face of Giants fans," wrote Mike Lupica in the *New York Daily News.*

Wellington's oldest daughter, Susan McDonnell, and his son Chris delivered readings.

Then Cardinal Egan, the archbishop of New York who celebrated the mass, rose to the pulpit to deliver his homily. The cardinal offered condolences to Well's wife Ann and to his children and family. He then quoted several kind statements about Wellington. And then he spoke about his departed friend.

"I have had the privilege of knowing Wellington Mara for over 20 years, and I believe that what made him what he was can be summed up in two simple and beautiful words—faith and family," said the cardinal.

"Wellington Mara, a man of deep faith, loved his God and lived his life as he understood his God would want him to live it. He participated in the Holy Sacrifice of the mass every morning, and he prayed frequently during the day, often with a rosary in his hands. Like Job in the first reading of our mass, Wellington Mara knew that his Lord, his 'Vindicator,' lived and that he would one day see Him face-to-face to be with Him for all eternity.

"Moreover, like St. Paul in our second reading, Wellington Mara had the utmost of confidence in the loving providence of the Almighty," the cardinal continued. He then spoke of Wellington and Ann's 51-year marriage, and their strong and large family. "Family gave Wellington Mara strength, peace, and deep unconditional love, and family was reflected in all of his other relationships and undertakings.

"Today, dear friends, in this cathedral of which Wellington Mara was a devoted trustee, we are joined in celebrating mass for the repose of his soul and the consolation of his beloved family. This is exactly as he would want it. For the mass meant the world to him; and the reason was very clear. It was his very special prayer, the one in which he felt most closely and intimately united with his God."

Following Egan's homily, daughters Maureen Brown and Meghan Brennan read the Prayer of the Faithful. Gifford then rose as the first of two eulogists.

"I had three stages of knowing Wellington Mara," Gifford said. "He was my boss for many years, then he became a father figure, then as we both got a little bit older, he became my dearest friend, someone I could always count on, somebody when I was troubled that I could go to.

"One of the most memorable times came when I went into the Hall of Fame and I asked him to be my presenter. He was eloquent, as he always was, and I was so honored that he was there. As we looked into the faces of all these people, Wellington turned to me and introduced, 'A man that any father would be proud to have as a son.' I will never forget that. And a few years later I had the opportunity to stand in the same place and say to the same audience, 'This is a man who any son would be proud to call a father.'" Gifford was elegant and controlled, if a bit visibly shaken.

Then John Mara rose. The eulogy is only represented here in part, but little can be put on the page to relay the emotional impact he had on the crowd. He gave them solace for their sadness and humor for their hearts. By all accounts it was one of the most memorable eulogies one can have delivered, and no small transcription can equal its breadth and delivery.

Said John: "One of the visions I will always have of him is sitting on the equipment trunk prior to Super Bowl XXXV, alone in his thoughts, a scene I had witnessed so many times over the years. No pregame parties or festivities for him. He was where he wanted to be, with his players and coaches, but off to the background so as not to interfere. During our road games, he always sat in the press box. Never one for a fancy suite or entertaining people during a game, his focus was on the game. He always maintained his composure and often tried with mixed results to calm his family down, more so his daughters than his sons. I remember one game years ago when a particular player was having a tough day and some of us became a little exasperated with him. At one point I yelled out, 'What is he doing out there?' My father put his hand on my shoulder rather firmly and said, 'What he's doing is the best that he can.'"

John recounted the story of his father digging in the closet of his Rye, New York, home, looking for clothing with the lowercase *ny* that he had saved for more than two decades. And he recounted the story of the wedding vow renewal and his love of his team and family. The crowd was heartened.

"He may be gone from this world and we certainly grieve over that," John said. "But we also rejoice over our good fortune in having had him with us for so long, for the extraordinary life he led and for his spirit, which will live on in his children and grand-children for generations to come. When my father's brother died 40 years ago, Arthur Daley, the well-known sportswriter of *The New York Times*, wrote a column lamenting the loss of his good friend Jack Mara. My father had that column on his desk for all these years and the last line from that column is a quote from Hamlet: "'Now cracks a noble heart. Goodnight sweet prince, and flights of angels sing thee to thy rest.'"

His eulogy ended, John took his seat, and many people in the cathedral were both saddened and encouraged—saddened at the loss of this sports legend, and encouraged by the fact that John and his brothers and sisters might carry inside of them the best of their father.

During the course of the funeral, Parcells turned and tapped Pittsburgh's Dan Rooney on the shoulder. Now the league's most senior owner, Parcells said to Rooney, "The torch has been passed to you."

After the mass was concluded, current and former players stood silently on either side of the steps as Mara's casket was loaded into a hearse. "A horse-drawn carriage led the funeral pro-cession as the sound of bagpipes filled Fifth Avenue—a little touch of St. Patrick's Day in October for the late Irishman," reported *The New York Times*.

AFTERMATH

At 10:00 AM on Saturday, October 29, 2005, 16-year-old "Sean Mara stood somberly amid the tree-clad hills of Gate of Heaven Cemetery in Westchester, watching the man he called Pop-Pop being lowered into his final resting place. It's the same cemetery that hold's Wellington's boyhood hero, Babe Ruth. Two hours later, Sean, a junior quarterback for Iona Prep, was putting on his No. 4 maroon-and-gold uniform, about to play the most emotional football game of his life, and the most meaningful," wrote Wayne Coffey for the *New York Daily News*.

Frank Mara, the director of promotions for the New York Giants, let his son Sean decide for himself whether he would play or not.

"The only thing I told him was, 'Pop-Pop would want you to play.' The game must go on," Frank Mara said.

John Mara, Frank's brother and now co-CEO, was on the hill now in the same place his father used to occupy. And so were about 30 Mara cousins, kids, and grandkids. Iona Prep has no stands. Fans bring their own chairs to the grass or stand through the games. The Maras ask for no special treatment, said school officials, and Sean was very much the same way.

Sean played well. Iona beat local powerhouse Monsignor Farrell 13–6.

"It's sad," Sean said. "I'm used to looking up on the hill and seeing my grandfather watching." Asked about his grandfather, Sean replied, "Nobody better. That's all I can say." After the game, Sean watched his team go in their separate directions, and joined his father Frank, his mother Lynn, and the rest of the Mara faithful at the top of the hill.

On October 30, 2005, the Giants had a home game against divisional rival Washington Redskins. The flags surrounding Giants Stadium that Sunday flew at half-staff in honor of Wellington. Before the national anthem there was a moment of silence. And then Wellington's granddaughter, Kate, one of the almost 40 that were at the game to honor their fallen grandfather, sang the national anthem. It was an emotional moment for the Mara family and the Giants family. At halftime a video was show on the jumbo screens showing video clips of Mara's induction into the Hall of Fame and clips of him from the 1986 and 1990 Super Bowl seasons.

The Giants team then paid tribute to Wellington and Tisch, by thrashing the visiting Redskins 36–0.

In the days and weeks that followed, those who had feared Well's wrath in life now felt free to tell the stories he would have preferred remain private.

His secretary of 21 years, Joann Lamneck, had eight feet of water in her basement after Hurricane Floyd hit in 1999. Wellington was the first person who called to find out how she made out, and wrote out a check to help her cover the damages.

Lamneck also recalled a time shortly before Well's illness when he came to the office without a hat on a cold day. It turned out he had given his hat to a maintenance worker at the stadium.

A longtime front-office employee was struggling to make ends meet when she moved to a new apartment. When Mara found out about it, he quietly gave her enough money to cover her costs.

Mara even wrote back to inmates who wrote to him from all around the country. He sent them media guides and Giants programs, autographed photos, and other items. On some occasions he sent gifts to their homes for their children.

"I really believe you are the only owner in the NFL whose picture is up in San Quentin," Lamneck chided Mara.

"Well, I can think of worse places," Mara would reply.

"Don Thum's letters would arrive at Giants Stadium every week, as inevitable as traffic on the Turnpike. They would be in the same scrawl, on the same yellow legal paper, from the same rural outpost—Fonda, New York—hard by Exit 28 on the New York State Thruway," wrote Wayne Coffey from the *New York Daily News*. "For more than 20 years, Thum, a 64-year-old retired state trooper, would send the letters to the team owner, most of them containing diagrammed plays and assorted personnel and draft suggestions. And for 20 years, the Giants owner, Wellington T. Mara, would answer them, every one, well over 1,000 in all. He would never use a form letter, or a signature stamp—not for Thum."

By October 2005, Thum had a bulging box of letters from Wellington in his attic. The correspondence was both unique and incredible in the modern sports era. "Thum never asked Wellington Mara for anything, but that didn't matter. Mara sent him tickets to a game in the first Super Bowl season. He invited Thum to visit him in Albany each year and come onto the field during training camp, and would introduce him to players and coaches," reported Coffey.

"This is my oldest pen pal," Mara would tell people. Mara used to tell people he should have listened to Thum and taken Shaun Alexander instead of Ron Dayne. Thum admitted he was wrong more than he was right. But he always looked forward to finding his friend's letters in the mail.

❧

Not long after Wellington's passing, Tisch, the co-owner of the New York Football Giants, also passed on. And the Giants were suddenly in the hands of the next generation.

"We're awful lucky to have both families," said Accorsi. "John Mara has been functioning as the CEO for quite a while. He's as fine a young executive as I've ever seen in this league. There's no concern in my mind as far as his leading his family.

"And what has been really encouraging has been the relationship he has struck with Steven and Jonathan Tisch [the Giants' VP and treasurer]. They get along great. The relationship and the affection that Wellington and Bob had, I see it with John and Steven and Jonathan. Because of that, I think we're rock solid. I have no concerns about the ownership foundation here."

"John Mara says that when he really thinks about it, the time he misses his father the most is when the game is over, and it is time to take the walk he always took with Wellington Mara down to the Giants' locker room," wrote Lupica after the Giants had beaten the Oakland Raiders in Oakland in the last game of the season to clinch the 2005 NFC Eastern Division crown. "His father lived for nights like this. They were the payoff for all the times, over all the year, when things didn't go his way."

"The walk we'd take after we'd win a game was always the best time," John said. "It was just that quiet few minutes between the end of the game and the locker room, making our way from the booth to the elevator, seeing that smile on his face. If you want to know when I feel his presence the most, that's when. I can still feel him right there next to me. ... He was always coming down the hall," the son said yesterday, "or around the corner."

EPILOGUE

Harry Carson had been there before. He had been mentioned as a candidate for the Hall of Fame many times. And he had missed out each time. The issue had become a yearly disappointment so painful for him that in 2004 he had actually written a letter to the Hall asking them to withdraw his name from future consideration. Luckily, that letter had been ignored.

Carson was one of Wellington's favorites. Quiet, smart, well-spoken, Carson was the classiest of former Giants. A local broadcaster and regional all-around legend, Carson was also among the most respected and loved of the Giants from the 1970s and 1980s. He had seen the team through from its roughest days to its return to glory. He was a captain of those teams.

In February 2006 it was announced that Carson had been elected to the Pro Football Hall of Fame. He would be inducted along with Reggie White, Troy Aikman, Warren Moon, John Madden, and Rayfield Wright.

Carson, stunned, had found out at an airport baggage carousel. As he was getting his bags, numerous people started coming up to him, congratulating him on the honor. He had no idea. He had been mistakenly congratulated in years past, but after a few minutes the moment seemed real, and the honor sunk in.

"I was never disenchanted with the Hall of Fame. I was always disenchanted with the process," he said. "Obviously, I will show up. The whole process sort of [had me] sour. But you look at the support I had, for me not to show up would be disrespecting those people who really went to bat for me.

"The Hall is a tremendous honor. Initially, I was thrilled about being even recognized as a potential Hall of Famer. As each year went by, it lost some of its luster because of the process—not the Hall, but the whole process involved in the selection and because it was so public.

"Where I had a change of heart was when Mr. Mara passed away. I know how strongly he felt about me being a Hall of Famer and I knew that if it did come, I couldn't tarnish his memory, because it is something he wanted for me," Carson said. "I would never embarrass his memory, the Giants organization, or the National Football League."

The moment was symbolic. The new executive duo of John Mara and Steve Tisch were now firmly in place, ready to lead the Giants organization into the future. Here were the sons of the fathers, applauding the champions of their fathers.

"Harry Carson's talent, humility, and passion for the game of football, as well as his passion for life, have been rewarded," Executive Vice-President Steve Tisch said. "The entire New York Giants organization and family are happy and thrilled that Harry Carson has his rightful place in the Pro Football Hall of Fame."

"The Giants organization is very happy for Harry. He is as deserving as any player this franchise has ever had. I know he's been frustrated over the last few years, as have all of us when he wasn't voted in. But now he takes his rightful place in the Hall of Fame," said John Mara, chief executive officer.

Asked how he thought his father would have reacted to the news, John replied, "This would have been very special for him. He was probably even more frustrated than Harry was over the last five years or so. I can remember him calling me a couple of times to tell me the inductees and I could hear the frustration and anger, really, in his voice. He could not believe that Harry was not voted in. He would have been very happy today, as we all are."

❧

On February 17, 2006, John and his mother Ann were asked to attend a ceremony. Throughout his life Wellington had remained loyal and connected with his high school, the Loyola School in Manhattan. Wellington had graduated in 1933.

The school had decided to rename its highly respected Christian Service Program the Wellington T. Mara Christian Service Program. The program was designed to encourage high school students to volunteer to help the poor.

John Mara spoke about Wellington's love for Loyola and his commitment to service throughout his life.

"As a general rule, he did not like things being named after him, whether it was buildings or awards, dinners, scholarship funds or anything like that," John said. "But as I told the students at Loyola, I can't think of any institution that he felt more warmly about or spoke more glowingly of or loved more than the Loyola School. He always attributed many of the values he had in his life to what he learned while he was at Loyola. So I think this would have been a particularly meaningful reward for him, because community service was so much a part of his life. It was certainly meaningful to us."

NOTES

PREFACE

"He built the team..." Needell, Paul. "Gifford Recalls Pal as 'Simple Man.'" Newark *Star-Ledger,* October 26, 2005.

"He was my owner..." Needell, Paul. "Gifford Recalls Pal as 'Simple Man.'" Newark *Star-Ledger,* October 26, 2005.

"Mara acquiesced, just for..." Needell, Paul. "Gifford Recalls Pal as 'Simple Man.'" Newark *Star-Ledger,* October 26, 2005.

"We made a little bit..." Gifford, Frank. Transcript: Frank Gifford Eulogy to His Friend Wellington Mara, St. Patrick's Cathedral, October 28, 2005.

"He hasn't spoken..." Gifford, Frank. Transcript: Frank Gifford Eulogy to His Friend Wellington Mara, St. Patrick's Cathedral, October 28, 2005.

"It was a beautiful night..." Gifford, Frank. Transcript: Frank Gifford Eulogy to His Friend Wellington Mara, St. Patrick's Cathedral, October 28, 2005.

CHAPTER 1 *A Son of Ireland*

At the height of the... Kinsella, Jim. The Kinsella Homepage, www.kinsella.com, August 2005.

For those who could not... Kinsella, Jim. The Kinsella Homepage, www.kinsella.com, August 2005.

"Wearing bright green..." Burrows, E. G. & Wallace, M. *Gotham: A History of New York City to 1898.* New York: Oxford University Press, 1999, 737–38.

"When city authorities..." Burrows, E. G. & Wallace, M. *Gotham: A History of New York City to 1898.* New York: Oxford University Press, 1999, 737–38.

This condition was... Kinsella, Jim. The Kinsella Homepage, www.kinsella.com, August 2005.

At one point in... Kinsella, Jim. The Kinsella Homepage, www.kinsella.com, August 2005.

Later, public officials... Kinsella, Jim. The Kinsella Homepage, www.kinsella.com, August 2005.

"A poor boy from Greenwich..." Daley, Arthur. "A Pioneer Passes." *The New York Times,* February 18, 1959.

"The horse lost, but..." Not attributed. "Tim Mara, 71, Dies, Owner of Giants." *The New York Times,* February 17, 1959.

"In the morning..." O'Toole, Andrew. *Smiling Irish Eyes.* Haworth, NJ: St. Johann Press, 2004, 50.

"On leaving school..." Not attributed. "Tim Mara, 71, Dies, Owner of Giants." *The New York Times,* February 17, 1959.

"[Mara] became a bookie..." Agee, James. "Saratoga." *Fortune,* August 1935.

"[Mara] has a place at..." Agee, James. "Saratoga." *Fortune,* August 1935.

"Tim Mara was a..." Smith, Red. "Little Arthur's Big Friend Tim." *The New York Times,* January 15, 1975.

Many hotels in... Pietrusza, David. *Rothstein: The Life, Times, and Murder of the Criminal Genius Who Fixed the 1919 World Series.* New York: Carroll & Graf Publishers, 2003, 52–60.

In the 1920s Rothstein's... Pietrusza, David. *Rothstein: The Life, Times, and Murder of the Criminal Genius Who Fixed the 1919 World Series.* New York: Carroll & Graf Publishers, 2003, 52–60.

"Tim operated a..." Smith, Red. "Little Arthur's Big Friend Tim." *The New York Times,* January 15, 1975.

"How was the..." Smith, Red. "Little Arthur's Big Friend Tim." *The New York Times,* January 15, 1975.

"Mara sat staring..." Smith, Red. "Little Arthur's Big Friend Tim." *The New York Times,* January 15, 1975.

Tim Mara was a... Cope, Myron. *The Game That Was.* New York: The World Publishing Company, 1970, 155.

"Tim Mara is a large..." Agee, James. "Saratoga." *Fortune,* August 1935.

Toots Shor... Klein, Dave. *The New York Giants: Yesterday, Today, and Tomorrow.* Chicago: Henry Regnery Company, 1973, 13.

"I never passed up..." Klein, Dave. *The New York Giants: Yesterday, Today, and Tomorrow.* Chicago: Henry Regnery Company, 1973, 16–17.

"A private clubhouse..." Robins, Tony. "Lost in Place." *New York,* October 10, 2005.

"There was 24-hour..." Walsh, George. *Gentleman Jimmy Walker.* New York: Praeger Publishing, 1974, 152–53.

The Roaring Twenties

"The 1920s in the..." Hirsch, Jr. E.D. & Kett, Joseph F., Trefil, James. *The New Dictionary of Cultural Literacy.* 3rd ed. New York: Houghton Mifflin Company, 2002.

Prohibition jump-started... Pick, Margaret Moos. "Speakeasies, Flappers & Red Hot Jazz: Music of the Prohibition." *Riverwalk Jazz,* National Public Radio, 2001.

My candle burns... Millay, Edna St. Vincent. "A Few Figs from Thistles." 1920.

"I remember as..." Eisen, Michael. *Stadium Stories: New York Giants.* Guilford, CT. Globe Pequot Press, 2005, 6–7.

"I remember it was..." Klein, Dave. *The New York Giants: Yesterday, Today, and Tomorrow.* Chicago: Henry Regnery Company, 1973, 17–18.

"My father had actually..." Mara, Wellington. Introduction with Whittingham, Richard. *Illustrated History of the New York Giants.* Chicago: Triumph Books, 2005, v.

"Last year we fielded 18..." Terzian, Jim. *New York Giants.* New York: Macmillan Publishing Company, 1973, 158.

"Sure. Any sports franchise..." Daley, Arthur. "A Pioneer Passes." *The New York Times,* February 18, 1959.

"The Giants were founded..." Daley, Arthur. "A Pioneer Passes." *The New York Times,* February 18, 1959.

"But you have to remember..." Klein, Dave. *The New York Giants: Yesterday, Today, and Tomorrow.* Chicago: Henry Regnery Company, 1973, 17–18.

"In New York, even..." Halas, George as told to Morgan, G. and Veysey, A. *Halas by Halas.* New York: McGraw-Hill Book Company, 1979, 94.

"I was betting on the..." Klein, Dave. *The New York Giants: Yesterday, Today, and Tomorrow.* Chicago: Henry Regnery Company, 1973, 18–19.

"The professional game was..." Lipsyte, Robert. "So Who Owns New York?" *The New York Times,* November 2, 1970.

"The only trouble with..." Cope, Myron. *The Game That Was.* New York: The World Publishing Company, 1970, 152.

"Tickets were a problem..." Klein, Dave. *The New York Giants: Yesterday, Today, and Tomorrow.* Chicago: Henry Regnery Company, 1973, 19.

"I can remember how..." Klein, Dave. *The New York Giants: Yesterday, Today, and Tomorrow.* Chicago: Henry Regnery Company, 1973, 19.

"I'm gonna try to put pro football..." Whittingham, Richard. *Illustrated History of the New York Giants.* Chicago: Triumph Books, 2005, 1.

"We were sitting on..." Whittingham, Richard. *What a Game They Played.* New York: Harper & Row, 1984, 132.

"What's a touchdown?" Steinbreder, John. *Giants: 70 Years of Championship Football.* Dallas: Taylor Publishing Company, 1994, 23.

"At least 5,000 tickets..." Klein, Dave. *The New York Giants: Yesterday, Today, and Tomorrow.* Chicago: Henry Regnery Company, 1973, 20.

"I used to pass out..." Steinbreder, John. *Giants: 70 Years of Championship Football.* Dallas: Taylor Publishing Company, 1994, 10.

Harold "Red" Grange

"Three or four men..." "100 Greatest Players of All-Time." Collegefootballnews.com, www.collegefootballnews.com/Top_100_Players/Top_100_Players_1_Red_Grange.htm, 2005.

"They knew he was coming..." "100 Greatest Players of All-Time." Collegefootballnews.com, www.collegefootballnews.com/Top_100_Players/Top_100_Players_1_Red_Grange.htm, 2005.

Partially successful STOP... Whittingham, Richard. *Illustrated History of the New York Giants.* Chicago: Triumph Books, 2005, 4.

"It looked like an invasion..." Klein, Dave. *The New York Giants: Yesterday, Today, and Tomorrow.* Chicago: Henry Regnery Company, 1973, 28–29.

"When I saw that..." Carroll, John M. *Red Grange and the Rise and Fall of Modern Football.* Urbana, IL: University of Illinois Press, 2004, 112.

CHAPTER 2 A Season of Woes
The Grange War of 1926 (and Then Some)

"He announced that he…" Carroll, Bob. "The Grange War: 1926." Professional Football Researchers Association, www.PFRA.com, 2005.

"I have the biggest star…" Klein, Dave. *The New York Giants: Yesterday, Today, and Tomorrow.* Chicago: Henry Regnery Company, 1973, 34.

"It was doomed…" Carroll, Bob. *The Grange War: 1926.* Professional Football Researchers Association, www.footballresearch.com, 2005.

"Mister Pyle's chin narrowly…" Klein, Dave. *The New York Giants: Yesterday, Today, and Tomorrow.* Chicago: Henry Regnery Company, 1973, 34.

"No blasted Irishman…" Halas, George as told to Morgan, G. and Veysey, A. *Halas by Halas.* New York: McGraw-Hill Book Company, 1979, 121.

"Ernie was very glad…" Cope, Myron. *The Game That Was.* New York: The World Publishing Company, 1970, 73–74.

"I'll tell you, kid…" Cope, Myron. *The Game That Was.* New York: The World Publishing Company, 1970, 74–75.

"What we've got to do…" Cope, Myron. *The Game That Was.* New York: The World Publishing Company, 1970, 74–75.

A Lot of Balls in the Air

Generally sponsored by promoters… "American Basketball League." Wikipedia, www.wikipedia.org, 2001–2005.

"Players were generally…" Selinker, Mike. "American Basketball League." Wikipedia, www.wikipedia.org, 2001–2005.

Gene Tunney and Jack Dempsey

During 1925, Tunney had… Kahn, Roger. *A Flame of Pure Fire.* New York: Harcourt, Brace and Company, 1999, 370–72.

"Mara's disparagement was…" Kahn, Roger. *A Flame of Pure Fire.* New York: Harcourt, Brace and Company, 1999, 370–72.

"Tim Mara, well-known sporting…" Not attributed. "Tunney Attracts Big Sunday Crowd." *The New York Times,* August 30, 1926.

"Tunney will beat Dempsey…" Not attributed. "Dempsey Is Picked by Large Majority." *The New York Times,* September 19, 1926.

"On the morning…" Pietrusza, David. *Rothstein: The Life, Times, and Murder of the Criminal Genius Who Fixed the 1919 World Series.* New York: Carroll & Graf, 2003, 234–43.

"I was laughed to…" Not attributed. "City Will Welcome Tunney Home Today: Mayor to Hail Him." *The New York Times,* September 19, 1926.

"Writer Ring Lardner…" Pietrusza, David. *Rothstein: The Life, Times, and Murder of the Criminal Genius Who Fixed the 1919 World Series.* New York: Caroll & Graf, 2003, 234–43.

"Get enough adrenaline…" Pietrusza, David. *Rothstein: The Life, Times, and Murder of the Criminal Genius Who Fixed the 1919 World Series.* New York: Caroll & Graf, 2003, 234–43.

"Private papers revealed..." Pietrusza, David. *Rothstein: The Life, Times, and Murder of the Criminal Genius Who Fixed the 1919 World Series.* New York: Caroll & Graf, 2003, 234–43.

The End of 1926

"I attend the games..." Whittingham, Richard. *Illustrated History of the New York Giants.* Chicago: Triumph Books, 2005, 11.

"Mara would look through..." Halas, George as told to Morgan, G. and Veysey, A. *Halas by Halas.* New York: McGraw-Hill Book Company, 1979, 127.

"Everyone on the Giants..." Whittingham, Richard. *Illustrated History of the New York Giants.* Chicago: Triumph Books, 2005, 10.

Later, after analyzing... Not attributed. "Pro Football Here to Stay, Says Mara." *The New York Times,* December 19, 1926.

"Many times my father..." Halas, George as told to Morgan, G. and Veysey, A. *Halas by Halas.* New York: McGraw-Hill Book Company, 1979, 132.

Gibson Gets Subpoena... Not attributed. "Gibson gets Subpoena." *The New York Times,* December 16, 1926.

"Christmas celebrations by..." Not attributed. "Christmas Spirit Pervades the City." *The New York Times,* December 25, 1926.

CHAPTER 3 *The Lean Years*
A Championship Season

"On defense, I came..." Halas, George as told to Morgan, G. and Veysey, A. *Halas by Halas.* New York: McGraw-Hill Book Company, 1979, 133.

"Come on, Halas..." Whittingham, Richard. *Illustrated History of the New York Giants.* Chicago: Triumph Books, 2005, 12.

Tim Mara versus Gene Tunney: Round 1

"Had the largest stable..." Desmond, Perry. "Remembering 'Boo Boo' Hoff." The American Mafia, www.onewal.com/maf-art07.html, 2003.

"First Gibson asked Tunney..." Heimer, Mel. *The Long Count.* New York: Atheneum, 1969, 14.

"According to newspaper accounts..." Desmond, Perry. "Remembering 'Boo Boo' Hoff." The American Mafia, www.onewal.com/maf-art07.html, 2003.

"The figures were disclosed..." Not attributed. "Tunney in 3 Years Earned $1,715,863." *The New York Times,* October 4, 1929.

"Engaged for the specific..." Not attributed. "Tunney Says Rickard Agreed to Make Him a World Champion." *The New York Times,* November 6, 1929.

"At that point..." Not attributed. "Tunney Says Rickard Agreed to Make Him a World Champion." *The New York Times,* November 6, 1929.

"Dempsey fought for..." Not attributed. "Tunney Says Rickard Agreed to Make Him a World Champion." *The New York Times,* November 6, 1929.

Wills for "big dollars..." Not attributed. "Tunney Tells Court of Big Bout." *The New York Times,* November 6, 1929.

"With Tunney refusing…" Not attributed. "Tunney Says Rickard Agreed to Make Him a World Champion." *The New York Times,* November 6, 1929.

"Tunney was being…" Not attributed. "Tunney Called Dupe of His Own Manager." *The New York Times,* November 11, 1929.

"Of this you can…" Not attributed. "Tunney Called Dupe of His Own Manager." *The New York Times,* November 11, 1929.

"Tunney was willing…" Not attributed. "Tunney Called Dupe of His Own Manager." *The New York Times,* November 11, 1929.

Benny and the Giants

"Benny Friedman did as…" Curran, Bob. *Pro Football's Rag Days.* Englewood Cliffs, NJ: Prentice-Hall, 1969, 59.

"After that year Tim Mara…" Curran, Bob. *Pro Football's Rag Days.* Englewood Cliffs, NJ: Prentice-Hall, 1969, 63.

"We need Friedman…" Klein, Dave. *The New York Giants, Yesterday: Today, and Tomorrow.* Chicago: Henry Regnery Company, 1973, 41.

"Ed would buy two…" Curran, Bob. *Pro Football's Rag Days.* Englewood Cliffs, NJ: Prentice-Hall, 1969, 63.

"He made us believers…" Klein, Dave. *The New York Giants, Yesterday: Today, and Tomorrow.* Chicago: Henry Regnery Company, 1973, 41.

"We had no problems…" Klein, Dave. *The New York Giants, Yesterday: Today, and Tomorrow.* Chicago: Henry Regnery Company, 1973, 43.

"In 1928, the year…" Curran, Bob. *Pro Football's Rag Days.* Englewood Cliffs, NJ: Prentice-Hall, 1969, 63.

"Tim Mara signed me…" Whittingham, Richard. *What a Game They Played.* New York: Harper & Row, 1984, 48.

"Red Badgro was…" Litsky, Frank. "Red Badgro, 95, Football Hall of Famer, Dies." *The New York Times,* July 15, 1998.

Santa Rockne Is Comin' to Town

"Tim, would you…" Rathet, Mike and Smith, Don R. *Their Deeds and Dogged Faith.* New York: Rutledge Books, 1984, 71.

"The Giants are big…" Maule, Tex. *The Game.* New York: Random House, 1963, 153.

"I think we ought…" Curran, Bob. *Pro Football's Rag Days.* Englewood Cliffs, NJ: Prentice-Hall, 1969, 67–68.

"How much time…" Maule, Tex. *The Game.* New York: Random House, 1963, 153.

"That was the…" Klein, Dave. *The New York Giants: Yesterday, Today, and Tomorrow.* Chicago: Henry Regnery Company, 1973, 68.

"We have no…" Curran, Bob. *Pro Football's Rag Days.* Englewood Cliffs, NJ: Prentice-Hall, 1969, 67–68.

"I know what…" Curran, Bob. *Pro Football's Rag Days.* Englewood Cliffs, NJ: Prentice-Hall, 1969, 67–68.

Other Distractions

"Pounded and battered..." Brouillard, Lou. BoxRec.com, www.boxrec.com/boxer_display.php?boxer_id=012330, as retrieved on May 29, 2005.

"Tim Mara lost $4,800..." Kieran, John. "Purely Personal, Sports of the Times." *The New York Times*, August 22, 1932.

"He hasn't much hope..." Kieran, John. "Phantom Fortune." *The New York Times*, July 12, 1933.

A Tammany Tiger by the Tail

"Investment banker"... Not attributed. "Smith Starts Tour to Win the West, Big Crowd Cheers." *The New York Times*, September 17, 1928.

The bank itself... Slayton, Robert A. *Empire Statesman: The Rise and Redemption of Al Smith*. New York: Free Press, 2001, 344–47.

"For others it was..." Slayton, Robert A. *Empire Statesman: The Rise and Redemption of Al Smith*. New York: Free Press, 2001, 344–47.

"Messers. Mara and Kenny..." Not attributed. "Raskob Donates $100,000 to Party." *The New York Times*, June 10, 1932.

An "accommodation..." Not attributed. "1928 Fraud Charged in Democrats' Fund." *The New York Times*, March 20, 1932.

"When we met..." Not attributed. "Says Raskob Spent $1,000,000 Too Much." *The New York Times*, March 26, 1932.

"The name should..." Not attributed. "Says Raskob Spent $1,000,000 Too Much." *The New York Times*, March 26, 1932.

"Smith testified in..." Slayton, Robert A. *Empire Statesman: The Rise and Redemption of Al Smith*. New York: Free Press, 2001, 344–47.

Tim Mara versus Gene Tunney : Round 2

"The majority opinion..." Not attributed. "Orders New Trial of Suit Tunney Won." *The New York Times*, July 2, 1932.

"I have no resentment..." Not attributed. "Tunney Pays Mara $30,000 to End Suit." *The New York Times*, January 15, 1933.

"It was urged upon..." Not attributed. "Tunney Remitts $30,000." *The New York Times*, January 22, 1933.

CHAPTER 4 *The Sons of the Father*

"I was permitted to..." Whittingham, Richard. *What a Game They Played*. New York: Harper & Row, 1984, 134.

"You can see..." Klein, Dave. *The New York Giants: Yesterday, Today, and Tomorrow*. Chicago: Henry Regnery Company, 1973, 21.

"You're a good friend..." Klein, Dave. *The New York Giants: Yesterday, Today, and Tomorrow*. Chicago: Henry Regnery Company, 1973, 70–71.

"I don't know..." Curran, Bob. *Pro Football's Rag Days*. Englewood Cliffs, NJ: Prentice-Hall, 1969, 103.

"You are three years..." Whittingham, Richard. *What a Game They Played*. New York: Harper & Row, 1984, 138.

"The Giants will give..." Curran, Bob. *Pro Football's Rag Days*. Englewood Cliffs, NJ: Prentice-Hall, 1969, 112–13.

"Well was much..." Klein, Dave. *The New York Giants: Yesterday, Today, and Tomorrow*. Chicago: Henry Regnery Company, 1973, 98–100.

"Jack, who befriended..." Klein, Dave. *The New York Giants: Yesterday, Today, and Tomorrow*. Chicago: Henry Regnery Company, 1973, 99.

"I'm not a football..." Klein, Dave. *The New York Giants: Yesterday, Today, and Tomorrow*. Chicago: Henry Regnery Company, 1973, 99.

"Smith is Named..." Not attributed. "Smith is Named in Company Row." *The New York Times*, October 11, 1933.

"I was a 10-year-old..." Coffey, Wayne. "Well Suited for Honor." *New York Daily News*, December 19, 2005.

"The Fordham campus..." Maraniss, David. *When Pride Still Mattered*. New York: Simon & Schuster, 2004, 32.

"Was occasionally seen..." Maraniss, David. *When Pride Still Mattered*. New York: Simon & Schuster, 2004, 32.

"Contrary to later..." Maraniss, David. *When Pride Still Mattered*. New York: Simon & Schuster, 2004, 153.

The Sneakers Game

"I wasn't sure then..." Klein, Dave. *The New York Giants: Yesterday, Today, and Tomorrow*. Chicago: Henry Regnery Company, 1973, 53.

"It's you! I'm tired..." Klein, Dave. *The New York Giants: Yesterday, Today, and Tomorrow*. Chicago: Henry Regnery Company, 1973, 53.

"The teams are..." Klein, Dave. *The New York Giants: Yesterday, Today, and Tomorrow*. Chicago: Henry Regnery Company, 1973, 55–56.

"When I went to..." Halas, George as told to Morgan, G. and Veysey, A. Halas by Halas. New York: McGraw-Hill Book Company, 1979, 179.

"It's bad..." Klein, Dave. *The New York Giants: Yesterday, Today, and Tomorrow*. Chicago: Henry Regnery Company, 1973, 79.

"We had a little..." Whittingham, Richard. *What a Game They Played*. New York: Harper & Row, 1984, 140.

"We were pretty..." Halas, George as told to Morgan, G. and Veysey, A. *Halas by Halas*. New York: McGraw-Hill Book Company, 1979, 179.

"Bronko Nagurski and..." Curran, Bob. *Pro Football's Rag Days*. Englewood Cliffs, NJ: Prentice-Hall, 1969, 120.

"Some of the..." Whittingham, Richard. *What a Game They Played*. New York: Harper & Row, 1984, 140.

"Good, step on their toes!" Halas, George as told to Morgan, G. and Veysey, A. *Halas by Halas*. New York: McGraw-Hill Book Company, 1979, 179.

"Dammit..." Klein, Dave. *The New York Giants: Yesterday, Today, and Tomorrow*. Chicago: Henry Regnery Company, 1973, 81.

"We were helpless..." Halas, George as told to Morgan, G. and Veysey, A. *Halas by Halas*. New York: McGraw-Hill Book Company, 1979, 180.

"By that time the..." Whittingham, Richard. *Illustrated History of the New York Giants.* Chicago: Triumph Books, 2005, 40.

"I still say we..." Curran, Bob. *Pro Football's Rag Days.* Englewood Cliffs, NJ: Prentice-Hall, 1969, 106.

"Steve Owen and..." Whittingham, Richard. *What a Game They Played.* New York: Harper & Row, 1984, 140.

"I wish I could..." Halas, George as told to Morgan, G. and Veysey, A. *Halas by Halas.* New York: McGraw-Hill Book Company, 1979, 180.

"My father and..." Halas, George as told to Morgan, G. and Veysey, A. *Halas by Halas.* New York: McGraw-Hill Book Company, 1979, 156.

"Tim said he needed..." Whittingham, Richard. *What a Game They Played.* New York: Harper & Row, 1984, 57.

Jack Grows into the Role

"Tim was easier to..." Whittingham, Richard. *What a Game They Played.* New York: Harper & Row, 1984, 57.

"Gee, I thought..." Obituary. "Jack Mara of Football Giants Is Dead Here of Cancer at 57." *The New York Times,* June 30, 1965.

"In the 1930s..." Obituary. "Jack Mara of Football Giants Is Dead Here of Cancer at 57." *The New York Times,* June 30, 1965.

"If you're going..." Obituary. "Jack Mara of Football Giants Is Dead Here of Cancer at 57." *The New York Times,* June 30, 1965.

"In every sport..." Not attributed. "Mara Suggests Substitution of Overtime." *The New York Times,* January 10, 1933.

"At the league meeting..." Halas, George as told to Morgan, G. and Veysey, A. *Halas by Halas.* New York: McGraw-Hill Book Company, 1979, 156.

"I thought the..." Halas, George as told to Morgan, G. and Veysey, A. *Halas by Halas.* New York: McGraw-Hill Book Company, 1979, 159.

"We had no..." Needell, Paul. "NFL, fans feel the loss as football giant dies." Newark *Star-Ledger,* October 26, 2005.

"I sent him a..." Whittingham, Richard. *Illustrated History of the New York Giants.* Chicago: Triumph Books, 2005, 43.

"With Tim Mara..." Cope, Myron. *The Game That Was.* New York: The World Publishing Company, 1970, 154–55.

"When my father..." Lowitt, Bruce. "Mara is Still a Football Giant." *St. Petersburg Times,* January 22, 2001.

"Art used information..." O'Toole, Andrew. *Smiling Irish Eyes.* Haworth, NJ: St. Johann Press, 2004, 65.

"We always wanted..." Cited in, Daly, Dan. "Everyone is in Rush for NFL Start." *The Washington Times,* August 10, 2003.

"Even without inside..." O'Toole, Andrew. *Smiling Irish Eyes.* Haworth, NJ: St. Johann Press, 2004, 67.

"I was up at..." Anderson, Dave. "For Rooneys, a Funeral and a Wedding." *The New York Times,* January 18, 1981.

"Jack was an..." Eisen, Michael. *Stadium Stories: New York Giants.* Guilford, CT: Globe Pequot Press, 2005, 7–8.

CHAPTER 5 *The Third Brother*

"Coach Owen had..." Neft, David S. and Cohen, Richard M. *The Football Encyclopedia.* New York: St. Martin's Press, 1991, 134.

"Back in 1935, I..." Izenberg, Jerry. *No Medals for Trying.* New York: Macmillan Publishing Company, 1990, 65.

"Most of the time..." Izenberg, Jerry. *No Medals for Trying.* New York: Macmillan Publishing Company, 1990, 65.

"George Preston Marshall was..." Povich, Shirley. "George Preston Marshall: No Boredom; No Blacks." Excerpted from *The Redskins Book.* Washingtonpost.com, www.washingtonpost.com/wp-srv/sports/redskins/longterm/book/pages/16.htm (accessed December 22, 2005).

"The relationship between..." Daley, Arthur. "Surprise Party." *The New York Times,* November 22, 1950.

"The success of the..." Klein, Dave. *The New York Giants: Yesterday, Today, and Tomorrow.* Chicago: Henry Regnery Company, 1973, 90.

"I didn't think..." Klein, Dave. *The New York Giants: Yesterday, Today, and Tomorrow.* Chicago: Henry Regnery Company, 1973, 90–91.

"He laid down the..." Needell, Paul. "NFL, fans feel the loss as football giant dies." Newark *Star-Ledger,* October 26, 2005.

"Mud, oodles of..." Povich, Shirley. "Redskins, Giants Play Scoreless Tie." *Washington Post,* October 2, 1939.

"Ten years ago..." Not attributed. *Time* magazine, December 11, 1939.

"Halloran never did..." Povich, Shirley. "George Preston Marshall: No Boredom; No Blacks." Excerpted from *The Redskins Book.* Washingtonpost.com, www.washingtonpost.com/wp-srv/sports/redskins/longterm/book/pages/16.htm (accessed December 22, 2005).

"The only thing..." Klein, Dave. *The New York Giants: Yesterday, Today, and Tomorrow.* Chicago: Henry Regnery Company, 1973, 128.

In March 1940... Not attributed. "Bookmakers Tell of Murray's Bets." *The New York Times,* March 28, 1940.

"Who could afford..." Not attributed. "Bookmakers Tell of Murray's Bets." *The New York Times,* March 28, 1940.

"The fact that..." Kieran, John. "The Shooting Party at the Polo Grounds." *The New York Times,* October 23, 1941.

"Attention please..." Maiorana, Sal. *Battle Cry.* Special to NFL.com, December 7, 2003.

"At halftime, Father..." Heller, Dick. "Tuffy Leemans Day turned tragic in 1941." *Washington Times,* December 5, 2005.

On the Home Front

"Even if we had..." Whittingham, Richard. *What a Game They Played.* New York: Harper & Row, 1984, 140–41.

"On more than one..." Bachelor, Jason. "James Carol Hecker." Brigham Young University, http://memorialhall.byu.edu/ww2/jhecker.html, (accessed February 22, 2005).

"Kept the National Football..." Not attributed. "Jack Mara of Football Giants Is Dead." *The New York Times,* June 30, 1965.

"The only boxed seats..." Whittingham, Richard. *Illustrated History of the New York Giants*. Chicago: Triumph Books, 2005, 62.

The All-American Footballll Conference

"It was hoped..." MacCambridge, Michael. *America's Game*. New York: Random House (Anchor Books paperback edition), 2005, 40.

"He'd have his..." O'Toole, Andrew. *Smiling Irish Eyes*. Howarth, NJ: St. Johann Press, 2004, 166.

"I think that it..." Whittingham, Richard. *What a Game They Played*. New York: Harper & Row, 1984, 140–41.

"I have to say..." Curran, Bob. *Pro Football's Rag Days*. Englewood Cliffs, NJ: Prentice-Hall, 1969, 42.

Scandal!

"I cannot discuss..." Klein, Dave. *The New York Giants: Yesterday, Today, and Tomorrow*. Chicago: Henry Regnery Company, 1973, 136–37.

"I didn't know what..." Klein, Dave. *The New York Giants: Yesterday, Today, and Tomorrow*. Chicago: Henry Regnery Company, 1973, 136–37.

"This game of yours..." Klein, Dave. *The New York Giants: Yesterday, Today, and Tomorrow*. Chicago: Henry Regnery Company, 1973, 136–37.

"The Giants' boss..." Not attributed. "Too Much Money." *Time* magazine, December 30, 1946.

"The biggest sport..." Not attributed. "Pro Careers End for 2 Giant Backs." *The New York Times*, April 4, 1947.

Alvin J. Paris had endeavored... Luchter, P.S. Historic records of the New York Giants, List of Amazing Sports Facts, as retrieved on December 26, 2005.

"Over the defense's..." Not attributed. "More Tapping Heard in Fix Trial." *The New York Times*, March 7, 1947.

"Filchock Admits He..." Not attributed. "Filchock Admits He Lied to Mayor." *The New York Times*, January 8, 1947.

"Paris Trial Data..." Not attributed. "Paris Trial Data Sought by Jersey." *The New York Times*, January 10, 1947.

"Bert Bell made a..." Not attributed. "Mara Approves Decision." *The New York Times*, April 4, 1947.

Conerly and Tunnell

"[Rickey] predicted the..." Smith, Red, from the *New York Herald Tribune*, 1948. Reprinted, Whittingham, Richard. *Illustrated History of the New York Giants*. Chicago: Triumph Books, 2005, 67.

"I don't know about..." Conerly, Perian. *Backseat Quarterback*. New York: Doubleday, 1963. Revised edition, Jackson, MS: University Press of Mississippi, 2003, 31.

"And if they don't..." Conerly, Perian. *Backseat Quarterback*. New York: Doubleday, 1963. Revised edition, Jackson, MS: University Press of Mississippi, 2003, 36.

"If you have enough..." Terzian, Jim. *New York Giants*. New York: Macmillan Publishing Company, 1973, 128.

CHAPTER 6 *The Golden Age of New York Sports*
The City of Champions

"The slab face and..." DeLillo, Don. *Underworld*. New York: Scribner, 1997, 18.

"Show me a man..." Gifford, Frank, with Waters, Harry. *The Whole Ten Yards*. New York: Random House, 1993, 210.

"On one side of..." Gifford, Frank, with Waters, Harry. *The Whole Ten Yards*. New York: Random House, 1993, 207.

"Need a ride?" Gifford, Frank, with Waters, Harry. *The Whole Ten Yards*. New York: Random House, 1993, 214.

"How can I..." Eskanazi, Gerald. *There Were Giants in Those Days*. New York: Grossett & Dunlap, 1976, 214–15.

A Hint of Greatness

"My brother Jack..." Klein, Dave. *The New York Giants: Yesterday, Today, and Tomorrow*. Chicago: Henry Regnery Company, 1973, 150–51.

"If we could..." Whittingham, Richard. *Illustrated History of the New York Giants*. Chicago: Triumph Books, 2005, 77.

"The Giants operated..." Gifford, Frank, with Waters, Harry. *The Whole 10 Yards*. New York: Random House, 1993, 82.

"We spend a lot..." Not attributed. "Football Giants Call TV Harmful to Attendance." *The New York Times*, March 4, 1953.

"Same with the..." Gifford, Frank, with Waters, Harry. *The Whole 10 Yards*. New York: Random House, 1993, 86.

"But I was..." Gifford, Frank, with Waters, Harry. *The Whole 10 Yards*. New York: Random House, 1993, 88.

"As much as the Maras..." Whittingham, Richard. *Illustrated History of the New York Giants*. Chicago: Triumph Books, 2005, 79–80.

"Years after lesser..." Daley, Arthur. "On Losing a Friend." *The New York Times*, July 1, 1965.

Jim Lee Howell

"Steve Owen, long..." Maraniss, David. *When Pride Still Mattered*. New York: Simon & Schuster, 1999, 152–53.

"In December of [1953]..." Blaik, Earl. *The Red Blaik Story*. New Rochelle, NY: Arlington House Publishers, 1960, 438.

"We tried Red Blaik..." Klein, Dave. *The New York Giants: Yesterday, Today, and Tomorrow*. Chicago: Henry Regnery Company, 1973, 150–51.

"When Army played..." Maraniss, David. *When Pride Still Mattered*. New York: Simon & Schuster, 1999, 153.

"When we fired Steve..." Klein, Dave. *The New York Giants: Yesterday, Today, and Tomorrow*. Chicago: Henry Regnery Company, 1973, 150–51.

"They are a great..." Terzian, Jim. *New York Giants*. New York: Macmillan Publishing Company, 1973, 115.

"Different as Daylight and Dark"—Vince Lombardi and Tom Landry

"At our last meeting…" Blaik, Earl. *The Red Blaik Story.* New Rochelle, NY: Arlington House Publishers, 1960, 438.

"I remember him…" Maraniss, David. *When Pride Still Mattered.* New York: Simon & Schuster, 1999, 154.

"Lombardi's philosophy was…" Golenbock, Peter. *Landry's Boys,* Chicago: Triumph Books, 2005, 33.

"[Landry] designed a…" Golenbock, Peter. *Landry's Boys.* Chicago: Triumph Books, 2005, 33.

"Mostly he is the…" Maraniss, David. *When Pride Still Mattered.* New York: Simon & Schuster, 1999, 160.

"If the question is…" Maraniss, David. *When Pride Still Mattered.* New York: Simon & Schuster, 1999, 160.

"I would like to say…" Terzian, Jim. *New York Giants.* New York: Macmillan Publishing Company, 1973, 112.

Wellington Gets Married

"It was a sporting…" Harris, David. *The League.* New York: Bantam Books, 1986, 83.

"Let's just take…" Golenbock, Peter. *Cowboys Have Always Been My Heroes.* New York: Warner Books, 1997, 366.

"We sat down…" Golenbock, Peter. *Cowboys Have Always Been My Heroes.* New York: Warner Books, 1997, 366.

"Recalled when the…" St. John, Bob. *Tex!* Englewood, NJ: Prentice Hall, 1988, 80.

"You can't talk…" Eisen, Michael. *Stadium Stories: New York Giants.* Guilford, CT: Globe Pequot Press, 2005, 9.

"The visiting coaches…" Eisen, Michael. *Stadium Stories: New York Giants.* Guilford, CT: Globe Pequot Press, 2005, 7–8.

"The Giants were…" O'Connor, Ian. "Giants' Big Win Brings Salve to Maras' Pain." *USA Today,* October 31, 2005.

The Second Sneakers Game

"Football is our…" Not attributed. "Owners of Football Giants Turn Down Offer of $1,000,000 for Franchise." *The New York Times,* December 29, 1955.

"Their television-radio…" Not attributed. "Owners of Football Giants Turn Down Offer of $1,000,000 for Franchise." *The New York Times,* December 29, 1955.

"You!" screamed Tim… Klein, Dave. *The New York Giants: Yesterday, Today, and Tomorrow.* Chicago: Henry Regnery Company, 1973, 24–25.

"Where the hell…" Klein, Dave. *The New York Giants: Yesterday, Today, and Tomorrow.* Chicago: Henry Regnery Company, 1973, 24–25.

"The Giants moved…" Neft, David S. and Cohen, Richard M. *The Football Encyclopedia.* New York: St. Martin's Press, 1991, 260.

"Wellington Mara once…" Terzian, Jim. *New York Giants.* New York: Macmillan Publishing Company, 1973, 118.

"I've been talking..." Robustelli, Andy. *Once a Giant, Always...* Boston: Quinlan Press, 1987, 22–23.

"The Maras were..." Terzian, Jim. *New York Giants.* New York: Macmillan Publishing Company, 1973, 106.

"The Giants...use..." Conerly, Perian. *Backseat Quarterback.* New York: Doubleday, 1963. Revised edition, Jackson, MS: University Press of Mississippi, 2003, 113–14.

"Boys," Mara said... Grier, Roosevelt, with Baker, Dennis. *Rosey.* Tulsa, OK: Honor Publishing, 1986, 84–85.

"All over the city..." MacCambridge, Michael. *America's Game.* New York: Random House, Anchor Books paperback edition, 2005, 99.

The Big Kick

"Nick Baldino, a friend..." Pennington, Bill. *Wellington Mara, All Dignity and Grace.* Neptune, NJ: Asbury Park Press, 2006.

"You'll never get..." Maraniss, David. *When Pride Still Mattered.* New York: Simon & Schuster, 1999, 183.

"I want you..." Daley, Arthur. "To Be or Not to Be." *The New York Times,* June 2, 1958.

"That point had..." Daley, Arthur. "To Be or Not to Be." *The New York Times,* June 2, 1958.

"That Summerall kick..." Eskanazi, Gerald. *There Were Giants in Those Days.* New York: Grossett & Dunlap, 1976, 136.

"What the..." Wallace, Bill. "Pat Summerall." *ProFootball Weekly,* September 17, 2001.

"I didn't see it..." Wallace, Bill. "Pat Summerall." *ProFootball Weekly,* September 17, 2001.

"What a kick..." Whittingham, Richard. *Illustrated History of the New York Giants.* Chicago: Triumph Books, 2005, 102.

The Greatest Game Ever Played

"For almost an..." Eskanazi, Gerald. *There Were Giants in Those Days.* New York: Grossett & Dunlap, 1976, 137–38.

It was a tough... Eskanazi, Gerald. *There Were Giants in Those Days.* New York: Grossett & Dunlap, 1976, 137–38.

"A tendency by..." Not attributed. "The Turning Point: The 1958 Championship Game—Baltimore Colts vs. NY Giants." Ravensnests.com, www.ravensnests.com/1958game/trngpt6.htm (accessed December 29, 2005).

"If you look..." St. John, Bob. *Tex!* Englewood Cliffs, NJ: Prentice Hall, 1988, 78–79.

"Pete Rozelle always..." Eskanazi, Gerald. *There Were Giants in Those Days.* New York: Grossett & Dunlap, 1976, 138–39.

"In the 1958 title..." MacCambridge, Michael. *America's Game.* New York: Random House, Anchor Books paperback edition, 2005, 113.

"The '58 Colts-Giants..." MacCambridge, Michael. *America's Game.* New York: Random House, Anchor Books paperback edition, 2005, 115.

CHAPTER 7 *A Death in the Family*
Death of a Giant

"We're gonna sell..." MacCambridge, Michael. *America's Game.* New York: Random House, Anchor Books paperback edition, 2005, 112.

"Perhaps pro football..." Daley, Arthur. "A Pioneer Passes." *The New York Times,* February 18, 1959.

"He died on a..." MacCambridge, Michael. *America's Game.* New York: Random House, Anchor Books paperback edition, 2005, 112.

"The National Football..." Daley, Arthur. "A Pioneer Passes." *The New York Times,* February 18, 1959.

More Good-Byes

"For a long time..." Steinbreder, John. *Giants: 70 Years of Championship Football.* Dallas: Taylor Publishing Company, 1994, 43.

"After the '55..." Golenbock, Peter. *Cowboys Have Always Been My Heroes.* New York: Warner Books, 1997, 54.

"I left the Giants in..." Steinbreder, John. *Giants: 70 Years of Championship Football.* Dallas: Taylor Publishing Company, 1994, 67.

Pete Rozelle

"If Jesus Christ..." MacCambridge, Michael. *America's Game.* New York: Random House, Anchor Books paperback edition, 2005, 138.

"Dan, it's got..." MacCambridge, Michael. *America's Game.* New York: Random House, Anchor Books paperback edition, 2005, 138.

"Great! Who the..." Harris, David. *The League.* New York: Bantam Books, 1986, 11.

A New League of Owners

"I went to New York..." Not attributed. "Flowers Is Irked by Giants' Stand." *The New York Times,* January 15, 1961.

"I received a contract..." Not attributed. "Flowers Is Irked by Giants' Stand." *The New York Times,* January 15, 1961.

"We have a legal contract with Flowers..." Not attributed. "Giants Threaten Suit." *The New York Times,* January 5, 1960.

"Giants Coach Jim Lee..." Miller, Jeff. *Going Long.* New York: Contemporary Books, McGraw-Hill, 2003, 18–19

The 1960 Season

"Jack always thought..." Eskanazi, Gerald. *There Were Giants in Those Days.* New York: Grossett & Dunlap, 1976, 212.

"Chuck knocked him..." Flatter, Ron. "More Info on Chuck Bednarick." ESPN.com, http://ad.abctv.com/classic/s/bednarikchuckadd.html (accessed February 22, 2005).

"Both parties recognized..." Maraniss, David. When Pride Still Mattered. New York: Simon & Schuster, 1999, 267.

"He said he had..." Klein, Dave. *The New York Giants: Yesterday, Today, and Tomorrow.* Chicago: Henry Regnery Company, 1973, 195.

Well never tried... Klein, Dave. *The New York Giants: Yesterday, Today, and Tomorrow.* Chicago: Henry Regnery Company, 1973, 194–95.

Hello Allie—The Second Choice

"I called Well..." Klein, Dave. *The New York Giants, Yesterday, Today, and Tomorrow.* Chicago: Henry Regnery Company, 1973, 194–95.

Art Modell

"It was a load..." MacCambridge, Michael. *America's Game.* New York: Random House, Anchor Books paperback edition, 2005, 167.

"Well was my..." Goldberg, Dave. "Giants owner Wellington Mara dies at age 89." *USA Today,* October 25, 2005.

Sharing the Wealth

"We should all..." MacCambridge, Michael. *America's Game.* New York: Random House, Anchor Books paperback edition, 2005, 172.

"We were able to..." Harris, David. *The League.* New York: Bantam Books, 1986, 14–15.

Glory Days

"The Giants may have..." Hall of Fame, Halloffame.com, as retrieved December 31, 2005.

Family Ties

"A headstrong..." Klein, Dave. *The New York Giants: Yesterday, Today, and Tomorrow.* Chicago: Henry Regnery Company, 1973, 104–05.

"For years, when..." Robustelli, Andy, with Clary, Jack. *Once A Giant, Always a Giant.* Boston: Quinlan Press, 1987, 216.

"As a child,..." Steinbreder, John. *Giants: 70 Years of Championship Football.* Dallas: Taylor Publishing Company, 1994, 22.

"Of course, there..." Steinbreder, John. *Giants: 70 Years of Championship Football.* Dalas: Taylor Publishing Company, 1994, 22.

Hall of Fame

"Johnny Blood, John..." Daley, Arthur. "Visit with the Immortals." *The New York Times,* September 9, 1963.

"Just think..." Klein, Dave. *The New York Giants: Yesterday, Today, and Tomorrow.* Chicago: Henry Regnery Company, 1973, 101.

The Ticket to Success

"We're going nuts..." Wallace, William N. "An Extra Ticket? Not a Chance!" *The New York Times,* October 11, 1963.

"One woman caller..." Wallace, William N. "An Extra Ticket? Not a Chance!" *The New York Times,* October 11, 1963.

"Why are we playing..." Hermoso, Rafael. "Pro Football: Relieved, Giants Support Commissioner's Decision." *The New York Times,* September 14, 2001.

"Singing full out for..." MacCambridge, Michael. *America's Game*. New York: Random House, Anchor Books paperback edition, 2005, 185–87.

Norman Mailer attended... MacCambridge, Michael. *America's Game*. New York: Random House, Anchor Books paperback edition, 2005, 185–87.

A Brother Returns

"It was Owen..." Exley, Fredrick. *A Fan's Notes*. New York: Random House, Vintage reprint, 1985, 70-71.

"I was glad Steve..." Klein, Dave. *The New York Giants: Yesterday, Today, and Tomorrow*. Chicago: Henry Regnery Company, 1973, 102.

The Crash of 1964

"They've gone too far..." Eskanazi, Gerald. *There Were Giants in Those Days*. New York: Grossett & Dunlap, 1976, 214–15.

"On paper it's..." Klein, Dave. *The New York Giants: Yesterday, Today, and Tomorrow*. Chicago: Henry Regnery Company, 1973, 202.

"Obviously I did..." Eskanazi, Gerald. *There Were Giants in Those Days*. New York: Grossett & Dunlap, 1976, 215.

CHAPTER 8 *The Wilderness Years*
Alone

"The family atmosphere..." Eskanazi, Gerald. *There Were Giants in Those Days*. New York: Grossett & Dunlap, 1976, 212.

"Jack was always..." Harris, David. *The League*. New York: Bantam Books, 1986, 83.

"You know, when..." Eskanazi, Gerald. *There Were Giants in Those Days*. New York: Grossett & Dunlap, 1976, 213.

"People said we..." Goldstein, Richard. "Wellington Mara, the Patriarch of the NFL, Dies at 89." *The New York Times,* October 26, 2005.

AFL Merger Talks

"My original plan..." St. John, Bob. Tex! Englewood Cliffs, NJ: Prentice Hall, 1988, 274.

But a wrench... MacCambridge, Michael. *America's Game*. New York: Random House, Anchor Books paperback edition, 2005, 220–21.

"This is a disgrace!..." MacCambridge, Michael. *America's Game*. New York: Random House, Anchor Books paperback edition, 2005, 221.

"It was bad enough..." MacCambridge, Michael. *America's Game*. New York: Random House, Anchor Books paperback edition, 2005, 223.

"If I try to get the..." MacCambridge, Michael. *America's Game*. New York: Random House, Anchor Books paperback edition, 2005, 223.

Broadway Joe

"Joe was the colorful..." Kriegel, Mark. *Namath*. New York: Viking, 2004, 111.

"They were giving people..." MacCambridge, Michael. *America's Game*. New York: Random House, Anchor Books paperback edition, 2005, 207.

Ah, Wilderness

"The most important thing..." Eskanazi, Gerald. *There Were Giants in Those Days*. New York: Grossett & Dunlap, 1976, 212–13.

"Our most expensive..." Fox, Larry. "Giants Traded for Future." *New York Daily News,* April 2, 1967.

"Unlike bachelor Joe..." Fox, Larry. "Giants Traded for Future." *New York Daily News,* April 2, 1967.

"Well, you've had..." Asinof, Eliot. *Seven Days to Sunday*. New York: Simon & Schuster, 1968, 18–19.

"I wish this club..." Asinof, Eliot. *Seven Days to Sunday*. New York: Simon & Schuster, 1968, 18–19.

"This is a war..." Miller, Jeff. *Going Long*. New York: Contemporary Books, 2003, 234.

"He was a wonderful..." Iorizzo, Pete. "Giants' owner was friend to region." *The Times Union,* October 26, 2005.

Good-Bye, Allie

"While the players..." Anderson, Dave. "Next Year is Today for Mara and Sherman." *The New York Times,* December 19, 1966.

"Were the same as..." Eskanazi, Gerald. *There Were Giants in Those Days*. New York: Grossett & Dunlap, 1976, 212–13.

"Allie believed the..." Eskanazi, Gerald. *There Were Giants in Those Days*. New York: Grossett & Dunlap, 1976, 215.

"He saw Coach..." Golenbock, Peter. *Cowboys Have Always Been My Heroes*. New York: Warner Books, 1997, 371.

"Well Mara reacted..." Klein, Dave. *The New York Giants: Yesterday, Today, and Tomorrow*. Chicago: Henry Regnery Company, 1973, 243.

"The most humiliating..." Lipsyte, Robert. "So Who Owns New York?" *The New York Times,* November 2, 1970.

"I really didn't..." Klein, Dave. The *New York Giants: Yesterday, Today, and Tomorrow*. Chicago: Henry Regnery Company, 1973, 205–6.

"I feel like I..." Klein, Dave. *The New York Giants: Yesterday, Today, and Tomorrow*. Chicago: Henry Regnery Company, 1973, 205–6.

"Either Al was..." Klein, Dave. Special report, Giants.com, August 3, 2001.

"Sure he got..." Klein, Dave. *The New York Giants: Yesterday, Today, and Tomorrow*. Chicago: Henry Regnery Company, 1973, 211.

"Wellington Mara yielded..." Daley, Arthur. "Alex Acknowledges He's Had Enough." *The New York Times,* December 13, 1973.

"I expect Allie..." Whittingham, Richard. *Illustrated History of the New York Giants*. Chicago: Triumph Books, 2005, 151.

The New NFL: AFC versus NFC

"It would emasculate..." MacCambridge, Michael. *America's Game*. New York: Random House, Anchor Books paperback edition, 2005, 257.

"It worked out..." Edleson, Steve. *Mara's Lasting Legacy*. Neptune, NJ: Asbury Park Press, 2006.

Father's Little Dividend

In April 1971... Not attributed. "Fordham's hall of fame to add four members." *The New York Times*, April 18, 1971.

"I thought it..." Not attributed. "The President is Calling." *New York Post*, July 9, 1971.

Maranoia

"The [1971] season was..." Tarkenton, Fran with Klobuchar, Jim. *Tarkenton*. New York: Harper & Row Publishing, 1976, 148.

"Poor Wellington Mara..." Merchant, Larry. "Maranoia III." *New York Post*, December 19, 1971.

"I happened to..." Tarkenton, Fran with Klobuchar, Jim. *Tarkenton*. New York: Harper & Row Publishing, 1976, 148.

"Why doesn't Wellington..." Tarkenton, Fran with Klobuchar, Jim. *Tarkenton*. New York: Harper & Row Publishing, 1976, 146–47.

"I just don't think..." Tarkenton, Fran with Klobuchar, Jim. *Tarkenton*. New York: Harper & Row Publishing, 1976, 149.

"It was abysmal..." Miller, Jeff. *Going Long*. New York: Contemporary Books, 2003, 149.

"It was tough..." Merchant, Larry. "Born Again." *New York Post*, October 15, 1972.

More Dark Years

"Of all the assistant..." Daley, Arthur. "Alex Acknowledges He's Had Enough." *The New York Times*, December 13, 1973.

"Once they were..." Anderson, Dave. "The Unbeaten Ex-Giants." *The New York Times*, October 28, 1973.

"The Webster rapport..." Daley, Arthur. "Alex Acknowledges He's Had Enough." *The New York Times*, December 13, 1973.

"At midseason I..." Anderson, Dave. "Giants Name Robustelli Director of Operations." *The New York Times*, December 18, 1973.

"[Webster] dropped a..." Daley, Arthur. "Alex Acknowledges He's Had Enough." *The New York Times*, December 13, 1973.

"Mistakes in personnel..." Amdur, Neil. "Decline of the Giants a Many-Sided Tale of Woe." *The New York Times*, December 28, 1973.

"Wellington's sense of..." Harris, David. *The League*. New York: Bantam Books, 1986, 83.

"Wellington's greatest virtue..." Wetzsteon, Ross. "What became of the New York Giants." *Sport*, December, 1984, 75–81.

"I just hope he..." Amdur, Neil. "Giants' Management Held Faulty." *The New York Times*, December 13, 1973.

"Morton's problem..." Golenbock, Peter. *Cowboys Have Always Been My Heroes*. New York: Warner Books, 1997, 371.

"I think the Jets..." Eskanazi, Gerald. *There Were Giants in Those Days*. New York: Grossett & Dunlap, 1976, 215.

"Losing cut him..." Robustelli, Andy with Clary, Jack. *Once a Giant, Always...* Boston: Quinlan Press, 1987, 138–39.

CHAPTER 9 *The Struggle*
The Return of Andy Robustelli

"When he succeeded..." Robustelli, Andy with Clary, Jack. *Once a Giant, Always...* Boston: Quinlan Press, 1987, 128.

"I wouldn't be here..." Anderson, Dave. "Robustelli Named Giants' Director of Operations." *The New York Times,* December 18, 1973.

"I told Well there'd..." Anderson, Dave. "Robustelli Named Giants' Director of Operations." *The New York Times,* December 18, 1973.

"He asked for an..." Harris, David. *The League.* New York: Bantam Books, 1986, 82–83.

"Lurtsema was a..." Tarkenton, Fran with Klobuchar, Jim. *Tarkenton.* New York: Harper & Row Publishing, 1976, 147–48.

"You have no..." Harris, David. *The League.* New York: Bantam Books, 1986, 82–83.

"You're damned right..." Harvin, Al. "An Embittered Lurtsema is dropped by the Giants." *The New York Times,* November 11, 1971.

"I'll be struggling..." Anderson, Dave. "Robustelli Named Giants Director of Operations." *The New York Times,* December 18, 1973.

"Wellington believed that..." Wetzsteon, Ross. "What became of the New York Giants." *Sport,* December 1984, 75–81.

"In retrospect I didn't..." Robustelli, Andy with Clary, Jack. *Once a Giant, Always...* Boston: Quinlan Press, 1987, 206.

The War Years: Tim and Well, 1969–1977

"[Tim and Dick] were seeking..." Robustelli, Andy with Clary, Jack. *Once a Giant, Always...* Boston: Quinlan Press, 1987, 128–29.

"I was doing..." Steinbreder, John. Giants: *70 Years of Championship Football.* Dallas: Taylor Publishing Company, 1994, 123.

"That's the way..." Robustelli, Andy with Clary, Jack. *Once a Giant, Always...* Boston: Quinlan Press, 1987, 138–39.

"Something of a..." Harris, David. *The League.* New York: Bantam Books, 1986, 84.

"I really don't..." Wetzsteon, Ross. "What became of the New York Giants." *Sport,* December 1984, 75–81.

"Did little to..." Robustelli, Andy with Clary, Jack. *Once a Giant, Always...* Boston: Quinlan Press, 1987, 214.

"I think Wellington..." Wetzsteon, Ross. "What became of the New York Giants." *Sport,* December 1984, 75–81.

"There has to..." DiTriani, Vinny. "The Mara Dynasty Giants." *The Record* (Bergen, NJ), August 11, 1986.

"I thought we..." Wetzsteon, Ross. "What became of the New York Giants." *Sport,* December 1984, 75–81.

Frank Gifford Goes to Canton

"I was certainly..." Gifford, Frank. Induction Speech, Pro Football Hall of Fame, Canton, Ohio, August 1977.

"For me, for 25..." Mara, Wellington. Introduction Speech, Pro Football Hall of Fame, Canton, Ohio, August 1977.

"If it hadn't been..." Mara, Wellington. Introduction Speech, Pro Football Hall of Fame, Canton, Ohio, August 1977.

"I had a lot..." Gifford, Frank. Induction Speech, Pro Football Hall of Fame, Canton, Ohio, August 1977.

Meadowlands Move
"Receptive to a possible..." Harris, David. *The League.* New York: Bantam Books, 1986, 84.

"We're not going..." Whittingham, Richard. *Illustrated History of the New York Giants.* Chicago: Triumph Books, 2005, 163.

"We're interested..." Daley, Arthur. "Boola, Boola for the Jersey Giants." *The New York Times,* May 7, 1971.

"Free office space..." Harris, David. *The League.* New York: Bantam Books, 1986, 84–85.

"The football Giants..." Fox, Larry. "Grid Giants Sign for Jersey Bounce." *New York Daily News,* August 27, 1971.

"What else can..." Harris, David. *The League.* New York: Bantam Books, 1986, 85.

"I'll tell you..." Harris, David. *The League.* New York: Bantam Books, 1986, 85.

"The new Giants Stadium..." Whittingham, Richard. *Illustrated History of the New York Giants.* Chicago: Triumph Books, 2005, 161.

"New York bankers..." Harris, David. *The League.* New York: Bantam Books, 1986, 87.

"By far the best..." Sullivan, Ronald. "Mara Still Set on Jersey Home." *The New York Times,* November 14, 1973.

"No public money..." Harris, David. *The League.* New York: Bantam Books, 1986, 87.

"New York–New Haven..." Whittingham, Richard. *Illustrated History of the New York Giants.* Chicago: Triumph Books, 2005, 159.

The NFL versus the Players Union
"He was a bright..." Harris, David. *The League.* New York: Bantam Books, 1986, 166–67.

"Encouraging," ... Harris, David. *The League.* New York: Bantam Books, 1986, 166–67.

"Described Mara's stance..." Harris, David. *The League.* New York: Bantam Books, 1986, 183.

"Everyone laughed..." Harris, David. *The League.* New York: Bantam Books, 1986, 225.

"IMPEACH MARA..." Miller, Norm. "How Long Can Giants Fans Wait for Revival?" *New York Daily News,* December 9, 1975.

Miracle of the Meadowlands
"A large banner held..." Miller, Norm. "Giants Play First Game at Meadowlands." *New York Daily News,* October 11, 1976.

"The fans were..." Miller, Norm. "Giants Play First Game at Meadowlands." *New York Daily News,* October 11, 1976.

"I'm looking forward..." Neft, David S., and Cohen, Richard M. *The Football Encyclopedia.* New York: St. Martin's Press, 1991, 640.

"To be a Giant..." Wetzsteon, Ross. "What became of the New York Giants." *Sport,* December 1984, 75–81.

"My first day there..." Miller, Stuart." *Where Have All Our Giants Gone?* Lanham, MD: Taylor Trade, 2005, 176.

"When the play..." Miller, Norm. "Last-Second Fumble." *New York Daily News,* October 20, 1978.

"We went back..." Miller, Stuart. *Where Have All Our Giants Gone?* Lanham, MD: Taylor Trade, 2005, 176.

"I remember the..." Steinbreder, John. *Giants: 70 Years of Championship Football.* Dallas: Taylor Publishing Company, 1994, 126.

CHAPTER 10 *That Championship Season*
Mr. Rozelle and Mr. Young

"Oh yes, I've..." Katz, Michael. "Heard on the NFL grapevine." *The New York Times,* December 17, 1978.

"During my five..." Robustelli, Andy with Clary, Jack. *Once a Giant, Always...* Boston: Quinlan Press, 1987, 205.

"Tim simply wouldn't..." Robustelli, Andy with Clary, Jack. *Once a Giant, Always...* Boston: Quinlan Press, 1987, 209.

"Those were some..." DuPont, *The Globe,* January 23, 1987.

"What made this..." Wetzsteon, Ross. "What became of the New York Giants." *Sport,* December 1984, 75–81.

"The poison of..." Wetzsteon, Ross. "What became of the New York Giants." *Sport,* December 1984, 75–81.

"Sure, it was a..." Wetzsteon, Ross. "What became of the New York Giants." *Sport,* December 1984, 75–81.

"I have not..." Katz, Michael. "Feuding Giants to Seek Coach." *The New York Times,* February 10, 1979.

"That's true, but..." Rosen, Byron. "How Can This Hurt Us Any More." *Washington Post,* February 6, 1979.

When Well and Tim passed... Wetzsteon, Ross. "What became of the New York Giants." *Sport,* December 1984, 75–81.

"My own choice..." Katz, Michael. "Feuding Giants to Seek Coach." *The New York Times,* February 10, 1979.

"Mr. Mara told me..." Berkow, Ira. "What's a Jersey Guy?" *The New York Times,* January 24, 1987.

"I got a call from..." Katz, Michael. "Feuding Giants to Seek Coach." *The New York Times,* February 10, 1979.

"Hear the latest..." Katz, Michael. "Heard on the NFL grapevine." *The New York Times,* December 17, 1978.

"Tim Mara has agreed..." Robustelli, Andy with Clary, Jack. *Once a Giant, Always...* Boston: Quinlan Press, 1987, 214.

"One of the..." Katz, Michael. "Feuding Giants to Seek Coach." *The New York Times,* February 10, 1979.

"That city has..." St. John, Bob. *Tex!* Englewood, NJ: Prentice Hall, 1988, 78–79.

"The fact that [Tim's]..." Robustelli, Andy with Clary, Jack. *Once a Giant, Always...* Boston: Quinlan Press, 1987, 209.

"What I think happened..." Izenberg, Jerry. *No Medals for Trying.* New York: Macmillan Publishing Company, 1990, 67–68.

"I started to get..." Steinbreder, John. Giants: *70 Years of Championship Football.* Dallas: Taylor Publishing Company, 1994, 133–35.

"And then all..." Izenberg, Jerry. *No Medals for Trying.* New York: Macmillan Publishing Company, 1990, 67–68.

"I want to have..." Whittingham, Richard. *Illustrated History of the New York Giants.* Chicago: Triumph Books, 2005, 188.

"Tim walked into..." Steinbreder, John. Giants: *70 Years of Championship Football.* Dallas: Taylor Publishing Company, 1994, 133–35.

"I thought that..." Whittingham, Richard. *Illustrated History of the New York Giants.* Chicago: Triumph Books, 2005, 187–88.

"It seems we've..." Katz, Michael. "Feuding Giants to Seek Coach." *The New York Times,* February 10, 1979.

"I had Frank Gifford..." Izenberg, Jerry. *No Medals for Trying.* New York: Macmillan Publishing Company, 1990, 67–68.

"I saw my first..." Steinbreder, John. Giants: *70 Years of Championship Football.* Dallas: Taylor Publishing Company, 1994, 149.

"Now we go on..." Izenberg, Jerry. *No Medals for Trying.* New York: Macmillan Publishing Company, 1990, 67–68.

"I only brought..." Steinbreder, John. Giants: *70 Years of Championship Football.* Dallas: Taylor Publishing Company, 1994, 134–35.

"Now remember, the..." Izenberg, Jerry. *No Medals for Trying.* New York: Macmillan Publishing Company, 1990, 67–68.

"About half a second..." Steinbreder, John. Giants: *70 Years of Championship Football.* Dallas: Taylor Publishing Company, 1994, 134–35.

"So George is in..." Izenberg, Jerry. *No Medals for Trying.* New York: Macmillan Publishing Company, 1990, 67–68.

"The war between..." Madden, Bill. "Dolphin Super Scout Young Takes Post." *New York Daily News,* February 15, 1979.

"He must be..." Wetzsteon, Ross. "What Became of the New York Giants." *Sport,* December 1984, 75–81.

"I wanted George..." Steinbreder, John. Giants: *70 Years of Championship Football.* Dallas: Taylor Publishing Company, 1994, 136–37.

"I imagine it gets..." Izenberg, Jerry. *No Medals for Trying.* New York: Macmillan Publishing Company, 1990, 67–68.

"I regard it as..." Dupont, *Boston Globe,* January 23, 1987.

Turnaround

"[Lawrence and I] came riding..." Gutman, Bill. *Parcells: A Biography.* New York: Carrol & Graf Publishers, 2000, 69.

"He was a tremendous..." Carson, Harry. "Thoughts and reflections on Wellington Mara." NFL.com, www.nfl.com/news/story/9003015 (accessed March 4, 2006).

"Kids were running..." Whittingham, Richard. *Illustrated History of the New York Giants.* Chicago: Triumph Books, 2005, 197.

"Because these gritty..." Lupica, Mike. "Rob Left, Rob Right, and the Giants Rob the Eagles." *New York Daily News,* December 28, 1981.

Mr. Parcells

"George told me..." Whittingham, Richard. *Illustrated History of the New York Giants.* Chicago: Triumph Books, 2005, 202.

"I grew up a Giants..." Steinbreder, John. Giants: *70 Years of Championship Football.* Dallas: Taylor Publishing Company, 1994, 135.

"Schnellenberger, whose Hurricanes..." Litsky, Frank. "Parcells Says Films Justify Holding Call." *The New York Times,* December 13, 1983.

"It took the threat..." Steinbreder, John. Giants: *70 Years of Championship Football.* Dallas: Taylor Publishing Company, 1994, 174.

"Wearing clubby sports..." Vecsey, George. "The Feud that Won Super Bowls." *The New York Times,* February 21, 1991.

"I try to get to the..." Eisen, Michael. *Stadium Stories: New York Giants.* Guilford, CT: Globe Pequot Press, 2005, 13–14.

"I'm not a glad..." Eisen, Michael. *Stadium Stories: New York Giants.* Guilford, CT: Globe Pequot Press, 2005, 13–14.

"He did not own..." Vecsey, George. "Wellington in California." *The New York Times,* January 20, 1987.

"We're people who..." Harris, David. *The League.* New York: Bantam Books, 1986, 617.

"Go back to last year..." Carson, Harry with Smith, Jim. *Point of Attack.* New York: McGraw-Hill, 1987, 173.

The Promised Land Once Again

"All that stuff about..." Anderson, Dave. "My Name is A-L-L-E-N Davis." *The New York Times,* June 25, 1986.

"We would have..." DiTrianni, Vinny. "The Mara Dynasty Giants." *The Record* (Bergen, NJ), August 11, 1986.

"I would not anticipate..." Not attributed. "Big 'Moral Victory' Claimed by Trump." *The New York Times,* July 30, 1986.

"The verdict sounded..." Not attributed. "Big 'Moral Victory' Claimed by Trump." *The New York Times,* July 30, 1986.

"I don't know." Not attributed. "Big 'Moral Victory' Claimed by Trump. *The New York Times,* July 30, 1986.

"The team is the..." DiTriani, Vinny. "The Mara Dynasty Giants." *The Record* (Bergen, NJ), August 11, 1986.

The reason this became... Hanley, Robert. "Giants Plan to Sell Luxury-Box Firm." *The New York Times,* August 29, 1986.

"We need George Preston..." Stellino, Vito. "Flashback, to the victor goes the title." NFL.com, a reprint from Game Day, http://www.nfl.com/news/story/6646278 (accessed March 4, 2006).

"Bill Parcells wasn't..." King, Peter. "A Coach's Man." *Sports Illustrated,* October 31, 2005.

"This was as warm…" Vecsey, George. "Wellington in California." *The New York Times*, January 20, 1987.

"I always said the…" Vecsey, George. "Wellington in California." *The New York Times*, January 20, 1987.

"Your father, Timothy…" Anderson, Dave. "Sinatra, Simms, Minelli." *The New York Times*, January 26, 1987.

"It was great…" Anderson, Dave. "Mara: A Grand Old Name Again." *The New York Times*, January 27, 1986.

"In actuality, nobody…" Anderson, Dave. "Mara: A Grand Old Name Again." *The New York Times*, January 27, 1986.

"I've watched the…" Barron, James. "No More Waiting for No. 1." *The New York Times*, January 26, 1987.

"We were Super Bowl…" Marshall, Leonard with Klein, Dave. *The End of the Line*. New York: New American Library, 1987, 168.

"Come on, Ed!" Rosenbaum, Bob. "Come on, Ed!" *The New York Times*, January 25, 1987.

"The team had…" Nelson, Karl with Stanton, Barry. *Life on the Line*. Waco, TX: WRS Publishing, 1993, 36.

"Charlie Conerly told…" Anderson, Dave. "Mara: A Grand Old Name Again." *The New York Times*, January 27, 1986.

"Taking a more active…" Wetzsteon, Ross. "What became of the New York Giants." *Sport*, December 1984, 75–81.

"Because of the…" Vecsey, George. "The Fued that Won Super Bowls." *The New York Times*, February 21, 1995.

"[Tim] has been…" Robustelli, Andy with Clary, Jack. *Once a Giant, Always…* Boston: Quinlan Press, 1987, 205.

"What's it been…" Dupont, Kevin Paul. "Giant Rift: Feuding Maras Are Silent Partners." *Boston Globe*, January 23, 1987.

"I told the agent…" Not attributed. "Rozelle Closes Door." *The New York Times*, January 31, 1987.

John Mara

"I really didn't…" DiTriani, Vinny. "The Mara Dynasty Giants." *The Record* (Bergen, NJ), August 11, 1986.

"He's intelligent…" DiTriani, Vinny. "The Mara Dynasty Giants." *The Record* (Bergen, NJ), August 11, 1986.

"I have given…" DiTriani, Vinny. "The Mara Dynasty Giants." *The Record* (Bergen, NJ), August 11, 1986.

The Cancer Scare

On August 29, 1987… Narvaez, Alfonso A. "Cancer Study Announced for Stadium." *The New York Times*, August 29, 1987.

"We think the…" Narvaez, Alfonso A. "Cancer Study Announced for Stadium." *The New York Times*, August 29, 1987.

"I grew up here…" Nelson, Karl with Stanton, Barry. Life on the Line. Waco, TX: WRS Publishing, 1993, 54.

"There had been a..." Nelson, Karl with Stanton, Barry. *Life on the Line*. Waco, TX: WRS Publishing, 1993, 54.

"I announced my..." Nelson, Karl with Stanton, Barry. *Life on the Line*. Waco, TX: WRS Publishing, 1993, 139.

Aftermath

"The people who..." Vecsey, George. "Brand X Football." *The New York Times*, September 23, 1987.

"I enjoy it..." O'Toole, Andrew. *Smiling Irish Eyes*. Haworth, NJ: St. Johann Press, 2004, 233.

"He longed for..." O'Toole, Andrew. *Smiling Irish Eyes*. Haworth, NJ: St. Johann Press, 2004, 224.

"If we were..." Anderson, Dave. "Farewell to the Chief." *The New York Times*, August 29, 1988.

The Old Guard and the New Commissioner

"This has been a..." Janofsky, Michael. "Owners Contend Rozelle Slowing Down." *The New York Times*, January 22, 1989.

"Rozelle heard of..." Janofsky, Michael. "Owners Contend Rozelle Slowing Down." *The New York Times*, January 22, 1989.

"We formed the..." Not attributed. "NFL Forms Search Committee." *The New York Times*, March 24, 1989.

"We have one..." George, Thomas. "The Selections Are in the Mail." *The New York Times*, April 14, 1989.

"In football, we'll..." Eskanazi, Gerald. "NFL Considers Making Changes at the Top." *The New York Times*, May 2, 1989.

"There's nothing wrong..." George, Thomas. "11 Make the Cut for the NFL Job." *The New York Times*, May 28, 1989.

"The selection process..." Eskanazi, Gerald. "Dissidents in NFL Join Search for Commissioner." *The New York Times*, July 15, 1989.

"I thought it..." George, Thomas. "Ultimatum for Panel as Vote for NFL Chief Stalls." *The New York Times*, October 26, 1989.

"What we might..." George, Thomas. "Old and New Guard Aim to Narrow Gap." *The New York Times*, October 29, 1989.

Another Ring

"I know New York..." Not attributed. "Landry to See Dallas Game." *The New York Times*, December 16, 1989.

"Bill Parcells is..." Anderson, Dave. "Coach with a Plan." *The New York Times*, January 27, 1991.

"Theirs was a relationship..." King, Peter. "A Coach's Man." *Sports Illustrated*, October 31, 2005.

Money, Money, Money

Despite their Super Bowl... Sandomir, Richard. "Records at NFL Show Trial." *The New York Times*, July 9, 1992.

"I feel right now…" DiTriani, Vinny. "NFL secrets revealed." *The Record* (Bergen, NJ), July 8, 1992.

However, the Giants… Sandomir, Richard. "Records at NFL Show Trial." *The New York Times,* July 9, 1992.

A Giant Embarrassment

"Sunday, the Super…" Quindlen, Anna. "Offensive Play." *The New York Times,* January 24, 1991.

"At the end of…" Bavaro, Mark. *Champions for Life.* Robustelli Productions, Athletes for Life, 1989.

"I hope and…" Martin, George. *Champions for Life.* Robustelli Productions, Athletes for Life, 1989.

"When I woke up…" Simms, Phil. *Champions for Life.* Robustelli Productions, Athletes for Life, 1989.

"No matter how…" Not attributed. "A Giant Embarrassment." *Sports Illustrated,* February 4, 1992.

"In later years…" Big Blue Blog, Saturday, October 29, 2005, www.nj.com, www.nj.com/weblogs/print.ssf?/mtlogs/njo_giants/archives/print090375.html (accessed January 15, 2005).

"We've written a…" D'Agostino, Joseph A. "Conservative spotlight: Chris Godfrey." *Human Events,* January 29, 2001.

Art Modell and Bob Tisch

"Bob, we now hear…" Vacchiano, Ralph. "Tisch's Super Secret in '91, Had to Wait on Giant Deal." *New York Daily News,* January 27, 2001.

"I was pretty well…" Vacchiano, Ralph. "Tisch's Super Secret in '91, Had to Wait on Giant Deal." *New York Daily News,* January 27, 2001.

"The Giants came into…" Eskanazi, Gerald. "Robert Tisch Agrees to Buy 50 Percent of the Champion Giants." *The New York Times,* February 21, 1991.

"Tim's sister Maura…" Vacchiano, Ralph. "Tisch's Super Secret in '91, Had to Wait on Giant Deal." *New York Daily News,* January 27, 2001.

"But this one was…" Eskanazi, Gerald. "Robert Tisch Agrees to Buy 50 Percent of the Champion Giants." *The New York Times,* February 21, 1991.

"It highlights again…" Pierson, Don. "Giants Internal Feud Over for Now." *Chicago Tribune,* February 24, 1991.

"At the closing…" Eskanazi, Gerald. "Just Call the Maras the Unspeakables." *The New York Times,* May 13, 1991.

"I'm looking forward…" Anderson, Dave. "Tisch Bought 15 Years of Fun with the Giants." *The New York Times,* November 15, 2005.

"Fifty years of a…" Concannon, Maura Mara. "Fairy Tale Ending for Giants and Me." *The New York Times,* February 24, 1991.

Parcells Leaves

"He's under contract…" Not attributed. "First 4-Team Super Bowl." *The New York Times,* January 27, 1991.

"They're treating me..." Not attributed. "First 4-Team Super Bowl." *The New York Times,* January 27, 1991.

"He's an unsettled..." Anderson, Dave. "5 Factors in Departure of Parcells." *The New York Times,* May 19, 1991.

"By not wanting..." Anderson, Dave. "5 Factors in Departure of Parcells." *The New York Times,* May 19, 1991.

CHAPTER 11 *A New Beginning*

John Joins the Giants

"It was one of..." DiTriani, Vinny. "Another Mara Joins the Giants." *The Record* (Bergen, NJ), April 26, 1991.

"I plan to be..." DiTriani, Vinny. "Another Mara Joins the Giants." *The Record* (Bergen, NJ), April 26, 1991.

Free Agency Redux

"The jury obviously..." Litsky, Frank. "Collins Profits and Mara Shrugs." *The New York Times,* September 12, 1992.

Good-Bye, Mr. Simms

"Young waited for..." Anderson, Dave. "Third Down, Coach to Go for Giants." *The New York Times,* January 20, 1993.

"The Maras are the..." Anderson, Dave. "What Parcells Didn't Say." *The New York Times,* January 22, 1993.

"May I have your..." George, Thomas. "Simms Will Remain a Giant." *The New York Times,* August 12, 1992.

"I've heard too..." George, Thomas. "Simms Will Remain a Giant." *The New York Times,* August 12, 1992.

"Quietly increased the..." Anderson, Dave. "Why Wellington Mara Deserves to Be in the Hall of Fame." *The New York Times,* January 20, 1992.

"A day of overwhelming..." Freeman, Mike. "A New, and Bitter, Mara Emerges." *The New York Times,* July 12, 1994.

"This is not the..." Freeman, Mike. "A New, and Bitter, Mara Emerges." *The New York Times,* July 12, 1994.

"I think Wellington..." Freeman, Mike. "Guiding the Giants with a Gentle Hand." *The New York Times,* July 22, 1997.

"I was convinced..." Freeman, Mike. "Guiding the Giants with a Gentle Hand." *The New York Times,* July 22, 1997.

Another Death in the Family

"I just blow up..." Thomas, Robert "McG." Jr. "Jim Lee Howell, Ex-Giant Coach, dies at 80." *The New York Times,* January 6, 1995.

"They hadn't been..." Eskanazi, Gerald. "Timothy J. Mara, 59, dies, Former Co-Owner of the Giants." *The New York Times,* June 2, 1995.

"Tim was a very..." DiTriani, Vinny. "Giant Family Loss." *The Record* (Bergen, NJ), June 2, 1995.

"A death in..." Eskanazi, Gerald. "Timothy J. Mara, 59, dies, Former Co-Owner of the Giants." *The New York Times,* June 2, 1995.

Well and Jerry

"We knew the nation..." Rhoden, William. "Cowboys' Owner Takes a Stand Against the NFL Welfare State." *The New York Times,* September 6, 1995.

"After the dust..." Rhoden, William. "Cowboys' Owner Takes a Stand Against the NFL Welfare State." *The New York Times,* September 6, 1995.

"I am for pooling..." Rhoden, William. "Cowboys' Owner Takes a Stand Against the NFL Welfare State." *The New York Times,* September 6, 1995.

"I don't think..." Smith, Timothy W. "Tagliabue Plans to Take Jones to Task." *The New York Times,* September 6, 1995.

"Wellington Mara has long..." Wojnarowski, Adrian. "Mara's Giant chance." *The Record* (Bergen, NJ), December 22, 2002.

"I think we are..." FreeRepublic.com, "A Conservative News Forum," posted July 18, 2001, www.freerepublic.com/forum/a3b55be06254c.htm#106 (accessed March 4, 2006).

"I am willing..." FreeRepublic.com, "A Conservative News Forum," posted July 18, 2001, www.freerepublic.com/forum/a3b55be06254c.htm#106 (accessed March 4, 2006).

Holding On

"It will be hard..." Freeman, Mike. "New Goal for the Giants, Hold on to That team." *The New York Times,* November 19, 1995.

Reeves, Parcells, and Fassel

"The one thing..." Freeman, Mike. "Young, Ever Loyal to His Team, Got to Leave the Giants on His Terms." *The New York Times,* January 11, 1998.

Helen Mara Nugent

On February 21, 1997... Not attributed. "Obituary: Helen Mara Nugent." *The New York Times,* February 21, 1997.

Maura had had... Not attributed. "Christine Concannon Plans to Wed." *The New York Times,* April 1, 1992.

Kathleen Mara Concannon... Not attributed. "Weddings: K.M. Concannon, David Anderson." *The New York Times,* December 18, 1994.

And Sheila Concannon... Not attributed. "Sheila Concannon, Taylor Melvin." *The New York Times,* October 5, 1997.

The Hall of Fame

"Naturally I'm very..." Eskanazi, Gerald. "It's Official." *The New York Times,* January 26, 1997.

"Three things are..." Eskanazi, Gerald. "It's Official." *The New York Times,* January 26, 1997.

"Right up front..." Gifford, Frank. Induction speech. Pro Football Hall of Fame, August 1997.

"I don't know..." Gifford, Frank. Induction speech. Pro Football Hall of Fame, August 1997.

"First of all..." Mara, Wellington. Induction speech. Pro Football Hall of Fame, August 1997.

"Laid down the..." Mara, Wellington. Induction speech. Pro Football Hall of Fame, August 1997.

Another Giant Loss

"He knows how..." Anderson, Dave. "Hampton Makes a Reappearance to Cheers and Chants." *The New York Times,* December 14, 1997.

"You heard it..." George, Thomas. "Old George Young Has Just Got Younger." *The New York Times,* December 14, 1997.

"We have a..." George, Thomas. "Old George Young Has Just Got Younger." *The New York Times,* December 14, 1997.

"My whole life..." Pennington, Bill. "Time Is Right: Young Leaves Giants for NFL Job." *The New York Times,* January 9, 1998.

"The Giants are..." Pennington, Bill. "Time Is Right: Young Leaves Giants for NFL Job." *The New York Times,* January 9, 1998.

"Hopefully, I'll do..." Pennington, Bill. "Time Is Right: Young Leaves Giants for NFL Job." *The New York Times,* January 9, 1998.

"It's new money now..." Anderson, Dave. "All of Those Billions: The Good and the Bad." *The New York Times,* January 18, 1998.

"George [Halas] told us..." Anderson, Dave. "All of Those Billions: The Good and the Bad." *The New York Times,* January 18, 1998.

"I worry that..." Pennington, Bill. "The N.F.L.'s Windfall Can Benefit Owners, Players and Fans." *The New York Times,* January 15, 1998.

"Wellington is strongly..." Freeman, Mike. "Mara's Opposition to Labor Deal Could Swing the Vote." *The New York Times,* March 22, 1998.

"If a player who..." Freeman, Mike. "Mara's Opposition to Labor Deal Could Swing the Vote." *The New York Times,* March 22, 1998.

"The situation was..." Freeman, Mike. "NFL Has a New Pact; Cleveland Back in Fold." *The New York Times,* March 24, 1998.

Friends and Hobbies

In November 1995... Not attributed. "Meadowlands Racing Attracts More Than Horse Fans." *TRC Thoroughbred Notebook,* November 22, 1995.

Wellington was a Fordham... Not attributed. Press release, "University Mourns Passing of Wellington Mara." ww.fordham.edu/Campus_Resources/Public_Affairs/topstories_582.html, (accessed October 6, 2005).

"Catholicism was a..." O'Connor, Ian. "Mara shows grace and dignity to the end." *Journal News* (Westchester, NY), October 26, 2005.

"When I worked..." Kirwin, Pat. "Mara was a Hall of Fame person, too." NFL.com, October 25, 2005.

"Leon would turn..." O'Connor, Ian. "Mara shows grace and dignity to the end." *Journal News* (Westchester, NY), October 26, 2005.

"He never ceases..." Not attributed. "New York Jets owner Leon Hess dead at 85." CNNSI.com, www.cnnsi.com/football/nfl/news/1999/05/07/news.obithess.html (accessed January 16, 2006).

"As a man of..." Anderson, Dave. "Glowing Words Amid Dark Suits, Dresses." *The New York Times,* May 11, 1999.

"He loved the fans..." Not attributed. "New York Jets owner Leon Hess dead at 85." CNNSI.com, www.cnnsi.com/football/nfl/news/1999/05/07/news.obithess.html (accessed January 16, 2006).

Wellington and LT

"Well, I still have..." Taylor, Lawrence and Serby, Steve. *LT: Over the Edge.* New York: Harper Collins, 2003, 52–55.

"Wellington Mara is one..." Taylor, Lawrence and Serby, Steve. *LT: Over the Edge.* New York: Harper Collins, 2003, 114–15.

"We owe it to..." Freeman, Mike. "Guiding the Giants with a caring hand." *The New York Times,* July 22, 1997.

"He has helped..." Freeman, Mike. "Guiding the Giants with a caring hand." *The New York Times, July 22, 1997.*

"Dad, I think it's..." Pennington, Bill. "Longevity has its rewards." *The New York Times,* January 26, 2001.

"You know I..." Taylor, Lawrence and Serby, Steve. *LT: Over the Edge.* New York: Harper Collins, 2003, 167.

"The Giants have..." Nobles, Charles. "Ex-Giant Taylor Is Arrested on Drug Charges in Florida." *The New York Times,* October 20, 1998.

"You may stay..." Nobles, Charles. "Ex-Giant Taylor Is Arrested on Drug Charges in Florida." *The New York Times,* October 20, 1998.

"The Giants have..." Freeman, Mike. "Taylor Enters Drug Clinic in Wake of Cocaine Arrest." *The New York Times,* October 27, 1998.

"Wellington Mara, as..." Freeman, Mike. "NFL Finds Labor Peace That Eluded Others." *The New York Times,* November 8, 1998.

"There's another man..." Taylor, Lawrence and Serby, Steve. *LT: Over the Edge.* New York: Harper Collins, 2003, 228.

One More Time

"The team boarded..." Pennington, Bill. "All Aboard! Giants Take the Train." *The New York Times,* September 3, 1999.

"By simply placing..." Eskanazi, Gerald. "Giants' New Uniforms Bring Their Past to Life." *The New York Times,* April 6, 2000.

"Each year our..." Mara, John. Eulogy for Wellington Mara, October 25, 2005.

"He loved participating..." Mara, John. Eulogy for Wellington Mara, October 25, 2005.

"We had breakfast..." Lowitt, Bruce. "Mara is still a football giant." *St. Petersburg Times,* January 22, 2001.

"Mara was one..." Not attributed. "Longtime owners Mara, Modell face off in Super Bowl." CNNSI.com, January 20, 2001.

"It was very..." Lowitt, Bruce. "Mara is still a football giant." *St. Petersburg Times,* January 22, 2001.

"I think [Art] may…" Lowitt, Bruce. "Mara is still a football giant." *St. Petersburg Times,* January 22, 2001.

"When I first…" Lowitt, Bruce. "Mara is still a football giant." *St. Petersburg Times,* January 22, 2001.

"Art is a man…" Not attributed. "Longtime owners Mara, Modell face off in Super Bowl." CNNSI.com, January 20, 2001.

"Wellington Mara and…" Not attributed. "Longtime owners Mara, Modell face off in Super Bowl." CNNSI.com, January 20, 2001.

"Wellington Mara is…" Not attributed. "Longtime owners Mara, Modell face off in Super Bowl." CNNSI.com, January 20, 2001.

"I asked Mara…" O'Connor, Ian. "Mara shows grace and dignity to the end." *Journal News* (Westchester, NY), October 26, 2005.

September 11, 2001

"The same feeling…" Hermoso, Rafael. "Relieved, Giants Support Commissioner's Decision." *The New York Times,* September 14, 2001.

"Even if it's high-fiving…" Hermoso, Rafael. "Relieved, Giants Support Commissioner's Decision." *The New York Times,* September 14, 2001.

"I don't know…" Not attributed. "Visions of smoke over New York convinced Mara not to play." Associated Press, September 13, 2001.

"How can you…" Not attributed. "Visions of smoke over New York convinced Mara not to play." Associated Press, September 13, 2001.

"Because I felt…" Hermoso, Rafael. "Relieved, Giants Support Commissioner's Decision." *The New York Times,* September 14, 2001.

"I think anything…" Stanton, Barry. "Decision to cancel right move by league." *Journal News* (Westchester, NY), September 14, 2001.

NFL spokesman Joe… Not attributed. "Visions of smoke over New York convinced Mara not to play." Associated Press, September 13, 2001.

"We would not…" Not attributed. "Visions of smoke over New York convinced Mara not to play." Associated Press, September 13, 2001.

One year a subscriber… Klein, Dave. "Wellington Mara." www.teamgiants.com/e-giants/e-giants102605.htm.

Over the years… Klein, Dave. "Wellington Mara." www.teamgiants.com/e-giants/e-giants102605.htm.

A Star-Studded Evening

"Good luck…" King, Peter. "A Coach's Man." *Sports Illustrated,* October 31, 2005.

"At the Tavern…" Eisen, Michael. "Giants Surprise Mara, Largest Assembly of Former Giants Turn out to Honor Owner." Giants.com, September 7, 2003.

"And since Wellington…" Eisen, Michael. "Wellington T. Mara (1916–2005)." www.giants.com, www.giants.com/news/press_releases/story.asp?story_id=10302 (accessed March 6, 2006).

"Frank told me…" Anderson, Dave. "Bitter taste from playoff debacle helps Giants." *Oakland Tribune,* September 8, 2003 (originally printed in *The New York Times*).

"We tried to keep…" Eisen, Michael. "Giants Surprise Mara, Largest Assembly of Former Giants Turn out to Honor Owner." Giants.com, September 7, 2003.

"I haven't slept..." Eisen, Michael. "Giants Surprise Mara, Largest Assembly of Former Giants Turn out to Honor Owner." Giants.com, September 7, 2003.

"We won the..." Eisen, Michael. "Giants Surprise Mara, Largest Assembly of Former Giants Turn out to Honor Owner." Giants.com, September 7, 2003.

"I do appreciate..." Vacchiano, Ralph. "Omar excited about 1st INT." New York Daily News, September 7, 2003.

"I'm at a little..." Eisen, Michael. "Giants Surprise Mara, Largest Assembly of Former Giants Turn out to Honor Owner." Giants.com, September 7, 2003.

"I know he enjoyed..." Not attributed. "Thoughts and reflections on Wellington Mara." NFL.com, www.nfl.com/news/story/9003015 (accessed March 5, 2006).

"This was a..." Eisen, Michael. "Giants Surprise Mara, Largest Assembly of Former Giants Turn out to Honor Owner." Giants.com, September 7, 2003.

The Mara Clan

"The most fun I..." Eisen, Michael. *Stadium Stories: New York Giants.* Guilford, CT: Globe Pequot Press, 2005, 14.

"The reason he's..." Anderson, Dave. "For Rooneys, a Funeral and a Wedding." *The New York Times,* January 18, 1981.

Francis X. Mara... Not attributed. "Lynn M. Hattrick to Marry Francis X. Mara." *The New York Times,* April 5, 1987.

"Wellington Mara had..." Coffey, Wayne. "Sean Mara wins one for Pop-Pop." *New York Daily News,* October 30, 2005.

Susan Ann Mara... Not attributed. "Susan Mara to be Bride." *The New York Times,* February 14, 1982.

Steven Vincent Mara... Not attributed. "Steven Vincent Mara Wed to Nancy Cassidy." *The New York Times,* March 13, 1983.

Sheila Marie graduated... Not attributed. "Sheila M. Mara Is Wed To Ryan John Durkin." *The New York Times,* May 30, 1987.

Kathleen Mary Mara... Not attributed. "Weddings: Kathleen Mara, Mark Morehouse." *The New York Times,* May 12, 1996.

Maureen Elizabeth Mara... Not attributed. "Maureen Mara Weds Douglas Allen Brown." *The New York Times,* July 2, 1988.

Ann Marie Mara... Not attributed. "Weddings: Ann Marie Mara, Timothy Cacase." *The New York Times,* March 7, 1993.

Meghan Ann Mara... Not attributed. "Meghan Mara, Charles Brennan." *The New York Times,* June 25, 2000.

Colleen Elizabeth Mara... Not attributed. "Weddings: Colleen Mara, Colin McLane." *The New York Times,* May 31, 1998.

Now Cracks Another Noble Heart

"One time...after..." Pennington, Bill. "Wellington Mara, all dignity and grace." *Asbury Park Press,* October 26, 2005.

"I was at a loss..." Pennington, Bill. "Wellington Mara, all dignity and grace." *Asbury Park Press,* October 26, 2005.

"More often than..." Pennington, Bill. "Wellington Mara, all dignity and grace." *Asbury Park Press,* October 26, 2005.

"My mother asked…" Mara, John. Eulogy for Wellington Mara, St. Patrick's Cathedral, October 28, 2005.

"I'm always hopeful…" Not attributed. NFL Report, www.orangemane.com/BB/archive/index.php/t-20046.

In early May… Vacchiano, Ralph. "Surgery for Cancer Fails to Slow Mara." *New York Daily News,* June 2, 2005.

"It doesn't appear…" Vacchiano, Ralph. "Surgery for Cancer Fails to Slow Mara." *New York Daily News,* June 2, 2005.

"During the afternoon…" Jones, Richard Lezin. "Giants' Longtime Owner in Treatment for Cancer." *The New York Times,* June 2, 2005.

"It was a big…" Vacchiano, Ralph. "Surgery for Cancer Fails to Slow Mara." *New York Daily News,* June 2, 2005.

"This is my publicity…" Benton, Dan and Lucca, Jason. "Three Weeks Later…" Giants 101, www.nygiants.mostvaluablenetwork.com/index.php?p=61.

"When I came…" Jones, Richard Lezin. "Giants' Longtime Owner in Treatment for Cancer." *The New York Times,* June 2, 2005.

"On July 29th…" Vacchino, Ralph. "Tom Lightens up on fragile Giants." *New York Daily News,* July 29, 2005.

"If I hear one…" O'Connor, Ian. "Mara shows grace and dignity to the end." *The Journal News* (Westchester, NY), October 26, 2005.

"Your team is really…" Coffey, Wayne. "Mara sportsman of the Year." *New York Daily News,* October 28, 2005.

"It was a faith…" Coffey, Wayne. "Mara sportsman of the Year." *New York Daily News,* October 28, 2005.

"Ronnie Barnes, who…" Lupica, Mike. "Mara Put The True In Blue. An Owner With Legacy as Team Player." *New York Daily News,* October 26, 2005.

"Nobody asked Ronnie…" Lupica, Mike. "Mara Put The True In Blue. An Owner With Legacy as Team Player." *New York Daily News,* October 26, 2005.

"Nobody took better…" Mara, John. Eulogy for Wellington Mara, October 25, 2005.

"Think good thoughts…" King, Peter. "Wellington Mara." Sports Illustrated. Reprinted by the Key Monk, "In Latter Days," Monday, October 24, 2005, thekeymonk. blogspot.com/2005_10_01_thekeymonk_archive.html (accessed March 5, 2006).

"Where am I?" O'Connor, Ian. "Mara shows grace and dignity to the end." *Journal News* (Westchester, NY), October 26, 2005.

"And that's what…" O'Connor, Ian. "Mara shows grace and dignity to the end." *Journal News* (Westchester, NY), October 26, 2005.

"I will be there…" O'Connor, Ian. "Mara shows grace and dignity to the end." *Journal News* (Westchester, NY), October 26, 2005.

"Make sure you…" O'Connor, Ian. "Mara shows grace and dignity to the end." *Journal News* (Westchester, NY), October 26, 2005.

"I hate to say it…" Pennington, Bill. "Wellington Mara, all dignity and grace." *Asbury Park Press,* October 26, 2006.

"Somewhere, Mara is…" Goldberg, Dave. "There will never be another Wellington Mara." *Canadian Press,* October 28, 2005.

Jerry Jones, in... Not attributed. "Thoughts and reflections on Wellington Mara." NFL.com, www.nfl.com/news/story/9003015, as retrieved on March 5, 2006.

"There was never..." Not attributed. "Thoughts and reflections on Wellington Mara." NFL.com, www.nfl.com/news/story/9003015, as retrieved on March 5, 2006.

"As we got older..." Not attributed. "Thoughts and reflections on Wellington Mara." NFL.com, www.nfl.com/news/story/9003015, as retrieved on March 5, 2006.

Bill Parcells said... Not attributed. "Thoughts and reflections on Wellington Mara." NFL.com, www.nfl.com/news/story/9003015, as retrieved on March 5, 2006.

Sherman said... Not attributed. "Thoughts and reflections on Wellington Mara." NFL.com, www.nfl.com/news/story/9003015, as retrieved on March 5, 2006.

Daniel M. Snyder... Not attributed. "Thoughts and reflections on Wellington Mara." NFL.com, www.nfl.com/news/story/9003015, as retrieved on March 5, 2006.

"The family followed..." Eisen, Michael. "Wellington Mara Laid to Rest." Giants.com, www.giants.com/news/eisen/story.asp?story_id=10454.

"The presence of NFL..." Not attributed. "NFL greats turn out for Mara's funeral." Foxnews.com, October 30, 2005.

"This was not..." Not attributed. "Blue sky welcomes Wellington Mara to heavens above." *The New York Times,* October 30, 2005.

"The current Giants..." Lupica, Mike. "Big Blue Family Comes Together as a Whole." *New York Daily News,* October 29, 2005.

"I have had the..." Egan, Cardinal Edward. "A Giant, Homily." St. Patrick's Cathedral, October 28, 2005.

"I had three stages..." Gifford, Frank. Eulogy for Wellington Mara, St. Patrick's Cathedral, October 28, 2005.

"One of the visions..." Mara, John. Eulogy for Wellington Mara, St. Patrick's Cathedral, October 28, 2005.

"He may be gone..." Mara, John. Eulogy for Wellington Mara, St. Patrick's Cathedral, October 28, 2005.

"The torch has been..." Shaughnessy, Dan. "It's hard to root against Man of Steel." *Boston Globe,* February 2, 2006.

"A horse-drawn carriage..." Anderson, Dave. "A Blue Sky, Naturally, Above All Those Who Were Touched." *The New York Times,* October 29, 2005.

Aftermath

"Sean Mara stood somberly..." Coffey, Wayne. "Sean Mara wins one for Pop-Pop." New York Daily News, October 30, 2005.

"The only thing I..." Coffey, Wayne. "Sean Mara wins one for Pop-Pop." *New York Daily News,* October 30, 2005.

"It's sad," Sean said... Coffey, Wayne. "Sean Mara wins one for Pop-Pop." *New York Daily News,* October 30, 2005.

"I really believe..." Coffey, Wayne. "Sean Mara wins one for Pop-Pop." *New York Daily News,* October 30, 2005.

"This is my oldest..." Coffey, Wayne. "Daily News tabs Mara as Sportsman of the Year." *New York Daily News,* October 28, 2005.

"We're awful lucky..." Vacchiano, Ralph. "Accorsi: Sons Just Fine." *New York Daily News,* November 17, 2005.

"John Mara says…" Lupica, Mike. "New Year Kicks Off With Old Memories of Great Men." *New York Daily News,* January 3, 2006.

"I go down on…" Lupica, Mike. "New Year Kicks Off With Old Memories of Great Men." *New York Daily News,* January 3, 2006.

EPILOGUE

"I was never…" Not attributed. "30 seconds with Harry Carson." Detroit News wire services, February 6, 2006.

"Harry Carson's talent…" "Carson is finally going to Canton." NFL.com, www.nfl.com/news/story/9208887 (accessed March 6, 2006).

"http://www.nfl.com/news/story/9208887 "This would have been…" "Carson is finally going to Canton." NFL.com, www.nfl.com/news/story/9208887 (accessed March 6, 2006).

"As a general rule…" Eisen, Michael. "Wellington Honored by Loyola School." Giants.com, February 17, 2006.

INDEX

A

B